# THE ARCTIC & ITS WILDLIFE

## BRYAN SAGE

With specialist contributions from

Dr Hugh Danks
Dr Eric Haber
Professor Peter G. Kevan
Dr Thomas G. Smith

**Facts On File Publications**
New York, New York • Oxford, England

*Wilderness is a non-renewable resource . . . wilderness constitutes an important — perhaps an invaluable — part of modern-day life; its preservation is a contribution to, not a repudiation of, the civilisation upon which we depend.*
Justice Thomas Berger

*The High Arctic is the world's largest desert. Filled with 'kenosis' — emptiness, the most precious resource the High North has to offer to the eternally product-hungry civilisation.*

Josef Svoboda

To Audrey and Annette

Library of Congress Cataloging in Publication Data

Sage, Bryan L.
The Arctic and its wildlife.
Includes index.
1. Zoology—Arctic Regions. 2. Botany—Arctic Regions.
3. Natural history—Arctic Regions.   I. Title.
QH84.1.S34 1986
574.5'2621      84-24745
ISBN 0-8160-1083-8

Printed in Italy by New Interlitho, Milan

10 9 8 7 6 5 4 3 2 1

# CONTENTS

# PLATES

Endpaper. Outlet glaciers near Bartholins Brae, Blosseville Kyst, Greenland, showing abrupt descent from the ice dome in two rock-walled troughs

Jacket photograph: A Gyrfalcon at its eyrie on Ellesmere Island in the Canadian High Arctic (D. Muir)

# TABLES

# FIGURES

# FOREWORD

Bryan Sage is a rare bird – an ecologist of note who has visited and worked at both ends of the world, and can write accurately about either. Recently he tackled the Antarctic in a memorable collaboration with photographer Eric Hosking. Now he writes of the Arctic, an area that has absorbed far more of his working life and thought, and in which he feels very much at home. In *The Arctic and its Wildlife* he collaborates with four specialist contributors to scan the whole white world of the Arctic – land, sea and air – and introduce its plants and animals. This is a big task, and Bryan Sage is one of very few people I know who could tackle it competently.

The Arctic sea basin and the cold lands surrounding it cover a huge area of the northern hemisphere. Polar boundaries can be drawn at the treeline, the Arctic circle or the 10° C summer isotherm, but we all know that polar influences spread far beyond any boundary line drawn by man. Ice-chilled seas spread far south down the coasts of North America and Europe; but for the North Atlantic Drift they would bite the toes of British and west European bathers, and give us a winter climate as harsh as Japan's. Winter and summer alike cold north winds blow chill down our necks. Air we breathe in Britain today may have crossed Greenland yesterday and Arctic Canada the day before; maverick winds from the Arctic carry frosts south to Florida and snow to southern Greece. Follow the cold air back to its source, and you find yourself in the strange world that Bryan Sage and his colleagues describe – a world of ice and snow, polar desert and semi-desert, tundra, tumbling glaciers, and cold, ever-circling sea-ice.

The Arctic has been known to temperate man for well over four centuries. For much of that time wildlife was the magnet drawing men north each short summer season. Exploitation, not appreciation, was the main attraction. Whale-bone and oil, furs and hides from sea-mammals and land-mammals alike were the prizes. Thousands of adventurers sought them across the northern oceans and continents; many died and a few made fortunes during the period of most ruthless exploitation, which has only recently passed from living memory. Indeed exploitation of fur seals and forest animals continues today, and will do so for as long as fine furs keep their popularity.

Yet most of our scientific knowledge of the Arctic has emerged from studies during the last 50 years, a surprising amount of it from the last two or three decades when the north has been explored systematically for oil and other minerals, and occupied in patches for military purposes. The Arctic's own indigenous peoples know their lands and wildlife well; they've had to, as a matter of survival. Southerners have learnt a little from them, though not enough for our own good. Had we acquired some of their wisdom and feeling for the Arctic at the time of learning, our impact over the years might well have been less destructive.

For impacts there have been, and damage has been done to the Arctic out of all proportion to the use we have made of it, or the benefits gained. Not long ago the epitome of purity, today the Arctic suffers radio-active fallout, chemical pollution of atmosphere and waterways, oil-spills and mechanical damage from pipeline installation, and a dozen other kinds of pollution drearily familiar to us in the industrial world. It is a conservation trouble-spot, and a tender one at that. We are meddlesome little apes, whose capacity for meddling has in the present generation begun to match world processes in magnitude. The amount of pollution entering the Arctic annually is measurable and considerable; it could, for example, be modifying local climates, and in doing so could not fail to modify climates elsewhere in the world.

But the Arctic is still an attractive and lively place, with a wealth of indigenous, sedentary plants and animals, and a whole plethora of migrants that fly, swim and trot northward each spring to take advantage of all it has to offer. Bryan Sage has moved north very frequently and knows his Arctic wildlife well. Here he tells us about it, in an attractive book that will help to keep all of us up to date and well informed on Arctic affairs.

Bernard Stonehouse
Scott Polar Research Institute
Cambridge

# ACKNOWLEDGEMENTS

A good many people have contributed to this book in diverse ways, some of them without knowing that they were doing so. The book really owes its genesis to discussions that I had in Alaska some 17 years ago with my valued friend and mentor, the late Sir Frank Fraser Darling, a man who was not only a fine ecologist but was also very much in tune with the wilderness ethic. Subsequently I owe much to discussions with numerous other ecologists of various nationalities who have worked in the Arctic. They are too many to list in detail, but I am conscious of a great debt of gratitude to them all, and to many others who have so kindly sent me copies of their publications. In my travels in the North American Arctic I have often received generous help and much kindness from officers of the United States Federal Fish and Wildlife Service, the State Department of Fish and Game in Alaska, and the Canadian Wildlife Service.

It goes without saying that I am extremely grateful to my four fellow contributors from Canada who have written on their respective specialised subjects. Without their contributions the book would have been quite incomplete.

I am indebted also to the librarians at the Scott Polar Research Institute in Cambridge, and at the Zoological Society of London, whose help has been invaluable. The Department of Zoology of the British Museum (Natural History) in London kindly assisted in resolving some taxonomic and distributional problems concerning small mammals. Dr Malcolm Ogilvie of the Wildfowl Trust generously provided me with data relating to breeding success in the Dark-bellied Brent Goose. I must also thank the Boreal Institute for Northern Studies at the University of Alberta, Canada, for the kind provision of English translations of Soviet ecological literature.

I must mention especially Dr Pavel Tomkovich of the Department of Ornithology at the Zoological Museum, Moscow, for not only providing a number of excellent colour photographs, but also for providing me with information on the breeding birds of the Soviet Arctic. I am indebted also to Dr Algirdas Knystautus for providing the colour photographs of Red-breasted Goose and Peregrine on the Taimyr Peninsula.

Every effort has been made to contact the copyright holders in respect of figures taken from other publications, and the following are thanked for permission to reproduce the figures indicated: 1.2 Princeton University Press. 1.3 and 10.2 Institute of Arctic and Alpine Research, University of Colorado. 1.4 and 7.4 Department of Energy, Mines and Resources, Ottawa. 1.5 The University of Alberta Press, Edmonton. 2.1 Methuen & Co. Ltd, London. 4.2, 9.2, 9.3 and 10.5 the Canadian Wildlife Service. 4.3 Macmillan, London and Basingstoke. 5.2 Edward Arnold (Publishers) Ltd, London, and the sources listed against Figure 3.3 in Washburn (1979). 5.3 and 5.4 Longman Ltd, Harlow, Essex. 5.5 Bell and Hyman, London. 9.1 University of Alaska. 9.5 and 9.6 Arctic Institute of North America. 10.1 Oregon State University Press. 10.7 and 10.8 Direktoratet For Naturforvaltning, Trondheim, Norway. 10.9 Cambridge University Press, and 10.10 British Columbia Ministry of the Environment and Nancy L. R. Le Blond. Table 3.1 is reproduced by permission of Springer Verlag, Heidelberg.

I would also like to thank the following for permission to reproduce as plates the photographs indicated: 9.15 and 9.52 Ardea. 9.9 and 10.12 Bryan and Cherry Alexander. 9.33 and 9.34 Dr D. Cabot. 10.4 and 10.9 W. Higgs. 10.17 J. Hout. 4.4 and endpapers Geodaetisk Institut, Denmark (Refs: 841190 12000-A 651 D-Ø 13 Aug. 1950; 841190 12000-A 651 B-N-V 11 Aug. 1951). 9.36 and 9.46 Dr A. Knystautus. 2.11, 2.13, 3.4, 3.6, 3.8, 5.6, 5.7, 5.8, 5.9, 9.27, 10.5, 10.10 and jacket R.D. Muir. 2.7, 2.9 and 9.32 Dr D.N. Nettleship. 9.50 Dr D. Norton. 10.13 and 10.18 C. Ott. 2.6, 2.8, 2.12, 9.2, 9.20, 9.26 and 9.56 Dr D. Parmelee. 10.7 Dr D. Pimlott. 9.60 Mike Reid. 9.39 Dr J.P. Ryder. 3.5, 4.3, 4.5, 5.4 and 9.30 P.J. Sellar. 3.2, 3.3 and 4.6 G. Shaw. 11.2, 11.3 and 11.4 Dr T.G. Smith. 10.8 W. Stribling. 10.16 A. Thayer (US Federal Fish and Wildlife Service). 2.10, 3.7, 4.1, 4.2, 9.5, 9.11, 9.13, 9.14, 9.16, 9.17, 9.24, 9.25, 9.31, 9.44, 9.58, 10.2 and 11.1 Dr P. Tomkovich. 3.1 G. Waterston. 9.23 Dr F. Wille. All other photographs are by Bryan Sage.

# INTRODUCTION

This book is about the Arctic landscapes and oceans and some of their associated wildlife, but the approach has, of necessity, had to be selective. The intention has been to give a background account of the physical characteristics of the Arctic terrestrial environment, particularly the various intriguing landforms, and then to discuss a variety of aspects of the fauna and flora. The marine environment is also covered, though it has not been possible to include the fish, despite their importance in some food chains. Also, for reasons of space, there is no separate discussion of the native peoples, economics, or development, important though these are. However, there are various other books which may be consulted by those seeking information on these aspects (e.g. Armstrong *et al* 1978, Müller 1981 and Stonehouse 1971). Neither has it been possible to deal with the all-important question of conservation, various aspects of which were discussed by Sage (1981).

There is now an enormous technical literature about the Arctic and its ecology, including many substantial books such as those of Bliss (1977), Bliss *et al* (1981), Ives and Barry (1974) and Tieszen (1978). The present work attempts to bridge the gap between these highly technical works on the one hand, and a purely general and non-technical approach on the other. The book is aimed at those readers who require, in one volume, a reasonably detailed account of the Arctic environment and its fauna and flora with plenty of 'meat' in the form of facts, figures and illustrations.

It is emphasised that the discussion throughout, unless otherwise stated, refers primarily to the Arctic as defined for the purposes of this book. Where common names of plants and animals are used the scientific name is also given at first mention, but not thereafter; all names will be found in the index. In terms of content and length, the various chapters are not entirely consistent. The chapter on terrestrial mammals, for example, is one of the longest in the book and contains much detail on breeding biology, while the chapter on birds contains rather less on that aspect. The reason for this difference is that there are many readily available books on birds, but few on mammals containing this sort of information. There is nothing wrong with inconsistency on occasion, although it may irk some reviewers.

The Arctic is threatened, and nobody should be under any illusions as to the seriousness of the situation. The main source of the threat is industrial development of one sort or another, but in particular the activities of the oil industry. In the Prudhoe Bay oil development complex on Alaska's Arctic Slope, some 6,000 people now live and work in what is for the most part a totally artificial environment. Oil and gas exploration in the Canadian north, with few exceptions, has existed only because of massive government subsidies (1.5 billion Canadian dollars in Petroleum Incentive Program grants since 1981) which has allowed the drilling of hundred of wells. One result of all the activity is that Panarctic Oils Limited is proposing to ship crude oil from its Bent Horn oilfield on Cameron Island south through Lancaster Sound – one of the most important areas for seabirds in the entire Arctic. Elsewhere in Canada, Little Cornwallis Island is the site of the world's most northerly metal mine. The Polaris lead-zinc mine, only 140 km from the magnetic pole, commenced production in November 1981.

The threats continue to multiply. Oil exploration is taking place in eastern Greenland; in October 1984 Norway's state-owned oil company Statoil announced that it had made the world's most northerly oil discovery deep inside the Arctic Circle on the edge of the Barents Sea; in March 1985, British Petroleum and Statoil engaged in a massive airlift of oil exploration equipment and accommodation into Svalbard. The Soviet Union has approved a plan to reverse the flow of its northern rivers so that they flow south instead of emptying into the Arctic Ocean; a drastic reduction in the amount of fresh water flowing into the Arctic Ocean could lower its temperature and increase its salinity, affecting the climate in much of Europe and North America. Oil and gas exploration (both onshore and offshore) continues in the North American Arctic. Recent advances in marine technology will allow year-round exploration, development, and transportation of oil and gas in Arctic waters, with the consequent increased threat of pollution. In a timely warning, Cameron (1983) pointed out that the federal mandate to explore the coastal portion of the Arctic National Wildlife Refuge may ultimately open an additional 650,000 ha to development, and that if all lands (in northern Alaska) identified as having oil and gas potential were eventually developed, approximately 12.5 million ha – nearly 60 per cent of the Arctic Slope – would be involved.

The problem was aptly summarised by Svoboda (1981):

> We must resist the pressure imposed on us by established opinion, shared unfortunately by many politicians, that the North is primarily of interest because of its non-renewable riches ... this popular, nevertheless, false concept of the North as a huge reservoir of oil, gas and ore for the South.

It is probably true to say that up to now actual physical damage to habitats and individual wildlife species has been minimal and localised, but what has happened is that the wilderness atmosphere of large areas has been destroyed. Such values are not important to the corporate mind since they cannot be interpreted in financial terms.

Nobody really knows what effects industrial activity in the Arctic will have in the long term on the fauna and flora, but the prospects are not encouraging. Another cause for concern is increasing tourism to remote areas. While hunting is now not a major threat to the Polar Bear, tourism and industrialisation are seen as growing dangers. Disturbing signs of indirect threats include the detection of toxic chemicals in Greenland seabirds although no pesticides are used in the country itself. The mercury content in Black Guillemots has doubled over a 20-year period, and six species have been found to be affected to varying degrees by DDE, PCB and aldrin (Salomonsen 1979). In Alaska and parts of northern Canada, thin eggshells, pesticide residues, and reproductive failures have all been noted in the Peregrine populations (Cade *et al* 1968, Cade and Fyfe 1970).

The Arctic as seen by the early explorers has largely gone, thanks to large-scale intrusion by the white man for military and industrial reasons. Although one of the most severe and harsh environments in the world, the Arctic has a unique assemblage of plants and animals living, for the most part, near the limit in terms of nutrient and energy requirements. This land has many faces; from the dark and biting cold of winter with its often violent winds and endless white wastelands, to the breathtaking displays of beauty by the Aurora Borealis, and the great flush of life in summer when the tundra flowers bloom, waterfowl and waders come north in their millions to breed, and the great herds of caribou move through the mountains and across the rivers to the tundra. The Arctic can be harsh and violent, peaceful and beautiful, and its pristine landscapes have aesthetic values sensed only by those whose reasons for being there are not dictated by commercial gain. Perhaps only those who have been privileged to undergo the 'wilderness experience' in the Arctic can truly understand its real value.

## Notes on the Editor and Contributors

Bryan Sage, Waveney House, Waveney Close, Wells-next-the-Sea, Norfolk NR23 1HU, England.

Dr Hugh V. Danks, Biological Survey of Canada (Terrestrial Arthropods), National Museum of Natural Sciences, Ottawa, Ontario K1A 0M8, Canada.

Dr Erich Haber, National Museum of Natural Sciences, National Museums of Canada, Ottawa, Ontario K1A 0M8, Canada.

Professor Peter G. Kevan, Department of Environmental Biology, University of Guelph, Guelph, Ontario N1G 2W1, Canada.

Dr Thomas G. Smith, Arctic Biological Station, Ste Anne de Bellevue, Quebec, Canada.

# 1
# DEFINING THE ARCTIC

Unfortunately there is no single, universally accepted definition of the Arctic, with the result that whatever definition is adopted it will be open to criticism from one or more quarters. The situation is further complicated by the fact that somewhat different criteria are required for the terrestrial and marine zones. (The marine environment is discussed in Chapter 4.)

The first definition which readily comes to mind is that of the Arctic Circle at 66° 32′ N, but this is a purely mathematical line of very limited practical significance from an ecological viewpoint, although it was used by Remmert (1980). Also, the Arctic Circle runs right across Greenland leaving a large proportion of that country's great polar ice-sheet to the south. Engineers and geomorphologists have often taken the occurrence of perennially frozen ground (permafrost) as the most important single element in the delimitation of the Arctic, but sometimes without distinguishing between continuous and discontinuous permafrost. Geophysicists, on the other hand, usually prefer to place the boundary of the Arctic around the area of strong magnetic storms, the Aurora Borealis, and radio blackouts. For the ecologist, the latter definition is of even less use than that of the Arctic Circle.

In his system of climatic classification, Wladimir Köppen (1900) defined as a polar climate one in which the mean temperature of the warmest month does not exceed 10° C. In practice, this places the 10° C July isotherm as the southern limit of the Arctic (Figure 1.1). This definition, despite some drawbacks, makes good ecological sense since there is commonly a very close correlation between the treeline (the northern limit of arborescent growth), or the northern limit of the boreal forest, and the 10° C July isotherm. In places the two lines diverge to varying degrees (up to about 160 km), because tree growth is limited not solely by summer temperature, but also by desiccating winds, the presence of permafrost, and poor quality soils.

This is the definition most often used by geographers and ecologists, and is basically the one adopted for the purposes of this book. A distinct advantage of this boundary (particularly the northern edge of the true forest) is that it can be readily identified with the aid of aerial photographs and satellite imagery. Also, at this boundary there occurs a sharp environmental change; to the north of it there occur very strong surface winds, and animals have to cope with a much more severe windchill than in the protection of the forests of the south. Drifting snow is also significantly more marked north of this boundary.

Although this definition of the Arctic is eminently suitable from an ecological point of view, it must be pointed out that the treeline (unlike the edge of the boreal forest) is frequently not sharply defined. In Alaska the situation is simplified by the fact that forest growth stops more or less abruptly on the southern slopes of the Brooks Range. In the Canadian and Soviet sections of the Arctic, however, there exists a zone of intergradation called the forest-tundra which has three basic types: isolated clumps of forest surrounded by tundra; scattered trees interspersed with tall shrubs; and extensive stands of willow and birch shrubs. As one proceeds northwards from the boreal forests, the first change usually noted is a thinning of the forest cover and a reduction in the size of individual trees. The habitat changes markedly from a shaded forest to an open bush area in which sunlight reaches the ground almost everywhere. Further north the trees become confined to the most sheltered and favourable areas such as river valleys and lake shores. Finally come tundras dominated by sedges, grasses, dwarf shrubs, or heaths, and last of all the polar deserts. In general, the northernmost trees are birches (*Betula*) in oceanic areas and spruces (*Picea*) in continental areas, replaced by larches (*Larix*) in extreme continental areas. Some authorities consider that in Canada (where the forest almost reaches the Arctic Ocean at 68° N in the Mackenzie Delta), the northernmost spruces are relicts from recent warmer periods and would not regenerate if destroyed (see, for example, Elliott 1979). The most northerly open woodland (forest-tundra) in the world is situated on the Ary-Mas Massif on the Taimyr Peninsula (about 75° N). Dahurian Larch *Larix dahurica* almost reaches the shores of the Laptev Sea at just over 70° N in northern Siberia, and a clump of Balsam Poplars *Populus balsamifera* flourishes near the Canning River (just a little below 70° N) on Alaska's Arctic Slope. The latter evi-

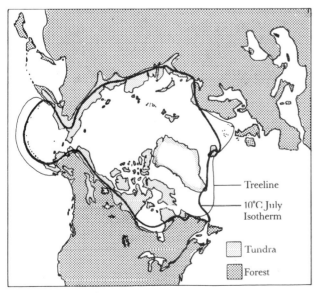

Treeline

10°C July Isotherm

Tundra

Forest

*Figure 1.1: The 10° July Isotherm in Relation to the Treeline*
*Source: Dr E. Haber.*

dently owe their existence to nutrient-rich ground-water and shelter from the wind.

In our relatively restricted definition of the Arctic, Fenno-Scandia is excluded. Because of the effects of the North Atlantic Drift, its climate, fauna, and flora are all closer to those in the temperate zone. Continuous permafrost has not been reported in that area (see Figure 5.2), and the 10° C July isotherm barely touches the northern extremity. The various land areas included in the Arctic for present purposes are shown in Table 1.1.

**Table 1.1:** Approximate Size of Land Areas in the Arctic (Figures in km²)

| Country | Total | Tundra[a] | Ice Areas |
|---------|------:|----------:|----------:|
| Soviet Union | 2,031,000 | 1,971,000 | 60,000 |
| Alaska | 209,790 | 207,200 | <2,590 |
| Canada | 3,086,450 | 2,918,400 | 168,050 |
| Greenland | 2,175,600 | 341,700 | 1,833,900 |
| Jan Mayen Island | 380 | 265 | 115 |
| Svalbard | 65,300 | 8,000 | 57,300 |
| Totals | 7,568,520 | 5,446,565 | 2,121,955 |

Note: a. Includes alpine tundra areas within the Arctic, and polar deserts, but not forest-tundra.
Source: Danks (1981).

The Arctic, as defined here, does not include the forest-tundra areas of Canada or the Soviet Union which, as suggested by Löve (1970), I prefer to regard as belonging to the Subarctic. Whilst this is a debatable point, in practice it makes very little difference in terms of animal species since it only excludes what are basically forest species which penetrate into the forest-tundra, but do not normally reach the true tundra zone.

Within the Soviet Union the tundra zone extends narrowly along the shores of the Arctic Ocean for some 25,000 km (see Figure 1.2), with further expanses on the Chukotka Peninsula in the extreme north-east. Arctic Alaska is taken to be the area defined by Pitelka (1974), with the southern boundary running from Cape Lisburne in the west, eastwards along the Continental Divide of the Brooks Range to the Canadian border (Figure 1.3). In Canada the picture is rather more complex since the forest extends much further north, but the distribution of the tundra habitats is shown in Figure 1.4. In Greenland (Figure 1.5), tundra and polar desert habitats (as opposed to the ice-sheet)

*Figure 1.2: Biotic Zones of the Soviet Arctic. Polar desert is present in the North of the Taimyr Peninsula, but does not show at this scale*

*Source: Adapted from Flint, Boehme, Kostin and Kuznetsov (1984). Reprinted by permission of Princeton University Press.*

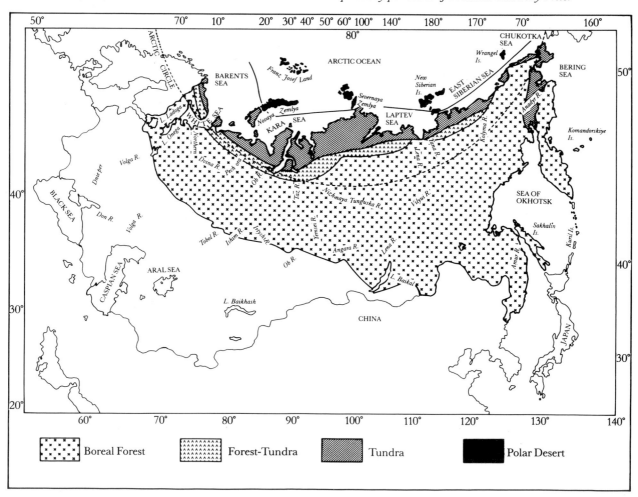

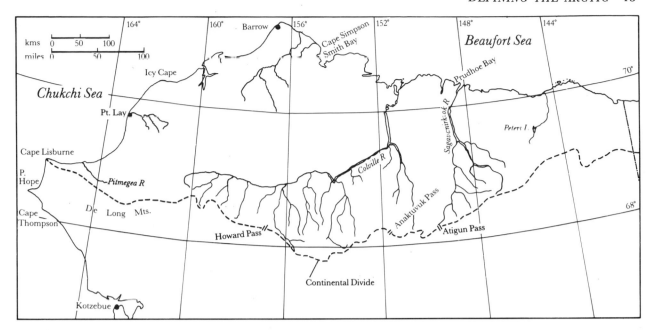

*Figure 1.3: Map of Northern Alaska. The dashed line running from Cape Lisburne eastwards along the Continental Divide of the Brooks Range to the Canadian border marks the southern boundary of Arctic Alaska as defined for present purposes*
*Source: Based on Pitelka (1974).*

*Figure 1.4: Major Ecosystems in Northern Canada   Source: Polunin (1951).*

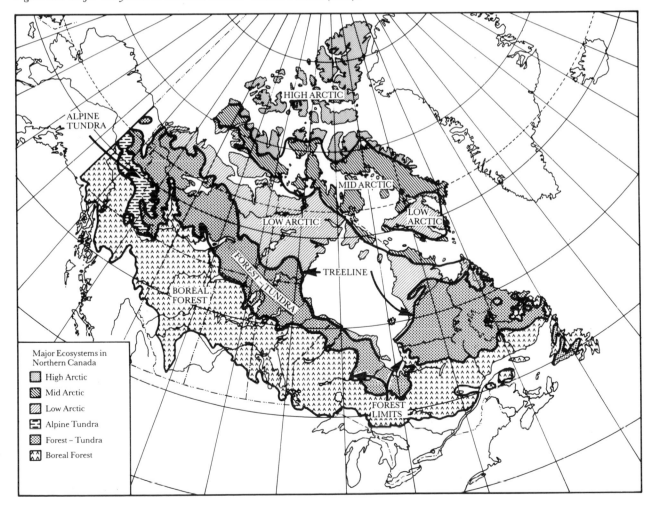

**Table 1.2:** Two Classifications of the Biogeographical Zones and Sub-zones of the Circumpolar Arctic

| Soviet Classification | Polar desert zone | | Tundra zone | | | | |
|---|---|---|---|---|---|---|---|
| | | | Arctic tundra | | Subarctic tundra | | |
| | Northern variant | Southern variant | Northern variant | Southern variant | Northern variant | Middle variant | Southern variant |
| American Classification | High Arctic zone | | | | Low Arctic zone | | |
| | Polar desert | Polar semi-desert | Mosaic of: Sedge-moss tundra (common), sub shrub, cottongrass, low shrub tundras (minor) | | Sedge-moss and grass-moss tundra | Cottongrass–sub shrub tundra | Low shrub–sub shrub tundra | Tall shrub tundra |

Sources: Alexandrova (1980) and Bliss (1975).

are confined to relatively narrow coastal regions, and to Peary Land in the north. This conception of the Arctic differs considerably from that used by some other authorities. Some, such as Stonehouse (1971), use a very wide definition which includes most of Iceland, western Alaska south of Cape Prince of Wales, and various of the Bering Sea islands, since all are treeless and therefore qualify as tundra by some

*Figure 1.5: Map of the North American High Arctic and Greenland Showing the Distribution of Polar Deserts, Polar Semi-deserts, Tundra and Sedge Meadows*
*Source: Bliss (1977).*

criteria. Iceland, however, is usually excluded from the Arctic on the basis of Nordenskjöld's studies of the vegetation (Nordenskjöld and Meckling 1928).

It is possible to divide the area into the Low and High Arctic at about the 5° C July isotherm. On this basis the latter includes all the Soviet Arctic Islands, the Canadian Arctic Archipelago (except southern Baffin Island), and all except the south of Greenland. It should be noted that in much Soviet ecological literature, the terms Subarctic and Arctic refer to what are called here the Low and High Arctic respectively (see Table 1.2).

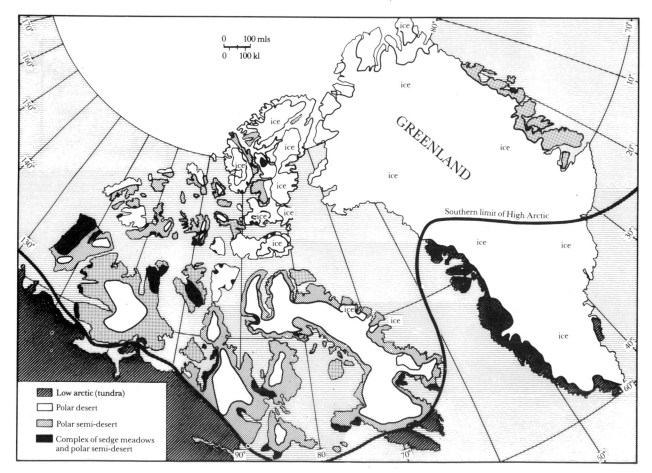

# 2
# GENERAL TOPOGRAPHY

## Introduction

Many of the most striking physical features of the Arctic landscape are discussed in Chapter 5, and the purpose of the present chapter is to outline the general topography. Within the Arctic, recently deposited and unconsolidated Quaternary deposits have made considerable impact on the topography, but these recent deposits lie over much older deposits and ancient rocks with a quite different scale of relief. Around the Arctic Basin, which averages over 3,500 m in depth, lie three great shields of resistant Precambrian rock: the Canadian Shield of Canada and Greenland; the Fennoscandian Shield of north-western Europe; and the Angara Shield of northern Asia. Extensive areas of extruded volcanic rock occur as lava plateaus on Jan Mayen Island and an adjacent area of Greenland. In addition, of course, past glaciations strongly influenced present-day landforms. Major features of the Arctic landscape include flat coastal plains (often with numerous lakes) extending inland to rolling tundra and mountain foothills, sparsely vegetated polar deserts, permanent snow and ice-fields, patterned ground and related phenomena, highland blocks, fold mountains and volcanic chains. Most areas have been subjected to upheavals and modifications over long periods of geological time. Tundra is a major Arctic habitat, and consists of a mosaic of plant communities varying from wet coastal to alpine tundras. The vegetation of tundras and of polar deserts is dealt with later (Chapter 7). The distribution of polar deserts and semi-deserts is shown in Figures 1.2 and 1.5.

## Alaska

The Continental Divide of the Brooks Range forms the southern boundary of the Alaskan Arctic. The Brooks Range, which is some 1,100 km from east to west, is a complex of fold mountains composed primarily of sedimentary rocks, and has its origin as a geologic and topographic entity in Canada's Yukon Territory about 130 km east of the international boundary in the vicinity of the Blow River. It first forms as a range of low hills known as the Barn Mountains whose highest point barely exceeds 1,220 m. West of the Barn Mountains, the British Mountains trend north-west towards the Alaskan border, increasing steadily in both width and altitude, so that by the time the border is reached there are peaks in excess of 1,525 m. Just over the

border in Alaska, the British Mountains take a nearly east-west trend to merge into the Romanzof Mountains. Here the Brooks Range reaches it highest and widest. The highest peaks are Mount Chamberlain 2,750 m, Mount Hubley 2,717 m and Mount Michelson 2,700 m. From here the range extends westwards to reach the sea at Cape Lisburne and Cape Prince of Wales.

In front of the whole range lies a plateau known as the Arctic Foothills with an elevation of 500 to 1,000 m which, in varying depth, follow the mountain range, terminating towards the north in the 200 km deep Arctic Coastal Plain. The plain is, in many respects, exceedingly monotonous, but is rich in small features such as thaw lakes and patterned ground, both of which are described in detail in Chapter 5. The foothills drop down to the coastal plain, mostly in a series of steep steps, and numerous rivers flow from the mountains across the plain to the sea. In many of these valleys are well developed willow thickets, particularly *Salix alaxensis*. The Arctic Coastal Plain covers an area of about 65,000 km² of which up to 40 per cent is wetland, and rises from the Arctic Ocean to a maximum altitude of 183 m at its southern margin. Frozen for some nine months of the year, the abundance of standing water is apparent when viewed from the air. There are thousands of thaw lakes, with additional surface water in a network of millions of low-centre polygons, variously shaped tundra ponds, oxbow lakes, streams and rivers.

The entire coast is backed by the coastal plain except in the extreme west where the mountain foothills approach the shore near Cape Lisburne. Quite high steep cliffs extend north from Cape Lisburne to Cape Beaufort, although some beaches do occur. A short distance north-east of Cape Beaufort, the shoreline changes to one in which barrier bars and narrow lagoons are the predominant forms. The coast from Icy Cape to Point Barrow consists of two long concave arcs with maximum curvature occurring at their south-west ends. East of Point Barrow there are a number of large bays and lagoons, and all along this coast the rivers are building deltas at their mouths. Some of the bays and deltas are open to the sea, some are separated from the sea by widely spaced barriers or offshore islands, and some have rather continuous barrier bars. The delta of the Colville River (600 km²), the largest river of the Arctic Slope, contains broad mudflats and extensive sand dune systems.

## Canada

From the Alaska/Canada border eastwards to Battle Harbour on the Labrador coast is some 4,800 km. The arctic coastal plain habitat extends eastwards from Alaska into northern Canada, where it is a relatively flat terrain that slopes from 300 m at its southern margin to sea level along the coast. Several large deltas (notably that of the Mackenzie) and many lakes are present on the formerly glaciated plain. East of the Mackenzie delta, numerous small and several large

*Plate 2.1 Galbraith Lake in the northern foothills of the Brooks Range, Alaska (June)*

bays indent the coastline. Along the coast and offshore, low-lying islands and spits have been formed by riparian deposits. The deposits from the Mackenzie River have formed a chain of out-lying islands of higher elevation than the rest of the delta. Much of the Mackenzie delta is sparse boreal forest and forest-tundra, giving way to true tundra near the coast. Excluding the Mackenzie delta, the coastal area from the Alaska/Canada border, east to Cape Perry and north to Sachs Harbour (Banks Island), is generally low, flat, wet tundra. At the Parry Peninsula, low-lying sand and gravel bars in the south give way to coastal cliffs and numerous offshore islands in the north. Further east, tundra extends to the shores of Hudson Bay, and north on the Boothnia and Melville Peninsulas, and is also present on the Ungava Peninsula on the east side of Hudson Bay.

The massive Precambrian block of the Canadian Shield occupies a large proportion of the land area of Arctic Canada and extends across Baffin Bay into Greenland. In addition to its extensive mainland area it occupies most of the central and eastern Arctic islands south of the Parry Channel, and sections of Devon and Ellesmere Islands further north. The eastern edge of the Canadian Shield stands markedly higher than the western and drops steeply to the sea. The highest land is along the eastern perimeter from Ellesmere Island, down through Baffin Island (with superb fjord scenery on its east coast), to the Torngat Mountains in northern Labrador where there are glaciated peaks of 1,500–2,100 m. The landscape of the Canadian Shield is one of wide horizons, broad lowlands, denuded hills, and low plateaus. Ice-scratched rocks, long morainal ridges and eskers demonstrate the effects of glacier-ice and melt-water at the end of the last glaciation.

The Canadian Arctic Archipelago has 14 large (including six of the 30 largest islands in the world) and many small islands totalling about 1,295,000 km². The largest is Baffin Island with its dissected chain of mountains exceeding 2,000 m. Fold mountain systems exclusive to the Arctic are found in the Sverdrup Islands in the northernmost part of the archipelago, with a continuation into Peary Land in north Greenland, and east Greenland. While Devon Island is ice-capped (with the summit nearly 2,000 m above sea level), most of the remaining islands have elevations below 300 m, with occasional uplands exceeding 600 m. The mountain range which extends from Labrador and Baffin Island, north through Devon, Ellesmere and Axel Heiberg Islands, is thus a major topographic feature. It has but two major gaps – the first in Hudson Strait which separates Ungava-Labrador from Baffin Island; the second is Lancaster Sound which separates Baffin from Devon Island. Most of the Arctic archipelago north of Lancaster Sound is polar desert or semi-desert, or covered by ice-fields.

The coastal plain of Arctic Canada is bordered to the south not by mountains, but by forest-tundra and then the boreal forest itself. East of the Blow River (where the Brooks Range begins) are the geologically distinct

*Plate 2.2 Cottongrass tussock tundra on the Arctic Slope of Alaska (June)*

*Plate 2.3 Low shrub tundra in the Sagavanirktok River valley, northern Alaska*

north-south trending Richardson Mountains which are the main physiographic feature bordering the west side of the Mackenzie River. It should be noted that the shrub-tundra habitat is virtually absent east and west of Hudson Bay, although it reappears in the Labrador Peninsula. This absence is correlated with the severe climate of the Hudson Bay area which depresses vegetational zones southward.

## Greenland

Greenland presents the greatest contrast in conditions of all the Arctic lands. At one extreme is the enormous perpetual ice-desert of the interior, while at the other are the coastal areas of the south-west with farms, wildflowers, and modern towns — thanks to the influence of a warm ocean current. It is the largest

island in the world and the distance from Cape Morris Jessup (83° 39′ N) south to Cape Farewell is 2,670 km. The island is widest towards the north where the distance from the most western point to the most eastern is 1,050 km.

Much of Greenland consists of a Precambrian shield of granites and gneisses, with high mountains in the east, but lower in the west; in the north there are Paleozoic sedimentary plateaus. The highest peak in Greenland is Gunnbjorn's Mountain 3,700 m at 69° N on the east coast. Also on the east coast are Mount Forel 3,360 m, and Petermann's Peak 2,940 m. About 80 per cent of the country is still ice-covered, and at Melville Bugt in the west and near Dove Bugt in the east the ice-sheet reaches the coast, though elsewhere it is separated from the sea by a band of ice-free and frequently mountainous land up to 200 km wide through which glaciers have cut deep valleys and narrow fjords.

The most prominent landforms of the ice-free areas are bare rock hillocks with irregular lakes and a complicated pattern of stream drainage. Large parts of south-west Greenland have landscapes of this type, evidently created by the scouring effect of an ice-sheet, though in other areas such as in Jameson Land in east Greenland the ice-sheet seems to have had little effect.

There are a number of superb glacial troughs, particularly in the fjord country of the north-east. For example, Nordvest Fjord, which runs from the ice-sheet towards Scoresby Sound, is about 75 km long, 5–10 km wide, and about 3,500 m deep from plateau surface to fjord bottom. Situations where ice erosion has been concentrated in a trough or series of troughs, and has left the intervening slopes or plateaus unmodified, produces what is known as *landscapes of selective linear erosion*. In east Greenland one can often stand on the edge of an essentially unmodified pre-glacial surface and look down into a trough over 1,500 m deep (Sugden and John 1984).

The most extensive ice-free region is Peary Land in the very far north, and Cape Morris Jessup is the most northerly land on earth. The area is mainly mountains, often with very steep sides, and in the central part is an alpine area with high peaks (e.g. Nordkronen 2,000 m).

Hot springs are found in a number of localities. Their temperatures vary from 2° C up to 62° C, and blue-green algae grow in most of them. The flora has been studied by Halliday *et al* (1974).

*Figure 2.1: Svalbard: Shading Indicates the Extent of the Ice-caps Source: Armstrong, Rogers and Rowley (1978).*

## Jan Mayen Island

Situated at 71° N 8° W, this is an elongated island about 55 km in length, consisting entirely of relatively recent volcanic materials, and dominated in the north-east by the volcano Beerenberg, a glacier-covered cone rising to 2,277 m which, though supposedly extinct, erupted early in 1985. Lower mountains occur at the south-western end, but shores all round the island are steep.

## Svalbard

The five major islands of the Svalbard group comprise the Spitzbergen Archipelago. The rocks of the islands are strongly folded in many regions, and the highest peaks are Newtontoppen and Perriertoppen (1,717 m) in north-east Spitzbergen. There is considerable contemporary ice-cover (see Table 5.1 and Figure 2.1); many glaciers reach the sea, and much of the coastline is permanently ice-covered, though a low strandflat, in some places more than 10 km wide, stretches along part of the coast. The landscapes are predominantly alpine, and there are many coastal fjords. On the west side of West Spitzbergen is a line of mountains, and inland run plateaus of flat sedimentary layers, mostly below 600 m. Tundra is found only locally, as for example in the middle of Edge Island (one-third ice-

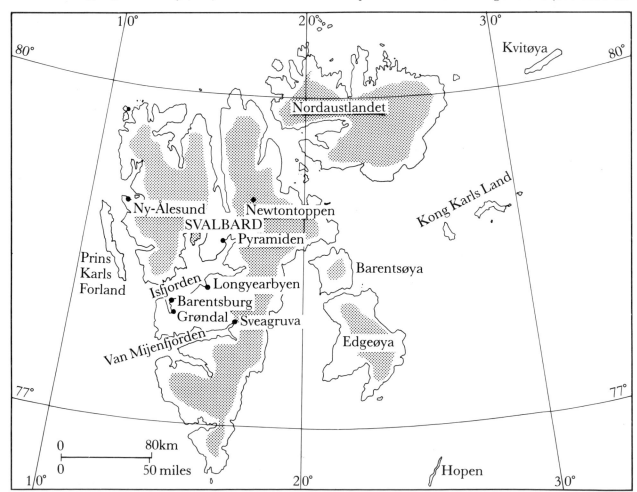

*Plate 2.4 North facing mountain ridges in the central Brooks Range, Alaska (April)*

*Plate 2.5 The Atigun Canyon in the northern foothills of the Brooks Range, Alaska, is an important lambing area for Dall Sheep*

covered), and in parts of West Barents Island and West Spitzbergen (54 per cent ice-covered); some bogs occur in the south-western part of the latter island.

## Soviet Union

The area of the Soviet Union covered by this book is predominantly flat and includes the northward extensions of the Russian Plain and of the West Siberian Plain, the two being separated by the Ural Mountains which rise to heights of between 1,000 m and 2,000 m. The fold mountain system of the Urals continues into Novaya Zemlya, and the Byrranga Mountains (which reach 1,500 m) of the Taimyr Peninsula extend into Severnaya Zemlya. Cape Cheluskin (77° 43′ N) on the Taimyr Peninsula represents the northernmost point of the Soviet mainland. On the Taimyr, tundra extends northwards for some 500 km at only 20 m elevation until the Byrranga Mountains are reached. Lake Taimyr (200 km long) lies to the south of these mountains and drains, via the Taimyr River which broaches the range, into the Arctic Ocean.

The great Siberian tundra stretches from the Urals for thousands of kilometres (gradually narrowing) eastwards beyond the Anadyr Mountains to the Chukotka Peninsula. Whilst the peninsula has mountains up to 2,000 m in height it is dominated by tundra; lowland areas of this habitat are elsewhere confined to a relatively narrow coastal strip bordering the Arctic Ocean. The general landscape is similar to that of the Arctic coastal plains of Alaska and Canada. Major rivers draining northwards into the Arctic Ocean include the Indigirka, Kolyma, Lena, Ob, Pechora and Yenesei. All are ice-bound for part of the year, and

*Plate 2.6 Breeding habitat of the Stilt Sandpiper on Jenny Lind Island, Arctic Canada*

*Plate 2.7 Breeding site for Brünnich's Guillemot, Prince Leopold Island, Lancaster Sound, Canada (June)*

since the headwaters of most are far to the south there is extensive annual flooding at the time of the spring thaw.

The Soviet Arctic islands of Franz Josef Land, Novaya Zemlya, and Severnaya Zemlya, are extensively glaciated (Table 5.1) and the two latter are mountainous. Franz Josef Land has a total shoreline of 2,700 km of which 500 km is flat beach, 600 km is steep mountains or cliffs, while the remaining 1,600 km is covered with glaciers which go straight into the sea. The New Siberian Islands further to the east are largely unglaciated and have maximum elevations of 300 to 525 m. They are poorly vegetated, and cliffs are present on some coastal stretches. Wrangel Island consists of lowlands and mountain ranges up to 1,100 m. Glacial and alluvial deposits cover large areas. All these islands are in the polar desert zone (see Figure 1.2).

*Plate 2.8 Breeding habitat of the White-rumped Sandpiper on Jenny Lind Island, Canada (June)*

*Plate 2.10 Ivory Gull colony on Graham Bell Island, Franz Josef Land (July)*

*Plate 2.11 The Mackenzie River, Canada, showing delta lakes and the Richardson Mountains*

*Plate 2.12 A stony alluvial plain on Bathurst Island, Arctic Canada, breeding habitat of the Sanderling*

*Plate 2.13 Coastal lowland at Berlinguet Inlet, south-west Baffin Island, Canada*

# 3
# THE ARCTIC CLIMATE

## Introduction

A knowledge of the main climatic features of the Arctic is essential background to an understanding of the flora and fauna. Complications obviously arise when trying to generalise. Significant local differences in climate are produced, for instance, by topography and the presence of bodies of water, and further down the scale comes the question of microclimates, which are briefly reviewed later in this chapter.

One aspect of particular importance which has to be borne in mind when considering the ecology of the Arctic is the fact that these regions are young. That is to say, they have only recently been exposed by the retreat of the Pleistocene ice-sheets. Some areas of Greenland and the eastern Canadian Arctic still remain much as they were when they first emerged from beneath the ice. The geological, palaeobotanical and biogeographic evidence clearly supports the conclusion that tundra is the most recently evolved of the world's major ecosystems; circumpolar Arctic tundra as seen today is a product of the Pleistocene. The time since the last glacial period, in which plant and animal communities have become established in the Arctic is in the order of 3,000 to 15,000 years, depending on the region. For example, Komárhová and Webber (1980) suggest a minimum age of 4,000 years for the development of complex tundra plant communities at Atkasook on the inland portion of Alaska's Arctic Coastal Plain. During the glacial periods not all of the Arctic was under ice. For example, the Arctic Slope of Alaska, certain areas in the Canadian Arctic Archipelago, and Peary Land in north Greenland, were probably largely unglaciated and therefore acted as refugia (Löve 1959, Matthews 1979).

An important factor to be considered when trying to explain the character of the Arctic environment is the extremely marked seasonal rhythm of these polar lands. In summary, the Arctic experiences prolonged cold, dark winters and brief, but bright summers. Winter may extend over eight or nine months, and during this time the temperature may never rise above freezing. On the other hand the days lengthen rapidly with almost continuous daylight in May, June and July, and by the early part of the latter month it is high summer and temperatures can remain above 10° C for week after week. Temperatures on rock surfaces and in the upper part of the soil can reach 30° C at this time, but by September winter conditions return.

Many people who have never been to the Arctic tend to envisage it as a dark and forbidding place, perpetually cold, and covered with snow and ice. Generally speaking it *is* cold in the Arctic, in fact so cold sometimes as to defy belief, but there is considerable variation in temperature and in the duration of cold periods from one part of the Arctic to another. Spring in the Arctic, coming as it does after the bitter cold and dark of the long winter, is an unforgettable experience. The sun is above the horizon 24 hours a day and the air shimmers above the white blanket of snow, just as it often does above the tundra in summer to the extent that mirages occur. Even quite early in spring it is possible to be comfortably warm in the sun, whilst temperatures in the shade will be well below freezing point.

In the spring the Arctic skies are a light blue (usually appearing green towards the horizon) and cirrus clouds are a characteristic feature. By summer the blue has increased in intensity, and grey stratus clouds replace the cirrus. Rain can, on occasion, be quite heavy and it may snow at any time. The great danger in the Arctic (particularly to man) is not the ambient air temperature itself, but the chill factor introduced by the wind (see Table 3.1). As an example, a 40 km per hour wind with an air temperature of −12° C results in an equivalent chill temperature of −34.5° C, at which point exposed flesh may freeze within one minute. Therefore, it is not locations with the lowest temperatures that pose a problem so much as those where cold and wind prevail together.

Wind is an important factor in the distribution of snow, and particularly windy sites may have little or no snow cover even in winter. The actual pattern of snow accumulation is a key factor in determining the distribution of plant communities both directly and indirectly, because of its influence on soil moisture and the disposition of available radiant energy at the surface.

Generally speaking, the winter regime in the Arctic is more clearly defined by latitude than is the summer regime. In the case of the High Arctic climates, temperatures rise above freezing for two to three months of the year. At Point Barrow, Alaska (71° N), for example, the total dark period lasts for about one month, whilst at Devon Island (75° N) in the Canadian High Arctic it extends over three months. The mean minimum winter temperature at Point Barrow is −32.8° C and at Devon Island −40.5° C. There is considerable climatic variation from year to year, particularly in summer air temperature, which in turn influences the temperature of the smaller aquatic habitats. From the 1930s to the late 1950s the Arctic climate was ameliorating, but this trend was then reversed and from 1961 to 1970 average temperatures showed that the Arctic was getting colder again. Collated temperature data for the area from Iceland and Svalbard, to Taimyr and Severnaya Zemlya show how the warming trend became clearly pronounced after the 1920s. The average difference in temperature between the beginning of the century and the 1950s was about 7° C for winter, 5° C for autumn, and only about 1° C for the spring and summer (Slessers 1966).

As pointed out by Lamb (1982), the cooling of the Arctic and Subarctic since 1950–1960 has been most marked in the very same regions which experienced the strongest warming in the earlier decades of the present century, namely the central Arctic and the northern-most parts of the two great continents remote from the world's oceans, and also the Norwegian-East Greenland Sea. In some places (e.g. the Franz Josef Land Archipelago near 80° N 50–60° E) the long-term average temperature fell by 3–4° C and the ten-year average winter temperatures became 6–10° C colder in the 1960s than in preceding decades. The increased flow of the cold East Greenland Current bringing polar water southwards has in several years brought more Arctic sea-ice to the coasts of Iceland than for 50 years.

## Pressure Systems

The primary framework of the Arctic polar climate is provided by the polar cap of low pressure in the middle and upper troposphere, i.e. above about 3 km (Barry *et al* 1981). In winter the westerly wind belt flows around this vortex in response to the equator-pole temperature gradient. At the surface in high northern latitudes, the vortex is obscured by a complex pattern of high- and low-pressure areas. Deep troughs of low pressure are located over eastern North America and eastern Siberia in winter and these have great influence on

**Table 3.1:** The Chill Factor Resulting from Wind Speed. The temperatures within the thicker line are hazardous to man: flesh freezes within one minute. Temperatures to the right are extremely hazardous; flesh freezes within 30 seconds
Source: Remmert 1980.

| Wind velocity in km/h | Temperature in −°C | | | | | | | | | | | | | | | |
|---|---|---|---|---|---|---|---|---|---|---|---|---|---|---|---|---|
| | 9 | 12 | 15 | 18 | 21 | 24 | 26 | 29 | 31 | 34 | 37 | 40 | 42 | 45 | 47 | 51 |
| 8 | 12 | 15 | 18 | 21 | 24 | 26 | 29 | 31 | 34 | 37 | 40 | 42 | 45 | 47 | 51 | 54 |
| 16 | 18 | 24 | 26 | 29 | 31 | 37 | 40 | 42 | 45 | 51 | 54 | 56 | 60 | 62 | 68 | 71 |
| 24 | 24 | 29 | 31 | 34 | 40 | 42 | 45 | 51 | 54 | 56 | 62 | 65 | 68 | 73 | 76 | 79 |
| 32 | 24 | 31 | 34 | 37 | 42 | 45 | 51 | 54 | 60 | 62 | 65 | 71 | 73 | 79 | 82 | 84 |
| 40 | 29 | 34 | 37 | 42 | 45 | 51 | 54 | 60 | 62 | 68 | 71 | 76 | 79 | 84 | 87 | 93 |
| 48 | 31 | 34 | 40 | 45 | 47 | 54 | 56 | 62 | 65 | 71 | 73 | 79 | 82 | 87 | 90 | 96 |
| 56 | 34 | 37 | 40 | 45 | 51 | 54 | 60 | 62 | 68 | 73 | 76 | 82 | 84 | 90 | 93 | 98 |
| 64 | 23 | 37 | 42 | 47 | 51 | 56 | 60 | 65 | 71 | 73 | 73 | 82 | 87 | 90 | 96 | 101 |

*Plate 3.3 Lindemansdalen from Store Sodal, A.P. Olsens Land, Greenland*

*Plate 3.1 Brilliant August colours in the Greenland landscape*

mid-latitude cyclones. Atlantic cyclones follow the line of the oceanic North Atlantic Drift, or move northward into Baffin Bay where they contribute significantly to the strongly oceanic regime of the eastern Canadian Arctic. The central Canadian Arctic and the central and eastern Siberian Arctic are dominated by high-pressure conditions in winter and also, particularly in the former area, in spring. The latter is the only season when there is a semi-permanent Arctic high-pressure system. In summer the polar vortex contracts and weakens. Although the major trough is at that time centred over Baffin Island, weak cyclonic activity is widespread in the Arctic. Lows on the Arctic front affect both northern North America and northern Siberia.

## Temperature

There is a surprising degree of uniformity in summer temperatures over the Arctic. From the southern edge of the area, where the mean temperature of the warmest month is 10° C, north to the endless surface of the permanent pack-ice, the difference is only 10° C. The mean of the coldest month may vary from −5° C or −10° C at the southern margin of the tundra, to −30° C or −35° C on the northern margins. Absolute minima below −70° C have in fact been recorded. Inevitably there is much variation. Over continental tundra areas daytime temperatures may reach 25° C, and even at 80° N latitude temperatures of 20° C are occasionally recorded. Water bodies may set up land-sea breezes, modify the structure of air masses, and induce cloudiness and precipitation. Thus, along the coast of Alaska's Arctic Slope the combined effect of stratus cloud cover and the cold sea results in summer temperatures several degrees lower than those inland. It has been demonstrated (Brown *et al* 1975) that the temperature increases inland in July by about 6° C per 100 km, with the steepest rise close to the coast.

In the Soviet Union data are available from the meteorological station of Ust-Tareya on the western Taimyr Peninsula, for 1967. During the course of that year there were 267 days with an average daily temperature below 0° C and 165 days with the temperature below −20° C. There were 5,500 degree-days below freezing and only 657 degree-days above. The average

*Plate 3.4 A High Arctic scene at Fluker Point, Ellesmere Island, Canada*

temperature for January was −31.3° C, and for July 10.5° C. The length of the frost-free period was only 59 days. There were only 269 degree-days above 10° C. However, during the short summer there were some very hot days, with an absolute maximum of 29° C (Romanova 1972). Cape Cheluskin (77° 43′ N) on the north of the Taimyr Peninsula represents the northernmost mainland in the Soviet Union and is in the Polar Desert zone. A mean temperature above zero is recorded only in July and August (1.8° C and 0.6° C respectively), but even during these months there are days with below zero mean temperatures (Chernov *et al* 1977). These data illustrate graphically the severity of the climate in some of the more northerly parts of the Arctic.

It is difficult to make neat divisions of the Arctic climate. A simple division, for example, into an ice-sheet climate where (like the Greenland ice-sheet) the warmest mean monthly temperature does not exceed 0° C, to a tundra climate where the comparable temperature lies between 0° C and 10° C, does not allow for the sort of variations produced by topography for example. Neither does it allow for the very important distinction between the maritime and continental portions of the Arctic. Whereas the northern periphery of Siberia, northern Alaska, and Arctic Canada are areas with a typical continental climate (i.e. low temperatures, minimal snowfall and, in terms of absolute humidity, very dry air), peripheral areas towards the Atlantic and Pacific rarely experience extreme low temperatures, but may receive considerable snowfall. Islands such as Jan Mayen and Svalbard have a markedly oceanic climate.

## Precipitation

Tundra climates become more desert-like (in terms of precipitation) with increasing latitude, since low temperatures limit the atmospheric water content. Although precipitation decreases towards the North Pole, at the same time the reduction in temperature reduces the ability of the air to hold water and the resultant high humidity (e.g. 84–85 per cent at Devon Island in June and July) minimises evapotranspiration, so that abundant moisture may be available in areas that are classified as polar desert. Various factors produce considerable irregularities in the distribution of precipitation, as for example the transport of snow by wind. In general, precipitation in the polar desert areas (including permanent ice) is light, ranging from 70 mm to, in isolated cases, in excess of 200 mm, most of it falling in solid form. Most of the northern Polar Basin is arid, probably receiving an annual average of only about 135 mm. Over most of Alaska's Arctic Slope the average snowfall is about 500–760 mm, increasing to more than 1,250 mm as the Brooks Range is reached, but dropping to under 375 mm at the higher elevations. Equivalent rainfall figures are about 100 mm on the Arctic coast to more than 200 mm near the Brooks Range. On the western part of the Greenland ice-sheet glaciologists have estimated that snowfall amounts of

*Plate 3.5 Svalbard—Austfjord, Einsteinfjellet (in cloud) and Sanderbreen Glacier*

up to 700 mm water equivalent occur over large areas. In contrast, at Ivigtut, West Greenland, most precipitation falls as rain; up to 1,400 mm has been recorded.

## Solar Radiation

The fundamental climatological driving force is solar radiation which, on a global scale, exhibits a marked zonation. As latitude increases so radiation plays an increasingly important role, but the lower the angle of incidence of the sun's rays, so the smaller the energy intake. Although the decrease in solar radiation because of low solar altitude is compensated for by increasing daylight (for example, a continuous polar 'day' of 3.5 months at latitude 75° N), a great deal of solar energy is nevertheless irradiated during the summer months. Also, the further north one goes, the greater the proportion of annual radiation required to melt the snow as opposed to acting as a source of energy – the primary input to the Arctic food web. The high reflectivity (or albedo) of snow also reduces considerably the amount of solar radiation actually absorbed by the tundra surface. In some parts of the Arctic the growing season may be as short as 40 days.

The biotic implications of climate are most strongly felt during the growing season, the period during which there is little or no frost. This period is critically important to the maintenance of the Arctic food web and is largely determined by the radiation regime.

## Microclimates

Microclimates are of great ecological importance in the Arctic, and a valuable synthesis is given by Corbet (1972). He defined microclimate (in the practical biological sense) as the physical environment of a particular organism, in that the concept has meaning only in terms of a given plant or animal. It therefore follows that at a single locality the microclimate available to a moss and a fungus, or a caribou and a mosquito, will be strikingly different. The majority of microclimates can be regarded as specialised parts of their general surroundings, and of the local climate. Many animals, especially invertebrates, can change their microclimate dramatically simply by changing their location. There is a stratum 10–15 cm thick next to the ground where temperature and air moisture fluctuate violently according to the sun's elevation and exposure. There is also a stratum a few millimetres thick where wind has no measurable effect owing to the frictional drag exerted by the substrate. Beneath the ground surface, in soil, gradients of temperature and moisture also exist. Because solar heat is distributed unevenly, the microclimatic conditions for plants and animals are likewise not uniform. The most favourable thermal regime occurs in the interface layer between the atmosphere and the soil, and maximum soil-surface temperatures of about 50° C have been recorded at 73° N (Sorensen 1941) and of 33° C at 82° N (Corbet 1967). The temperature of a surface is affected greatly by its albedo (which itself depends on the nature of the surface), and also by aspect and the degree of slope.

*Plate 3.6 Polar desert habitat in northern Greenland*

*Plate 3.7 North-west Taimyr Peninsula—wet tundra with Brent Goose nest in foreground*

Generally speaking, while the sun is above the horizon, mounds and hummocks are significantly warmer than the surrounding level ground. In the absence of near-surface temperature inversions, ground temperature remains above the ambient air temperature recorded at standard screen height, and diurnal temperature variations are small.

One of the most obvious examples of a favourable microclimate is found in moss cushions and the low-growing cushion-type plants (for example, Moss Campion *Silene acaulis*) so characteristic of some Arctic habitats. Here is a microclimate so sheltered that even a gale force wind has very little effect. In northern Greenland, at 82° 29′ N, during the month of May

*Plate 3.8 Ketil (2,010 m), Tasermiut, southern Greenland*

above the snow. Winters of unusually shallow snow cover and cold subnivean conditions may well inhibit winter survival of lemmings. The air temperature under snow cover is not only very stable compared with that above at the snow surface but, as already mentioned, is generally higher, particularly where there is little or no insolation. In the High Arctic, subnivean temperatures of 0° C may occur when it is −33° C only 40 cm away at the snow surface.

when the ambient air temperature at noon was −12° C, a Swedish botanist recorded a temperature of 3° C among the dead leaves of a tuft of saxifrage and 10° C inside a cushion of dark coloured mosses. Another example is cottongrass *Eriophorum* spp. which produces its own insulation, protecting the developing seedhead in a ball of cotton inside which the temperature may be 20° warmer than that of the surrounding air.

For nine months of the year, the Arctic coastal plains of Alaska, Canada and Siberia are covered with dry, wind-packed snow. Distinct features of the snow include a thin wind-swept sastrugi surface (i.e. ridges on the surface of the snow) and large drifts along banks. Provided a good depth of snow is present, lemmings are able to live in a favourable subnivean environment where temperatures are significantly higher than those

# 4
# THE MARINE ENVIRONMENT

## Introduction

Oceanographers and marine biologists are concerned with the seas and the life therein, and their definition of the Arctic is somewhat different to that used for the land areas. They define Arctic water as having a temperature at or near 0° C and a salinity of approximately 30 parts per thousand. The surface waters of the Arctic Ocean exhibits these characteristics as do portions of the adjacent seas. Another definition takes as the Arctic marine zone the area which is covered by sea-ice in the midwinter months, and having surface waters with negative temperatures and salinities below 34.5 parts per thousand (Dunbar 1968).

The marine area of the Arctic may also be divided into High and Low Arctic (or Polar and Subpolar) zones, the boundaries in this case being based on the physical properties of water masses. High Arctic water, as defined above, spreads across the Arctic Basin and through the Canadian Arctic Archipelago. In addition, a long narrow tongue of the same cold waters stretches southwards down the east coast of Greenland. At its southern limit the High Arctic water meets and overrides warmer and saltier water. The southern limit of the Low Arctic marine zone is the somewhat ill-defined boundary between the mixed waters and the pure northern Atlantic and Pacific Ocean waters. The boundaries of the High and Low Arctic marine zones are shown in Figure 4.1. A wide zone of mixed Arctic and Atlantic water extends from the Kara Sea and Novaya Zemlya in the east to Baffin Bay, Labrador and Newfoundland in the west. On the Pacific side, mixed Arctic and Pacific Ocean waters flow eastwards along the north coast of Alaska, and west as far as Wrangel Island and the southern Chukotka Peninsula.

The polar region above 80° N is an ocean-filled basin – the Arctic (or Polar) Basin – some of which is well over 4,000 m below sea level. Recent research suggests that the connections to the Atlantic and Pacific Oceans did not emerge until after the end of the Cretaceous (about 65 million years ago) or even later. The Arctic Basin should not be confused with the Arctic drainage basin (most of the immense expanse between 55° N and 80° N) which is a huge watershed from which all running water drains eventually into the Arctic Ocean and which, confusingly, has sometimes been referred to in the literature as the Arctic basin.

The area of the Arctic Ocean as a whole is approximately 14 million km². In the Eurasian section of the Arctic, peninsulas and islands result in separation of the area into five marginal seas – Barents, Kara, Laptev, East Siberian and Chukchi. Together they occupy about 36 per cent of the area of the Arctic Ocean, but only two per cent by volume of its water. All the major continental rivers of the Arctic drainage basin (with the exception of the Colville River in Alaska and the Mackenzie River in Canada) flow into these five seas. As a result of this these shallow seas, with a high ratio of exposed surface to volume and with a substantial input of fresh water in summer, greatly influence the surface water conditions in the Arctic Ocean.

A major underwater ridge (the Lomonosov Ridge rising 3,000 m above the surrounding ocean floor) lies between the New Siberian Islands (Novosibirskiye Ostrova) and Ellesmere Island in the Canadian Arctic. With a minimum depth of about 900 m and a sill depth of about 1,500 m, the ridge divides the Arctic Ocean into two major basins – the Amerasia and Eurasia Basins. The Eurasia Basin (about 5,122 m at its deepest point) is connected with the Atlantic Ocean via the Greenland and Norwegian Seas. Since the opening between Svalbard and Greenland is 460 km wide and has a sill depth of more than 2,500 m, large amounts of water may be exchanged between the Atlantic and the Arctic Oceans.

The Amerasia Basin (which itself contains two sub-basins, the largest of which is the Canadian Basin) is connected with the Pacific Ocean via the Chukchi and Bering Seas by the narrow (64 km) and shallow (45 m) Bering Straits. It has been calculated that the total annual influx through these straits from the Bering Sea is 10 times that from the Siberian rivers. This results in a marked Pacific influence on the upper 150 m of water in the Canadian Basin. The Amerasia Basin has a uniform depth of about 3,800 m in the south and depths in excess of 4,000 m near the North Pole.

## Stratification

Generally speaking, the Arctic Ocean can be said to have three main strata of water or water masses, and these are:–

1. The surface layer (Arctic water).
   This has varying characteristics but is generally cold (at or near freezing point), and is relatively dilute at 28–32 parts per thousand at the surface, but below about 50 m the salinity increases sharply with depth. In these cold Arctic waters temperature has less influence on density than does salinity, so that the vertical distributions of salinity and density are nearly parallel. Below about 100 m in the Eurasia Basin and 150 m in the Amerasia Basin, the temperature also rises.

2. The layer immediately below the Arctic water (the Atlantic layer).
   This layer, from about 150 or 250 m down to 900 m,

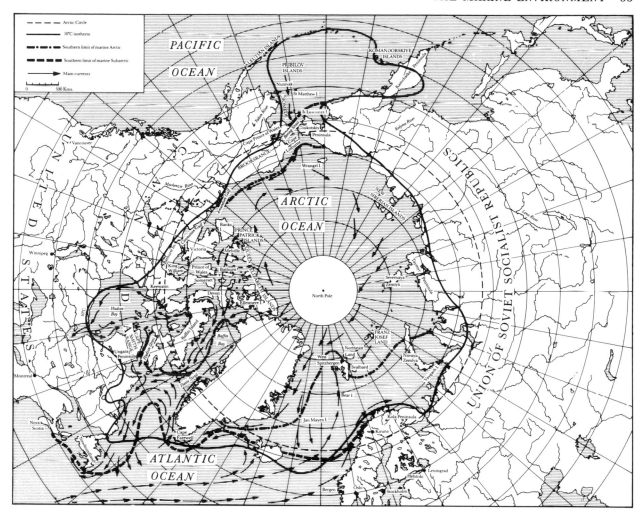

*Figure 4.1: Marine Zones of the Arctic   Source: Adapted from Stonehouse (1971).*

has temperatures above 0° C (as high as approximately 3° C) and a quite uniform salinity of 34.9 to 35.1 parts per thousand.

3. The layer from the Atlantic water to the bottom. This stratum is occupied by 'bottom water' with almost uniform salinities between 34.9 and 35.0 parts per thousand. Its temperatures are nearly uniform also: in the Eurasia Basin they are −0.70° C to −0.80° C and in the Amerasia Basin from −0.30° C to −0.40° C.

In the Candaian Basin, warmer, fresher water flooding north through the Bering Strait mixes with colder, more saline water in the Chukchi Sea forming a layer with temperature and salinity characteristics such that it flows over the underlying Atlantic water and under the purely surface waters as part of the clockwise circulation in the Beaufort Sea area.

## Continental Shelves

The Arctic Ocean is surrounded by shallow continental shelves with a combined area exceeding 2.5 million km² (Dunbar 1982). On the North American side the shelf is quite narrow (37–93 km), whereas the section bounded by Europe and Siberia (from Svalbard east to the Bering Strait) has a broad shelf the edge of which, near Franz Josef Land, is more than 1,500 km from the mainland. The biological productivity of these continental shelf areas is more intense than on land. It is in the peripheral seas where ice-cover disappears briefly in summer, and cold waters from the Arctic meet those of the warmer oceans, that marine life in the Arctic is most abundant. The whole Barents Sea region belongs to the continental shelf, having depths mostly between 200 and 400 m.

## Sea-Ice

In summer the boundaries between sea and land in the Arctic are mostly clearly apparent. In winter, however, ice and snow means there is little visible difference. The Arctic Ocean is covered year-round by a more or less continuous expanse of pack-ice of varying thickness. In the North American Arctic a large-scale surface current moves the sea-ice in an irregular clockwise circulation, while in the Eurasian shelf areas it is moved counter-clockwise by several complex circular currents. At its annual maximum, the pack-ice reaches 10 million km² (almost 30 per cent of the world's sea-ice), and it plays a critical role in the generation of climates.

Pack-ice, to the inexperienced eye, appears featureless and unproductive. It is, in fact, a varied substrate, providing many different niches for a rather impressive number of sea mammals. It can be split into two main types. Ice forming in bays and along complex coastlines is anchored to the land and is known as 'landfast', or simply 'fast-ice'. It is a stable expanse usually containing annually-formed ice 1.5 to 2.0 m thick. Deformation by winds and tides of such ice-sheets results in ice-hummocks, pressure ridges of varying size, open leads and cracks. Some fast-ice areas contain polynas, areas of open water, which form in the same place from year to year and are discussed further below. Fast-ice will sometimes be more than one year old. Such ice is encountered in bays at high latitudes.

More abundant in total extent than land-fast ice is the shifting ice made up of pans or ice floes, and generally referred to as the pack-ice. This not only covers extensive areas of the Arctic seas, but also extends south into other seas such as the Bering and Okhotsk. Depending on existing currents, wind and temperature, pack-ice can cover varying proportions of the water bodies. The ice in such areas is constantly moving and interspersed with open water. Both fast-ice and annual pack-ice provide a floating platform for bears and seals.

## Polynas

Ice-cover on the Arctic seas is never absolutely complete. A variety of factors, the most important of which are currents, tidal fluctuations, wind and upwellings, cause leads and open areas of water to occur. It is these open areas that are known as polynas, and they are found particularly over shallows and near headlands. The most recent useful study of polynas is that by Stirling and Cleator (1981).

Polynas vary in size from quite small holes to extensive areas of open water. There are two categories of recurring polynas – those that remain open throughout the winter, and those that may be ice-covered through the coldest months in some years. In the latter case, open water usually appears in late March or early April. Probably the largest polyna of the first type is the North Water, an area about the size of Switzerland in the northernmost part of Baffin Bay between Greenland and southern Ellesmere Island. The distribution of recurring polynas (see Figure 4.2) may be quite localised, as in the Canadian Arctic.

In addition to the types of polyna just described, there are extensive systems of shoreleads throughout the Arctic where variable-sized areas of semipermanent open water are maintained largely by offshore winds and, to a lesser degree, by local currents. These leads tend to be linear in shape and are among

*Plate 4.1 Scene near the Lenivaya River, northern Taimyr Peninsula showing clumps of Glacier Avens* Geum glaciale

*Plate 4.2 View on the north-west Taimyr Peninsula showing flowers of the Arctic Milk Vetch* Astragalus umbellatus

the areas where open water is found most constantly during winter and early spring.

In terms of biological significance, it is the recurring polynas that are most important, and they are used extensively by marine mammals. There is evidence to suggest that they are also of critical importance to Arctic marine birds for feeding, reproduction and migration.

## Biological Aspects

The Arctic Ocean (High Arctic) ecosystem differs in several important respects from that of the Low Arctic, and even more so from that of temperate marine ecosystems. Characteristic features of the Arctic Ocean include low species diversity, low productivity, lifecycles adapted to very short timetables and changes, and the presence of distinctive sub-ice biological communities. The overall effect is an ocean with a relative biological barrenness and ecological simplicity that is unusual among major circulating water bodies of the world. Compared to open water, sea-ice permits only some one per cent of the energy exchange between the sea and the atmosphere, and reduces photosynthesis to less than one tenth the amount that would occur without ice-cover. The production of phytoplankton, the basis of the marine food chain, is therefore reduced, and there is a sparse and strongly oscillating nutrient supply for plants and lower animals.

In contrast, in the areas (in the Low Arctic) where the Arctic Ocean meets and mixes with the Atlantic and Pacific waters, the biological productivity matches that of any other portion of the world's oceans. The ice-cover is responsible for most of the special characteristics of the Arctic marine ecosystem. It provides a substrate for a special category of primary producers, namely the ice biota – mainly diatoms – which probably represent between 10 and 30 per cent of the total Arctic Ocean planktonic production. The ice flora supports a special group of grazers and species in higher trophic levels, including amphipods, copepods,

some worms, and two species of polar cod. The system also includes seabirds (especially auks) and Ringed Seals *Phoca hispida* (Dunbar 1982). Figure 4.3 represents the High Arctic and Low Arctic marine food web, though it is a simplified version of a much more complex pattern. Superimposed on top of the food web as shown here are the Polar Bear *Ursus maritimus* and Arctic Fox *Alopex lagopus*, the one as a predator and the other as a predator and scavenger.

The most productive areas, where turbulence or upwelling has disrupted the stable water stratification, allow mixing of water masses with sustained currents that can gather and concentrate nutrients from a large area. Where warm waters (those of the North Atlantic Drift for example) meet cold Arctic water masses the warm water becomes cold and sinks to the bottom. It is

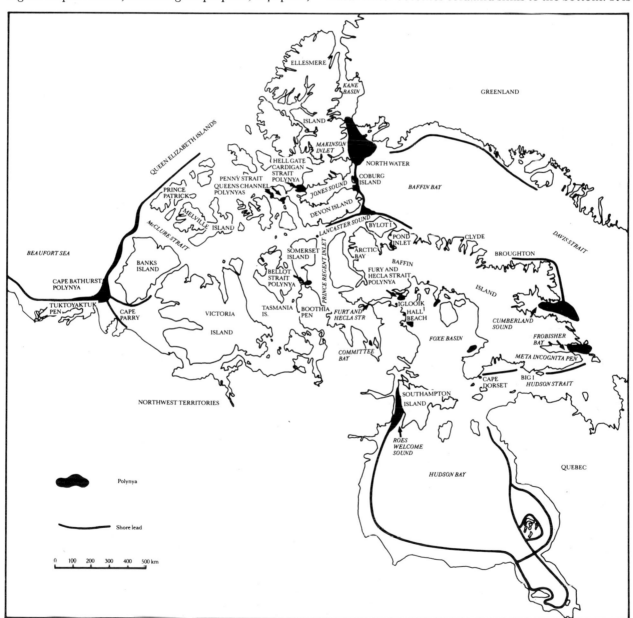

*Figure 4.2: Map of the Canadian Arctic Showing the Distribution of Recurring Polynas*
*Source: Stirling and Cleator (1981).*

Plate 4.3 Reinsdyrflya is the largest area of low-lying ground in Svalbard, and an important breeding area for waders

Plate 4.4 Landscape exhibiting selective linear erosion, Nordvestfjord, east Greenland

*Plate 4.5 Prins Karls Forland on Svalbard's westerly seaboard attracts bad weather*

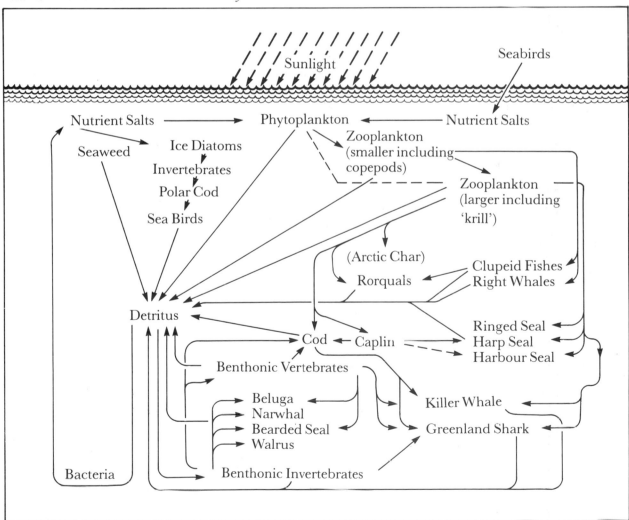

*Figure 4.3: Simplified Presentation of the Biological Cycle and Food Web in the Arctic Marine Zone  Source: Dunbar (1982).*

*Plate 4.6 Dry hummocky tundra near Mesters Vig, north-east Greenland*

replaced by nutrient-rich deeper-lying polar water. The vertical circulation (convergence) renews the nutrients in the upper water layers, an essential condition for plant production. A particularly important area is Lancaster Sound in the Canadian Arctic Archipelago.

It is possible that more than 33 per cent of all the breeding seabirds of eastern North America north of the subtropics breed or spend part of the year in this one restricted area at 75° N, and that 40 per cent of the North American populations of the Beluga *Delphinapterus leucas* and Narwhal *Monodon monoceros* move into or through Lancaster Sound in the summer months (Dunbar 1982). Among the factors responsible for the unusual productivity of Lancaster Sound are channel morphology, temperature and salinity gradients in three intersecting passages, freshwater run-off from glaciers, and wind patterns.

The Barents Sea likewise exhibits high primary production and is one of the most densely populated seabird areas in the world. This situation is due to a combination of three basic factors as outlined by Norderhaug *et al* 1977:–

1. Temperature – which, in the area of the North Atlantic Drift is relatively higher than it is elsewhere so far north.
2. Availability of light – which, because of the extreme light conditions of the polar regions is continuous day and night during the summer season.
3. Abundance of dissolved nutrients – which, because of vertical circulation within the water mass, are present in the upper water layer all year round.

The average zooplankton abundance in the Barents Sea is 140 mg m$^{-3}$ of water; in the most productive area, the figure fluctuates between 200 and 2,000 mg m$^{-3}$ and even attains 6–8 g m$^{-3}$. The total mass of zooplankton in the Barents Sea in summer has been calculated to be *ca*. 100 million tonnes. The greatest part of this figure is made up of copepods (*Calanus* spp.) which have only one generation a year. Not less than 1,000 million tonnes of phytoplankton provides the food for this great mass of zooplankton. The yearly production of phytoplankton in the Barents Sea may be of the order of 2–3,000 million tonnes. These figures give a good indication of just how biologically rich some Arctic waters can be, given the right conditions.

# 5
# THE TERRESTRIAL ENVIRONMENT

## Introduction

Once snow-melt has uncovered those areas not permanently covered by snow and ice, the Arctic landscape is seen to possess a variety of striking features many of which are due, directly or indirectly, to the presence of permafrost. These, and other aspects, are briefly dealt with below.

## Permafrost

Permafrost is naturally occurring earth material whose temperature has been below 0° C for several years regardless of the state of any moisture that might be present. This is the definition given by Lachenbruch (1968), but in point of fact it is a complex subject and there are minor differences of opinion regarding its definition. However, from a biological point of view the semantic arguments are not particularly important. The term describes only the thermal condition of the ground, not its composition, which may be almost any kind of material – bedrock, clay, gravel, sand or silt.

We can recognise two main types of permafrost – dry permafrost containing little excess ice, as usually found in areas of rock, gravel or coarse sand; and wet permafrost which generally has a high ice content, and is found in fine-grained soils such as Pleistocene and recent (as for example on the Arctic coastal plains of Alaska and Canada). Some of the features of the permafrost environment are illustrated in Figure 5.1. The biological effects of permafrost are considerable. In much of the Arctic its presence prevents the growth of plant species with deep root systems. At the same time, because of its impervious surface, the limited precipitation is retained in the overlying soil and concentrated in shallow ponds, and an extensive cover of shrubs, mosses and sedges is able to flourish that could not otherwise survive.

Permafrost may be described as the hidden face of the Arctic landscape, although its presence is revealed by sundry surface features. The importance of permafrost is best appreciated when it is realised that it underlies approximately 26 per cent (including glaciers) of the earth's land surface, the majority of it in the northern hemisphere. The distribution of the various categories of permafrost in the northern hemisphere is shown in Figure 5.2. In the high latitudes of the northern hemisphere, where it has existed for thousands of years, it is known as *continuous permafrost*, which is very much a feature of the Arctic as defined for the purposes of this book. Excluding mountains, continuous permafrost covers about $7.64 \times 10^6$ km² of the northern hemisphere. The southern limit of continuous permafrost in general relates to the mean annual air isotherm of −8° C.

Permafrost thickness has been measured at various places in the Arctic (see Washburn 1979). In general, it is true to say that permafrost in the Soviet Union is thicker than in North America. In the continuous zone the depth increases northwards from 300 m at the southern limit to over 600 m along the Arctic coastal plain in the Verkhoyansk-Kolyma region. On the Taimyr Peninsula permafrost reaches 610 m in thickness. In North America the maximum thickness recorded is about 1,000 m on Ellesmere Island. Other permafrost depths reported in Arctic Canada include 700 m on Cameron Island (north-west of Bathurst Island) and 400 m on Cornwallis Island. In Alaska, just over 600 m has been recorded at Prudhoe Bay and 204–405 m at Barrow. Recorded depths on Svalbard range from 241 to 305 m. At Thule, Greenland, 518 m has been reported.

Climate is basic to the formation and continued existence of permafrost, and also has a profound influence on the active layer (see below). The development of permafrost and its thickness are influenced by various factors that affect the transfer of heat between the air and the ground – for example, the type of vegetation cover, snow cover, the nature of the component rock and soil, cloud cover, microclimatic conditions, and hydrology. Permafrost cannot be considered in isolation, either in its origin and formation, its degradation, or its ecological effects. It forms a complex, dynamically-balanced system with climatic history, vegetational history, recent climate, current vegetation, substratum, topography, solifluction and animal activity all interacting. If any one of the individual factors changes, the permafrost regime may shift.

## Coastal Erosion

Where coasts are developed in permafrost terrain composed of unconsolidated and ice-rich sediments, rapid and dramatic coastal retreat may be associated with the melting and release of excess ice. For example, the entire coast from Point Barrow, Alaska, east to the Canadian border, and the adjacent 500 km coastline of Canada's Yukon Territory, is characterised by the thermal erosion of permafrost during the annual thaw period (Lewellen 1970). The shoreline recession slumping, and permafrost degradation, is caused by wave action and thawing air temperatures. In the vicinity of Point Barrow, average retreat rates of 2–4 m per annum appear to be typical for sections of coast with no protecting beach gravels. Along the Yukon Territory coast and in the Mackenzie district of Canada the same pattern of rapid coastal retreat is

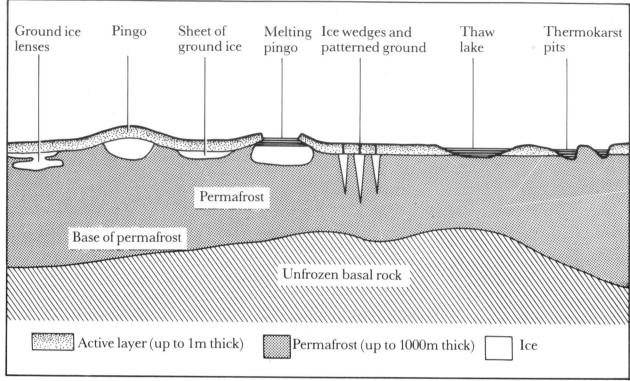

*Figure 5.1: Simplified Diagrammatic Representation of Surface Features on Tundra Underlain by Continuous Permafrost  Source: Author.*

evident, and similar conditions exist in Siberia along the coastline bordering the Laptev Sea, where retreat rates of 4–6 m per annum are not uncommon, and up to 100 m per annum has been reported elsewhere. A remarkable example of erosion is that of the island of Semenowski Ostrow in the Soviet Arctic. In 1823 it was about 15 km long, but by 1956 it had completely disappeared. Large extents of coastline in the central and eastern Canadian Arctic, Greenland and Svalbard are developed in relatively resistant and coherent rock in which retreat rates are slow (French 1976).

## The Active Layer

The active layer is a surface layer of soil and rock which lies above the permafrost, and which freezes in winter and thaws in summer when its temperature rises above 0° C for a short period. It is the layer through which heat and moisture movement take place between the permafrost and the atmosphere. The term 'active layer' is very appropriate because most physical, chemical and biological activity takes place in this seasonally thawed layer. Phase changes from ice to water and back to ice, moisture changes through the thermal season, decomposition of organic matter and weathering of mineral soil, movement of soil through frost action, biological activity of soil fauna and flora, as well as root penetration by plants all take place in this layer almost exclusively. The entire active layer is not, in fact, utilised by plants, as most growth is completed by late July, long before the full development of the active layer is reached. Generally speaking, by far the greatest

*Plate 5.1 An example of coastal erosion on the Beaufort Sea coast of Alaska*

portion of plant roots are concentrated in the top 10 cm of soil, although in some locations roots may reach 25 cm.

The thickness of the active layer in a given climate depends greatly on a variety of factors, including soil texture and type, water content, the type of habitat, and the degree of vegetation cover. The latter affects the active layer by shielding it (and the permafrost) from the thawing effect of summer air temperatures. The depth of thaw, therefore, is obviously related to the type of habitat. In Arctic tundra meadows, for example, it thaws to some 30–40 cm, compared to 80–100 cm on drier sites. The Truelove Lowland, on Devon Island in the Canadian High Arctic, is underlain by deep and cold permafrost. On the crest of this lowland the active layer reaches a maximum of 80–100 cm in August, but is shallower (40–70 cm) on

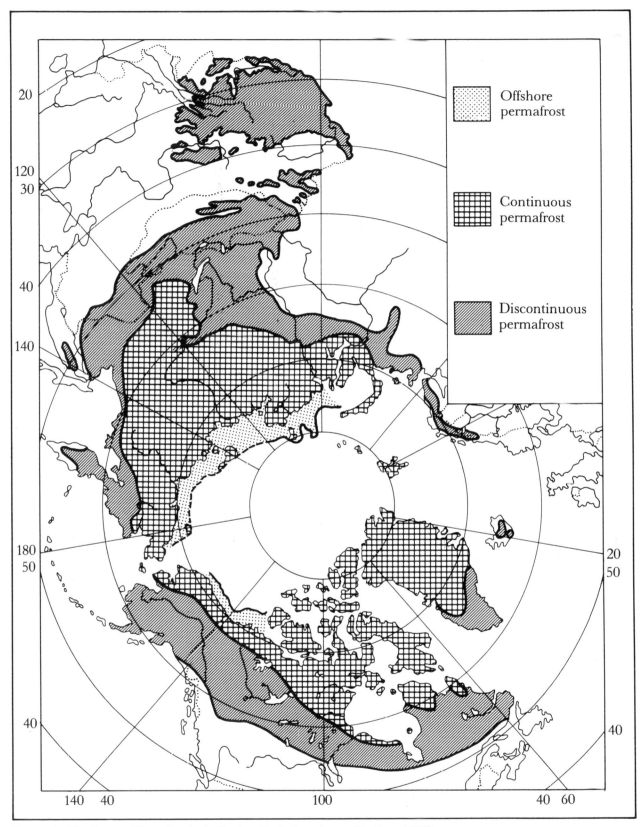

*Figure 5.2: Distribution of Permafrost in the Northern Hemisphere  Source: Washburn (1979).*

slopes and even more shallow (25 cm) in the transition zone to a meadow. After snow-melt it takes about three days for the active layer depth to reach 25 cm during which time the soil warms only slowly (Svoboda 1977). On the western Taimyr Peninsula in the Soviet Union the depth of the active layer fluctuates from 35 to 70 cm in the loams, and from 70 to 90 cm in the sands. In those soils with a clearly developed peaty horizon the depth of seasonal thawing does not exceed 15–35 cm (Vasil'evskaia *et al* 1973). In the continuous permafrost zone the active layer usually extends downwards to the permafrost table, although in some situations (as for example in the vicinity of water bodies) it may not do so.

## Arctic Soils

Following mention of the active layer it seems logical to deal with the soils of the Arctic. The cold, coupled with the existence of an impermeable substratum (the permafrost) dominates soil-forming processes. The net result is that, in the broad sense, one can divide Arctic soils into two main groups: (a) poorly drained soils and (b) well-drained soils. The polar deserts of the High Arctic have soils (where they exist) of a somewhat different type, and many mountainous areas lack any soil. Despite this apparently relatively simple situation, soil patterns in the Arctic are often as complex as those anywhere. Arctic soils have been classified by Rieger (1974) and FitzPatrick (1980).

Arctic soils are, in general, very shallow, very wet, and deficient in nutrients (primarily nitrogen and phosphorus), and poorly drained soils that are usually or always saturated throughout the thaw period probably occupy 85–90 per cent of the tundra region. They cover most areas of low relief from the low coastal plains to rolling foothills, and tend to mantle landscapes from ridge tops to valley bottoms. Modest areas of well-drained soils do occur in certain locations leading to localised mosaical effects, and the properties of the wet soils themselves vary to some extent. Temperatures in these soils are always low and, except for brief periods at the surface, rarely exceed 10° C, decreasing rapidly towards the permafrost. These poorly drained mineral soils all have essentially the same sequence of horizons consisting, first, of a mat of organic materials at the surface; then a greyish or bluish mineral layer (often mottled with other colours); and then a greyish perennially frozen layer. The well-drained soils occur almost entirely in stony, gravelly, or coarse sandy materials on steep slopes, ridges, elevated flood plains and so forth. They have good surface drainage and are usually underlain by bedrock or dry permafrost.

In the polar desert zone of the High Arctic, not only are there fewer areas with abundant moisture and vegetation suitable for tundra and bog soil development, but also the soil-forming potential decreases. The soils in such environments are termed polar desert soils. In this zone, tundra soils are restricted to the lower parts of valley side slopes, especially below snow patches and other localised areas of abundant moisture or poor drainage. Polar desert soils are defined as those mature well-drained soils of the ice-free polar regions having a sparse cover of higher plants. They are usually found on the higher landscape features, but are also present on some low-lying areas (for example on morainal or fluvial deposits). The almost complete absence of vascular plants and the low temperatures and precipitation mean that the organic content scarcely enters the soil system. A common morphological feature of terrain underlain by these free-draining polar desert soils is a veneer of coarse particles resting on the surface. It is the removal of the finer soil particles by wind erosion that results in the concentration of pebbles and stones at the surface. This type of landscape is termed a 'desert pavement' and is a feature found, in fact, in many arid regions of the world. Salt efflorescences at the surface are common, particularly on soils of hummocky ground after long dry periods. Frost fissures and sand wedges (see below) forming extensive polygonal networks are also characteristic. Polar desert soils tend to be neutral, but a characteristic feature of many is their predominantly saline or alkaline reactions (pH 7.0 to 8.0).

Finally, mention must be made of the occurrence of sand dunes in various parts of the Arctic. For example, a broad belt of Quaternary aeolian sands extends westwards from near the Colville River on Alaska's Arctic Slope. Ancient stabilised sand dunes are found on some 13,000 km² of the Arctic Coastal Plain, and represent primary landform elements. In Greenland, where mountains meet the sea and there is little shore development it is not possible to find parallel dune systems, and any sand accumulations are confined to the heads of fjords, such as Hurry Fjord in Scoresby Land, or to coastal inlets or basins.

## Ground Ice and Patterned Ground

Large bodies of ice, generally referred to as ground ice, are commonly found within permafrost. The two main types of massive ground ice are pingo-ice (pingos are discussed below) which shows no foliation, and ice-wedges which show vertical or inclined foliation. Ice lenses of varying size are also of common occurrence, and these are frequently associated with silt. As the saturated sediments slowly freeze, crystalline ice forms in the larger pores, thus attracting fluid water which moves towards it and freezes. The resultant ice lens may be many metres thick.

What are possibly the thickest and most extensive massive ice bodies in the world are to be found in the coastal and aggradational lowlands of northern Siberia around the Laptev Sea. Ice exposures over 70 m high are reported from the cliffs bounding the lowland areas of the New Siberian Islands. In the North American Arctic, segregated ice, in the form of icy sediments and massive ice, has been widely reported from coastal lowlands bordering the Beaufort Sea in Alaska and Canada. Usually this massive ice occurs beneath Pleistocene sediments, commonly till, reworked till, or glaciofluvial or lacustrine sediments. The nature of such massive ice bodies can be seen, for example, in numerous coastal exposures east of Herschel Island in the Mackenzie Delta (French 1976).

Segregation of ice in the ground leads to the development of a variety of most unusual Arctic landforms, of which polygonal patterned ground is one of the most remarkable since it usually has a striking geometrical appearance. Patterned ground is widely distributed in the Arctic and is frequently very conspicuous, and signifies the presence of a mobile surface. There are several varieties of patterned ground including ice-wedge polygons and circles formed by a net of pebbles, and tundra circles. In the Point Barrow region of Arctic Alaska there are three general types of polygons which make up the tundra surface. These are the wet, low-centre polygons; high-centre polygons which are relatively dry; and flat polygonised 'tundra meadows'. The characteristic relief and associated vegetation of low and high-centred ice-wedge polygons is shown in Figure 5.3. The polygonal form is generated by the thermal contraction of frozen ground during the winter. These contraction processes, a function of the annual freeze-thaw cycle, form vertical tension cracks in a honeycomb pattern. If these cracks are to become a permanent feature of the landscape they must be kept open when the seasonal thaw takes place. In the case of ice-wedge polygons (the type which predominates in silt plains) which are so much a feature of the Alaskan

Arctic coast, Arctic Canada around the Beaufort Sea, and the Siberian coastal plains, waters from the melting snow and ice drain down into the cracks and form a vein of ice which eventually becomes a wedge-shaped mass of ice (Figure 5.4). The development of a large ice-wedge is a long and repetitive process since the growth increment in one winter is typically 0.5 to 1.00 mm. It follows that large ice-wedges, which may be several metres across, must be thousands of years old. The diameter of a polygon is usually 15–30 m although many considerably exceed this. Leffingwell (1919) demonstrated that large ice-wedges form a network under the troughs between large low-centre polygons. The largest wedges, which are sometimes buried under sediments or peaty soils, are at least 6–10 m across at the top. They can be as much as 14,000 years old in the vicinity of point Barrow. Because of bounding sediments only rarely do single ice-wedges exceed 3 m in width, although they can extend down to a depth of 10 m, and on the Siberian coast there are examples which penetrate to more than 30 m.

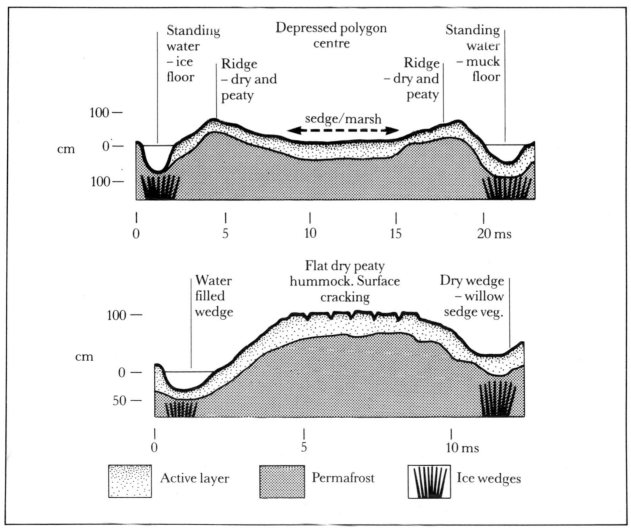

Figure 5.3: Typical Relief and Vegetation of Low- and High-Centred Ice-Wedge Polygons
Source: French (1976).

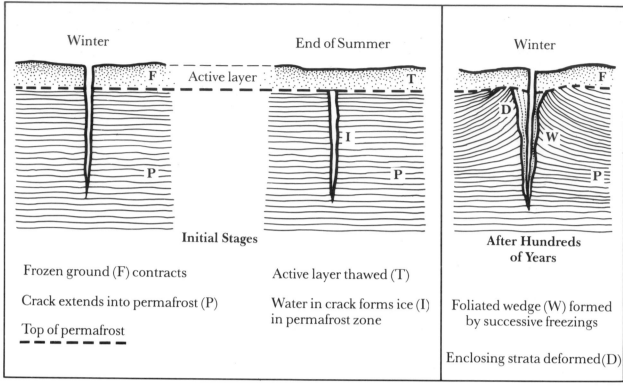

*Figure 5.4: Stages in the Progressive Development of an Ice-Wedge Showing Deformation of Surrounding Material
Source: Money (1980).*

The pattern of polygons and circles formed by a net of pebbles is usually caused by the fissuring of desiccated soils. The fissures in this case are kept open by the movement into them of small stones and gravel from the surface. The sorting process which leads to the separation of coarser and finer particles in exposed soils is responsible for the formation of the tundra circles that were mentioned above. These usually take the form of oval or circular areas of bare soil in vegetated areas. Where such bare patches are numerous the intervening vegetation may form a polygonal pattern. It should also be mentioned that ground patterning of quite different appearance occurs on slopes as a result of, for example, frost action and solifluction. A common type of downslope patterned ground consists of a series of parallel lines of gravel or coarser debris which may be separated by strips of vegetation. Sometimes several different types of patterned ground may be seen in one general area, as for example inland from Thule, Greenland, where an area of several hundred square kilometres of landscape between the sea and the ice-sheet exhibits a variety of forms.

Another type of polygon (the sand-wedge polygon) is usually confined to outwash plains, terraces and elevated deltas, and may commonly be seen in the eastern Canadian Arctic. Sand-wedges, like ice-wedges, form in frost fissures that develop from the thermal contraction of the ground. In this case, however, because of extreme aridity there is no moisture available to penetrate the crack and to subsequently freeze. Instead, the crack is filled with windblown sed-

iments or other materials. Sand-wedges occur in arid regions, with less than 100 mm of precipitation per year, and the enclosing sediments are usually coarse-grained sands and gravels. In no cases so far reported do sand-wedges produce the same dramatic surface relief as ice-wedges.

## Frost Boils and Earth Hummocks

The many forms of patterned ground in the Arctic include frost boils (or frost scars) where mineral soils are actively heaved during the seasonal freeze-back. It is these which give a characteristic spotty appearance to many tundra landscapes when viewed from the air. Frost heaving is the predominantly upward movement of mineral soil during freezing caused by the migration of water to the freezing plane, and its subsequent expansion upon freezing. The greatest heave is usually measured in those areas of abundant moisture, and takes place during the autumn period as the winter freeze-up occurs. Average amounts of soil heave vary from locality to locality. Frost heave of 1–5 cm is probably typical, but much higher values have been recorded.

Vegetation plays an important role in outlining many patterns in which there is localised soil movement. Some of these patterns are mainly developed in vegetation, and in this category are clay and earth hummocks (also known as thufur). They are well developed in High Arctic regions. If frost heaving is concentrated into discrete areas, the resulting soil movement often produces small mounds or hummocks. Where they occur widely, these frost mounds represent a form of patterned ground. While some may owe their origin entirely to the tussock-forming habit of some common tundra plants, most exhibit an updoming of mineral soil. The initial cause of the frost heaving is usually related to the presence of an insulating vegetation cover. During freeze-up, moisture from the adjacent areas migrates, causing differential frost heave and the segregation of localised ice-bodies. The earth hummocks are a major relief form varying from a few centimetres to several metres high (but rarely more

*Plate 5.2 Polygonal patterning in sedge-grass tundra in northern Alaska*

*Plate 5.3 Aerial view of polygonal patterned ground in northern Alaska*

*Plate 5.4 Stone polygons on Svalbard*

*Plate 5.5 Two pingos on the Arctic Coastal Plain of northern Alaska with cottongrass tussock tundra in the foreground*

*Plate 5.6 A typical Mackenzie Delta-type pingo, Canada*

*Plate 5.7 An esker near the Thelon River, Northwest Territories, Canada*

than about 30 cm) and often cover extensive areas.

In the Canadian Arctic, extensive areas of central and western Axel Heiberg Island, and the Fosheim Peninsula of Ellesmere Island, have ice-free land covered with fine-grained soils, and an abundance of unsorted polygons and hummocks of varying sizes. A complex of environmental factors has produced these phenomena; some have developed by growth and others by erosion (clay hummocks) for example. A detailed study of these hummocks is given by Beschel (1963a and 1963b). Turf hummocks are a conspicuous feature of the landscape in the Mesters Vig area of north-east Greenland. These hummocks are formed by

the radial proliferation of mosses from central starting points to more or less dome-shaped masses. A comprehensive study of these hummocks is that by Raup (1965).

## Pingos

Pingo is a word of Inuit origin meaning conical hill, and was apparently first used by the Inuit of Canada's Mackenzie Delta exclusively to denote the numerous hills, for the most part regularly conical, which rise to heights of 50 m above the gently rolling landscape of the north-east part of the delta.

*Plate 5.8 Glacier in northern Ellesmere Island, Arctic Canada*

*Plate 5.9 A coastal glacier in northern Baffin Island, Canada*

Pingos are a permafrost phenomenon and are perhaps the most dramatic of the various surface expressions of the presence of permafrost. True pingos are hill-like formations, generally circular or oval in shape and conical in profile, which are found in the active state (as opposed to fossil pingos) only in permafrost regions. The core of a pingo lies inside the permafrost and this phenomenon is probably the best criterion for defining a true pingo. Although rarely rising more than 100 m above the surrounding terrain (and usually much less) they can be several hundred metres in circumference. The sides of pingos are nearly always quite steep (20–30°). Their internal structure is characterised by the presence of a massive ice lens or beds of ice. Painstaking research (Mackay 1973), over many years, has established that the core of ice develops by increments of as much as 25 cm per year, after being initially formed during development of permafrost. Pingos are always covered with vegetation and their surface soil or peat is the same as that of the surrounding tundra. The top may form an unbroken dome, or alternatively the dome may be breached by an open crater. Various factors, including external thawing temperatures, begin a process of disintegration of the pingo, but the whole process of formation and eventual decay is very slow. For example, two pingos some 150 m apart on Banks Island in the Canadian Arctic are probably between 4,500 and 7,000 years old.

Probably the largest group of pingos in the world are those in the former (Pleistocene) delta of the Mackenzie River. This lies east of the present delta and contains at least 1,400 pingos, almost all of them in shallow lakes or former lake beds. In the delta, pingos up to about six metres high are known to have formed after 1935, following coastal recession that led to draining of lakes. Others have formed since 1950. Further west, pingos are locally common on the Arctic Coastal Plain of Alaska.

It is customary to recognise two main types of pingo – the East Greenland type and the Mackenzie type – both based on the pioneer studies by Muller (1963).

Pingos of the East Greenland type are associated with the expansion of existing, or the formation of new taliks (gaps in the permafrost), and the ascension of subpermafrost water and gases under hydrostatic pressure. This produces massive ice formation and updoming but also a central zone of weakness in which crater formation is evident, and from which fissures tend to radiate. Because the water is circulating in an open system, repetitive formation is normal and new pingos may appear within the remains of older ones, and associated groups are likely to occur.

Mackenzie type pingos on the other hand are associated with the contraction and extinction of taliks, and, since such a sequence is most commonly caused by the disappearance of a lake, these pingos are usually found on old lake floors. As the permafrost closes, the increase in volume associated with freezing causes an upward ascent of water and sediments in a comparatively narrow vertical channel. Growth ceases once the talik has been eliminated. Since, unlike the East Greenland type of pingo, the water is circulating in a closed system, reactivation and group association are unlikely.

## Eskers

There has been a certain amount of confusion in the literature concerning the nomenclature of eskers, and their variety of form and composition suggest that they are of varying origin. However, there is general agreement that in all cases they are formed during the retreat phase of a glacier. The best developed eskers are located where the continental ice-sheets were at their maximum, as for example in Canada on either side of Hudson Bay, and especially in Labrador. An example of a Canadian esker is shown in Plate 5.7. Eskers are used by some birds for nesting, and because of their composition, height, and porous nature they are important to mammals such as foxes and wolves for denning purposes.

Typical eskers are narrow, sinuous ridges of well-drained glacial till (glaciofluvial material such as gravel and other debris). The most commonly held opinion is that they are formed by deposition in sub-glacial meltwater tunnels, and thus represent the aggraded beds of streams left standing as ridges by the disappearance of the ice. Eskers vary greatly in length, width and height. The largest may stretch for many kilometres and be 400–700 m wide and 40–50 m high. Shorter examples may be only 200–300 m in length, 40–50 m wide, and 10–20 m high. The slope of the sides can vary from as much as 20° to as little as 5–10°. In cases where the ridge broadens, the esker is said to be *beaded*.

## Glaciers

Glaciers are important both because of their geological role and their relationship to climate. They are also important ecologically. The Greenland ice-sheet, for example, severely limits the movements of caribou and musk-ox by confining them to the peripheral ice-free

**Table 5.1:** Approximate Present Extent of Arctic Glaciers (Figures in km²)

| Soviet Arctic | | |
|---|---:|---:|
| Franz Josef Land | 13,735 | |
| Novaya Zemlya | 24,300 | |
| Severnaya Zemlya | 17,500 | |
| Miscellaneous (De Long Islands) | 400 | 55,935 |
| **Svalbard** | | 57,300 |
| **Jan Mayen Island** | | 115 |
| **Greenland** | | |
| Ice-sheet | 1,757,700 | |
| Independent glaciers | 76,200 | 1,833,900 |
| **Canada** | | |
| Mainland | | 16,940[a] |
| Arctic Archipelago | | |
| Ellesmere Island | 80,500[b] | |
| Axel Heiberg Island | 11,750 | |
| Devon Island | 16,200 | |
| Melville Island | 160 | |
| Baffin Island | 37,000 | |
| Bylot | 5,000 | |
| Remaining islands | 500 | 151,110 |
| **Alaska** (Brooks Range) | | <2,590[c] |
| Total | | 2,117,890 |

Notes: a. This is in the mountains in the north-west.
b. Includes 500 km² of the ice-shelf.
c. There is little accurate data on the size of glaciers in the Brooks Range, many of which are retreating.

Sources: Alaska Geographic Society (1982), Danks (1981), and Hattersley-Smith (1974).

land, and the richness of plant life in many areas is controlled by the availability of meltwater from glaciers. Glaciers develop when snow survives over the summer for several years, gradually metamorphosing into firn (consolidated snow-ice found above the climatic snow line), and later into glacier ice. The climatic snow line (or equilibrium line) varies in its altitude above sea level. The mean height of the equilibrium line on the Greenland ice-sheet is 1,100–1,200 m. In Peary Land, the most northerly part of Greenland, there are only localised mountain glaciers because of the low precipitation, and the equilibrium line is at about 600 m. At the northern end of Ellesmere Island it is at sea level and a so-called ice-shelf (see below) some 500 km² in extent has developed, a phenomenon possibly unknown elsewhere in the Arctic. At the northern end of Severnaya Zemlya also the equilibrium line drops locally to sea level. In heavily glacierised Svalbard it is located at 300–700 m.

With the exception of Greenland, the Arctic today is relatively sparsely glacierised. With certain exceptions it is none too easy to arrive at precise figures regarding the extent of glaciers in the various areas, although figures have been given by Hattersley-Smith (1974) and Danks (1981), see Table 5.1. Leaving aside Greenland, it is clear that considerably less than 10 per cent of the land surface of the Arctic is currently covered by glaciers. Greenland now accounts for over 85 per cent of the land surface that is still glacierised, followed by the Canadian Arctic islands.

A classification of the main types of glacier is shown in Table 5.2. The difference between an ice-sheet and an ice-cap is basically one of size. According to Armstrong *et al* (1973) ice-sheets are generally accepted as covering areas in excess of 50,000 km², whereas smaller areas are known as ice-caps. Ice-shelves, of which there are very few in the Arctic, are floating glaciers fed by snowfall in the same way as other glaciers, but with a different appearance and a different mode of behaviour because, although attached to the land, they are floating on the sea's surface. The best known is the Ward Hunt ice-shelf on the north coast of Ellesmere Island. This shelf extends for 75 km across the mouths of three fjords. Although over 50 m thick, its upper surface is seldom more than 10 m above sea level, and the outer shelf edge attains a height of only 5 m. Summer melting on this ice-shelf creates quite complicated patterns of ponds, stream courses, ice ridges and hummocks.

The great ice-sheets, like that in Greenland, behave more or less independently of the details of topographic relief. The Greenland ice-sheet blankets a vast area

**Table 5.2:** A Simple Morphological Classification of Glaciers

| | |
|---|---|
| Ice-sheets and ice-caps (unconstrained by topography) | Ice domes Outlet glaciers |
| Ice-shelves | |
| Glaciers constrained by topography | Ice-fields Valley glaciers Cirque glaciers Other small glaciers |

Source: Sugden and John (1984).

and conceals mountains, plains, high plateaus, and deep valleys. The thickness of ice in the centre of the ice-sheet reaches 3,410 m and depresses the ground 365 m below sea level. Nevertheless, regardless of the bedrock forms which are present at depths of 2,000 m or more, the ice flows steadily seawards. Smaller ice-caps elsewhere in the Arctic also behave in this manner. Beneath the greater part of an ice-sheet or ice-cap surface, the ice moves more or less radially away from the centre. The ice movement is caused by a number of mechanisms, generally termed *sheetflow*, of which internal deformation is the most important. Most of the larger glaciers or ice-caps assume a basically dome-shaped cross-profile, with a steep gradient close to the margin lessening gradually towards the centre.

*Plate 5.10 A massive ice lens revealed by bank collapse in the Atigun River valley, Brooks Range, Alaska*

The outlet glaciers which transport ice from the interior of the ice-sheets or ice-caps are often very impressive features. Those in Greenland flow at very high velocities. For example, the Jakobshavn Isbrae maintains a rate of over 7 km per year, and the Rinks Isbrae over 10 km per year. The former, constantly calving at its snout, produces over 142 million tonnes of icebergs every day (John 1979).

Mountains that are surrounded by glaciers tend to have a characteristic form and display steep straight slopes. Where isolated, such mountains may form upstanding horns with three or four distinct faces. Sometimes they may be linked by arêtes (steep-sided ridges). Such features occur both in mountain chains and in massifs or nunataks which stand above ice-sheet surfaces. Nunataks are of particular importance in the disjunct geographical distribution of many plants and invertebrates (see for example, Ives 1974, Löve and Löve 1963 and 1974).

## Rivers

At high latitudes the land slopes generally towards the north, so that approximately 14 per cent of the land area of the world drains into the Arctic Ocean and adjacent cold seas by major rivers. The geometry of the Arctic Ocean provokes the convergence of the circumpolar runoffs coming from adjacent continents. From Siberia and North America, powerful rivers (including some of the world's largest) carry hundreds of megatonnes of fresh water into the polar seas. At the present rate, the Yenisei, Ob-Irtysh system, Lena, Kolyma and Mackenzie Rivers, draining a continental area in excess of 10 million km², together bring to the Arctic Ocean some 90,000 m³ s⁻¹ of fresh water (Rey 1982). The deltas of many rivers, particularly the large ones like the Mackenzie River in Canada, are a maze of channels and shallow lakes.

The majority of the large rivers flowing into the Arctic Ocean (other than those in Alaska) have their origin south of the tree-line and therefore display the combined effects of flow through climatic and vegetative areas that are non-Arctic. One typical example is the Mackenzie River whose drainage basin covers nearly one-fifth of the total land area of Canada. One result of this fact is that the runoff of major rivers is more evenly distributed throughout the year than that of streams originating and contained within tundra areas whose runoff rises sharply in late spring due to the melting of winter snow and ice. In virtually all Arctic rivers a great part of the annual discharge occurs in a period of 10–21 days in June or early July. For example, data collected on Alaska's Colville River in 1962 showed that 43 per cent of the annual discharge occurred in a three-week period.

One feature common to all Arctic water bodies is that for some six months of the year they are completely or partially covered by ice. The timing is related to a number of factors, including latitude. The Mackenzie River, for example, is normally frozen from at least November to May. Streams (and lakes) on the Cana-

dian Arctic islands freeze earlier and thaw later than those on the mainland.

River channels may be of a single or multiple type. The most distinctive and common type in the Arctic is the multiple or braided one. The majority of braided channels occur in high-energy streams flowing in non-cohesive sediments and carrying heavy sediment loads. Bank erodibility is obviously a relevant factor which can lead to very wide channels forming. Braiding is also related to rapid and large variations in runoff. The

large-scale collapse of river banks adds sediment to the river as well as broadening the channel. The importance of abundant bedload sediment in producing braided stream channels is illustrated by the absence of well-developed braided stream channels in those areas where bank erodibility is limited, and where debris suitable for transport is scarce.

In a study of streams and rivers on part of the Arctic Slope of Alaska (Craig and McCart 1975), the streams were divided into three types, and this classification can be applied elsewhere in the Arctic:

1. Mountain Streams: these originate in the mountains and derive from two main sources – springs and surface runoff. They were the largest streams in the study area with cold waters (usually less than 10° C) and flow about five months of the year. Arctic Char

*Plate 5.11 Elusive Lake in the Ribdon River valley, northern Alaska, is an example of a moraine lake*

*Salvelinus alpinus* is the common fish species and the density of benthic invertebrates is typically low (100 organisms m$^{-2}$).

2. Spring Streams: these are small spring-fed tributaries of the Mountain Streams. Perennial springs were located in many of the latter, and most were of fresh water with temperatures of 3° to 7° C although thermal and mineral springs do occur. The Spring Stream habitat is relatively stable and this appears to have a profound biological influence. Streambanks are often overgrown with vegetation and the bed is covered in most places with a heavy growth of moss or algae. These are all small streams, generally less than 1.5 km long and only a few metres wide. The springs are inhabited by Arctic Char and high densities of benthic invertebrates (10,000 organisms m$^{-2}$).

3. Tundra Streams: these drain the tundra-covered slopes of the mountain foothills and the coastal plain. They tend to be small meandering streams, 30–65 km in length, which flow directly into Mountain Streams or directly into the Beaufort Sea. They flow for $3\frac{1}{2}$ to $4\frac{1}{2}$ months of the year. Their waters are stained brown and have a lower pH and less calcium than found in Mountain or Spring Streams. Summer water temperatures may exceed 16° C. These streams are used as spawning and rearing areas by Grayling *Thymallus arcticus*. Densities of benthic invertebrates are between the other stream types. Various characteristics of these streams are summarised in Table 5.3.

## Lakes

Lakes are a common feature of the Arctic, but their distribution is very irregular, the highest density being reached on flat coastal plains. The largest lakes are on mainland areas, the biggest lakes on islands being Nettilling (5,525 km²) and Amadjuak (3,105 km²), both on Baffin Island. The borders of many lakes, particularly the smaller ones, are indeterminate since they gradually merge into swampy tundra. On the basis of maps then available, Rawson (1953) estimated that there were 250 lakes of a size exceeding 65 km² in area, and hundreds of thousands of smaller ones, within the tundra region of Canada alone. The number of lakes and lake basins on the Arctic Slope of Alaska is probably tens of thousands.

Despite morphological differences, these high-latitude lakes share a number of characteristics. Many Arctic lakes are ultra-oligotrophic and considerably less productive than most oligotrophic lakes of the north temperate zone (Kalff 1970) and, in general, are characterised by their biological simplicity. Many of the smaller lakes have only one species of herbivore (a copepod crustacean), and one species of primary carnivore (usually a mysid or an amphipod). Water temperatures are low, except in the extremely shallow lakes, thermocline formation is rare, and they are subject to severe seasonal variation in insolation. The chemistry of large Arctic lakes is remarkable for the near-absence of annual cycles and the low quantities of dissolved solids. Shallow tundra ponds often appear brown due to dissolved humic materials and are turbid because of continual wind mixing. Many large lakes contain suspended glacial material. On the other hand a few Arctic lakes are remarkably clear, examples being Anguissoq Lake in Greenland (Barnes 1960) and Kongressvatn Lake in Svalbard (Amren 1964). Eutrophic lakes are, of course, present in the Arctic, as for example in the Mackenzie Delta. Lakes in this delta were studied by Gill (1973) who found that they were not equally

**Table 5.3:** General Characteristics of Spring Streams, Mountain Streams, and Tundra Streams. Mean values are followed by the range of observed values

| Features | Spring[a] Streams | Mountain Streams | Tundra Streams |
|---|---|---|---|
| *Physical and chemical* | | | |
| Flow – Surface | minimal | late May–mid-October | late May–mid-September |
| Groundwater | perennial | minimal | none |
| Summer discharge (m³ sec$^{-1}$) | 0.1–1.5 | 0.3–100+ | 0.1–7+ |
| Temperature (° C) | | | |
| Summer | 7 (4–11) | 10 (4–15) | 10 (5–20) |
| Winter | 2.5 (0–5) | 0–1 or frozen | frozen |
| Annual variation | 4 | 10 | 17 |
| Colour | clear | clear/turbid | stained |
| pH | 8.0 (7.5–8.5) | 8.0 (7.0–8.5) | 7.6 (6.4–8.5) |
| Conductivity ($\mu$mhos cm$^{-1}$) | 241 (149–322) | 176 (78–285) | 116 (17–230) |
| Ca$^{++}$ (mg/l) | 45 (35–55) | 28 (16–37) | 9 (3–16) |
| | | | |
| *Benthic invertebrates* | | | |
| Standing crop (no. m.$^{-2}$) | 10,000 | 100 | 1,000 |
| Relative diversity | high | 102 | moderate |
| | | | |
| *Fish* | | | |
| Most abundant species | Arctic Char | Arctic Char | Grayling |

Note: a. Excludes thermal or mineral springs. Source: Craig and McCart (1975).

eutrophic. About one-third are bounded by high levees and receive an input of nutrients through sediment transport only during high floods, thus reducing aquatic vegetation. Most such lakes are subject to bank recession, and littoral plant succession is absent. Approximately another third of the lakes are highly eutrophic, maintained in this condition through transport of nutrient-rich sediments by small channels during flood stages and during channel flow reversals. There is evidence that the biological productivity of these high-latitude lakes is to some extent inversely related to their size and depth.

Lakes (which freeze earlier than rivers) are markedly influenced by the long-lasting ice cover that persists from September or early October until June or July. Some, such as Anguissaq Lake in Greenland, are in contact with ice-fields or snow-fields and have more or less permanent ice-cover. Others may not become ice-free every summer. The snow-melt pools and many of the permanent ponds or lakes are small enough for their temperature regimes and ice-free periods to be related to those of the surrounding land. In the larger lakes there is a seasonal lag, with a later melting and freeze-up, and during the ice-free period there is a buffering of the short-term temperature variations in the surrounding atmosphere. In general the larger lakes have a shorter ice-free period than the smaller lakes and ponds (Roen 1962), as well as very low temperatures and a lag in ice break-up. For example, Lake Hazen (Ellesmere Island) becomes ice-free only in some years, and its temperature in 1957 did not exceed 3° C. Most lakes in the High Arctic are free of ice for only 50–60 days, whilst in the Low Arctic the ice-free period may be 100 days or more (Uspenskii 1984).

On the Arctic Slope of Alaska, lakes vary greatly in number and size, and on some parts of the coastal plain (as also in Canada and Siberia) they may occupy as much as 90 per cent of the surface area. These are known as thaw lakes and are discussed in more detail below. In the previously glaciated portions of the Brooks Range and foothills glacial lakes are numerous (see below), and along most rivers and in most deltas floodplain lakes are common. The 160 km wide Mackenzie River delta in Canada is dissected by many channels, contains many sand bars, and is dotted with islands on which numerous large and small lakes are present.

A rather different type of Arctic pond or lake is that which might be considered an Arctic member of the family of *perched lakes*. A perched lake has been defined as a perennial lake which has a surface level lying at a considerably higher elevation than that of other waterbodies directly adjacent or closely associated (Veatch and Humphreys 1964). In order to meet this definition a highly irregular local relief is necessary, so most tundra lakes are excluded. However, the Arctic Coastal Plain of northern Alaska does contain numerous sand dune areas in which local relief may reach 10 m, thereby allowing the development of perched ponds. One example is the delta of the Colville River, where many such ponds are found in the dunes (Walker and Harris 1976). In order for perched lakes to exist, an aquaclude must be present between the water table associated with the lake and the regional water table. In the present instance permafrost, developed in a basin, is the aquaclude.

The truly unique Arctic lakes are known as thermokarst (thaw) lakes – shallow bodies of water formed by the melting of the permafrost. Lakes of this type occur in large numbers on the north coasts of Siberia, Alaska and Canada. They are in fact ubiquitous in flat lowland areas wherever silty alluviums with high ice content are present. Fluviatile terraces, outwash plains, and Arctic coastal areas are the most favoured localities for their widespread development. The absence of underground drainage because of the presence of permafrost, and the flatness of the terrain, result in great numbers of lakes on the flat coastal plains. The Alaskan coastal plain is covered by parallel, elongated, thaw lakes that have their long axis aligned 10–15° west of north and perpendicular to the prevailing winds. They are known as oriented lakes, are rarely deeper than 3 m, ranging in length from several hundred metres to several kilometres.

The thaw lake cycle, first hypothesised by Britton (1957), described a process during which lakes advance across the landscape, merge, drain, and reform over thousands of years. It is an important geomorphic process because it implies that all land surfaces on the coastal plain of Alaska's Arctic Slope (and also of course elsewhere) alternate between terrestrial and aquatic phases over a period of thousands of years. Britton's main hypothesis is neatly summarised by Billings and Peterson (1980): thaw lakes come into existence as sediments rise above the sea; the lakes grow to maturity by thermokarst erosion of shorelines and central basins; they are then captured and drained by small streams; the drained, flat basins slowly change to low-centre polygons with ponded centres; and, finally, some of the low-centre polygons coalesce into thaw ponds which grow by marginal erosion into thaw lakes similar to the originals.

There are, of course, other types of lakes. Many are the result of Pleistocene ice-sheets, when ice-scouring formed depressions now filled with water. These are termed ice-scour lakes, and the numerous small, irregular lakes of the Canadian Shield are good examples. Ice-dammed lakes are common in the Arctic and have one margin formed by ice. They occur in mountains and in association with ice-sheets. In Greenland this type accounts for all the large lakes. Moraine lakes are formed by the damming action of glacial moraines. Elusive Lake, Chandler Lake, Lake Peters and Lake Schrader, are all typical examples in the Brooks Range of Alaska, and there are also numerous examples in northern Canada. Kettle lakes result from the melting of buried glacial ice and are much rarer. Ox-bow lakes formed by abandoned river channels are common in the valleys of most large Arctic rivers.

# 6
# ADAPTATIONS OF ANIMALS & PLANTS TO THE ARCTIC ENVIRONMENT

## Introduction

Arctic animals and plants exhibit a variety of adaptations – behavioural, morphological and physiological – to the rigours of their environment. Plants, unlike animals, cannot move to a more favourable site in order to avoid adverse conditions, so obviously only those species capable of enduring protracted periods of intense frost without injury can survive. Arctic animals have evolved mechanisms by means of which they maintain sufficient activity for their survival in an environment of low heat budget.

## Adaptations of Mammals and Birds

In both these groups we find examples of behavioural adaptations. The most obvious strategy is to completely avoid the severity of winter by moving (migrating) elsewhere, and this is the strategy used by the vast majority of Arctic birds which head south before freeze-up. In the case of mammals, a number of species go into hibernation or deep sleep through the winter period. True hibernation may be defined as a periodic phenomenon in which body temperature ($T_b$) falls to a low level, approximating to the ambient, and in which heart rate, metabolic rate and other physiological functions fall to correspondingly minimal levels. It is an adaptation to overcome periods of climatic stress associated with food shortage, and examples of true hibernators include the Alaska Marmot *Marmota broweri* and Arctic Ground Squirrel *Spermophilus undulatus*. The Grizzly Bear *Ursus arctos*, by contrast, is not a true hibernator even though its reactions are similar to those of small hibernating mammals. The bear goes into a state of dormancy at nearly normal $T_b$, does not eat, drink, urinate or defecate, and metabolises fat reserves almost exclusively as a source of energy.

The Arctic Fox is particularly interesting in that it exhibits a variety of adaptations. It remains active all year and in winter assumes a dense, white, well-insulated coat; even the paws are covered, top and bottom, with fur. Adaptive features of the breeding cycle include, as an adaptation to the Arctic environment, the relatively high litter size. They include also, as adaptations to fluctuating prey abundance, relatively infrequent breeding on the part of young vixens, and an efficient mechanism for litter reduction – possibly activated through the precocious development of dominance hierarchy among siblings (Macpherson 1969). So well adapted is the Arctic Fox to the Arctic winter that heat production is not increased until the ambient temperature ($T_a$) reaches about $-40°$ C, and only a small increase in metabolic rate is required in order to ensure survival in the most extreme conditions. The fox can thus sleep on open snow at $-80°$ C for an hour without any decrease in core temperature.

The Arctic Hare *Lepus arcticus* has the lowest minimal thermal conductance (i.e. greatly increased insulation) of any lagomorph, and is the only one which shows a depression in basic metabolic rate (BMR). Its $T_b$ on the other hand is within the normal range of other lagomorphs. It is apparent that the reduced BMR and reduced thermal conductance represent distinct physiological assets in terms of energy conservation for a species living in areas of low primary productivity and low $T_a$ in every month of the year (Wang *et al* 1973).

Small mammals, because of their large body surface in relation to size, cannot entirely compensate for heat loss by increasing their surface insulation. What they in fact do is increase their metabolic rate rather than their insulation – precisely the opposite strategy to that of the Arctic Fox. They can compensate to some extent for their lack of effective insulation by utilising that provided by the environment – the snow cover. Living most of the winter beneath the snow, sheltered in burrows and nests, and with an increased BMR to compensate for the low $T_a$, small mammals can survive through the winter providing enough food is available.

Tundra birds remaining in winter become physiologically acclimatised to the low temperatures through insulative and metabolic means. Two species of over-wintering birds show adaptations similar to those of mammals. Ptarmigan increase their feather density and acclimatise by reducing their metabolic response to low temperatures (West 1972). Also, they may burrow into snow when resting overnight, thus helping to reduce heat loss. Redpolls cannot increase their plumage to the same extent as ptarmigan, but they can move under an insulating cover of snow where they are able to forage. Even with high metabolic demands during winter, they can maintain their $T_b$ because of their high metabolic capacity (Pohl and West 1973).

The Snowy Owl *Nyctea scandiaca* has the lowest level of thermal conductance recorded for birds (Gessaman 1972), a value three to four times lower than that of the well-insulated Willow Ptarmigan *Lagopus lagopus*. The feet of this owl have foot pads that are covered by big, cornified papillae which are poor conductors of heat and also reduce the area of contact with the cold substrate to a minimum. The feet of the Raven *Corvus corax* have a similar but even better developed heat insulating mechanism.

Heat loss is a more immediately critical problem for eggs and young birds than it is for adults, and nests on the open tundra are not renowned for their insulative properties. Perhaps the most striking metabolic adaptation among breeding birds is that of the thermolability of wader chicks. Weighing less than 10 g at hatching, and becoming independent of the nest and adults (except for periods of brooding) within hours of hatching, their small size, thin downy plumage, and requirement for freedom to forage actively, essentially eliminates insulative specialisations. These free-living chicks are able to consistently reduce the gradient between core and $T_a$ by allowing $T_b$ to drop to 30°–35° C while remaining functional, alert and active (Norton 1973).

## Adaptations of Arctic Insects
### (Professor P. G. Kevan and Dr H. V. Danks)

Like the higher animals, insects have adapted to the Arctic environment in anatomical, behavioural, metabolic and biochemical ways (MacLean 1975; Downes 1965).

One of the notable features of Arctic insects is that they seem to be darker, smaller and hairier than their southern counterparts. The darker colours and general hairiness of Arctic butterflies is especially noticeable in species of *Boloria* and *Colias*. Even Arctic aphids are darker than those in the south, and species with distributions extending south of the Arctic are melanic in the alpine zone as well as in the north. This is contrary to 'Gloger's Rule', which states that vertebrates tend to be white towards the north, presumably for camouflage in snowy conditions. For animals that are unable to regulate their body temperatures by internal, metabolic means, radiative warming is important, and dark-coloured insects can warm faster by basking in the sun or absorbing heat from the ground. This activity, which will be discussed below, is widespread among Arctic insects. Nevertheless, not all arthropods in the Arctic are melanic: the crab spider *Xysticus deichmanni*, like crab spiders (Thomisidae) of the south, waits in flowers for its prey and seems to be able to change its colour to match that of the flower it uses. Hairiness helps in the absorption of solar radiation, and especially in insulating the warmed insect and so conserving its heat. In the dark-coloured fuzzy caterpillars *Gynaephora rossii* (Lymantriidae), the hairs seem to accelerate warming and reduce the rate of convective heat loss compared with caterpillars that have been shaved (Kevan *et al* 1982). The smaller size of Arctic insects may also favour faster warming, or it may be related to lack of food, severe climate or other factors that are not understood. Arctic insects are often of compact appearance with low surface to volume ratio, and thus they lose heat and moisture less rapidly. Such reduction in the length of the limbs is especially evident in the wings. As in a wide variety of alpine insects, brachyptery (shortened wings) or aptery (lack of wings) are known in Arctic insects, especially in stone flies (Plecoptera), crane flies (Tipulidae), midges (Chironomidae), and some moths (Lepidoptera). In some of these species, flightlessness may affect only the females. Some moths have reduced flight muscles but well developed wings (e.g. *Gynaephora*). In the alpine zone, and on oceanic islands where this phenomenon is also frequently encountered, it has been suggested that winglessness aids the individuals in staying put under windy conditions, but other explanations have been put forward, including those related to conservation of energy, type of microhabitat, and so on. Reduction in sensory organs has also been reported for Arctic insects; the antennae of the males of some midges and moths are reduced, as are the eyes of some noctuid moths (perhaps in response to conditions in the land of the midnight sun).

Arctic insects show activities and activity patterns by which they take advantage of relatively benign local conditions in their environment and of scattered resources such as heat, food, mating sites, oviposition sites, etc. Arctic insects always fly close to the ground, in the warmest layer of air, and often restrict their activities to sheltered valleys and the lee of hills. Butterflies are conspicuous sunbathers in the Arctic (Kevan and Shorthouse 1970). The Pieridae (*Colias* spp.) bask with their wings folded over their backs and they lean so that the sun beats directly on the flat surface of the wings; the fritillaries (*Boloria* spp.) bask with their wings opened flat, and adpressed to the substrate and angled so that the sun shines directly on them; the blues (Lycaenidae) bask with their wings half open and their bodies orientated to catch the sun along the dorsal mid-line. Blow flies oviposit on insolated carcasses and the development of the fly larvae is faster on the south side. The larvae of mosquitoes follow the sun as it warms the shallow water at the edges of ponds. The adults of these and other flies bask in the sun as well. They sit in holes and on hummocks as well as man-made structures such as tents, and follow the sun throughout the day. Some midges also bask within the warm embrace of willow catkins and Purple Saxifrage *Saxifraga oppositifolia* flowers. Some flowers act as solar furnaces, constantly facing the sun. Inside these flowers, the air is many degrees warmer than the surroundings: insects such as mosquitoes, dance flies and hover flies act as pollinators and also use the warmth in the flowers. Only the Arctic bumblebees are capable of producing heat themselves. These remarkable insects rapidly vibrate their wing muscles to produce heat; they can maintain the temperature in their nests above 30°C to rear their brood (Richards 1973).

Despite these behavioural and anatomical adaptations for becoming and staying warm, many Arctic insects are active only during good weather. This is especially noticeable among the hover flies (Syrphidae), muscoid flies (Muscidae, Anthomyiidae), butterflies (Lepidoptera), blow flies (Calliphoridae), bristle flies (Tachinidae), ichneumon wasps (Ichneumonidae), and some mosquitoes (Culicidae) and midges (Chironomidae). Nevertheless, these insects can become active at lower temperatures than their relatives in the south, even though the sun may not shine. Some, such as *Aedes* mosquitoes, can fly at temperatures as low as 1.7° C, and other mosquitoes may feed even when temperatures are close to freezing. Most mosquitoes from temperate regions become active at dawn and dusk; those from the Arctic are active whenever it is warm enough (Corbet 1966). This opportunism for activity is probably widespread among Arctic insects as they must reproduce in the short period available to them. Although many temperate and tropical insects have characteristic patterns of daily activity that are triggered by light intensity, daily changes in light intensity are much less marked in the Arctic and air temperatures are likely to be a more reliable indicator of suitable conditions. Desiccation may pose a risk to some Arctic insects, which restrict most of their activities to periods of dampness (e.g. some springtails Collembola) or seek refuge in damp moss (e.g. *Culicoides* sp. Ceratopogonidae).

Insect mating activities in the Arctic tend to be simplified, even in groups with elaborate mating behaviour in temperate areas. The flightless females of *Gynaephora* merely rest on their cocoons, emitting a chemical signal (pheromone) into the air to attract the flying males for mating. Although swarming by some Arctic midges and mosquitoes is conspicuous, it takes place only during fine weather, usually close to the ground, and for short periods. In other species, swarms are so reduced that mating takes place on the ground. The specialised eyes and auditory antennae characteristic of males in swarming species, by which they recognise the females by sight and wing-beat frequency (sound), are reduced in those species that mate on the ground.

Arctic insects are metabolically adapted to their cold environment. The threshold for development of eggs and larvae is close to freezing in a number of Arctic midges that inhabit deep lakes, and High Arctic mosquito larvae develop and grow at temperatures near 1° C. In some insects that range south of the treeline the individuals from northerly populations have lower thresholds for development and activity than those from the south; in other insects there is no such disparity. Despite the lower thresholds for development and activity, many Arctic insects do not show higher rates of metabolism than temperate insects. They can metabolise at lower temperatures, but not elevate the metabolic rate. This suggests that metabolism in the Arctic may be governed by the energetic balance of the organisms, which is limited by the speed of feeding and assimilation.

One might expect winter survival to be the most important factor in the life of Arctic insects, but little is known of the overwintering sites of Arctic species. Mosquitoes overwinter as eggs at the edges of ponds, and some midges overwinter as larvae in the unfrozen deeper parts of some ponds and lakes; others must freeze-in as shallow ponds become solid ice continuous with the permafrost. Blow flies seem to be able to overwinter as adults or as larvae, adults seeking shelter beneath stones, twigs, leaves, etc., and the larvae in their food source of a carcass or dung. Most Lepidoptera overwinter as larvae; none do so as adults, and it is not known whether any Arctic species can overwinter as eggs. Bumblebees overwinter as inseminated queens only, and psyllid bugs also overwinter as adults. Some insects overwinter on fully exposed ridges, which are swept free of snow in the winter, others may burrow a short distance into the ground, but most probably seek some protection among the vegetation. Nevertheless, except for those species living in bodies of water that do not freeze, all are exposed to long, unrelenting, bitter cold.

In temperate areas, some insects can overwinter by supercooling; that is by remaining unfrozen at temperatures below 0° C. They do this by preventing the formation of ice crystals in their bodies, often synthesising glycerol to assist in this. However, freezing cannot be avoided in most Arctic habitats and though the exact survival mechanisms are unclear some general features are known (Danks 1978, 1981): some insects dehydrate for winter, and at least some species build up ice-nucleators in the haemolymph, thus presumably directing the freezing process to minimise or prevent damage. Some frozen Arctic insects cannot survive repeated thawing and re-freezing, and most cannot tolerate freezing once the period of summer activity has started and before they prepare again for the next winter.

Many temperate and tropical insects complete their lives from egg to adult in one year or less. In the Arctic, the shortness and coolness of the active season preclude rapid development and the arthropods have extended life spans. Some stone flies and midges illustrate this point. In these organisms, individuals inhabiting cooler (northern or higher) habitats take longer to develop and live for two years, whereas the same species at lower latitudes or altitudes complete their life-cycles in one year. The midge *Tanytarsus gracilentus* has two generations per year in Iceland, but takes several years to complete its life-cycle in the High Arctic. The springtail *Hypogastrura tullbergi* (Collembola) may complete a generation in as little as two months in the temperate zone but can take three to five years in the High Arctic.

Life cycles of Arctic arthropods seldom have been measured directly (see Chernov 1978). Inferences, from ecological studies, suggest that some midges take from two to seven years (Butler 1982), crane flies four or more years, horse flies at least three years, the 'woolly bear' caterpillar *Gynaephora rossii* 13 years or more and its parasitic wasps and bristle flies three or more years (Kukal 1983) and so on. The variability in life-span reflects the opportunistic nature of the insects: they take advantage of warm weather and then may grow relatively rapidly, but have reduced developmental rates under adverse conditions (e.g. Corbet and Danks 1973; Danks and Oliver 1972). Nevertheless, some insects such as bumblebees and some midges (e.g. *Chironomus*) (Butler 1982) have fixed life-spans.

As noted above, most Arctic insects do not over-winter as adults. During the short summer, the activity of the adults of one species is often closely synchron-ised. The males usually emerge first, as in other parts of the world, but only by a narrow margin. Climatic factors are clearly important in providing cues for syn-chrony of behaviour, but additional precision might often be required within a season. Given that some Arctic insects have long, somewhat indeterminate life-spans, that individual rates of development vary, and so on, precise synchrony could be difficult to achieve. One way that insects can overcome this problem is through an obligate period of dormancy. Some Arctic insects enter such periods at a given life stage, no matter what part of the summer season prevails. Some midges pupate and emerge only at the outset of spring, even though they may have become fully grown larvae early in the previous year.

One might expect that food specificity would not be pronounced in Arctic insects, favouring opportunistic feeding. To some extent this may be true. Many of the herbivores are more or less polyphagous, but rigorous testing has not been widely carried out. When experi-ments have been conducted, most of these insects have proved to eat only a few species of plants. Perhaps the incidence of monophagy is low among herbivores, but many of the specialised, parasitic, carnivorous bristle flies, parasitic wasps (Ichneumonidae, Braconidae) and ectoparasites of mammals and birds are mono-phagous. Other predatory insects, spiders, and mites are probably generalists and, like the Arctic sap-rophages, take a variety of foods, and may feed in a mixed fashion. Nevertheless, the Arctic arthropods fol-low the general feeding patterns of their more southerly relatives.

Some of the adaptations of Arctic insects appear to favour 'opportunism'. This word carries with it the idea of ability to take advantage of conditions as they arise and implies that some variability exists to allow for this. Thus one might expect an opportunistic insect, living in the Arctic, to be anatomically, behaviourally, physiologically, and ultimately genetically, variable. This is indeed true of most Arctic insects. Mating and the mixing of genetic information from generation to generation is an important part of life strategy every-where, including in the Arctic. However, sex is almost, or completely, unknown in a number of Arctic insects. In these species, which include caddis flies (Trichop-tera), stone flies, midges, black flies (Simuliidae), and plant sucking bugs (Psyllidae, Coccidae, and Miridae), males are rare or unknown, the females reproducing parthenogenetically. Presumably, the genetic information these females carry represents a 'winning combination' for the species and allows it to succeed despite the harsh conditions of the Arctic. In plants, this situation is well known amongst weeds (colonising species of disturbed and unstable habitats) and the Arctic flora. A few insects appear to have come upon the same solution to the same sorts of problems. In both the plant and insect species with these capabilities, the chromosome complement is often larger (polyploid) than in sexually reproducing rela-tives.

## Adaptations of Arctic Plants
(Dr E. Haber)

All adaptations, whether they pertain to the morphol-ogy, physiology, or reproductive processes of the species, are ultimately controlled at the genetic level. In some cases, the phenotype (morphological appear-ance of a plant) is the end result of the interactive process between the environment and the genetic com-plement of the plant. When the morphology can be changed under different environmental conditions, the plant is said to exhibit phenotypic plasticity. In other plants, the appearance cannot be influenced by the environment in the same way, and the plants are only capable of a limited variability because they have become genetically adapted to a specific set of environmental conditions; such plant populations are considered to be ecotypes. Many ecotypes may be pre-sent in some species, but in others the adaptability of the species may be due primarily to its phenotypic plasticity. In the bitter-cress *Cardamine bellidifolia*, a circumpolar Arctic-alpine species, plants from alpine locations in Alaska, British Columbia, and the Yukon have been shown, through transplant studies under temperate conditions, to grow into tall plants; conse-quently, such plants exhibit phenotypic plasticity. However, seeds of this species collected on Ellesmere Island and tested under the same conditions grew only as dwarfed specimens, therefore representing dwarf ecotypes of the species (Savile 1972). The Arctic Wil-low *Salix arctica* is an example of a genetically prostrate species. In contrast, the stunting of some other Arctic shrubs such as various willows and birches is usually due to snow abrasion in which the twigs and buds are killed above a certain height.

### Morphological Adaptations

One of the most obvious adaptations is the low or dwarfed size of Arctic plants. This reduces desiccation from winds that are usually stronger at greater heights above ground, minimises snow blasting of exposed parts, and permits the plants to be covered to a greater degree by the limited snowfall. The low stature is also beneficial for the production of flowers and seeds. Temperatures near the ground are generally much higher. The overall effect of dwarfing allows the plants to grow in an ameliorated microclimate where flowers can be produced earlier and have an extended season. Some Arctic plants have an additional adaptation of overwintering well developed flower buds which enables flowering to start at the earliest opportunity in the new season.

Other temperature-related adaptations are the dense basal rosettes of leaves of many species, and the formation of mats of low vegetation that provide a suitable environment for heat build-up in the air pock-ets around the clustered leaves. Dark coloration of leaves and stems results in greater heat absorption, particularly when combined with a dense leafy growth form. A 15° C difference has been recorded between the temperature within a clump of saxifrage and the surrounding air. The cushion growth form has evolved in unrelated families with Arctic species, and represents an example of parallel evolution.

The presence of coloured floral parts assists in the heat-trapping process that promotes the development and maturation of the flowers and seeds. Even the parabolic shape of some flowers in species such as poppy *Papaver* and mountain avens *Dryas*, whose flowers track the sun, probably serve as heat concentrating devices. Besides increasing metabolic activity, the temperature increase also benefits the flowers by ameliorating the microhabitat for insect pollinators which are frequently seen basking there.

Dense layers of hair on stems, leaves and flowers may be of some use in reducing moisture loss by decreasing air movement, particularly on the lower surface of leaves where the pores are primarily located. On surfaces exposed directly to sunlight, the presence of a dense felty layer of hairs may serve in an analagous manner to the glass panes of a greenhouse. The hairs increase the temperature next to the surface of the plant by radiating back some of the heat rays that would otherwise all escape. Species in the genera *Antennaria*, *Pedicularis* and *Potentilla* commonly have abundant hair, as do the catkins of Arctic Willow.

Certain adaptations, such as fleshy roots or tuberous storage organs, as well as evergreen leaves, may permit rapid and early seasonal growth and photosynthesis at any time when the tissue temperatures are suitably elevated. Fleshy roots and tuberous rhizomes occur in various plants including Mountain Sorrel *Oxyria digyna*, and species of *Pedicularis*, *Polygonum* and *Taraxacum*. The roots of some species also tend to be stratified, being restricted to the warmer, upper, better-drained layer of soil. This contrasts with many alpine plants whose roots penetrate more deeply into the soil.

Most Arctic species that have evergreen leaves, such as the various shrubs of the heather family (Ericaceae) and some saxifrages, occur most abundantly in the Low Arctic regions where snowfall gives the leaves some protection from snow abrasion. The year-round presence of leaves makes photosynthesis possible at any time when climatic conditions are suitable. In the High Arctic, winter protection for the evergreen Arctic White-heather *Cassiope tetragona* is afforded by its occurrence in areas of snow accumulation. A few species of evergreen saxifrages withstand snow abrasion by their compact cushion growth form (*Saxifraga oppositifolia*), or leafy, tufted habit in which the growing points are protected within the clumps of old leaves and stems (Spotted Saxifrage *S. bronchialis* and Prickly Saxifrage *S. tricuspidata*).

Species with wintergreen leaves are more numerous. In such species, the younger leaves produced in one growing season remain green and function at least during the early part of the following season. The rosette growth form of these plants, in which the older leaves remain on the plant, provides a means of protection for the younger, evergreen leaves found near the centre of the plant. Plants of this type include Snow Saxifrage *Saxifraga nivalis* and *S. tenuis*, most members of the pink family (Caryophyllaceae), mustard family (Brassicaceae), as well as Thrift *Armeria maritima*, mountain avens, and poppies. In the majority of the monocotyledonous plants, in particular the grasses and sedges, the basal parts of the leaves remain green over the winter, with mainly the ends of the narrow blades being killed.

## Physiological Adaptations

Experiments with some wide-ranging Arctic-alpine species, in particular Mountain Sorrel and Alpine Meadow-rue *Thalictrum alpinum*, have shown that Arctic plants of these species are better adapted to the lower light intensities and temperatures, and long photoperiods than are alpine plants from southern localities (Bliss 1962). This is shown in their higher photosynthetic rates at given levels of low illumination and temperature, and better growth under long daylight periods.

Just as the northern treeline is regulated to a large extent by the availability of a minimum level of summer warmth, plant hardiness in the Arctic is dependent on frost hardiness during the growing season (not winter hardiness), combined with the ability to resume metabolic activity immediately upon thawing. In temperate regions, woody plants and even the subterranean parts, once physiologically hardened late in the year, can withstand very low winter temperatures. Once frozen, the absolute temperature is not as critical as desiccation by warm drying winds during winter when groundwater is still frozen and unavailable to the plants. Arctic plants generally have exceptional tolerance to summer frosts, even at the normally critical flowering stage.

# 7
# FLORA OF THE CIRCUMPOLAR ARCTIC

Dr E. Haber

## Introduction

North beyond the fringe of the nearly continuous expanse of predominantly coniferous forest that encircles the northern hemisphere lies a treeless barren, the Arctic tundra. The word tundra is of Finnish origin referring to a treeless rolling plain; it is a very descriptive term for much of the Arctic landscape. The northernmost limit of arborescent growth, however, is not the edge of the closed forest, but the tenuous northern edge of the transitional forest-tundra. This zone is a mosaic of open barrens and coniferous trees that become progressively more stunted and scattered northward. (While some authorities regard the forest-tundra as part of the Arctic, it is not regarded as such in the present work; see Chapter 1.)

## History of the Arctic Flora

Of all the major biomes in the world, the Arctic tundra is the most recently evolved. There are indications that forest-tundra vegetation may have existed in the latter part of the Miocene, about 10 million years ago in the most north-western region of the Canadian Arctic Archipelago and northern Greenland as well as in northern Siberia (Matthews 1979a). Unlike the Arctic today, these two main regions did not form a continuous circumpolar belt, but were separated by a band of coniferous and mixed conifer-hardwood forests that stretched throughout most of present day Arctic and Subarctic regions.

Within this forested belt, the mixed conifer-hardwood forest extended as far north as Banks Island. The climate of the time was considerably warmer, allowing temperate hardwood species and mixed deciduous-coniferous forests to thrive at high latitudes. The species of the early forest-tundra communities at the fringe of the forested belt probably consisted of forest plants that were more tolerant of the colder, drier conditions that existed beyond the limits of the continuous forest and in the upper elevations of highland regions within the forested zone.

These first areas of forest-tundra communities in the high latitudes probably did not expand to form a cir-

cumpolar zone of tundra until the late Pliocene, about 3 million years ago, during a time of gradual climatic deterioration that led to the start of the Pleistocene glaciations. During the Pleistocene epoch that began about 2 million years ago, the circumpolar Arctic was repeatedly fragmented into isolated refugia and reconstituted as a consequence of several major periods of worldwide glaciation.

During glacial periods, as much as 30 per cent of the earth's land surface was covered by ice and permanent snowfields. In North America, four major glacial periods have generally been recognised, each representing several advances and retreats of ice fronts. The last glacial period began as much as 100,000 years ago and ended about 14,000 years ago. During the time of maximum glaciation, most of Canada as well as the northern United States was covered in ice (Figure 7.1), probably over 2,000 m thick. In Europe, ice-cover was never as extensive as that in North America, with most of the continuous ice being restricted to northern Europe and north-western Siberia.

### Glacial Refugia

Based on geological evidence and the distributional patterns of plants and animals, a number of areas within glaciated regions are known to have been ice-free during the last glacial maximum (Lindsey 1981). These have served as refugia for Arctic species. Northern glacial refugia that are known or assumed include the interior of Alaska and Yukon, Kodiak Island (Karlstrom and Ball 1969), western Banks Island (Vincent 1982), eastern Siberia and the land area exposed during glacial times between Siberia and Alaska (see Figure 7.2) called Beringia (Hopkins 1967), localised sites on Svalbard (Rönning, 1963),

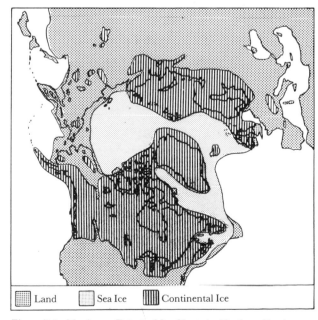

Figure 7.1: Maximum Extent of Ice-Sheets in Northern North America at the Height of the Last Glaciation
Source: Dr E. Haber.

the north-western coast and mountain tops of Scandinavia (Dahl 1955; Gjaerevoll 1963), Iceland (Steindórsson 1963), eastern Baffin Island (Löken 1966), northern Ellesmere Island (Schuster *et al* 1959) and parts of western Greenland (Böcher 1963). Areas to the south or along the fringe of continental glaciers also served as refugia. A number of these are found in the Gulf of Saint Lawrence, and in various mountainous regions in North America and Eurasia where Arctic and Arctic-alpine species are still found.

The most important and largest refugia in the north for Arctic species were the interior of Alaska and Yukon, eastern Siberia, and the region between the two continents, Beringia, that became exposed as the sea levels dropped by more than 100 m at times of glacial advance (Hopkins 1967; Murray 1981; Matthews 1982). As it became exposed or inundated by the fluctuating sea levels during periods of glacial advance and retreat, Beringia served intermittently as a corridor for the spread of plants and animals. About 10,000 years ago this land connection was severed for the last time. The vegetation of Beringia consisted primarily of a steppe-tundra that was dominated by plants such as grasses and sagebrush *Artemisia*, with groves of poplar in favourable sites. Large herds of grazing animals such as bison, horse and mammoth wandered over the rolling terrain (Matthews 1979b).

Eastern Beringia (Alaska and Yukon) was in essence a biological extension of north-eastern Asia. Indeed, most of the movement of species was in an easterly direction, perhaps as a consequence of the continuous and extensive unglaciated region of forest and mountain vegetation of central Asia that connected with eastern Siberia and Beringia (Yurtsev 1972). Alaska and Yukon, during the glacial maximum, was basically a cul-de-sac, receiving many Asian species but probably having no exit to the interior of the continent, except possibly a narrow corridor between the abuting Cordilleran and Laurentide ice-sheets.

The Arctic vegetation of today is the result of the recent migration of species that survived in unglaciated refugia, and from areas of the continents to the south of the ice-fronts, into newly exposed lands, some of which have only been free of ice for several thousand years. The variable community structure of the Arctic vegetation and the localised differences in species diversity are a reflection not only of local environmental differences, but of the species composition of the refugia from which the colonising species spread and the time available for establishment.

The rate of migration of the Arctic flora during post-glacial times from centres harbouring Arctic species was dependent on the dispersal capabilities of each. On the mainland, in areas of relatively uniform

*Figure 7.2: The Beringian Land Connection, a Major Refugium for Plants and Animals, During the Last Glacial Maximum Source: Dr E. Haber.*

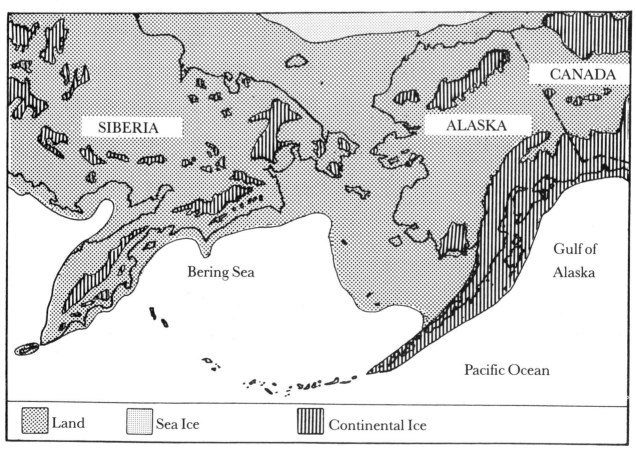

topography and climate without mountain barriers, species movements and the spread of the Arctic vegetation proceeded relatively unhampered. Such an area was the vast northern continental plain of Canada over which developed a relatively uniform Arctic tundra vegetation. In the Arctic islands, the spread of Arctic species was much more haphazard.

The present Arctic vegetation is the result of the vagaries of chance and time working on the stocks of Arctic plants that remained at the end of the last glaciation. It is a transient phase in the evolution of species adapted to cold and dry environments that has been shaped by successive climatic fluctuations of different magnitudes over the past 3 million years.

## Environmental Factors Controlling Plant Growth

The Arctic is characterised by a harsh cool climate that averages only 5° C in mid-summer and −32° C in mid-winter. Annual precipitation is normally below 38 cm, but commonly, in the interior of continents and large islands, is less than 25 cm, with two-thirds of it falling as summer rain. Winter snowfalls are light and are regularly swept off windward slopes and level ground by the frequent gales. In the summer, winds off permanent sea-ice and summer ice-floes cool the air, and the cold waters cause frequent fogs to occur, particularly in some coastal areas, as a consequence of the cooling of water evaporating from the saturated land surface during the continuous daylight.

Below ground, the entire Arctic is held in a state of deep freeze by the permafrost (see Chapter 5). The southern boundary of continuous permafrost coincides approximately with the Arctic treeline. Where the permafrost extends to within about 60 cm of the surface, the soil becomes too waterlogged in summer for tree growth to occur. During the summer, the permafrost may only thaw to depths of 15 to 30 cm in the northern Arctic, but this may extend to three metres in the lower forested latitudes of discontinuous permafrost. Much of the Arctic, however, would be a lifeless desert if it were not for this layer of permanently frozen soil and water a few centimetres below the surface that prevents the meagre summer rain and meltwater from penetrating below the reach of plant roots.

Plant growth is also greatly influenced by the short growing season that may be less than 50 days between late and early frosts. The effects of a shortened growing season are partly counteracted by the nearly continuous daylight that prevails for one to four months (depending on latitude), but total illumination received by plants is offset by the low elevation of the sun that changes the light quality and reduces its intensity. The frequent cloud cover in summer also reduces light intensity.

Arctic soils are generally acid because of poor drainage and therefore poor aeration. Consequently, organic decay by soil bacteria is extremely slow with the result that levels of nitrogen for plant growth are low. Plant growth is relatively slow in the Arctic and may be caused by the low levels of nutrients as well as

the uniformly low soil temperatures. Some woody plants such as dwarfed shrubs may take years before they mature sufficiently to produce flowers and fruits.

## Zonation of Vegetation

Attempts have been made to subdivide the Arctic on the basis of the general and progressive depauperation of the vegetation that occurs with increased latitude. Three main belts dividing the Arctic have been recognised, as shown in Figure 1.4 (Polunin 1951). The Low Arctic is characterised by the presence of nearly continuous vegetation over most areas, the Middle Arctic as containing large areas of continuous vegetation (but perhaps most commonly in low lying areas), and the High Arctic by the extensive rock barrens where plants and localised communities are highly scattered and where closed vegetation cover is restricted to only the most favourable habitats. The term tundra perhaps best describes the large tracts of rolling waterlogged terrain, covered in large part by a surface layer of peat, that are the common features of the landscape in the Low Arctic. Such a landscape covers approximately the southern half of the continuous zone of permafrost that underlies the Arctic from the treeline northward.

Another approach that has been taken to divide the Arctic into latitudinal zones was that by Young (1971). The basis for his Arctic zonation was the premise that one overriding climatic factor, the amount of available warmth during the growing season, controlled the northern limits that common circumpolar species could attain. Certain groups of circumpolar species with similar northern limits to their distributional ranges serve as markers for the northern limits of each

*Figure 7.3: Species Diversity in the Arctic in Relation to the Four Floristic Zones (Stippled and Hatched) of Young (1971). (Notes: 1. Cape Dezhnen; 2. Cape Prince of Wales; 3. Alaska and Yukon; 4. Melville Island; 5. Ellef Ringnes Island; 6. Continental Northwest Territories, Ungava and North Labrador; 7. South-west Greenland; 8. Lake Hazen, Ellesmere Island; 9. Alert, Ellesmere Island; 10. Iceland; 11. Svalbard; 12. Zemyla Frantsa Iosifa; 13. Severnaya Zemyla; 14. Taimyr Peninsula; 15. Tiksi Bay; 16. Aion Island.) Source: Dr. E. Haber.*

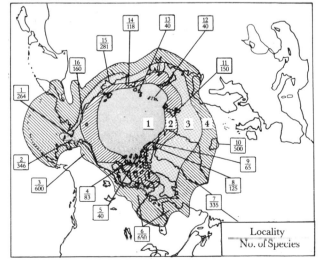

of Young's floristic zones. He viewed the use of these representative species as being analogous to the delimitation of the northern treeline on the basis of the conifers that form the boundary between the Subarctic and Arctic zones. Young recognised four floristic zones in the Arctic, as shown in Figure 7.3.

Zone 1 includes the northernmost regions of the Arctic where the impoverished flora usually consists of fewer than 50 species, and in which no vascular cryptogams (ferns and other spore-bearing plants) occur. The species are found in a variety of habitats, but few form extensive colonies. The majority are circumpolar in distribution. Zone 2 includes portions of the northernmost land areas of the polar continental regions. The flora is somewhat richer, consisting of 75–125 species at a representative site, and includes mainly circumpolar and wide-ranging species. At least seven species of vascular cryptogams occur in the zone. Both Zones 1 and 2 fall within the region traditionally called the High Arctic. Zone 3 represents a transition between the relatively depauperate two northern zones and the floristically richer Zone 4. Within Zone 3, in the less isolated regions, there are usually about 250 species or more at a locality, and there is a greater differentiation between the floras of the various regions in the zone. Zone 4 consists primarily of mainland areas and includes a total land mass equivalent to that of Zones 1 to 3 combined. This region of the Low Arctic has a flora several times richer than that found in Zones 1 and 2, but the number of characteristic species found is not substantially different from that of the other zones. Within this region, the composition of the floras varies greatly between areas, and the percentage of circumpolar species is considerably reduced.

These zones are not correlated with historical factors, climatic differences such as mean annual temperature or precipitation, day length, or soil types. The main controlling factor is the amount of summer warmth available for plant growth.

Aleksandrova (1980) recognised two main geobotanical regions in the Arctic – the tundra region and the region of the polar deserts. Her classification of Arctic vegetation takes into account both the continuity of vegetation and the degree of floristic diversity. The region of the polar deserts, in her treatment, agrees with Young's floristic Zone 1. The tundra is subdivided into two subregions – the Subarctic tundras and the Arctic tundras (see Table 1.2).

The Subarctic tundras are characterised by the presence of semiprostrate shrubs such as the birches *Betula nana*, *B. glandulosa*, and dwarf shrubs, including Bilberry *Vaccinium uliginosum* s.l., Crowberry *Empetrum nigrum*, and Labrador Tea *Ledum palustre*. In the Arctic tundras, Arctic-alpine and Arctic dwarf shrubs such as Polar Willow *Salix polaris*, the avens *Dryas octopetala*, *D. punctata*, *D. integrifolia*, and Arctic White-heather predominate. Thickets of shrubs disappear and there are no snow-dependent meadow-like communities.

The High Arctic has also been subdivided into broad categories based primarily on the availability of moisture (Babb and Bliss 1974). Four units were recognised: polar deserts with very sparse vegetation, polar semi-desert with only local areas of continuous vegetation, areas of diverse terrain where tundra or sedge-moss meadows are more frequent, and sedge-moss meadows with nearly continuous cover occurring mainly in lowlands.

Studies by Edlund (1983) in the Queen Elizabeth Islands in the north-western Canadian Arctic Archipelago have shown that a bioclimatic zonation based on vegetational patterns is roughly correlated with regional climatic trends. She recognised four zones in these islands (Figure 7.4): Zone 1 has a very depauperate flora consisting only of herbs, with the number of species less than 35; Zone 2 includes a few dwarf shrubs but consists mainly of herbs with the total number of species ranging between 35 and 60. The boundary between these two zones she recognises as a 'mini-treeline'. Zone 3 supports about 60–100 species and includes dwarf shrubs and sedges (Cyperaceae). These, together with Zone 4, she regards as constituting a 'mini-forest'. Zone 4 has the richest and most diverse flora. Edlund's studies indicate that the limit of vascular plant growth is controlled by a mean daily July temperature of just over 2.5° C. The limit for the growth of woody plants is 3–3.5° C, and 3.5–4° C for the occurrence of dwarf shrub communities.

There is no concensus on the number of phytogeographic units that should be used to subdivide the Arctic into regional divisions. Those proposed by Polunin (1951) were adopted primarily as conveniences for locating species distributions within broad geographic sectors. The latitudinal belts corresponding to the High Arctic, Middle Arctic, and Low Arctic tend to be widely recognised, probably because there is a readily evident phytogeographical gradient poleward. The subdivision of the Arctic into east-west units is more subjective in that a greater number of factors such as major physiographic differences in the landmasses, climatic variability, and historical factors have influenced the distributional patterns of plants.

## Species Diversity in the Arctic Flora

Species diversity is dependent on climate, habitat diversity, and historical factors such as the age of the flora, but there is generally a progressive decrease in the numbers of species with increasing latitude. Such a reduction in the numbers of species northward can be readily shown.

In North America, for example, in the warm temperate climates of Texas and California, the numbers of species are approximately 5,000 and 4,000 respectively. In contrast, the flora of all of Canada is less than 5,000 species. The northern continental portion of Canada comprising the Northwest Territories has a flora of less than 1,200 species. In the Arctic zone of the continental Northwest Territories and the Ungava Peninsula, there are only 650 species, and the flora of the Canadian Arctic Archipelago, an area of about $1.34 \times 10^6$ km², comprises only about 340 species of vascular plants. Over a latitudinal spread greater than

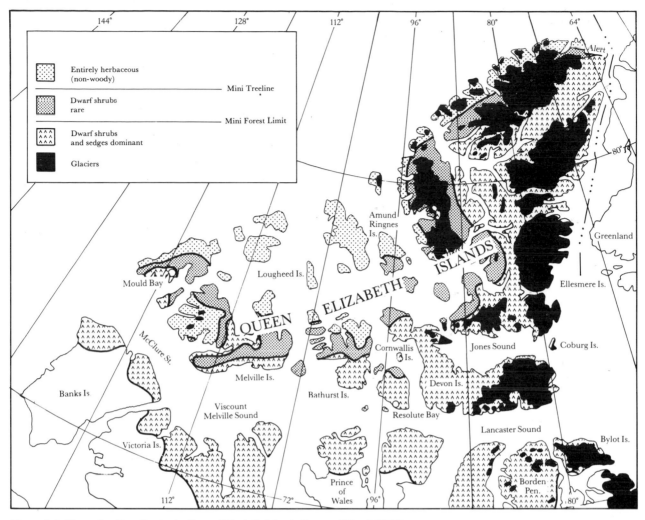

*Figure 7.4: Vegetation Zonation in the Queen Elizabeth Islands Source: Edlund (1983).*

1,600 km from the continent to the northernmost Arctic islands, a further marked decrease in species numbers occurs. This considerable reduction in numbers of species northward is only in part due to the decrease in land surface available for colonisation. In northern Ellesmere Island, the flora is reduced to 65 species, and on Ellef Ringnes Island in the north-western Archipelago, the flora consists of only about 50 species of plants (see Figure 7.3).

Woody plants are even more susceptible than perennial herbs to the increased climatic rigours northward. Within the Canadian Arctic Archipelago, shrubs decrease rapidly in number with increasing latitude, and are completely absent over large areas in the Queen Elizabeth Islands along the western fringe of Axel Heiberg Island and the north-west coast of Ellesmere Island.

The Arctic zone in Eurasia does not extend over such a broad latitudinal span as in the North American Arctic, but consists primarily of a narrow and somewhat fragmented band along the northern continental coast and a few small island groups in the Arctic Ocean. As a consequence, the rapid species reduction northward in the Siberian Arctic occurs over a distance of less than 65 kilometres in some areas.

The flora of the circumpolar Arctic has been estimated to be about 900 species (Polunin 1959), although with the imperfect state of knowledge for this immense region, the number may very well be closer to 1,000. Roughly 600 species are considered to be endemic to the Arctic, and of these about 200 are circumpolar, although some are Arctic-alpine species that extend into the alpine tundra of mid-latitudes. Within the whole of the Arctic region, there are fewer than 70 families of vascular plants, with a total of about 230 genera. The families with the greatest number of species represented, in order of importance are as follows: the grass family (Poaceae), sedge family (Cyperaceae), daisy family (Asteraceae), mustard family (Brassicaceae), pink family (Caryophyllaceae), saxifrage family (Saxifragaceae), buttercup family (Ranunculaceae), willow family (Salicaceae), bean family (Fabaceae) and rose family (Rosaceae). The grass and sedge families have by far the greatest number of Arctic species of any of these families. In the polar deserts of the High Arctic, certain groups and families such as the ferns, the lily family (Liliaceae), the birch family (Betulaceae), and the crowberry family (Empetraceae), are completely absent. The genera with the largest numbers of species, for the most part, are those that occur in the ten families listed: *Carex, Saxifraga, Salix, Ranunculus, Draba, Potentilla, Oxytropis, Puccinellia, Pedicularis*, and *Eriophorum*. In general, Arctic floras are characterised by large numbers of genera that are represented by only a single species.

Floristic diversity is in part a function of climate, as is clearly evident in the universal phenomenon of the reduction in the numbers of species poleward. It is also related to such factors as habitat diversity and the age and origins of the flora. The Arctic zone of the continental Northwest Territories in Canada, for example, is an extensive region of interior plains with only low to moderate relief and a uniformly dry, continental climate. Habitat diversity as a consequence is low, resulting in a flora of only about 650 species that occur relatively uniformly across the region (Porsild 1955). The size of the flora as well as the presence of only a few endemic species may also be a reflection of the relatively short time available for colonisation and diversification of species during post-glacial times (less than 8,000 years), and of the barrier which the Mackenzie River Valley provides to the eastward spread of species with Asian and Cordilleran affinities.

To the west of the central continental Arctic region in Canada, the flora of the Arctic regions of the Yukon and Alaska combined consists of over 600 species, and in number is comparable to that in the Arctic continental Northwest Territories. The species comprising the flora are, however, much more varied in their phytogeographic affinities, and in addition the region is rich in endemic species. This diversity is in large part due to the greater age of the flora. Large parts of Alaska and the Yukon were never ice-covered during the last glaciation, and these areas were also connected during glacial times with the east Asian floras via the broad land shelf of Beringia. These unglaciated regions, containing a relict flora rich in endemics and species that had migrated eastward from a large unglaciated region in eastern Asia and northward from the alpine tundras of the Cordillera during inter-glacial times, served as the source of plants for the colonisation of the newly developing Arctic zones in Alaska and the Yukon. Indications are that the migration from Asia to North America was mainly of Arctic-alpine species. The reverse migrational pattern consisted mainly of Arctic and Subarctic species, with the net result that Asia played a greater role as a source of species for the Arctic regions of north-western North America (Derviz-Sokolova 1966).

The flora of the narrow Arctic zone of continental Eurasia is relatively impoverished (Tolmachev 1966). Aion Island, just off the coast west of the Chukotka Peninsula, has a flora of about 160 species of Arctic and Arctic-alpine affinity. Further west, at Tiksi Bay near the mouth of the Lena River, 281 species have been found. The flora has a continental aspect in view of the large numbers of continental Arctic, Arctic-alpine, and Subarctic species. Because of the strong winter winds that cause heavy drifting, 30–40 per cent of the habitats

are essentially snowless, supporting little plant growth, and Arctic-alpine species tend to comprise the largest group in the flora. In the Taimyr Peninsula, the most northerly continental promontory on the globe, habitat variety is minimal, with large areas of wet tundra predominating. In this region of severe climate and recent land availability following glaciation, the Arctic flora consists of only about 118 species.

Some of the most depauperate floras of the entire Arctic occur in the Soviet Arctic Archipelagoes (Young 1971). At a latitude of about 80° N, Zemlya Frantsa Iosifa and Severnaya Zemlya each have only about 40 species of vascular plants. In contrast, the Norwegian archipelago of Svalbard, at the same latitude, has a flora of over 150 species, but this comparatively rich flora is probably due to the influence of the North Atlantic Drift.

## Habitats and Plant Cover

Within the vast expanse of the Arctic, there is considerable physiographic diversity, local and regional climatic differentiation and distinctive poleward gradients in the climate. The combined action of these variables results in a mosaic of habitats with differing conditions that, to varying degrees, are conducive to or inimical to the growth of plants. In spite of the influence on plant growth of such variables as substrate, exposure, slope and moisture availability, the overriding factor controlling the occurrence of plants in the Arctic is the amount of summer warmth available. Given these variables, the plants themselves have their own specific requirements and tolerances that control their survival and reproductive successes.

Plants with similar environmental tolerances regularly occur together as recognisable associations. In different habitats, generally a different mix of species occurs, and the relative abundances change as well. Numerous plant associations can be recognised in the Arctic flora. For convenience, the vegetation is here described in terms of some of the common species that occur in several broad habitat types and in certain specialised microhabitats (Polunin 1948; Porsild 1951, 1955): rock deserts and barrens, tundra habitats and vegetation, snowflush vegetation, marine strand vegetation, freshwater habitats and manure-enriched habitats.

### Rock Deserts and Barrens

In the Low Arctic, fell-fields and barrens are found mainly at higher elevations, and in exposed sites, particularly near the coast; the lower elevations are covered by tundra vegetation. In contrast, vast tracts of rocky terrain dominate the landscape in the High Arctic. These appear as monotonous expanses of rock rubble and barrens, nearly devoid of plants except for the scattered tufts and cushions that dot the landscape.

Typically, rock deserts or fell-field habitats consist of various sizes of frost-shattered rock with fine mineral soils interspersed. Areas of this kind characteristically have very scant vegetation that never forms a closed ground cover. Soils have a limited development, tend to be relatively dry, and in the high latitudes little snow-cover accumulates. In some of the more extreme areas, plant-cover may be as low as 2 per cent of the surface. Various species of crustose and foliose lichens lend colour to the rocks, and a variety of species of flowering plants such as the Arctic Poppy *Papaver lapponicum* s.l., Moss Campion, species of *Draba*, saxifrages (Tufted Saxifrage *Saxifraga caespitosa*, Nodding Saxifrage *S. cernua*, Purple Saxifrage and Prickly Saxifrage), grasses and sedges occur scattered throughout. Ferns, such as *Woodsia glabella* and *W. ilvensis* and the sweet-scented shield fern *Dryopteris fragrans*, root within crevices where water may be more readily available. In more severe habitats, only the occcasional plant of Arctic Poppy or Purple Saxifrage may be found. Species that predominate in these stony wind-swept rock deserts tend to form dense tufts or flattened cushions.

Barrens consist of smaller, more uniformly weathered particles of rock that occur as pavements and rocky flats and plains. In such areas, species diversity is low, but the plants that occur tend to form conspicuous colonies, frequently arranged in the form of islands or strips, patterning the terrain. Purple Saxifrage, Arctic Avens *Dryas integrifolia*, and Locoweed *Oxytropis arctica* are common species of rock barrens.

During the brief Arctic summer, many of these rock deserts are transformed into showy rock gardens. Out of a seemingly barren landscape, springs a colourful mosaic including the whites of the Arctic Avens, chickweeds (*Stellaria* and *Cerastium*) and Large-flowered Wintergreen *Pyrola grandiflora*, the yellows of *Arnica* and locoweeds, and the purples of Broad-leaved Willow-herb *Epilobium latifolium* and Mountain Vetch *Astragalus alpinus*. Dwarf shrubs of willow *Salix* and heaths, including blueberries *Vaccinium*, Labrador Tea *Ledum decumbens*, Arctic White-heather, and Lapland Rosebay *Rhododendron lapponicum* also occur scattered throughout these rocky habitats.

## Tundra Habitats and Vegetation

Extensive tundra is characteristic mainly of Low Arctic regions, particularly in the Canadian continental Northwest Territories and in northern Siberia. The tundra consists of a nearly continuous, although at times thin, cover of vegetation, commonly 15–35 cm high in which sedges and grasses are dominant. Scattered among the grassy vegetation, in places forming a conspicuous layer, are various species of mosses, a variety of flowering herbs and a few species of scrubby and dwarfed shrubs of willows and birches.

In the Low Arctic, tundra vegetation is generally denser and more vigorous in growth. Tall shrubs of Alaska Willow *Salix alaxensis* 3–5 m tall occur along rivers and lakes. Other willows such as Northern Willow *S. glauca*, birches *Betula glandulifera*, and Alder *Alnus crispa* form an understorey among the taller shrubs. In better-drained sites, dwarfed specimens of *S. glauca*, *S. pulchra*, and *Betula nana exilis* predominate. Associated with these shrubs are heaths such as Mountain Cran-

berry *Vaccinium vitis-idaea*, Bilberry, Crowberry, Labrador Tea, Bearberry *Arctostaphyllos alpina* and *A. rubra*, and Arctic White-heather. Characteristic herbs of these thickets include Fireweed *Epilobium angustifolium*, Lapland Buttercup *Ranunculus lapponicus*, Northern Windflower *Anemone parviflora*, *Petasites*, *Senecio*, louseworts (*Pedicularis labradorica*, *P. sudetica*, and *P. lanata*), Arctic Lupin *Lupinus arcticus*, Cottongrass *Eriophorum angustifolium* and various grasses including Blue-joint *Calamagrostis canadensis*. This dwarfed shrub and heath tundra attains its best development in areas such as the interior coastal plains of northern Alaska, continental Northwest Territories north of Great Bear Lake, and central Keewatin District.

Large areas of wet tundra and marshy habitats tend to occur mainly in the low flats along the coastlines. Drainage is poor in such areas due to the low relief and presence of underlying permafrost. Tussocks of sedges, cottongrass and grasses grow over an underlying layer of poorly decomposed humus and protrude above the standing pools of water accumulated from the snow meltwater. Where the landscape is more elevated and the soils better drained, the moisture-loving mosses and dense growth of grassy vegetation of the wet flats give way to various species of reindeer lichens *Cladonia* that dominate the upland areas. Their intermingled growth patterns the landscape in a mixture of muted hues of greys, browns and whites. Scattered within the mat, tufted grasses, sedges, and dwarfed shrubs of birch, willow, and rhododendron add some relief to the vegetation.

The most exposed and elevated, well-drained tundras of the Low Arctic may have rather sparse vegetational cover. Here, species more tolerant of xeric conditions tend to predominate. Rock Sedge *Carex rupestris*, Alpine Holy-grass *Hierochloe alpina*, Northern Wood Rush *Luzula confusa*, and Alpine Bistort *Polygonum viviparum* are common, with dwarfed Arctic Willow and various species of avens *Dryas* that may form extensive colonies.

## Snowflush Vegetation

Areas of regular snow accumulation and persistence such as occur on sheltered slopes, in depressions, ravines, and along lakeshores develop a characteristic snowflush vegetation, almost all herbs. Characteristically, when several species occur together, they grow in zones beginning from the outermost extent of the snow and moving inwards. The zonation is the result of the differing needs of the plants for moisture, tolerances to shortened growing season, and their ability to persist vegetatively for several seasons in the event of unusually high accumulations of snow.

The snowflush vegetation varies in composition depending on the geographical location. In the Low and Middle Arctic of the Canadian Arctic Archipelago, the outer fringe frequently consists of dwarfed willows (*Salix herbacea* and *S. pseudopolaris*), an inner darker region of Arctic White-heather, and in the centre a sparsely vegetated region with herbs such as the sedge *Carex scirpoidea*, Mountain Sorrel, Dwarf Buttercup *Ranunculus pygmaeus* and Alpine Clubmoss *Lycopodium alpinum*. In the northern Arctic, the only healthy vegetation may be in such snow drift areas. Arctic White-heather is one of the few widespread species that commonly occurs in such sites.

### Marine Strand Vegetation

The beaches and sand dunes of coastal shores are the preferred habitats of species such as Lyme Grass *Elymus arenarius*, brome grass *Bromus pumpellianus*, Sea Lungwort *Mertensia maritima*, Sea Purslane *Arenaria peploides* and a few less conspicuous grasses and halophytic sedges. In wet places, such as in muddy or sandy marshes, grow a number of characteristic grasses such as Alkali Grass *Puccinellia phyryganoides*, Pendent Grass *Arctophila fulva*, Tundra Grass *Dupontia fischeri*, sedges and rushes (*Juncus balticus* and *J. castanea*). These marshes are also the habitat for flowering herbs such as buttercups *Ranunculus pallasii* and Marsh Marigold *Caltha natans*.

### Freshwater Habitats

Large Arctic lakes, for the most part, are relatively depauperate in aquatic vegetation. The waters remain cold and only become ice-free for short periods. Small ponds and shallow lakes with dark bottoms, in contrast, warm up quickly and are suitable habitats for various aquatic vascular plants. Common species include pondweeds, *Potamogeton*, bladderworts *Utricularia*, aquatic buttercups (e.g. *Ranunculus hyperboreus*), and Mare's-tail *Hippuris vulgaris*. Such aquatics have overwintering propagules called winter buds (turions) or overwinter as rhizomes; these organs ensure that continued growth in successive years is possible even though seeds may not have matured during particularly short growing seasons. In the more

northern areas, the aquatics may exist only in the vegetative state.

Ponds and shallow lakes are often fringed with aquatic sedges, in particular Water Sedge *Carex aquatilis*, cottongrass and true grasses such as Pendent Grass that form luxuriant beds of marshy vegetation. In the Low Arctic, boggy areas dominated by *Sphagnum* mosses are the characteristic habitats of Cloudberry *Rubus chamaemorus*, a widespread member of the rose family.

### Manure-enriched Habitats

Areas within the immediate vicinity of any localised animal activity are always distinctive by virtue of their relatively lush vegetation. In view of the low nutrient levels of most Arctic substrates, any organic nutrients derived from microbial action on skeletons and manure or by the leaching of such organic substrates has a marked effect on the vigour of plant growth. Because of the low temperatures and limited precipitation over much of the Arctic, the decay processes are slow, with the result that low levels of nutrification continue over long periods of time.

One of the most common examples of nutrient-rich microhabitats are the miniature oases formed around rocks and promontories in the landscape that serve as owl perches. Enriched by the ever-increasing supply of rodent and occasional bird skeletons, a turf of grasses and associated species forms over the remains. In addition to the grasses, a host of other species find this habitat a suitable place to send down roots. Some of these associated species include Northern Wood-rush, pinks (*Arenaria rubella*, *Melandrium affine*), mustards (*Erysimum pallasii*, *Cochlearia officinalis*, *Draba*), Alpine Cinquefoil *Potentilla pulchella* and composites (*Arnica alpina*, *Taraxacum*).

Nesting cliffs are invariably excellent sites of nutrient enrichment. Nests tend to be located on the warm south sides of cliffs, and here, on the ledges and scree slopes, are found a broad spectrum of flowering plant species, in addition to the normal encrustation of rock lichens, especially species of *Xanthoria* and *Physcia*. Nesting and feeding sites of geese are similarly man-

*Plate 7.1 Lapland Rosebay* Rhododendron lapponicum *grows primarily in dry rocky or heathy habitats*

*Plate 7.2 The Glacier Avens* Geum glaciale *is an upland species of stony slopes or dry heaths, ranging from Novaya Zemlya east into Canada*

ured by droppings as are lowlands and sheltered valleys where sedge-grass meadows serve as grazing areas for musk ox. Animal burrows, such as the dens of wolves and foxes, are also sites of local soil enrichment and are, consequently, conspicuous in the landscape because of the lush growth surrounding the entrances.

## Distributional Patterns of Arctic Plants

When distribution maps of Arctic plants are compared, certain recurring patterns become evident. Based on these, groups of species exhibiting overall similarities in their ranges have become commonly recognised. Some of these distributions are circumpolar, amphi-Atlantic, amphi-Beringian, regional, and endemic in nature. The similarities in the ranges of species within each group reflect the similar adaptiveness and historical background of the species.

The distributional patterns of plants can be grouped in a variety of ways, depending on the degree of variation present and the criteria by which they are recognised. These patterns serve as clues to probable historical events that have enabled plants to expand their ranges and exhibit the present-day distributions. The fragmented nature of some distributions may, on the other hand, be a reflection of the soil preferences of the plants, or represent gaps in the collection data of the species.

*Braya humilis* and some other members of the mustard family (Brassicaceae), for example, tend to prefer calcareous soils formed from Paleozoic sediments; others, particularly species of the heather family (Ericaceae) are universally found on nutrient-poor and generally acidic soils that develop on the ancient Precambrian rocks such as those of the Laurentian Shield and are absent on calcareous substrates. Such soil preferences tend to result in a discontinuous pattern of distribution for these species, except in regions where there are vast areas of preferred substrates.

Within the overall geographical limits of the range of a species, some plants only occur in specific habitats. Littoral species, including Scurvy-grass *Cochlearia officinalis*, Tundra Grass and *Carex maritima*, are seashore plants. Their occurrence inland, sometimes at high elevations on the Arctic islands or miles from the coast in the continents, is of historical interest. Their presence in such places generally marks the position of former sea levels before the elevation of what were beaches. During post-glacial times, such uplifts were in the magnitude of over 200 m in some parts of the Canadian Arctic islands.

### Circumpolar Plants

The widespread Arctic distribution of this group of plants is a reflection of their considerable adaptability and tolerance of severe climatic conditions, variation in day length and substrate. It is a group that has been well documented (Hultén 1964, 1971) and includes a large percentage of the Arctic flora. Most of the species are perennials, and only a few are woody. In Canada, where the Arctic region covers the broadest latitudinal expanse found anywhere in the world, the circumpolar flora has been divided into species that have High Arctic, Arctic-alpine, and Low Arctic distributions (Porsild 1955).

High Arctic plants, with few exceptions, such as the Arctic Willow, are all herbs. Species in this group extend to the northernmost Arctic regions where vascular plants have been found, but may also have a broad range extending south across the continental Arctic. Some even extend into alpine regions. Examples of such species are the Arctic Buttercup *Ranunculus sulphureus* (Figure 7.5), the mustard *Eutremia edwardsii*, Alpine Foxtail *Alopecurus alpinus*, Scurvy-grass and Tufted Saxifrage.

Arctic-alpine plants also range widely in the Arctic and may extend as far north as the High Arctic species. This group, however, tends to occur considerably further south into Subarctic regions of the taiga, and

*Plate 7.4 The Spider Plant* Saxifraga flagellaris *is an example of a species with an Amphi-Atlantic distribution*

*Plate 7.3 Purple Saxifrage* Saxifraga oppositifolia *occurs as far north as land extends in the High Arctic*

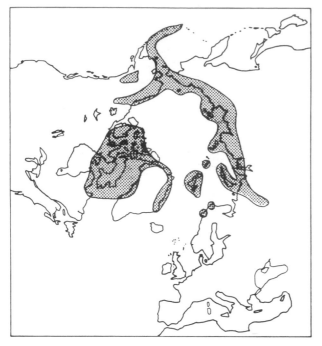

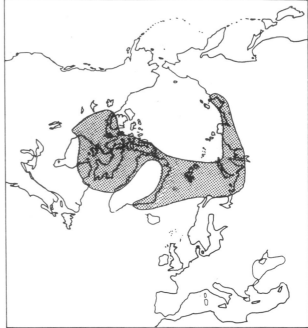

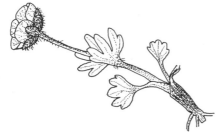

*Figure 7.5: Circumpolar Distribution of an Arctic Buttercup*
Ranunculus sulphureus
*Source: Dr E. Haber.*

*Figure 7.6: Amphi-Atlantic Distribution of the Pink Lousewort*
Pedicularis hirsuta
*Source: Dr E. Haber.*

into the high alpine of southern mountain ranges. Common species include the herbs Mountain Sorrel, Northern Wood-rush, Large-flowered Wintergreen, Purple Saxifrage, Alpine Bistort and Broad-leaved Willow-herb. A few common woody plants are also found in this group, such as Arctic White-heather, Crowberry and Bilberry.

Low Arctic species comprise the largest subdivision of the circumpolar plants. These are some of the most common and ubiquitous tundra and mountain species. Their main range tends to lie south of the Arctic treeline in the northern coniferous forest. Plants in this group have a narrower range of adaptiveness to polar climates, consequently, most of the species barely extend into the Arctic islands, or are found only infrequently in unusually favourable habitats in the High Arctic. Some of the most showy plants include the perennial herb Cloudberry and the shrubs Mountain-heather *Phyllodoce coerulea*, Lapland Rosebay and Mountain Cranberry. Many of the common sedges and grasses also belong in this group.

### Amphi-Atlantic Plants

Species in this group occur on both sides of the Atlantic

(Hultén 1958). It is a diverse group that consists of plants that are found both in the Arctic and Subarctic regions. In North America, species of this group rarely occur west of Hudson Bay. Their European populations are commonly found in the highlands of Scotland and Scandinavia, with some even reaching the mountains of central Europe and northward across western Siberia. The more southern elements may have survived the last glaciation to the south of the ice-sheets and in various mountain and coastal refugia; the northern Arctic species probably survived in unglaciated refugia in the Arctic.

The Arctic species of this group are distinctly more continental in their range. They tend to occupy considerable areas of the eastern Canadian mainland, northern Europe, and the western Siberian Arctic, with the plants in these areas of the two hemispheres being linked by way of populations in Greenland and the eastern Arctic islands. Examples of plants in this group are Pink Lousewort *Pedicularis hirsuta* (Figure 7.6), Dwarf Willow-herb *Epilobium arcticum*, Arctic Cinquefoil, Spider Plant *Saxifraga flagellaris* and Semophore Grass *Pleuropogon sabinei*.

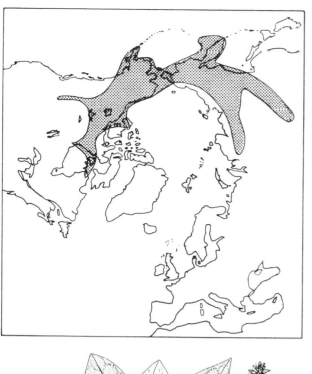

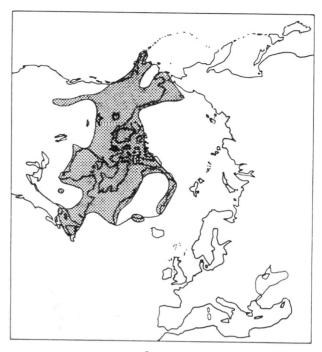

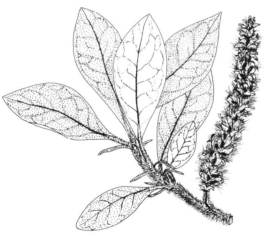

*Figure 7.7: Amphi-Beringian Distribution of the Alaska Willow* Salix alaxensis
*Source: Dr E. Haber.*

*Figure 7.8: Distribution of a Western Hemisphere Endemic, the Arctic Avens* Dryas integrifolia
*Source: Dr E. Haber.*

### Amphi-Beringian Plants

The ranges of species in this group include both sides of the Bering Sea. Because of the previous Beringian land connection, species that survived the glacial periods in unglaciated Alaska and Yukon and in eastern Siberia could spread from these centres across the land bridge to the opposite continent. About one-third of the flora of Alaska and Yukon consists of species with an amphi-Beringian distribution (Porsild 1951).

For the most part, the plants of this group are not primarily Arctic, but species that also occur throughout the forested regions of the continental interior. A few common members of the group are the cottongrass *Eriophorum vaginatum*, *Parrya nudicaulis*, *Hedysarum alpinum*, the sagebrush *Artemisia tilesii*, and the Alaska Willow (Figure 7.7).

### Regional and Localised Endemics

Within the Arctic flora, there are species that are found in only one region of the Arctic, although it may be quite a sizeable area in some cases, and the species may be quite common. A species with this type of distribution is Arctic Avens (Figure 7.8), a North American endemic (Porsild 1958). It occurs from east Greenland to western Alaska and easternmost Arctic Siberia, frequently dominating dry clay or gravel barrens. It has one of the broadest distributions of all Arctic plants in the western hemisphere.

In contrast are species that are endemic to rather localised areas. The Pigmy Aster *Aster pygmaeus* is a rare species, only infrequently found in the Canadian Arctic in the Coronation Gulf–Great Bear Lake area (Figure 7.9). In the eastern hemisphere, the Spitsbergen But-

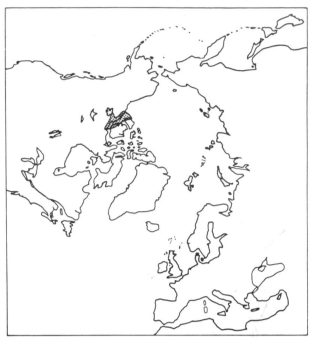

*Figure 7.9: Distribution of a Localised Canadian Endemic, the Pigmy Aster* Aster pygmaeus
*Source: Dr E. Haber.*

tercup *Ranunculus spitsbergensis* has an even more restricted range, occurring only in the Inner Fjord district of the island.

## Plant Dispersal

Arctic plants are adapted in various ways for the dispersal of their seeds and fruits. Only a few of these involve animals as the primary agents of dispersal, as occurs more commonly in temperate regions. The low density of animals (Savile 1972), together with the slow rate of evolution of plants in the Arctic, the disruptive influence of glacial ages, and the stringent requirements of the climate probably all contribute to the lack of specialisation to animal dispersal, particularly in the High Arctic.

Fleshy, edible fruits are produced by Low Arctic shrubs such as Cloudberry, bearberries (*Arctostaphyllos alpina, A. rubra,* and *A. uva-ursi*) and Mountain Cran-

berry, and a few shrubs such as Bilberry and Crowberry occur throughout the Arctic. Plants with hooked fruits that can cling to fur and feathers are quite rare and include only a few species of bedstraw *Galium* in Low Arctic areas and the sedge *Carex microglochin*. Aquatic birds may be instrumental in long-range transport of certain minute aquatic plantlets such as duckweeds *Lemna* on their legs and lower bodies as well as the seeds and fruits of wetland plants in their intestines and gizzards.

The greatest number of plants have their seeds, fruits, or vegetative propagules spread by the action of the wind. This agent can be quite effective because of its strength, duration, and frequency year-round. Plumed seeds and fruits occur in cottongrass *Eriophorum*, willow-herbs *Epilobium*, fleabanes *Erigeron*, mountain avens *Dryas*, willows *Salix*, and dandelions *Taraxacum*. Birches *Betula* and docks *Rumex*, common in the Low Arctic, have winged seeds and fruits, as does the wide-ranging Arctic-alpine Mountain Sorrel. The seeds of some plants such as *Diapensia* and *Pyrola* are minute and readily carried aloft by the wind.

One of the most effective means of dispersal of plant parts in the Arctic is that of wind transport during the winter months (Savile 1972). Arctic snow tends to consist of small, needle-like crystals that compact into a smooth hard layer, and seeds, fruits and vegetative propagules such as bulbils can be blown over the snow and ice for considerable distances. In the Canadian Arctic where the land mass is fragmented into numerous islands extending northwards over a great distance, the sea is but a small obstacle to plant migration, for in the western two-thirds of this region there is a continuous cover of sea-ice for about nine months of the year. It is possible that some plants of Iceland and northern Svalbard were derived from Greenland during the course of the last several thousand years at times of particularly extensive winter ice formation.

The gradual release of seeds seems to be a common phenomenon. It ensures, particularly in species that flower and fruit throughout the growing season, that seeds are available for dispersal over a long period of time, even into the winter months, thereby increasing the chances for the occurrence of conditions conducive to dispersal and germination. Fruits such as those of mountain avens and cottongrass may not be fully released until the following season.

## Reproductive and Genetic Specialisation

As a consequence of the selective process of a rigorous environment, the majority of Arctic plants are perennials. These include both herbaceous species with adaptations for ample food storage such as fleshy roots, rhizomes, and tubers that permit overwintering for periods up to nine months or more, or even survival until the second season, and woody plants in which food storage can be in both above- and below-ground structures. The perennial habit ensures an individual's survival and possible future reproductive success in spite of unfavourable conditions during years when the season is too short to permit the maturation of seeds. Annuals, such as *Koenigia islandica*, and biennials, such as Scurvy-grass, are relatively few in number.

The opportunities for reproductive success are also enhanced in some species that exhibit aperiodic growth (Savile 1972). *Arenaria rossii*, *Braya humilis*, *Oxyria digyna*, *Potentilla hyparctica* and various grasses continue to grow throughout the summer, as long as conditions are favourable, without cessation of activity at a genetically predetermined stage as in plants exhibiting periodic growth. Most monocotyledonous plants, with the exception of some grasses, exhibit periodic growth – a mechanism that minimises the risk of winter injury, but also reduces the opportunities for prolonged growth and seed production, a feature characteristic of aperiodic plants. *Braya humilis* is an extreme example of a species with aperiodic growth in that it can overwinter, with its inflorescences at any stage of development, and continue its growth undamaged the following season.

In addition to the limitations and advantages of periodic and aperiodic growth, there is still the overriding control on productivity imposed by the Arctic climate. With increased latitude, the flowering capability of plants and their successful production of fruit is reduced. Even on a local basis where topography varies, there is a considerable difference in flowering and fruiting success, depending on the localised severity of the microhabitats. For example, plants on exposed ridges tend to flower less profusely than on sheltered slopes and areas of snow accumulation.

In contrast with the floras of warmer climates where self-sterility and cross-pollination are common mechanisms that promote genetic diversity, Arctic plants, to a large extent, are self-fertile, but also maintain the capability for outcrossing. Although insect pollinators, including Diptera, Lepidoptera, and bumblebees occur in the Arctic, they are not as varied or abundant as in more southern regions. Their movements and, therefore, effectiveness, are probably much more influenced by the climate than in southern latitudes. The high level of self-fertility in Arctic plants ensures that adequate seed is matured during most years. Self-fertility reduces genetic variability and future adaptability to changing environments. In the Arctic, this may be of advantage, however, at least along the more critical edge of a species' range, in ensuring that those genetic traits that confer adaptability undergo minimal recombination in the majority of the seeds produced. Consequently, the proportion of unfit seedlings, if outcrossing were the predominant means of pollination, would be reduced.

### Apomixis

Sexual reproduction with the formation of seeds occurs in nearly all Arctic plants, wherever the climate permits flower formation. A considerable number of Arctic plants can, however, also reproduce by agamospermy. This is a specialised form of apomixis (asexual reproduction) in which viable seeds are formed without the sexual union of gametes, the egg and sperm nuclei. Diploid ($2n$) cells (i.e. having the same compliment of paired chromosomes as is present in the cells of the parent plant), rather than haploid ($n$) ones (as in egg cells), are produced within the ovule by one of several means. The embryo develops without fertilisation from the diploid cells within the seed and usually represents a clone of the parent plant, identical to it in genetic makeup. Many Arctic species in the genera *Arnica*, *Hieracium*, *Poa*, *Potentilla* and *Taraxacum* are apomictic.

Vegetative reproduction other than by the more specialised process of agamospermy is also important in the Arctic, as in other areas of adverse environments. Because many grasses and sedges are rhizomatous, vegetative reproduction is a common means by which they persist and increase locally under marginal conditions where they may rarely set seed. Various species of grasses are also viviparous, forming small vegetative bulbils within the floral bracts in place of flowers, as in the Viviparous Fescue Grass *Festuca vivipara* and the Arctic Red Fescue Grass *F. rubra* s.l. These bulbils root and produce new clones of the parent plant. Bulbils are also produced by Alpine Bistort and the Nodding Saxifrage, an Arctic-alpine species that rarely produces seeds in the Arctic.

In contrast to the use of underground rhizomes, species such as the Spider Plant produce above-ground runners that form plantlets at their tips. Many Arctic plants, however, have no vegetative means of reproduction, and persist only as short-lived perennials, depending on the production of seeds in sufficient numbers and at regular intervals to maintain their population levels.

# 8
# ARCTIC INSECTS

Professor P. G. Kevan
and Dr H. V. Danks

## Introduction

Insects are the most numerous of Arctic animals; some are conspicuous; all are important to the ecosystem of the Arctic and its wildlife. In summer, human visitors to the Arctic often find the mosquitoes next to intolerable. Both migratory and resident Arctic animals are plagued by hordes of biting insects. Nevertheless, these, and the myriad non-biting midges, together with often small detritus-, carrion-, dung- and fungus-eating flies, root-maggot flies and their relatives, bristle and hover flies, colourful butterflies, moths, parasitic wasps, and the large bumblebees, all play their own unique roles in the functioning of the Arctic ecosystem.

In this chapter, we will examine the diversity and distribution of Arctic insect life, and the role of insects in the Arctic ecosystem. The adaptation of insects to the Arctic environment is discussed in Chapter 6. Because over half of the land that can be defined as Arctic is principally North American (Canada, Alaska and Greenland), because a high proportion of the Arctic insect fauna is Holarctic (i.e. found in North America and Eurasia), and because information from the northern reaches of the Soviet Union is not easily available, we can justifiably rely heavily on knowledge from North America. Fortunately, the terrestrial arthropods of Arctic North America have been recently reviewed in detail by Danks (1981).

## The Diversity of Arctic Insects

Britain has about 25,500 species of terrestrial arthropods, of which 22,000 are insects; the North American Arctic has but 2,100 arthropods, of which some 1,550 are insects. If we allow for the fact that the British fauna is so much better known than the North American Arctic fauna, and the fact that we have made no provision for the Arctic Arthropoda of Eurasia (even though many Arctic species there are shared with North America), we project that the Arctic arthropod fauna for the world would be only about one-quarter as large as the arthropod fauna of Britain.

The Arctic fauna is relatively little known because collections and specimens are lacking, and this is coupled with the difficulty of taxonomic studies and a paucity of entomologists to conduct the studies of certain insect groups. The sawflies (Tenthredinidae), ichneumon wasps (Ichneumonidae), braconid wasps (Braconidae) and midges (Chironomidae) are especially inadequately known. The Arctic is not an easy part of the world for travel and entomological collecting, and therefore many areas are not represented in collections and some areas are represented only by dint of cursory visits. In some places, certain species may be very abundant in a given year but completely lacking in others. Some habitats are difficult to collect from (e.g. bird roosts on cliffs) or highly localised (e.g. mammal burrows) yet may harbour interesting Arctic arthropods. Nevertheless, we know enough to make some generalisations.

As might be expected, the groups most commonly encountered in other parts of the world, especially the temperate zone, are represented in the Arctic insect fauna. Nevertheless, the balance of representation is not the same. For example, the butterflies and moths (Lepidoptera) make up about 11 per cent of the North American insect fauna and 10 per cent of the Arctic fauna (a balanced representation), whereas the beetles (Coleoptera) are underrepresented in the Arctic, making up only 12 per cent of the insect fauna *versus* 33 per cent in all of North America. On the other hand, the true flies (Diptera) are overrepresented at 53 per cent of the Arctic insect fauna, but only 19 per cent of the North American.

For the purposes of this chapter, we define Arctic insects as those that occur beyond the treeline, though many such species also occur south of this limit, both in forested areas and in alpine tundra. Very few insects are restricted to Arctic tundra. Through the next few paragraphs, which summarise information on named species from North America only, species restricted to the Arctic (Arctic endemics) will be noted as being of special interest.

Among the mayflies (Ephemeroptera), dragonflies (Odonata), and stone flies (Plecoptera), there are few Arctic endemics, and no species reach the High Arctic. The situation for the grasshoppers and their allies (Orthoptera) is more pronounced, with perhaps only one species, *Melanoplus frigidus*, restricted to the Arctic, though it only occurs close to the treeline. The true bugs (Hemiptera) occur in relatively low diversity in the Arctic. The aphids (Aphididae) are the best represented family, with about 20 species, three of which occur in the High Arctic. They suck plant saps, and their food plants are prostrate willows *Salix*, mountain avens *Dryas*, saxifrages *Saxifraga*, louseworts *Pedicularis*, chickweeds *Cerastium*, sedges *Carex*, etc. In temperate areas, these insects typically produce several generations of different forms, sometimes on different host plants, but in the Arctic the number of generations is reduced and alternation of host plants is eliminated from their life history. The leafhoppers (Cicadellidae), seed bugs (Lygaeidae), plant or leaf bugs (Miridae) and psyllids (Psyllidae) are also small, plant-sucking insects, a few species of which inhabit the Arctic. Predatory bugs are less well represented, with a single species, *Anthocoris melanocerus* of Anthocoridae (minute pirate bugs). Aquatic bugs are similarly few, with two species of water boatman (Corixidae) and a few species of shore bugs (Saldidae). Water striders (Gerridae), damsel bugs (Nabidae), assassin bugs (Reduviidae), ambush bugs (Phymatidae), stink bugs (Pentatomidae), most families of the Homoptera, and many others which occur abundantly in temperate climes are entirely absent from the Arctic. Even thrips (Thysanoptera) are represented by only a small number of species in the Arctic, although they have been collected in the High Arctic.

Despite the fact that the beetles (Coleoptera) form the largest order of insects in the world (about a quarter of a million species named), less than 200 species have been reported from the North American Arctic. Even then, most species are restricted to the southernmost tundra. Some familiar families are entirely absent, as for example the June beetles (Scarabeidae), sap beetles (Nitidulidae), checkered beetles (Cleridae), and most wood-boring families. The ground beetles (Carabidae) of the Arctic, like their southern relatives, are chiefly predatory as adults and larvae. Only one species, *Amara alpina*, can be found in the High Arctic, although 78 species are recorded from the North American tundra. The rove beetles (Staphylinidae) follow the same pattern, with only two, as yet unidentified, of the 15 recorded Arctic species occurring in the High Arctic. Even the predatory diving beetles (Dytiscidae) extend to the High Arctic with two, *Hydroporus polaris* and *H. morio*, of their 19 species recorded from far northern locations. Water scavenger beetles (Hydrophilidae), click beetles (Elateridae), and ladybirds (Coccinellidae), are represented by five or six species each in the Low Arctic tundra. The herbivorous leaf beetles (Chrysomelidae) and weevils (Curculionidae) are more diverse (12 and 10 species) as well as being more northerly in maximum range.

As mentioned above, the Diptera (true flies) are well represented: 721 species in 39 families have been reported from the Arctic of North America, and about 20 per cent of these enter the High Arctic. Some families, such as the pomace flies (Drosophilidae), small dung flies (Sphaeroceridae), flesh flies (Sarcophagidae) and snipe flies (Rhagionidae), drop out a short distance north of the trees, and other families that are well known in temperate countries are rare or absent from the Arctic, e.g. horse flies (Tabanidae), robber flies (Asilidae), bee flies (Bombyliidae), and fruit flies (Tephritidae).

The crane flies (Tipulidae) have larvae which feed, for the most part, on organic detritus in aquatic and semi-aquatic habitats. More than 42 species of these large flies are recorded from the Arctic, especially in the west. Many have been recorded nowhere else. Because they are large and often numerous they are important foods for birds. Of the mosquitoes (Culicidae), few are widespread true tundra species. *Aedes impiger* and *A. nigripes* are very widespread, both in alpine and Arctic environments, and both breed in the High Arctic. These, and the Subarctic species that encroach on the tundra occur in uncountable numbers. The females lay their eggs on or near still water in which the larvae develop, eating fine particulate material. The adult females feed on the blood of various vertebrates, but, unlike many of their southerly relatives, can mature a small batch of eggs autogenously, that is without partaking of this protein meal. Although they are the scourge of the north woods, most black flies (Simuliidae) do not extend their ranges far on to the tundra. Most Arctic black flies are, like the mosquitoes, autogenous. Their larvae are filter feeders in running waters, where they attach themselves to rocks and other substrates. Biting midges or no-see-ums (Ceratopogonidae) in the Arctic do not feed on vertebrate blood. These small insects are inadequately known taxonomically and biologically.

By far the most abundant and diverse of Arctic insects are the non-biting midges. In some places they may contribute up to half the insect diversity! The aquatic and semi-aquatic larvae feed on fine particulate matter, algae, detritus, and so on. The life-spans of some of these species are very long, perhaps more than six years, although the adults of some species may live up to a few weeks. Some lake-inhabiting species emerge as the adults crawl through the candled, thawing ice in the early summer, others emerge much later in the season. Most of the species of shallow ponds, the most productive habitats, emerge relatively early. Some species of chironomids never feed as adults, but others feed extensively on floral nectar. In places, they emerge in such vast numbers that they may cloud one's vision. In warmer regions, these midges form dense mating swarms, which may resemble small funnel clouds that dance in one place or move slowly over minor landmarks, such as the edges of tundra polygons. Swarming is less conspicuous, or even absent, in some High Arctic species. These insects are an important part of the ecological web, functioning as herbivores, detritivores and as food for other insects, fish and the large numbers of migratory birds, especially waders, which inhabit the Arctic tundra in the summer. Five other families of gnats and midges are recorded from North American Arctic tundra, but are inadequately known. These include fungus gnats (Mycetophilidae and Sciaridae), gall midges (Cecidomyiidae), march flies (Bibionidae) and minute black scavenger flies (Scatopsidae).

Among the short-horned flies (suborder Brachycera), the dance flies (Empididae) are the most conspicuous and range northward the farthest. Five species of the genus *Rhamphomyia* are recorded from the High Arctic. These, like the related long-legged flies (Dolichopodidae), also recorded in high diversity (28 species) from the Arctic, are predatory as adults. At least some species are also predatory as larvae. The dance flies are well known for their interesting habits in mating swarms, in which the males of some species present the females with a nuptial gift of prey, or prey in spittle, or merely just spittle (Downes 1970).

The hover flies (Syrphidae) of the Arctic are conspicuous flower visitors throughout their range. About 17 named species are recorded from Arctic localities, and five penetrate into the High Arctic. Most species have larvae that feed on aphids, but one genus (*Helophilus*) is aquatic and similar in habits to the familiar rat-tailed maggot *Eristalis*. Leaf-mining flies (Agromyzidae) are also widespread in the Arctic. The larvae make characteristic, vermiform mines in the leaves of various vascular plants, including grasses, sedges, poppies, and fleabanes. The small, usually grey, adults are inconspicuous, but may be found feeding on floral nectar, sometimes of their host plant. There are about 13 other families of such small, inconspicuous flies represented in the Arctic records, mostly restricted to the southern reaches of the tundra.

Most species of muscoid flies (Calypteratae) are larger in size. Dung flies (Scathophagidae) feed as larvae on decaying organic matter or on plant tissue (e.g. roots), and some species are predatory. The adults prey on other insects, some of which may be captured at flowers. About 25 species are known for the Arctic, and five reach the High Arctic. The Anthomyiidae is one of the most diverse of Arctic insect families, with over 130 species recorded so far; however, only six reach the High Arctic. Their larval habits are varied, but in general they feed on decaying organic matter, or roots (as in the root maggots, *Delia*) or other plant tissues. The adults feed at flowers, taking nectar and sometimes pollen. The closely related Muscidae (the family to which the house fly belongs) is similarly diverse, both taxonomically (more than 160 species, 20 in the High Arctic) and biologically. One genus, *Spilogona*, is especially diverse in the Arctic, making up nearly half the species list for the family. At least some of these species are predatory as larvae, feeding on midge larvae. The adults feed extensively on floral nectar, and some eat pollen as well. The blow flies (Calliphoridae) are conspicuous from their size, metallic coloration, and sometimes numbers near human habitation. Although most species, of which twelve are known from the Arctic, feed on decaying matter, carrion, and filth, some like living meat: *Protophormia terraenovae* may cause subcutaneous lesions (myiases) in caribou and *Protocalliphora sapphira* is parasitic on nestling birds. Notorious for their appetites for living flesh are the bot and warble flies (Oestridae). Females of *Cephenemyia trompe* lay their living first-instar larvae in the nostrils of caribou. These larvae develop and overwinter in the nasal cavities, and drop to the ground the next year, often being expelled by the sneezing of the unfortunate animals. The warbles *Hypoderma tarandi* start life as eggs attached to caribou hair. On hatching, the larvae penetrate the host's skin and migrate, subcutaneously, to near the mid-line of the back. There the warbles develop, making an opening through the skin by which to breathe. Equally parasitic are the bristle flies (Tachinidae). However, these flies use other insects as their hosts. They lay their eggs on or in other insects. Of the seven recorded Arctic species (four from the High Arctic), most use moth caterpillars as the host. The larvae develop within the host, eventually killing it. Many more species of this family are expected to be discovered.

Turning now to more pleasant entomological thoughts from the Arctic, let us consider the butterflies and moths (Lepidoptera). The moths are not as well represented as the butterflies. Of the 136 Arctic species of Lepidoptera in 17 families, 51 species in 6 families are butterflies. Among the moths, some are small, inconspicuous, and inadequately known. Species of the families Tortricidae, Noctuidae, Geometridae (inchworms), Lymantriidae, and Noctuidae are the best known. Even so, little is known about their larval habits. Most, as caterpillars, probably eat a diversity of vegetation. They may live in the larval stages for prolonged periods. It has been estimated that the conspicuous 'woolly bear' caterpillars of *Gynaephora* spp. (Lymantriidae) in the High Arctic may live for 13 years or more before pupating and emerging as adults in the last season of their lives (Ryan and Hergert 1977; Kukal 1983). The larvae of the butterflies probably share the same sorts of life strategies, although some appear to have a restricted range of host plants. One of the Arctic blues, *Rumicia phlaeas*, feeds only on Mountain Sorrel or dock *Rumex*. Some adult moths do not feed, others are frequently encountered as they feed at flowers. In some instances it is only the males that feed and fly, while the females are sedentary egg producers, which call in their mates by chemical attractants. Adult butterflies are active fliers, but in Arctic regions they tend to stay close to the ground and to frequent sheltered creek courses. There, in the bright sunlight of the summer season, one may see sulphur butterflies (Pieridae), blues and coppers (Lycaenidae), and brush-footed butterflies (Nymphalidae) flitting from flower to flower, settling to bask in the sun (Kevan and Shorthouse 1970), and in courtship flight even in the High Arctic: the satyrs (Satyridae) are quite diverse in the Arctic, but occur mostly in the south. The skippers (Hesperiidae) and swallowtails (Papilionidae) are restricted to the most southerly parts of the Arctic tundra.

About 15 species of caddisflies are known from mostly southern Arctic locations. The northern caddisflies (Limnephilidae) are the most diverse, but only one, *Apatania zonella*, extends into the High Arctic. The larvae of caddisflies in this family are detritus feeders in lakes, ponds and streams, where they dwell protected in tube-like cases or caddises (built of materials such as small twigs or stones) which they carry about.

The order Hymenoptera (sawflies, parasitic wasps, ants, wasps, and bees) is well represented. There are about 34 named species of sawfly in Arctic North America, but little is known of their biology. The larvae are phytophagous: many eat leaves, but others inhabit galls on leaves or stems. The adults feed at flowers. The petiolate (or wasp-waisted) Hymenoptera (suborder Apocrita) includes the ichneumon wasps and their relatives. Most of these are parasitoids, i.e. they are fatally parasitic on other insects. The females lay eggs inside their hosts by piercing the latter's integument with their ovipositor. The parasitoid larvae consumes the host from inside and when fully grown it metamorphoses, usually using the host's remains for its own protection. It is usually only at this point that the host finally dies. In the Arctic the family Ichneumonidae is represented by over 100 species and many more species await description. The other dozen or more families of parasitoids are inadequately known, and mostly recorded from the southern Arctic. Gall wasps (Cynipidae) are included amongst these parasitoids taxonomically, but these insects are phytophagous, as the name suggests.

Among the stinging Hymenoptera (Aculeata), the ants (Formicidae) are notably absent from the tundra. Only one species, the chiefly boreal ant *Leptothorax muscorum* regularly makes incursions on to the most southerly Arctic tundra. The social wasps (Vespidae) live in nests of paper. The adults forage at fruit and other sweet materials, and on dead and living arthropods for their own sustenance and to raise their brood. Only two species have been recorded from just north of the treeline. Among the bees (Apoidea), by far the majority are bumblebees; twelve species of *Bombus* have been recorded, and three of these reach the High Arctic. Even in that extreme environment these social bees forage actively at flowers, gathering nectar and pollen. The queens mate at the end of the summer, and overwinter in the frozen ground. They emerge in the spring, feed, search out nest sites, which are often abandoned mammal burrows, and establish nests, which they provision with honey and pollen and maintain at an elevated temperature. In the Arctic, the queen raises only one generation of worker brood before depositing the eggs destined to become drones and queens. Despite the bumblebees' precarious lifestyle, social parasitism occurs. In the High Arctic the two common species are *Bombus polaris* and *B. hyperboreus*. Queens of the latter emerge from overwintering later than those of the former. These queens seek out the established nests of *B. polaris* and try to usurp them. In the ensuing battle, the smaller queens of *B. polaris* may be killed, and the queens of *B. hyperboreus* take over the colony of workers, using them to rear the eggs they deposit, which are destined to become sexual forms only (Richards 1973).

One group of insects that we have not yet discussed includes the ectoparasites of vertebrates. The bird lice (Mallophaga) and sucking lice (Anoplura) of the order Phthiraptera are closely associated with their hosts, as are the fleas (Siphonaptera). It is questionable that the fleas and bird lice parasitic on migratory birds should really be defined as 'Arctic'. Those lice and fleas that are parasitic on the resident mammals are blood-suckers protected from the Arctic environment by the warmth of their hosts. Nevertheless, the High Arctic may restrict the ranges of some of these insects, especially the fleas, in which larvae live away from the host. For example, the lemming flea *Megabothris groenlandicus* has not followed its host to the most northern tundra.

## Distribution Patterns of Arctic Insects

Because the terrain is so homogeneous over vast areas at high latitude, the proportions of circumpolar species within each group of Arctic insects is of special interest. For the mosquitoes (Culicidae) and brush-footed butterflies (Nymphalidae), over 85 per cent of the Arctic species are circumpolar; for the blow flies (Calliphoridae) and sawflies (Tenthredinidae) the figure is 75 per cent; for non-biting midges (Chironomidae), Anthomyiidae, Muscidae and Noctuidae about half of the species are circumpolar. Amongst the leaf beetles (Chrysomelidae), crane flies (Tipulidae), black flies (Simuliidae), dance flies (Empididae), hover flies (Syrphidae), ichneumon wasps (Ichneumonidae) and bees (Apidae) the Arctic regions of Eurasia and America share about one-fifth to one-third of the fauna.

These generalisations may be examined in finer detail. For example, it is apparent that the proportion of circumpolar species increases in the more northerly fauna. Thus, very few species in the High Arctic are not circumpolar. Arthropods characteristic of the northern Arctic are the moth *Gynaephora groenlandica* and two species of spiders, a wolf spider *Alepecosa exasperans* (Lycosidae) and a dwarf spider *Erigone psychrophila* (Erigonidae). Even among the far northern Arctic bumblebees the species are the same in North America, Europe and Asia. Although insects with this sort of distribution, such as *Bombus polaris*, the blow fly *Boreellus atriceps* and the mosquito *Aedes nigripes*, are widespread, these characteristic northern forms are not as far-ranging as the few 'cosmopolitan' species which enter the Arctic and also occur far to the south. Most of these are soil-inhabiting arthropods, such as the springtail *Isotomurus palustris*, which is recorded throughout the northern hemisphere and well south of the equator.

Some more restricted ranges are also particularly interesting, notably those termed 'amphi-Beringian', i.e. found either side of the Bering Sea in north-western North America (Alaska, Yukon) and in the far eastern Soviet Union (see Chapter 7). The rove beetle *Tachinus brevipennis* and the ground beetles *Pterostichus nivalis* and *P. similis* are good examples.

'Amphi-Atlantic' insects are found on either side of the Atlantic Ocean, and although their ranges often extend eastwards well into Asia, their distributions show substantial gaps. There are few examples of amphi-Atlantic species, but one is the moth *Sympistis lapponica* (Noctuidae), which is known from mountainous and northern Scandinavia, Greenland, and Canada.

Within North America there are a number of characteristic types of Arctic distribution. We have already mentioned the few northern Arctic species. A number of insects are restricted to the Arctic in general, living only north of the treeline. The best understood examples are among the dung flies (Scathophagidae) and Muscidae. Those Arctic insects that occur only in the southern Arctic often extend into the boreal zone or into alpine areas. Some butterflies, such as Ross' Satyr *Erebia rossii* and some fritillaries (*Boloria* spp.), may be found far south of the tundra in the vicinity of cold acid bogs. A wide variety of different insects occur in southern alpine tundra as well as in their Arctic range, and these should be thought of as Arctic-alpine tundra species, rather than as southern Arctic-boreal types.

Many species also inhabit the northern boreal forest as well as the tundra proper.

So far, we have examined distributions on a continental basis and on a north-south axis. In North America, some east-west restrictions in the ranges of insects can be identified in the southern Arctic, although many insects are 'transcontinental' in range, including most of the circumpolar species as well as insects such as the wasp *Vespula albida* and some dung flies known only from North America. However, a few insects are restricted to the eastern parts of the Arctic (i.e. east of Hudson Bay). Examples include a stone fly *Nemoura trispinosa* with a sister species, *N. arctica*, occurring in the west. The range of the amphi-Atlantic moth *Sympistis lapponica* is also restricted in North America, extending west of Hudson Bay but not beyond the Canadian Shield. Hudson Bay may not pose a great barrier to the dispersal of Arctic insects: a narrow band of treeless habitat extends almost completely around the southern shore, and a chain of islands forms a potential northern route of dispersal. Nevertheless, a number of western species of insects range no further than Hudson Bay. In the west, it appears that the Mackenzie River valley and the mountain ranges have produced another biogeographic barrier: there are flies, spiders and beetles that seem to be restricted to Alaska, the Yukon Territory, and the Mackenzie River Delta region. Several of the species with western Arctic ranges in North America are also amphi-Beringian. Some disjunct range types pose interesting biogeographical puzzles; the mosquito *Aedes pullatus* is distributed in the Arctic and Subarctic east of Hudson Bay and in the northern part of the western cordillera from Alberta to the Yukon, but does not occur in between. Other flies and beetles show similar distributions.

## Arctic Insects in the Ecosystem

Within all ecosystems, organisms interact with one another. The food habits of arthropods provide a basis for understanding these interactions through the places of arthropods in the food chain, that is their trophic relationships. *Saprophages* feed on dead and decaying plant and animal matter. Soil-inhabiting organisms, such as crane fly larvae (Tipulidae), many midge larvae (Chironomidae), some root-maggots (Anthomyiidae), blow flies (Calliphoridae), fungus flies (Mycetophilidae and Sciaridae), springtails (Collembola), and many mites (especially Oribatei), fall into this category. Even so, many of these organisms are probably polyphagous, and consume living fungal hyphae, various kinds of algae, bacteria, protozoa, and perhaps larger animal prey, as well as decaying matter. Many northern saprophages are dependent, indirectly, on vertebrates. They dine on vertebrate dung, or on the wastes associated with burrows, nests and denning sites, as well as on carcasses.

*Herbivores* are relatively scarce, making up as little as 17 per cent of the insect fauna in the High Arctic. There are relatively few species of vascular plants upon which to feed, but even so, herbivorous arthropods are more greatly reduced in Arctic regions than are the plants. Most herbivores eat leaves (e.g. caterpillars) or suck sap (e.g. aphids). Alaskan psyllids feed on willow catkins, and the moth *Sympistis zetterstettii labradoris* eats the flowers of Arctic Avens. There are seed- and fruit-eating bugs *Nysius groenlandicus* (Böcher 1972), cecidomyiids and sawflies. Some arthropods feed on plant roots, such as *Bradysia* (Sciaridae), a crane fly *Tipula lionota*, *Lepyrus* weevils and some larval Anthomyiidae. The Arctic mosses, like mosses everywhere, are not often attacked by herbivores, but mites and springtails have been found eating these plants.

Nectar and pollen are important food resources for Arctic insects (Kevan 1973), in fact almost all adult insects that have a prolonged life and are active fliers in the Arctic probably feed at flowers. Nectar is mainly a sugar solution and provides the fuel for insect flight, even for mosquitoes. Pollen is consumed by a few Arctic insects, including some springtails, flies, possibly some beetles, and of course, bumblebees. For these insects, pollen is an important and often vital source of protein and other nutrients. Plants benefit from the attentions of the insects through pollination (Kevan 1972), and although many Arctic plants do not require pollination for seeds to be formed the most common flowers of the High Arctic such as willows, Purple Saxifrage, Arctic Avens and louseworts (*Pedicularis* spp.) do depend on insect-mediated pollination. It has been estimated that two-thirds of the tundra plants of the Soviet Union are insect pollinated. The spectrum of pollinators in the Arctic is different from elsewhere. In the Arctic, the flies are the most important group in general, with butterflies, moths and bumblebees playing a secondary role.

*Carnivores* among Arctic arthropods are varied. Among the *predators* are spiders, a number of families of mites and a few insects. The smallest spiders feed on springtails, mites and immature insects, whereas the larger ones feed chiefly on flies. The mites prey on other mites, springtails, insect eggs and small insects. Among the adult insect carnivores are the dance flies (Empididae), the long-legged flies (Dolichopodidae) and dung flies (Scathophagidae). Some of the latter wait beside flowers to ambush hover flies there. The shore bugs (Salididae), ground beetles (Carabidae) and diving beetles (Dytiscidae) are also predatory as adults wherever they occur. Among the aquatic insects, the stone flies, some caddisflies, and dragonflies are predatory as larvae, as are some muscid flies (*Spilogona*) and the crane fly *Pedicia hannai* which eats the small pale, earthworm-like, enchytraeid worms that are characteristic of Arctic soils. Arctic predators are not specialists; their habits reflect the availability of prey. The *parasitoids*, which develop with their hosts and kill them, are probably more specialised, but little is known of them; in fact, the hosts of most parasitoids that have been found in the Arctic are unknown. The caterpillars of *Gynaephora* are host to at least seven species of parasitoids, including ichneumon wasps (Ichneumonidae), braconid wasps (Braconidae), and bristle flies (Tachinidae). Some of these parasitoids may be restricted to this host, but others may attack additional species of Lepidoptera. The Ichneumonidae are parasitoids of a wide variety of hosts, even in the Arctic, where their hosts include butterflies and moths, sawflies (Tenthredinidae), other ichneumon wasps, beetles, and various true flies (Diptera) such as hover flies (Syrphidae), muscoid flies and some fungus and gall midges (Mycetophilidae and Cecidomyiidae).

Some arthropods are *ectoparasitic* on other animals, living on their skin or integument. These include the lice, fleas and mites of vertebrates, as well as mites that infest other insects. Arctic bumblebees often carry with them numerous mites which feed on the host's haemolymph (blood) through the thin and flexible membranes between the body segments. Water mites (Hydracarina) are sometimes found on various Arctic insects, particularly nematocerous Diptera. The bot and nasal flies of caribou are *endoparasitic*, living within their host.

The interactions that Arctic arthropods have among themselves, with plants, and as agents in the recycling of organic debris are evidently of great importance to Arctic ecosystems (Ryan 1981). No less important, however, is their role as food for vertebrates. Northern fish, notably Arctic char, feed extensively on midges, especially when these are in the larval and pupal stages, and it has been suggested that three-quarters of the midge production of Char Lake on Cornwallis Island is consumed by the char there. Among waders, the largest species generally consume fewer but larger prey insects than the smaller birds, which eat a larger number of smaller insects. Nevertheless, the birds tend to be opportunists, eating whatever species of prey is most abundant and accessible.

The interactions outlined above demonstrate clearly that energy and material are cycling through Arctic ecosystems. The sun's rays, along with moisture, nutrients, and nitrogen and carbon dioxide are captured by green plants (the primary producers) and turned into organic matter (gross primary productivity). The productivity is used by various consumers, as they become secondary producers.

Accurate quantification of the flow of matter and energy in ecosystems is very difficult, but some qualitative comparisons can be made (see Bliss 1977). The primary productivity of the Arctic is low, limited by cold, low light intensity and short growing season. Furthermore, the supply of nutrients in Arctic soils is low. Net primary productivity (gross primary productivity less maintenance costs such as respiration) on Arctic tundra, even in the best sites, has been estimated to be about one-tenth that of temperate grasslands and forests, and in High Arctic deserts may be less than one-hundredth of grassland and forest productivity. The amount of organic matter present at a given time is also low, but is greatest in moist situations. The roles of insects in cycling nutrients and energy in the Arctic are poorly understood. Invertebrate herbivores probably consume less than 2.5 per cent of primary production, and insectivores probably consume a comparable fraction of insect productivity. Thus, insects appear to metabolise relatively little organic matter directly in the Arctic, yet their influence in stimulating decomposition and in pollination may be highly important to the system.

We may now ask how numerous are insects in Arctic habitats. Already, readers can appreciate that insect populations may be very high but at the same time highly localised; insects in the Arctic are normally aggregated into microhabitats with the most suitable conditions of moisture, insolation, temperature, nutrients, plant cover, food and so on. In the High Arctic desert, stream courses and ponds provide oases for insect activity between large tracts of inhospitably dry and sparsely vegetated tundra. In wetter areas of tundra, such as the extensive sedge-moss meadows of some coastal areas and the Low Arctic, insect habitat is more or less continuous, with tracts of drier fjeldmark comprising islands of lesser insect productivity and activity. Specialised habitats, such as owl mounds, mammal burrows, bird nests, vertebrate cadavers, etc., are nutrient-rich islands, which are colonised by a variety of insects, sometimes in high numbers.

It is difficult to estimate the populations of Arctic insects because habitats are heterogeneous and may change from year to year. Moreover, a variety of factors cause numbers to fluctuate from place to place and from one season to another. Springtail (Collembola) populations have been studied in various locations: in Barrow, Alaska, about 24,000 individuals $m^{-2}$ were found in the centres of polygons, which are usually wet and cold, *versus* 180,000 $m^{-2}$ at the polygon edges and troughs, which are more diversely vegetated, better drained and warmer. On Svalbard, it was found that dry lichen tundra had populations of 38,000 $m^{-2}$, whereas in wet sites 243,000 $m^{-2}$ were found. It has been suggested that Collembola may achieve populations of up to a million $m^{-2}$ around old and grassy fox dens. Mites also occur in high numbers but are usually less numerous than are springtails; populations of 2,000 to 83,000 $m^{-2}$ have been noted from various sites. The populations of midges (Chironomidae) are also high in some ponds. In Char Lake, Cornwallis Island, 6,000 to 9,000 larvae $m^{-2}$ have been found, and up to 27,000 $m^{-2}$ have been recorded in some shallower and more nutrient-rich ponds. Most insects do not occur in these huge numbers, however. For the larvae of flies on rich tundra on Svalbard, 40–60 $m^{-2}$ has been recorded, and for adult butterflies and for caterpillars of *Gynaephora* densities of one individual per ten or more square metres seem typical.

Although the average populations of different insects may be very high or very low, they are likely to fluctuate greatly. A season of bad weather may depress adult populations of midges, mosquitoes, crane flies and other insects as the larvae wait for more equable conditions before they become adult. Fewer eggs are produced in such years, and the effects may become manifest much later. Some insects, such as carrion-feeding blow flies *Boreellus atriceps* fluctuate with the populations of lemmings, which are a major source of carrion.

# 9
# BREEDING BIRDS

## Introduction

In most areas of the northern part of the northern hemisphere birds are only relatively recent colonists, since the region was largely uninhabitable during the major glaciations. Since the end of the Ice Age a terrestrial avifauna has evolved and become adapted to the present Arctic tundra environment, and other species are adapted to the marine environment of the polar seas. The carrying capacity of many habitats exhibits very marked seasonal changes, and Arctic regions are an extreme example. They can support large numbers of individuals in the summer because of the high levels of productivity at that time but, in the winter, conditions are too severe to support many individuals.

The total number of species currently breeding in the Arctic is 183. (These are listed in Appendix 1 which also indicates their presence or absence in the Arctic regions of Alaska, Canada, Greenland, Svalbard and the Soviet Union. The nomenclature used is that of Voous (1977). The number of species breeding in each of these countries is shown in Table 9.1.) The total of 183 species recognised here as breeding in the Arctic differs from that given by some other authorities such as, for example, Salomonsen (1972) and Uspenskii (1984). These differences are due not only to varying views concerning the boundaries of the Arctic, but also to the availability of more up to date data concerning breeding distribution.

Certain species have been omitted from the list entirely. The Eskimo Curlew *Numenius borealis* for example is not quite extinct, but its present breeding area is not known. It formerly bred in the northwestern Mackenzie area of Canada and on the north coast of the Chukotka Peninsula in the Soviet Union. The Swallow *Hirundo rustica* has bred on the Arctic Slope of Alaska (once at Cape Sabine and possibly once at Barrow), but is certainly not an Arctic species. A similar comment applies also to the Common Sandpiper *Actitis hypoleucos* and the Brambling *Fringilla montifringilla*, both of which bred on the Yamal Peninsula in the Soviet Union in 1950 (during a period of climatic amelioration) but not subsequently. Other species have been omitted from individual country totals. For

example, the Teal *Anas crecca* may have bred in east Greenland in 1974; the Golden Plover *Pluvialis apricaria* bred in Svalbard in 1965; the Ruff *Philomachus pugnax* bred at Point Lay on Alaska's Arctic Slope in 1977; and the Savannah Sparrow *Ammodramus sandwichensis* has bred once on the Chukotka Peninsula. These all come under the category of isolated events.

Included in the total of 182 breeding species are 39 that can be regarded as of marginal occurrence in the Arctic (these are indicated by an asterisk (*) in Appendix 1). They include the Lesser White-fronted Goose *Anser erythropus* and European Wigeon *Anas penelope* which nest only in the extreme south of the tundra in the Soviet Union; the Lesser Sand Plover *Charadrius mongolus* which breeds only on the southern Chukotka Peninsula; four species of seabird – the Pigeon Guillemot *Cepphus columba*, Horned Puffin *Fratercula corniculata* and Tufted Puffin *Lunda cirrhata* which just enter the Arctic by virtue of breeding at Cape Lisburne in north-west Alaska, and the Great Skua *Stercorarius skua* which nests only on Svalbard; and several other species such as the Sedge Warbler *Acrocephalus schoenobaenus*, Chiffchaff *Phylloscopus collybita* and Willow Warbler *P. trochilus* which, in the Soviet Union, just penetrate into the tundra from the forest-tundra zone, usually along wooded river valleys.

The breeding birds of the Arctic can be analysed using the concept of 'faunal types' as originally proposed by Voous (1963). That a species represents a faunal type implies that it is a characteristic element of

*Plate 9.1 The Arctic Tern is a circumpolar colonial-nesting species*

the particular regional fauna and that in its origin, evolution and distributional history it is a product of this affiliation. Excluding the 39 marginal Arctic species, the application of this analysis to the remaining 144 species gives the result shown in Table 9.2.

Arctic birds can be divided into two distinct groups, the first fairly strictly confined to this particular environment, while the second comprises ubiquitous species whose ecological flexibility allows them to cope with tundra conditions. The highly specialised Arctic birds include the Gyrfalcon *Falco rusticolus*, Knot *Calidris canutus*, Sanderling *C. alba*, Snowy Owl and Snow Bunting *Plectrophenax nivalis*, for example. The second

**Table 9.1:** Geographical Distribution of Arctic Breeding Birds

| No. of | Soviet Union | Alaska | Canada | Greenland | Svalbard |
|---|---|---|---|---|---|
| **species** | 136 | 113 | 105 | 61 | 31 |

**Table 9.2:** Analysis of the Breeding Birds of the Arctic According to Their Faunal Type

| Faunal Type | No. of species |
|---|---|
| Arctic | 73 |
| Canadian | 7 |
| Siberian | 9 |
| Siberian-Canadian | 5 |
| Siberian-Beringian | 1 |
| Holarctic | 14 |
| Nearctic | 14 |
| Palearctic | 6 |
| European | 1 |
| North Atlantic | 3 |
| Angaran | 4 |
| Tibetan | 1 |
| Montane (Rocky Mountains) | 1 |
| Paleomontane (Old World) | 2 |
| Cosmopolitan | 3 |
| Total | 144 |

group consists primarily of those species that are present in the tundra habitat only during the summer months. While the breeding range of some of these species may be predominantly Arctic, the distribution of others extends much further to the south.

Very few species may be considered winter residents in the Arctic tundras of North America and Eurasia. Species in this category include the Gyrfalcon (occasionally), Willow Ptarmigan, Rock Ptarmigan *Lagopus mutus*, Snowy Owl, Raven and Arctic Redpoll *Carduelis hornemanni*. Ptarmigan can winter up to 75° N, and when food is available the Snowy Owl may live further north than any other species, having been seen at 82° N on Ellesmere Island in winter (Gessaman 1978).

## Migration

With the exception of the few species that are able to reside year-round on the Arctic tundras, those birds utilising food resources there during the summer are faced with just two basic alternatives when conditions deteriorate and freeze-up approaches: they can move out of the area, or die. In order to make long migratory flights, birds require substantial reserves of energy. These are provided by the laying down of fat, and the amounts which have to be laid down are considerable. In the case of the Sanderling which migrates from the High Arctic to temperate shores the normal weight is about 50 g, but prior to migration this increases to about 110 g. In Arctic-nesting geese, energy reserves available to birds at the beginning of the breeding season constitute one of the major determinants of reproductive success. Tundra-nesting geese are heavy and have large fat reserves on arrival at the nesting grounds.

Lesser Snow Geese *Anser caerulescens caerulescens* from breeding grounds in the Mackenzie River and Anderson River deltas, and other Canadian nesting areas, migrate westwards to a major autumn staging area between the Canning River delta in north-east Alaska

*Plate 9.2 A Sanderling on Bathurst Island, Canada*

and the Blow River in the Yukon Territory. In September 1979 some 80,000 were seen between the outer Canning delta and Barter Island (Derksen *et al* 1981). For a period of two to four weeks in late summer, before they depart for their wintering grounds, the geese feed on the coastal plain. The length of time that the geese feed in the area is variable from year to year and the date of departure is triggered by the arrival of the first winter storms. Studies in September 1973 showed that during the average 17-day stay, body weights increased 14.3 per cent in adult males, 17.1 per cent in adult females, 9.5 per cent in juvenile males, and 23 per cent in juvenile females (Patterson 1974).

Migratory birds travel to and from the Arctic by a number of overland and coastal routes in enormous numbers. The springtime arrival of these vast numbers of birds, coinciding with the rise in temperature and increasing daylight is, along with the flush of new plant growth, one of the most spectacular and exciting sights in the annual cycle of events in the Arctic. The various patterns of migration in Eurasia and North America are discussed by Mead (1983).

In late April and early May a lead (linear area of open water) develops from the eastern Bering Sea north through the Chukchi Sea to Point Barrow. This is known as a flow lead, which forms when the free-floating pack-ice separates from the more stable landfast ice. The formation of this flow lead is an annual occurrence, the first major event in the decomposition of the pack-ice in the Arctic Ocean off northern Alaska. A number of marine bird and mammal species use the lead as a migration pathway to breeding grounds in northern Alaska and the Canadian Arctic (Woodby and Divoky 1982). Other species move overland, and radar observations at Oliktok Point in northern Alaska revealed a broad front of eastward migration across the Arctic Slope extending at least 75 km south of the Beaufort Sea coast. The movements of some species (particularly some of the waders and virtually all of the passerines) are made entirely overland.

Some Arctic nesting species cover enormous distances between their breeding areas in the north and wintering grounds far to the south. The most spectacular migration is undoubtedly that of the Arctic Tern *Sterna paradisaea* which breeds north of the Arctic Circle and winters in the Antarctic. Another example is Baird's Sandpiper *Calidris bairdii* which winters in the Andes of South America, while its northernmost breeding range extends from the eastern High Arctic of Canada through to Greenland. The species' total range therefore spans over 100° of latitude.

It is of interest to discuss briefly the actual migration patterns of some Arctic-nesting species. The Wheatear *Oenanthe oenanthe* has a very wide circumpolar breeding distribution with populations in Alaska, north-east Canada and Greenland. All the Arctic populations, together with those breeding across Europe and Asia, winter in Africa. The subspecies nesting in Greenland, *O.o.leucorhoa*, performs one of the most remarkable land-bird migrations in the world. In autumn, in order to make their first landfall in the British Isles or in Iberia, these birds cross 2,000–3,000 km of open ocean. In contrast, Snow Buntings breeding in western Greenland travel, via the islands of the Canadian Arctic Archipelago, to the North American mainland where they winter southwards from southern Alaska and Canada.

The Tundra Swan *Cygnus columbianus* is a species with a disjunct circumpolar distribution whose autumn movements are overland to traditional coastal wintering areas. Adults and young set off together in late summer, remain as a unit through the winter and return (still together) to the same breeding areas. In the case of the populations in the Eurasian Arctic, this involves a journey of some 5,000 km or more. The Barnacle Goose *Branta leucopsis*, has three distinct populations. Two of these (those of east Greenland and Svalbard) cross extensive areas of ocean to reach their wintering grounds in the British Isles, while the Siberian population moves overland to coastal wintering areas in the Netherlands. A much more complex pattern of movements is shown by the Brent Goose *Branta bernicla* which undertakes the longest migration of all geese, and some of whose populations have to move considerable distances east or west from the breeding areas to reach the continental shores along which they migrate. Many of those breeding in the Canadian Arctic move east across Greenland to Iceland, and then southwards to their wintering grounds in Ireland.

Mention must be made of two species of wader, the Knot and the Sanderling, which breed in the highest latitudes attained by migratory birds. They are very long distance migrants, although both have wintering populations in temperate northern latitudes. Some Eurasian breeding Knot reach South Africa and New Zealand, while Sanderling breeding in North America move as far south as South America in winter. Finally, the Lesser Golden Plover *Pluvialis dominica* performs some of the longest trans-oceanic movements of any wader. Siberian birds regularly winter in Oceania, Australia and New Zealand, while American birds fly out over the Atlantic to reach wintering grounds in South America.

Not all species migrate by flying. A number of marine species evade the winter by swimming southwards and remaining south of the edge of the pack-ice, returning north the same way in spring. The species which exhibit this pattern of behaviour are primarily the Arctic Alcidae (auks) and one or two species of gull, notably the Ivory Gull *Pagophila eburnea*. Brünnich's Guillemots breeding in eastern Greenland follow the drift-ice south to winter off the south-east coast. The majority of those from western Greenland follow the Labrador Current to wintering areas on the Newfoundland Grand Banks, but many adults winter in the southern Davis Strait.

A certain amount of mystery surrounds the movements of Ross's Gull *Rhodostethia rosea*. The autumn migration of this gull is observed regularly at Point Barrow during north-westerly gales, and during any one season several thousand birds may be seen. These

*Plate 9.3 A Willow Ptarmigan in winter plumage in northern Alaska*

gulls are mainly heading north-east towards the polar pack-ice, and this, given the time of year and the geographical location of Point Barrow, is an unexpected direction. Equally interesting is the fact that no return migration of the same magnitude in the reverse direction has ever been recorded.

In 1980 a minimum of 670 individuals were seen between the north of Svalbard and Franz Josef Land between 3 July and 6 August, and at least 116 between 23 August and 10 September in the east Greenland ice between Svalbard and north Greenland. The large numbers observed, together with the westerly migration in July and the easterly migration observed in September, suggest that the highly productive polar ice bordering the Barents and Greenland Seas serves as an important feeding and moulting area for non-breeding Ross's Gulls during the summer (Meltofte *et al* 1981).

The sheer volume of spring migration into the Arctic is best appreciated by observation at favoured vantage points, such as Point Barrow, past which migrants traditionally move. During one six-week migration period 240,000 birds of 50 species were recorded passing just one spit of land on Canada's north Yukon coast, and during one spring week in 1974, 175,000 divers, Long-tailed Ducks *Clangula hyemalis* and eiders were counted in a single large polyna. However, even these large numbers are exceeded by counts at Point Barrow where, on 26 May 1976, 360,000 King Eiders *Somateria spectabilis* passed during a period of ten hours; this was the peak of the migration. The total number of birds estimated to have passed Point Barrow between 6 May and 4 June 1976 included 802,556 King Eiders, 153,081 Common Eiders *S. mollissima*, 32,141 Long-tailed Ducks and 3,537 Glaucous Gulls *Larus hyperboreus* (Woodby and Divoky 1982).

The spring migration of King Eiders eastward along the Arctic coast of North America begins in late April and reaches a peak in mid-June (sometimes in late May). The movement is usually well offshore but comes close in at Point Barrow and a few other points on the mainland. Many birds subsequently branch off

to nesting sites on Banks Island and Victoria Island. It was estimated by Barry (1968) that a total of some 1,108,000 King and Common Eiders use the Beaufort Sea migration route in spring.

Large numbers of birds may also be noted during the autumn period, and this applies particularly to waterfowl which concentrate in favoured feeding areas (see the section on Post-breeding Concentrations and Moult Migration). Post-breeding congregations of water birds have been recorded in nearshore waters of the Chukchi and Beaufort Seas, and on freshwater lakes on the Arctic Coastal Plain of northern Alaska. Shallow coastal lagoons protected by barrier islands are important to Long-tailed Ducks during moult in August and September. Johnson (1979) counted 106,000 birds in Simpson Lagoon 25 km west of Prudhoe Bay in September 1977.

Another phenomenon of interest applies to a few Arctic-nesting species, and this is movement away from the direction of their normal migratory flight in autumn. An example here is the Grey Phalarope *Phalaropus fulicarius* which, before their final migration from the Soviet Arctic, travel in large numbers to areas located further to the north of their nesting locations. Thus in autumn they appear in numbers on Wrangel Island where very few breed (Portenko 1981).

Finally, mention must be made of the interesting behaviour of the Willow Ptarmigan of Arctic Alaska. These have a definite migratory pattern which leaves the adult males on the breeding grounds north of the Brooks Range in winter, the juvenile males in the passes of the Brooks Range, and the females south of the range (Irving *et al* 1967). This distribution pattern may result in slightly different energy demands and definitely results in different diets of the four age-sex groups of the population (West and Meng 1966). It has been estimated that approximately 50,000 ptarmigan move southward and northward through Anaktuvuk Pass annually, with the autumn migration reaching a peak in mid-October, and the peak movement northwards coming in late April.

*Plate 9.4 The Glaucous Gull is a predatory species with a circumpolar distribution*

*Plate 9.5 Within the Arctic, Ross's Gull breeds in scattered localities in the Soviet Union, Canada and Greenland*

### Mortality in Migrant Waterfowl

The relative unpredictability of weather and temperature fluctuations in the Arctic is a major hazard for the earliest spring migrants. Once open leads of water appear in the pack-ice large numbers of duck begin to assemble, and should a sudden drop in temperature subsequently occur and freezing conditions return, the results can be very serious.

The King Eider is particularly vulnerable in this respect since males precede the females in the easterly movement along the north coasts of Alaska and Canada which begins in late April. Sudden local freezes have been responsible for trapping eiders in late April and early May. This happened in Arctic Canada, for example, in the spring of 1960 when temperatures of −40° C froze the open leads. The 1964 season was one of the most severe in the recent history of the Canadian western Arctic. Close pack-ice was present nearly continuously and it was one of the few years when continuous ice stretched from the mainland to Banks Island. Even the normally well defined polyna in the Amundsen Gulf off Cape Parry froze over and remained frozen from January until mid-July. It was estimated by Barry (1968) that approximately 100,000 King Eiders perished from starvation caused by the unusually bad ice conditions in the Beaufort Sea in the spring of that year. Heavy losses can also be caused by freeze-up occurring before the birds reach the flight stage in the autumn.

### Post-breeding Concentrations and Moult Migration

From late June to early July a movement of non-breeding and post-breeding adults of several species of waders occurs on the coastal plain of northern Alaska, with flocks utilising habitats at the edge of small coastal lagoons and nearby brackish pools. In late July and early August, flocking adults also move into littoral areas prior to commencing their southward migration (Risebrough 1976). A similar pattern of events involving waders occurs also in other parts of the Arctic, the timing and numbers involved varying according to geographical location and local environmental conditions. In the Soviet Arctic, for example, when broods of Little Stints *Calidris minuta* abandon the breeding sites they concentrate first on the banks of streams and rivers in large numbers, and later move to the shores of lakes and to the coast (Uspenskii 1984).

The really spectacular post-breeding concentrations involve ducks and geese and are related to moult migration. Post-breeding concentrations of waterfowl have long been known to occur in nearshore waters of the Chukchi and Beaufort Seas, and on freshwater lakes on the Arctic Coastal Plain. Many male Pintails *Anas acuta* fly west along the north coast in early July, but most seem to travel only a short distance, and tens of thousands subsequently moult in various lagoons on the coast (Johnson and Richardson 1982). Similarly, brackish shallow waters of Canada's Mackenzie delta provide moulting grounds for some 600,000 Long-

Plate 9.6 *The Common Eider is essentially a colonial-nesting species in the Arctic*

Plate 9.7 *The King Eider is one of the most northerly ranging of the Arctic-breeding ducks*

tailed Ducks, scaup and scoters. The males of most other populations of Long-tailed Ducks do not undertake long moult migrations, but northward moult movements to Wrangel Island and northern Greenland have been reported.

Males of the Surf Scoter *Melanitta perspicillata* and Velvet Scoter *M. fusca* begin to congregate in the Mackenzie delta in mid-June, and in late June and July thousands of male Surf Scoters fly west near the Yukon and Alaskan coast to moulting areas in lagoons. This flight, unlike moult migrations of most scoters, is not directed towards the wintering areas. Several thousand

Surf Scoters moult annually at Herschel Island, Yukon Territory, in July and early August.

The King Eider has a remarkable moult migration which begins soon after incubation has commenced with males gathering on freshwater areas away from the nesting sites. Shortly thereafter the movement begins, more or less in the direction of the winter range, and continues for up to several weeks. Huge numbers eventually arrive at traditional moulting locations and become flightless. One such location is along the south-west coast of Novaya Zemlya. From the western North American Arctic there is a massive movement of both Common and King Eiders (several hundred thousand males) past Point Barrow. These birds are *en route* from breeding areas in the Beaufort Sea to moulting areas believed to be in the Chukchi Sea or northern Bering Sea. From the eastern section there is heavy migration out of the central Canadian Arctic, principally across the central portion of Baffin Island, to waters along the coast of central western Greenland, a movement of up to 2,500 km (Palmer 1977). About 100,000 males and immatures may be found in Davis Strait.

Moult migration is especially common in geese, which do not breed until two to four years of age, and during the period of moult the birds tend to become wary and to select remote sites. The large groups which are seen at this time probably comprise immature non-breeders and failed breeders, since pairs rearing young tend to moult separately near the nesting area.

Moulting locations often are long distances from the breeding areas, occasionally involving long flights over the sea. A classic example is the massive movement of thousands of non-breeding Pink-footed Geese *Anser brachyrhynchus* from Iceland to east Greenland early in June (Christensen 1967). Large concentrations of Bean Geese *A. fabalis* moult in southern Novaya Zemlya. These originate from mainland western Siberia. Other concentrations are found on the Yamal Peninsula, western Taimyr Peninsula and in the Lena delta. All of these presumably originate from the breeding grounds further south (Owen 1980).

The numbers of geese moulting along the Beaufort Sea coast of Alaska are considerable. It was estimated by King (1970), for example, that there were 15,000 moulting Canada Geese *Branta canadensis* along the coast from Smith Bay to the Canning River (a distance of about 300 km), and suggested that most of these were non-breeding birds from interior Alaska south of the Brooks Range. According to Ogilvie (1978), the numbers of White-fronted Geese *Anser albifrons* on the Arctic Slope at the end of the breeding season may be about 50,000, far in excess of the breeding population. The deltas of the Mackenzie and Anderson Rivers in Canada also hold large numbers of this species, with an estimate for the two of 40,000 at one time. The Queen Maud Gulf area is probably the most important site in the east with at least 10,000 birds there by late summer, and a further 2,000 or so on the islands to the north.

The area near Cape Halkett, north of Teshekpuk Lake, where there are about 30 elongated lakes from 1.6 to 6 km in length, was identified as an important site for moulting geese. Surveys were carried out there in July 1976, 1977 and 1978 (Derksen *et al* 1979) and the numbers of geese seen in those years is shown in Table 9.3. The moulting area is about 2,000 km² and extends from Cape Halkett in the east to Drew Point on the west, and south to the north shore of Teshekpuk Lake. The area is the only known moulting area for

non-breeding geese on the Arctic coast of Alaska, and ringing returns have demonstrated that the geese are drawn from populations in Canada and Siberia. The habitat ecology of the geese moulting in the Teshekpuk Lake area has been the subject of detailed research by Derksen *et al* (1982).

## Aspects of Breeding Biology

The purpose of this section is to review briefly some of the wider aspects of breeding in Arctic birds. Some further information on individual species will be found in the species accounts later in this chapter.

While the majority of tundra-breeding species are absent during the winter period, thus avoiding the extreme low temperatures, high potential heat loss, and the restricted day length of mid-winter, they nevertheless do have to confront a series of environmental problems. These are partly similar to those faced by winter residents, partly the opposite extreme conditions, and partly quite unrelated problems arising from their migratory habits. Seven such problems are listed by West and Norton (1975):–

A. Direct Factors
  1. The shortness of the breeding season
  2. Factors promoting heat loss, including low temperatures, wind, radiative and evaporative heat loss
  3. Long or continuous daylight hours
  4. Lack of vertical habitat structure (song perches, topographic relief)
  5. Long-distance migrations between wintering and breeding ranges
B. Indirect Factors
  6. Vagaries of weather
  7. Patchiness of suitable habitat through space and time

In polar regions, where the onset of spring and winter occur abruptly, the timing of breeding can be absolutely critical in determining reproductive success. Species breeding in the Arctic experience abrupt seasonal changes with unpredictable environmental

**Table 9.3:** Populations of Moulting Geese Near Teshekpuk Lake, Alaska

|  | 1976 23 July | 1977 13 July | 1978 18 July |
|---|---|---|---|
| White-fronted Goose *Anser albifrons* | 4,872 | 2,687 | 1,943 |
| Snow Goose *Anser caerulescens* | 718 | 179 | 87 |
| Canada Goose *Branta canadensis* | 12,079 | 12,490 | 14,388 |
| Brent Goose *Branta bernicla* | 14,243 | 22,075 | 32,720 |
| Totals | 31,912 | 37,431 | 49,138 |

Source: Derksen *et al* (1979).

*Plate 9.8 The Black-throated Diver nests on lakes from the Arctic tundra south into the boreal zone*

*Plate 9.9 The Ivory Gull is essentially a High Arctic species*

conditions that may affect the time of egg-laying. The time of spring melt-off and ice break-up can vary considerably among years and can have a marked effect on the timing of breeding and breeding success: success is lower in late years (see, for example, the remarks under Brent Goose later in this chapter). The timing of egg-laying is particularly important since the season is so short. Any delay at the commencement of the breeding season may mean that birds are unable to complete the cycle before autumn freeze-up starts.

Waterbirds are particularly affected by the time of spring melt-off. Late thaws in spring are not at all unusual and in some years almost entire populations of divers, geese, waders, and seabirds may fail to rear young (Birkhead and Nettleship 1982; Perrins and Birkhead 1983). Species which nest on offshore islands (for example, eiders, Glaucous Gull, and Arctic Tern), do not normally start to breed until the ice breaks up, thereby opening up nearby feeding areas and reducing the probability of access by predators such as the Arctic Fox. Similarly, those species nesting on tundra pools or lakes, such as the Red-throated Diver *Gavia stellata*, Black-throated Diver *G. arctica* and Long-tailed Duck, do not breed at all if the ice does not thaw early enough. Even if the spring thaw is not delayed and the birds are able to nest, there are years when the autumn freeze-up comes abnormally early thereby catching young birds before they are able to fly: the young of divers are particularly vulnerable in this respect.

While, in many Arctic-nesting species, the commencement of breeding is clearly related to the timing of snow-melt, this rule does not apply throughout the Arctic since there are some exceptions. For example, studies of four species of *Calidris* sandpipers in Alaska and of Knots and Turnstones *Arenaria interpres* on Ellesmere Island indicate that they time their nesting so that the young hatch when their food – small adult dipterans on the tundra surface – is most abundant (Holmes 1966; Holmes and Pitelka 1968; Nettleship 1973, 1974). On the other hand, in north-east Greenland where conditions are drier than in Alaska and where snowfall is heavier than on Ellesmere Island, research in 1974 showed that there were marked differences in the date and duration of the wader breeding season in different valleys, and that these were clearly associated with differences in the time of snow-melt (Green *et al* 1977). Nevertheless, Meltofte (1979) in his studies of waders in north-east Greenland showed that nests can survive even when snow-covered.

### Non-breeding in Arctic Birds

Each spring enormous numbers of birds assemble in traditional breeding locations in the Arctic. Many of them, the actual proportions varying from year to year, do not breed. The phenomenon of partial or total non-breeding in the Arctic is well known in such species as the geese, ducks, skuas, gulls (e.g. Glaucous Gull, Ivory Gull), Arctic Tern and Snowy Owl. Even now there are many unresolved questions concerning this behaviour. In particular, the true Arctic non-breeding in which, in a given area, the majority of birds of all species do not lay eggs, is difficult to explain.

Partial or total non-breeding is a characteristic feature of several species of high-latitude marine birds, but it is interesting to note that seasons without breeding are unusual among the colonial seabirds that nest on cliffs in the Arctic. In the case of the gulls mentioned above, and the Arctic Tern, it is perhaps significant that they are species feeding mainly on food gathered from the surface waters, and are therefore certainly affected by late break-up of the sea-ice.

As suggested by Uspenskii (1984), there seems little doubt that peculiarities in the hydrological regime are one of the main factors responsible for partial or total non-breeding (particularly in the case of marine birds), although the way in which they influence the birds varies in different instances. Among the ducks which nest in the Arctic, non-breeding is a common phenomenon in the case of the Common Eider. The reason here is that failure of the ice to melt allows predators to cross to the nesting islets and wreak havoc. It was pointed out by Freuchen and Salomonsen (1958) that in those years when snow lies late on the tundra and ice covers the waters, Red-throated Divers and King Eiders may never settle down to nest. Following his research on the oceanic island of Jan Mayen at 71° N, Marshall (1952) stated that non-breeding in sexually mature birds may be caused variously by lack of safe nest sites due to fox predation, lack of nesting cover or food shortage. Absence or shortage of food (lemmings) is the primary cause of non-breeding in the Pomarine Skua *Stercorarius pomarinus* and the Snowy Owl, both of which are virtually obligatory predators on these rodents.

Non-breeding in Arctic waders is discussed by Hobson (1972) who stresses the food-shortage factor, particularly the scarcity of suitable food for the young. In his studies of the Knot at Eureka, western Ellesmere Island, he found that a number of pairs did not breed, and suggests that inadequate food was the reason. The only insect life on the tundra at the time was numbers of caterpillars of the moth *Byrdia*. It also proved to be a non-breeding year for the Long-tailed Skua *Stercorarius longicaudus*, and Snow Buntings were very scarce. Light snowfall the previous winter caused abnormally dry conditions so that by the end of June the terrain was completely dried out and there were no marshes or ponds.

Food shortage as a cause of partial or total non-breeding in the Kittiwake *Rissa tridactyla* is described by Uspenskii (1984) who shows that the effects differ between breeding localities according to the diversity of food available. In eastern Murmansk and Novaya Zemlya only partial non-breeding (and a reduction in clutch size) occurs, but on the New Siberian Islands where a very limited range of food species is available, total non-breeding may be found in some years.

### Clutch Size in Relation to Latitude

One of the most striking and long-established variations in clutch size both between and within species is the increase with latitude. The explanation originally

Plate 9.10 *The Pectoral Sandpiper breeds in a variety of tundra habitats*

Plate 9.11 *A Baird's Sandpiper on its nest on the Chukotka Peninsula in the Soviet Union*

proposed to explain this trend is that in the northern hemisphere summer days get longer the further north one goes, and since birds then have a longer day in which to obtain food for their young, they are able to lay larger clutches and rear more young.

This plausible theory does, however, present problems as was shown by the work of Hussell (1972) on clutch size in Arctic passerines. This showed that Snow Buntings breeding far north of the Arctic Circle lay larger clutches than those breeding close to the Arctic Circle, yet birds at both extremes have very nearly 24 hours of daylight each day at the time when they are rearing young. Precisely the same situation was found to exist in the case of the Lapland Bunting *Calcarius lapponicus* (see Table 9.4).

Subsequent research, for example that of Ricklefs (1980), suggests that the most likely explanation for the marked latitudinal trend in clutch size has more to do with the relative productivity of the area rather than with daylength. In general, Arctic habitats show greater variations in seasonal productivity than do habitats at lower latitudes. It was demonstrated by Ricklefs that clutch size is directly related to seasonal variation in actual evapotranspiration (AE), which is proportional to primary production. Clutch size is directly related to the ratio between summer AE and winter AE, and additionally is inversely related to winter AE, but is independent of summer AE. This implies that the number of breeding individuals is regulated in winter and that population size exerts a density-dependent influence on resources available to each individual for reproduction. Clutch size is shown to be directly related to the ratio between summer productivity and the density of breeding adults. It is suggested that geographical trends in clutch size are caused primarily by factors that limit populations outside the breeding period rather than by the abundance of resources *during* the breeding season.

### Diurnal Rhythms in Arctic Birds

The phenomenon of long or continuous daylight hours permits, or perhaps forces, birds on the tundra to remain active and alert, and therefore metabolically active, to a greater degree than is the case elsewhere. Theoretically, continuous daylight should enable birds to be active throughout the 24 hours. However, most species do not lose a diurnal rhythm, and in all regions north of the Arctic Circle activity is still synchronised with the rotation of the earth. The resting period of light-active song-birds shifts further into the evening with lengthening light period.

The research on diurnal rhythms in Arctic birds has concentrated on passerines in which it is so clearly defined and obviously governed by a physiological clock. Non-passerines are capable of activity under very varied conditions, and continuous activity has been noted in ducks, auks, gulls and terns. Although there can be no doubt that these birds do possess a physiological clock and are able to synchronise it with the rotation of the earth, even in the High Arctic, this does not seem to have been demonstrated. The fact that these species exhibit continuous activity does not exclude the physiological clock hypothesis.

A particularly interesting study is that by Krüll (1976) concerning research done in the very narrow valley of Longyearbyen, Svalbard's largest town. The valley only receives direct sunlight around midnight, and for the rest of the 24 hours is entirely in the shadow of surrounding high mountains. It was found that there was no difference in the activity of birds (for example the Snow Bunting) in the valley and on the open tundra. They all rested at about midnight, which means that birds in the Longyear valley were asleep during the only part of the day when direct sunlight fell on the valley. This being so, it is clear that light intensity itself is not the only factor controlling this behaviour. It is of interest to note that in the case of the Willow Ptarmigan there is a definite seasonal change in its activity pattern in summer. The normal bimodal pattern is lost and activity remains continuous throughout the 24 hours (West 1968).

There have of course been a number of studies on the activity patterns of diurnal Arctic birds. Investigations on nesting Wheatears in Scoresbyland, Greenland (72° N), for example showed that every 'night' both male and female had a distinct period of inactivity which lasted on average from 02.39 to 07.25 hours, a mean period of 4 hours 46 minutes. It was also found that the inactive period for the Wheatear was two to three hours later in the day than for Snow Buntings

**Table 9.4:** Geographical Variation in Clutch Size of Lapland Bunting *Calcarius lapponicus* and Snow Bunting *Plectrophenax nivalis* in Selected Arctic Localities

| Species and Locality | Latitude (°N) | 1 | 2 | 3 | 4 | 5 | 6 | 7 | 8 | Total | Mean |
|---|---|---|---|---|---|---|---|---|---|---|---|
| Lapland Bunting | | | | | | | | | | | |
| Churchill, Manitoba | 59 | | | 2 | 3 | 9 | 1 | | | 15 | 4.60 |
| Frobisher Bay, Baffin Is. | 64 | | | 1 | 4 | 9 | 1 | | | 15 | 4.67 |
| Aberdeen Lake and vicinity, Keewatin | 65 | | | 1 | 4 | 4 | | | | 9 | 4.33 |
| Cumberland Peninsula, Baffin Is. | 67 | | | | 2 | 4 | 5 | 2 | | 13 | 5.46 |
| Brooks Range, Alaska | 68 | | | | 4 | 4 | 1 | | | 9 | 4.67 |
| Cape Thompson, Alaska[a] | 68 | 1 | 1 | 4 | 23 | 65 | 17 | | | 111 | 4.81 |
| Cambridge Bay, Victoria Is. and Jenny Lind Is. | 69 | | | | 9 | 22 | 33 | | | 64 | 5.38 |
| Clyde Inlet, Baffin Is. | 70 | | | | 2 | 4 | 2 | 2 | | 10 | 5.40 |
| Sachs Harbour, Banks Is. | 72 | | | | 1 | 2 | 3 | 1 | | 7 | 5.57 |
| Bylot Island | 73 | | | 2 | 6 | 3 | 4 | | | 15 | 4.60 |
| Devon Island | 76 | | 1 | 4 | 12 | 16 | 17 | 4 | | 54 | 5.04 |
| Snow Bunting | | | | | | | | | | | |
| Frobisher Bay, Baffin Is. | 64 | | | | 2 | 10 | | 1 | | 13 | 5.00 |
| Cumberland Peninsula, Baffin Is. | 67 | | | | 1 | 3 | 3 | 2 | | 9 | 5.67 |
| Cambridge Bay, Victoria Is. and Jenny Lind Is. | 69 | | | | | 2 | 6 | 9 | | 17 | 6.41 |
| Devon Island | 76 | | | 1 | 10 | 31 | 24 | 3 | | 69 | 5.25 |
| Eureka, Ellesmere Is. | 80 | | | | | | 2 | 5 | 1 | 8 | 6.88 |

Note: a. Not within the boundaries of the Arctic as defined for the purposes of this book.

Source: Based on Hussell (1972).

(22.32–02.46 hours), although the length of the inactive period was the same for both species. It was suggested that the different timing of the inactive periods might be related to differences in the types of food brought to the nestlings of the two species (Asbirk and Franzmann 1979). It was clear that the daily activity pattern of Snow Buntings in continuous daylight coincided with the daily cycles of light and temperature. However, these factors are so variable from day to day that it seems likely that the birds' activity patterns are mainly determined by an endogenous rhythm. The daily cycles of light and temperature may entrain this rhythm. The daily activity of invertebrates followed a similar pattern to that of the Snow Buntings. It is too variable to be the proximate factor determining the birds activity patterns but feeding efficiency is probably the ultimate factor determining them. The period of rest coincided with the coolest part of the day, when the preferred food was least active (Asbirk and Franzmann 1978).

These findings are in accord with the statement by Uspenskii (1984) based on studies in the Soviet Union, to the effect that Snow Buntings, Lapland Buntings, and Red-throated Pipits *Anthus cervinus* are most active in the morning hours (from 02.30–03.00 hours), with the activity level falling at noon, then rising again slightly in the hours before dusk; the birds rest from 24.00 to 02.30 hours. The resting period coincides with the hours when the sun is low over the horizon and the atmospheric temperature is low.

## Metabolic Demands of Breeding

It is a well known fact that in most birds there is an increased requirement for calcium and protein during egg-laying, and this is followed by a major increase in energy requirements associated with intensive feeding of the young. Some species (such as geese, ducks, waders and ptarmigan) have precocial young able to forage for themselves soon after hatching and so avoid this additional energy requirement. It follows that for this strategy to succeed, the timing of hatching must be such that suitable food is readily available for the rapidly growing chicks, whose foraging time is limited because of brooding by the adults.

Breeding birds of the tundra satisfy the energetic demands of maintenance and reproduction on a variety of diets. In the case of species such as the Lapland Bunting, Snow Bunting and *Calidris* sandpipers, animal protein supports tundra breeding to a very striking degree, often representing a complete reversal of food preferences outside the breeding season. The energetic advantages of invertebrate food (higher calorific value, increased digestibility) strongly suggest that the growth of young is optimised with some proportion of animal food, even in the case of species that are nominally herbivorous.

The question of calcium availability for tundra-nesting waders at the time of egg-laying is of particular interest, since egg production is an exercise of considerable magnitude for waders in an Arctic environment. As stated by MacLean (1974), there is considerable variation in the time between the laying of successive eggs by sandpipers, and in the case of the Dunlin the interval is 24 hours in northern Alaska and 36 hours in coastal Finland. The deviation from a diurnal cycle suggests that eggs are laid at intervals determined by the ability of the female to mobilise some resource such as fat, protein or calcium. MacLean then shows that significant amounts of lemming remains (teeth and bones) were found in the stomachs of Semipalmated Sandpiper *Calidris pusilla*, Baird's Sandpiper, Pectoral Sandpiper *C. melanotos* and Dunlin *C. alpina* on the Arctic tundra of northern Alaska. He suggests that the abundant supply of lemming skeletal remains in northern Alaska may favour rapid calcium accumulation and thus allow a shorter interval between laying eggs.

## Predation on Breeding Birds

Predation is probably the primary cause of nesting failure among Arctic-breeding waterfowl, waders and passerines (Jehl 1971), and the Arctic Fox plays an important role in this context as is discussed in detail by Larson (1960). As he pointed out, it is generally accepted that the breeding of so many Arctic bird species on minor islands off the coast or in lakes, and on inaccessible cliffs, is a direct consequence of the threat posed by this animal. In some areas during the nesting season Arctic Foxes feed extensively on eggs and young birds, particularly if fox populations are at a high level. Avian predators include the skuas, Glaucous and Herring Gulls *Larus argentatus*, Snowy Owl and Raven, but their level of predation on other birds is normally relatively low compared to that exerted by the Arctic Fox and to a lesser extent by weasels.

On Devon Island, predation on the nests of all birds is usually heavy. Predators destroyed 25 per cent of the nests found in 1970, 60 per cent in 1971 and 63 per cent in 1972. Arctic Foxes were the most important predators, followed by Ermine *Mustela erminea* and skuas (Fitzgerald 1981). On Eskjer Island, west Svalbard, out of a total Common Eider population of about 3,300 pairs and a total annual egg production of approximately 20,500 eggs only *ca.* 5,500 young or 27 per cent are hatched. Almost all the difference, *ca.* 15,000 eggs or 73 per cent, is consumed by predators (Ahlen and Andersson 1970).

Research on Ross's Goose *Anser rossii* in Canada's Perry River region (Ryder 1967) revealed that in the first week of June 1964 foxes destroyed 144 Ross's and 122 Lesser Snow Goose nests on one island. In another study (MacInnes and Misra 1972) a single fox destroyed all 200 snow goose clutches in a 3 km² area in five days, systematically removing the eggs from one nest after another and burying them. On Wrangel Island, Arctic Fox predation on the Lesser Snow Goose colonies accounts for 40–80 per cent of goose production losses each year (Bousfield and Syroechkovskiy 1985).

Some Arctic birds of prey are highly specialised predators on birds. One example is the Gyrfalcon whose distribution is very clearly linked with the presence of ptarmigan which usually account for more than

*Plate 9.12 A female Grey Plover on its nest on dry lichen-dominated tundra*

95 per cent of its food, except in parts of the High Arctic of Canada, and in some coastal regions where seabirds are utilised.

The ecology of the Pomarine, Arctic and Long-tailed Skuas has been studied in detail by Maher (1970a, 1970b and 1974). The Pomarine Skua can be described as an obligatory predator on microtine rodents. Breeding birds at three localities in northern Alaska fed predominantly on microtine rodents (approximately 80 per cent of their food supply), but in non-breeding populations rodents formed less than half of the food, and waders (sandpipers, Grey Phalaropes), ptarmigan, and eggs were amongst the alternative prey.

Breeding Arctic Skuas also have more specialised food habits than non-breeding ones, although the contrast is not as extreme as in the case of the preceding species. Breeding individuals specialise either on birds or on birds and microtine rodents. In the case of Arctic Skuas breeding in the Kaolak River area on the Arctic Slope of Alaska, the total number of birds taken was 75 per cent of all food items in 1957, 81 per cent in 1958 and 88 per cent in 1959. The percentage of passerine birds in the total number of prey items varied from 45

in 1957, to 66 in 1958 and 75 in 1959. Two pairs nesting at Peters Lake and Schroders Lake in north-east Alaska preyed almost entirely on birds. Eighty seven per cent of the 245 food items identified were passerine birds, and six per cent were waders – a total of 93 per cent avian food items.

In the case of the Long-tailed Skua, the data indicate clearly that it is by preference a microtine rodent predator, which is also able to prey successfully on birds, primarily passerines (e.g. Snow Bunting and redpolls) and some juvenile waders. In the case of breeding birds at the Kaolak River, birds comprised more than half of the total prey in 1957 and 1959 and slightly less than half in 1958.

The Glaucous Gull, although omnivorous, takes predominantly animal food and this includes eggs and young birds. These gulls will patrol seabird colonies on cliffs and have been seen to catch newly fledged Brünnich's Guillemots in flight. In Canada numerous observations were made of young Ross's Geese being snatched off the water and devoured whole (Ryder 1967). Also, Barry (1956) noted that Glaucous Gulls (and skuas) took a heavy toll of the eggs and young of

*Plate 9.13 The Great Knot nests on dry alpine tundras in the Soviet Union and only just qualifies as an Arctic-nesting species*

*Plate 9.15 The Purple Sandpiper has a disjunctive, high latitude, circumpolar breeding distribution*

*Plate 9.14 A Little Stint on its nest near the Uboinaya River, north-west Taimyr Peninsula*

*Plate 9.16 The Sharp-tailed Sandpiper inhabits the coastal plain tundra of eastern Siberia from the Lena River eastwards to the vicinity of the Chaun Gulf*

Brent Geese at a colony in the Northwest Territories.

Predation on nesting birds in the Arctic is very variable and in some areas the situation may be quite complex. At Point Barrow, for example, in years when weasels are plentiful and lemmings are in decline, weasels prey heavily on the eggs and young of birds. In some years non-breeding Arctic and Long-tailed Skuas may be sufficiently numerous to reduce substantially the number of young sandpipers fledged (Fitzgerald 1981).

### Breeding Strategies of Some Arctic Waders

Among the best studied of the Arctic-nesting waders are the sandpipers of the subfamily Calidridinae. The social systems of the species concerned fall into four basic patterns, each representing an adaptive strategy evolved primarily in response to the highly variable and unpredictable tundra resources, but also modified through other selective pressures such as predation. This fascinating subject is discussed in detail by Pitelka *et al* (1974).

In a majority (14) of the species, populations are dispersed through a strongly developed territorial system, with strong monogamous pair bonds and only minor yearly fluctuations in numbers. The second pattern is seen in three species in which the female of a pair

may lay two sets of eggs in quick succession, one for each member of the pair to incubate. This opens opportunities for facultative polygyny or polyandry ('serial polygamy') and for the evolutionary weakening of the strong pair bond seen in the first pattern. The third and fourth patterns are those of polygyny (three species) and promiscuity (three species). These six species show clumped dispersions; their year-to-year fluctuations tend to be strong; the males defend compressible, often small, territories; and high densities can occur locally. The species in these four groups are listed in Table 9.5, which also shows the role of the sexes in incubation and the main types of nesting habitat.

It has been suggested that the pattern of overdispersion and monogamy represents a conservative mode of adapting to high-latitude environments, while the pattern of clumped dispersion with polygyny or promiscuity represents an opportunistic mode in that the birds are concentrated into breeding areas where and when weather, food, and/or some other environmental factors are particularly favourable. Apparently falling evolutionarily between these two basic patterns are several species conservative in their life styles, but polygamous at least occasionally and showing some features of opportunism.

**Table 9.5:** Breeding Strategies and Habitats of Some Arctic Nesting Sandpipers

| | Incubating Sex(es) | Territorial and Spacing Patterns of Males | Main Habitat Type |
|---|---|---|---|
| **Group 1.** (Monogamous) | | | |
| Great Knot *Calidris tenuirostris* | M+F | Widely dispersed. | Dry alpine tundra. |
| Knot *Calidris canutus* | M+F | Large territories, males spaced far apart. | Stony, barren polar desert (away from sea and main feeding areas) with scattered vegetation. Nearly all nests near water. |
| Semipalmated Sandpiper *Calidris pusilla* | M+F | Evenly spaced but dense. | Drained tundra near coast and along rivers, damp grassy flats, and bare tundra. |
| Western Sandpiper *Calidris mauri* | M+F | Densely packed. | Slightly raised and well drained ground, ridges and hummocks in marshes. |
| Rufous-necked Sandpiper *Calidris ruficollis* | M+F | No information. | In Siberia, high ground away from flat low tundra. Nests in mossy places with shrubs in areas near dry ridges or rocky debris. |
| Least Sandpiper *Calidris minutilla* | M+F | Evenly spaced. | Mostly Subarctic within treeline, but on Arctic Slope of Alaska breeds locally inland on tussock-heath tundra. |
| Baird's Sandpiper *Calidris bairdii* | M+F | Evenly spaced. | Well-drained microhabitats on wet tundra near coast, and also inland on alpine tundra. |
| Purple Sandpiper *Calidris maritima* | M+F | Dispersed evenly over habitat. | Dry tundra from sea level inland to alpine tundra. |
| Rock Sandpiper *Calidris ptilocnemis* | M+F | Widely dispersed over available habitat. | Mesic tundra with mosses, lichens and dwarf willows on rolling plains and in low mountains. |
| Dunlin *Calidris alpina* | M+F | Large territories. | Various types of tundra. Nests on dry raised areas with lichens, and mossy and grassy tundra. |
| Spoon-billed Sandpiper *Eurynorhynchus pygmeus* | M(+F?) | No information. | Grassy areas near freshwater, and in dry meadows. |
| Broad-billed Sandpiper *Limicola falcinellus* | M+F | Closely tied to small territories. | Wet tundra. Nests in sphagnum moss bogs or grassy swamps with hummocks, away from the coast. |
| Stilt Sandpiper *Micropalama himantopus* | M+F | Pairs spaced. | On most northerly breeding area at 70° N on Victoria Island nests in a variety of habitats from wet tundra with well developed willows to higher and drier slopes. Sometimes nests on dry hummocks in lichen tundra. |
| **Group 2.** (Serially Polygamous) | | | |
| Sanderling *Calidris alba* | M+F | Widely scattered, but dispersion may be clumped. | Nests mostly on alpine lichen tundra. |
| Little Stint *Calidris minuta* | M+F | Widely scattered. | Nests on a variety of tundra habitats near the coast: among dwarf willows by swampy areas, among moss hummocks, and on dry tundra. |
| Timminck's Stint *Calidris temminckii* | M+F | Males on small territories. | Nests usually near water, and inland up to at least 1,000 m a.s.l. on flat ground with sparse vegetation, but also between hummocks. |
| **Group 3.** (Polygnous) | | | |
| White-rumped Sandpiper *Calidris fuscicollis* | F only | Variable-sized territories containing one or more nests and most feeding areas. | Mainly near the coast. Lowland and upland tundra, with nests among grass tussocks or hummocks near water, and sometimes on dry ridges. |
| Sharp-tailed Sandpiper *Calidris acuminata* | F only | Variable-sized territories from 0.9 to 7.1 ha. | Nests in sedge-grass tundra marshes. Selects the wettest habitats of all the *Calidris* sandpipers. |
| Curlew Sandpiper *Calidris ferruginea* | F only | Variable-sized territories with one or more nests and most feeding areas. | Dry moss-lichen tundra, nests on raised areas. At Barrow, nests were located on low mounds among well-developed polygons. |
| **Group 4.** (Promiscuous) | | | |
| Pectoral Sandpiper *Calidris melanotos* | F only | Variable-sized territories, often small and may or may not include nest(s), but include most feeding sites for male. | Ranges from coastal to inland tundra up to at least 550 m a.s.l. Nests in all varieties of tundra providing it is well drained and has continuous cover of grass or sedges. |

| | Incubating Sex(es) | Territorial and Spacing Patterns of Males | Main Habitat Type |
|---|---|---|---|
| Buff-breasted Sandpiper *Tryngites subruficollis* | F only | Groups of 2–10 males on clumped display sites; females feed and nest at variable distances but not on male territories. | Well-drained grassy tundra. |
| Ruff *Philomachus pugnax* | F only | Groups of 2–20 males on traditional display sites; feeding and nesting elsewhere. | Wet marshy tundra with grassy or hummocky vegetation. |

Note: M=male.  F=female.  a.s.l.=above sea level. Source: Partly based on Pitelka *et al* (1974).

On the open tundra the reproductive success among waders depends on effective temporal organisation of incubation effort, which has to contend with low temperatures, unpredictable weather and diurnal temperature cycles. A fairly high level of nest attendance appears to be a necessary attribute of Arctic sandpipers. Studies at Point Barrow by Norton (1972) of the incubation schedules of Semipalmated, Baird's and Pectoral Sandpipers and Dunlin revealed:–

1. A rapid transition from desultory to nearly continuous incubation during the latter part of the egg-laying stage among the two-sex incubators.
2. Nest attentiveness of 85 per cent by female Pectoral; nest attendance of 96.5 per cent by Baird's Sandpiper pairs and 97.5 per cent by Dunlin pairs.
3. A strong diurnal periodicity in incubation parameters of Pectoral Sandpiper, weaker periodicity among Dunlin and Baird's Sandpiper pairs; these rhythms functionally afforded more constant covering of all nests during colder hours of the 'night' despite the continuous daylight at Barrow.
4. Optimisation and synchronisation of hatching time by stimuli largely controlled by adult behaviour just prior to and during hatching.

In some species of the two-sex incubators desertion by one parent occurs at various stages of the breeding cycle. For example, on the Chukotka Peninsula, female Baird's Sandpipers on early nests remain with the chicks for several days, whereas females from late nests leave at or prior to hatching (Myers *et al* 1982). In the case of the Great Knot *Calidris tenuirostris*, the females abandon the nest shortly before hatching and only males have been seen with broods. In at least one species, the Sanderling, different strategies seem to be displayed in different populations. In Greenland, for example, both adults share incubation and care of the young, whilst on Bathurst Island it seems that in favourable years two clutches may be laid, each incubated by one adult (Pienkowski and Green 1976). It is clear that the breeding season available for Arctic-nesting waders is too short for any one adult to be involved in the rearing of more than one clutch.

Both the Red-necked Phalarope *Phalaropus lobatus* and Grey Phalarope are sociable breeders, usually dispersed in small diffuse groups, and with incubation entirely the province of the male. The females of both species are now known to be polyandrous (included in Group 2 above) particularly when there is an excess of males. Polyandry in Grey Phalaropes at Barrow is discussed by Schamel and Tracy (1977).

## The Structure of Tundra Bird Communities

A striking feature of tundra bird communities is the number of wader species, all of which are entirely or primarily insect predators. Most members of the terrestrial avifauna depend on freshwater resources, and these diverse wetland habitats (lakes, pools, marshes, peatbogs) offer abundant food supplies since their productivity is significantly higher than the adjacent tundra or polar desert habitats. The feeding activities of these insectivorous birds serves to bring energy and nutrients from below-ground components of the tundra ecosystem into circulation above ground. A portion of the large nutrient reserves in sub-surface components is thus transferred into avian production and secondarily into vertebrate carnivores.

Even a simple analysis at the order level is adequate to show the dominance of certain groups. Applying such an analysis to the species in Appendix 1, and omitting the marginal Arctic species, reveals three major groupings – Charadriiformes 62 species (43.06 per cent), Passeriformes 35 species (24.31 per cent) and Anseriformes 29 species (20.14 per cent). In practice, however, at many Arctic locations, bird communities are dominated by waders and waterfowl, and passerines are relatively unimportant. This subject is discussed later, but it is worth noting that many passerine species that nest on the tundra are in fact boreal forest or forest-tundra species that reach the tundra habitat via wooded river valleys and are most prominent near the southern edge of the tundra zone.

Terrestrial arthropods play an important part in the ecosystem, and it is noteworthy that most of the waders feed on them while breeding, and this applies even to those species which take marine Crustacea and molluscs when on migration or in their wintering areas. Flies (Chironomidae and Tipulidae) and their larvae are especially important as food resources. The herbivorous birds are represented primarily by geese, ducks and ptarmigan. The place of birds in the tundra ecosystem and their relationship with other components is shown in Figure 9.1, which is based on the terrestrial tundra habitat at Prudhoe Bay in northern Alaska.

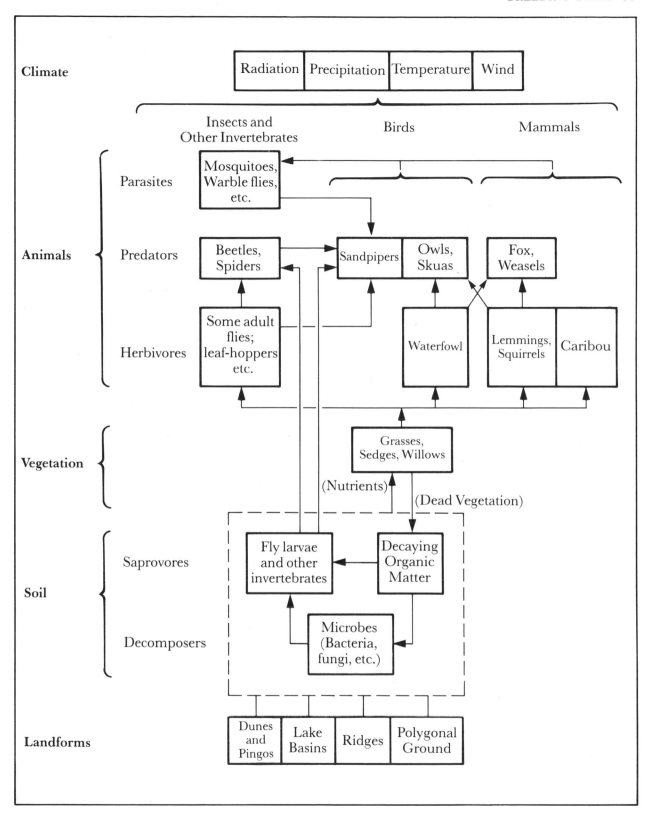

*Figure 9.1: Flow Diagram of Major Components of the Prudhoe Bay,*
*Alaska, Terrestrial Tundra and Their Relationships*
*Source: Brown, Haugen and Parrish (1975).*

Although relatively few bird species breed at the higher latitudes, they nevertheless play a key role. Different species fill the niche of primary consumers, first level carnivores, top carnivores, and scavengers. This is of particular interest when the limited number of vertebrate species is taken into account.

The situation is well illustrated by research carried out at the high latitude location of the Truelove Lowland on Devon Island (76° N). Birds were found to occupy quite specific trophic levels. Primary consumers – Snow Goose and Rock Ptarmigan – had a biomass of 1 kg km$^{-2}$; secondary consumers – the ducks, waders and buntings – together provided 8.2 kg km$^{-2}$; tertiary consumers – Red-throated Diver, skuas and terns – amounted to 4.9 kg km$^{-2}$, and finally the quaternary consumers – Peregrine Falcon *Falco peregrinus* and Snowy Owl – contributed 0.04 kg km$^{-2}$. In addition, scavenging gulls and Ravens amounted to 2.4 kg km$^{-2}$, giving the entire lowland 16.5 kg km$^{-2}$ (Pattie 1977).

Only a few avian predators of small mammals breed regularly in tundra ecosystems, and those that do are migratory and particularly dependent upon small mammal populations during the breeding season. Once they have nested, their food supply must be gathered relatively close to the nest (Batzli 1975). Some of the species concerned, notably the skuas, were mentioned in the previous section, and to these can be added the Snowy Owl and the Short-eared Owl *Asio flammeus*.

The factors making insectivory a feasible strategy for breeding birds at Barrow appear to be the unusual proportion of primary production entering the litter category susceptible to consumption by saprovores, the consequent high standing crops of larval saprovores, and the interdigitation of moist and dry tundra on a fine scale that permits birds to select from radically different feeding habitats within short distances. Prudhoe Bay tundra differs from that of Barrow in lacking the extreme variability of microrelief and moisture over short distances. Nevertheless, tundra resource use by terrestrial birds at the latter location is essentially similar in pattern to that at Barrow, despite differences in species composition and density (Norton *et al* 1975).

Of the 34 known or suspected breeding species at Prudhoe Bay, only 12 (35 per cent) regularly use primarily terrestrial resources to support breeding, and waders dominate this group (7 of 9 species or 78 per cent, excluding the suspected breeding species). At Barrow only 22 species breed regularly and 11 of these (50 per cent) utilise primarily terrestrial resources when breeding. Waders again dominate this group (9 of 11 species or 82 per cent). Data given by Norton (1973) in his studies of waders at Barrow were used to estimate that insectivorous species there ingest some $4 \times 10^5$ kcal km$^{-2}$ yr$^{-1}$ from the tundra arthropod resources. A similar estimate for Prudhoe Bay was somewhat lower at 75 per cent of the Barrow system. The comparable figure for the Truelove Lowland, Devon Island (where only three insectivorous species are present) is $6 \times 10^4$ kcal km$^{-2}$ yr$^{-1}$ (Norton *et al* 1975).

Plate 9.17 *A Curlew Sandpiper on its nest on the north-west Taimyr Peninsula*

Plate 9.18 *A Red-necked Phalarope on its nest in northern Alaska*

Plate 9.19 *Female Grey Phalaropes on a tundra pool in northern Alaska*

Some Arctic locations have breeding bird communities dominated by passerines. One such example is the Sarqaqdalen area of north-west Greenland (70° N) where, in July 1965, eight species were recorded of which four passerines – Lapland Bunting, Snow Bunting, Wheatear and Redpoll – comprised 88 per cent of the total community, and the Lapland Bunting alone accounted for half of all pairs (Joensen and Preuss 1972). For a similar type of habitat at 67° N on Baffin Island, Watson (1963) recorded five pas-

*Plate 9.20 A Stilt Sandpiper at its nest on Jenny Lind Island in the Canadian Arctic*

*Plate 9.21 A Least Sandpiper on its nest on the Canadian tundra*

*Plate 9.22 Large numbers of Snow Geese breed in the Canadian and Soviet Arctic*

serine species of which Lapland Bunting (61 per cent) and Snow Bunting (22 per cent) made up the greater part of the total bird population.

## Nesting Densities in Arctic Habitats

The carrying capacity of many habitats exhibits marked seasonal variations, and the Arctic is an extreme example. The absolute numbers of birds present in some Arctic habitats may be enormous, particu-

larly during the post-breeding and migration periods. For example, despite the low breeding densities of some species, large numbers of waterfowl and waders annually use the Arctic Coastal Plain of Alaska. Surveys of the coastal plain (excluding the western foothills) in the early 1970s gave rough estimates of minimum pre-breeding populations of $11 \times 10^6$ birds. These included 170,000 geese, 200,000–500,000 dabbling ducks, $1 \times 10^6$ to $2 \times 10^6$ scabirds, $5.5 \times 10^6$ waders, and $2.75 \times 10^6$ passerines (Arctic Institute of North America 1974). Aerial surveys of 94,697 km$^2$ of the Arctic Coastal Plain in July 1977 and 1978 gave estimated populations of $5.4 \times 10^6$ and $4.9 \times 10^6$ waterbirds respectively. Waders represented 91 per cent of the total in 1977 and 93 per cent in 1978 (King 1979). Waterfowl densities in the inshore waters (within 8 km of the coast) of the Beaufort Sea exceed mainland densities. Densities have been known to range from 41.3 to 530.9 ducks km$^{-2}$, with a mean of 167.9 ducks km$^{-2}$. These were mainly Long-tailed Ducks and eiders (Bartels 1973).

Not surprisingly, extreme examples of high nesting density are found in colonial birds such as the waterfowl (and seabirds – discussed later), and one or two examples will serve to illustrate this point. Nesting density in the main Lesser Snow Goose colony on Wrangel Island fluctuates within very wide limits. It depends both on relief and exposure, which determine when the snow melts, and on the condition of the grass. The nesting density in 1964, a year when the spring weather was extremely unfavourable for reproduction, is shown in Table 9.6, together with some comparative data from other areas. Obviously nesting density may vary in different areas at one location. For example, in the case of Wrangel Island in 1964 the mean number of nests km$^{-2}$ varied from 1,200 to 6,400.

The average density of breeding White-fronted Geese on Wrangel Island is given by Uspenskii (1984) as 2,000–5,000 nests km$^{-2}$. This species is not, however, normally a colonial nester and these figures probably represent an exceptional situation. On the Arctic Coastal Plain of northern Alaska, mean seasonal densities of breeding White-fronted Geese varied from 0.7 birds km$^{-2}$ at Meade River near the Beaufort Sea, to 2.7 birds km$^{-2}$ at Singiluk 138 km inland (Derksen *et al* 1981). East of Point Barrow small colonies of 23–30 pairs km$^{-2}$ have been recorded.

Nesting Common Eiders vary within wide limits in the degree of clumping. Individual nests may be several hundred metres apart, or less than one metre. On Eskjer Island, west Svalbard, in 1967 there was a nesting density of 1,000+ pairs on 0.3 ha, equivalent to $3.3 \times 10^5$ nests km$^{-1}$ (Ahlen and Andersson 1970). Ground surveys on part of Alaska's Arctic Coastal Plain estimated breeding duck densities at 8.9 to 19.2 birds km$^{-2}$ in 1977 and 9.8 to 11.7 birds km$^{-2}$ in 1978 (Derksen *et al* 1981).

Generally speaking, the density of breeding waders is very clearly related to habitat-type, topography and snow conditions. Some species achieve quite high densities in optimum habitats. Baird's Sandpiper pro-

**Table 9.6:** Snow Goose *Anser caerulescens* Nesting Densities at Selected Arctic Localities

| Location | Year | Total Area Surveyed (km²) | Approximate No. of Nests | Mean Nest Density km⁻² |
|---|---|---|---|---|
| Wrangel Island | 1964 | 37.0 | 114,200 | 3,086 |
| Baffin Island | | | | |
|   Bowman Bay | 1973 | 193.7 | 91,900 | 474 |
| Banks Island | | | | |
|   Egg River | 1976 | 605.3 | 82,511 | 136 |
| Hudson Bay (West) | | | | |
|   McConnell River | 1973 | 249.4 | 163,000 | 654 |
|   Wolf Creek | 1973 | 60.1 | 22,500 | 374 |
| Southampton Island | | | | |
|   Boas River | 1973 | 384.0 | 64,800 | 169 |
|   Bear Cove | 1973 | 1.6 | 400 | 250 |

Sources: Kerbes (1975 and 1983) and Uspenskii (1965).

**Table 9.7:** Breeding Densities of Baird's Sandpiper *Calidris bairdii* at Selected Arctic Locations

| Locality | Year | Pairs km⁻² | Source |
|---|---|---|---|
| Uelen, Chukotka Peninsula, Soviet Union | ? | 0.14–0.28 | Myers *et al* 1982 |
| Barrow, NW Alaska | 1971–72 | 24.8 | Norton 1973 |
| Sarcpa Lake, Melville Peninsula, Canada | 1981–82 | 3.8 | Montgomerie *et al* 1983 |
| Bylot Island, Canada | 1954 | 10.0 | Freedman & Svoboda 1982 |
| Alexandra Fjord, Ellesmere Island, Canada | 1980–81 | 0.8–1.0 | Freedman & Svoboda 1982 |
| Truelove Lowland, Devon Island, Canada | 1970–73 | 0.5 | Freedman & Svoboda 1982 |

**Table 9.8:** Breeding Densities of Five Species of Wader in North-east Greenland Expressed as Pairs km⁻²

| Locality | Year | Study Area (km²) | Ringed Plover *Charadrius hiaticula* | Knot *Calidris canutus* | Sanderling *Calidris alba* | Dunlin *Calidris alpina* | Turnstone *Arenaria interpres* |
|---|---|---|---|---|---|---|---|
| Denmarkshavn | 1969 | 7.6 | 6.9 | — | 1.8 | 3.03 | 1.84 |
| | 1969 | 7.6 | 2.76 | — | 2.04 | 2.37 | 2.24 |
| | 1975 | 4.49 | 4.7–4.9 | 2.2 | 2.9–3.3 | 4.0–4.5 | 3.8 |
| Hochstetten Forland | 1976 | 20.0 | 0.35 | 0.01 | 1.5–2.0 | 0.95 | 1.80 |
| Kong Oscars Fjord | 1974 | 133.0 | 0.85 | 0.11 | 0.27 | 0.43 | 0.26 |
| Pearyland | 1973 | 8.6 | 0.58 | — | 0.70 | — | 0.93 |

Sources: Green (1978) and Meltofte (1979).

vides a good example and, as can be seen from Table 9.7, high densities are found at Barrow, where suitable habitat (e.g. dry polygon ridges) is widespread.

A great deal of research on wader ecology has been carried out in Greenland as a result of which there is a lot of data concerning breeding density. The breeding densities of five species of wader are shown in Table 9.8 and, as can be seen, there is considerable variation within and between species. In the case of north-east Greenland, it was found that nearly all wader territories are located on ground less than 200 m above sea level and mostly below 100 m. This distribution is dictated by the topography of steep-sided, U-shaped valleys dissecting rugged mountainous country with many snow-fields and glaciers. Waders breed in the valleys and on other low ground because these are the only near-barren areas from which the snow clears early enough in the year. As Table 9.8 shows, populations are generally sparse, and all species show localised pockets of dense population related to the location of suitable habitat and the date of spring melt-off (Green 1978).

The Lake Hazen area at 82° N on Ellesmere Island is a classic example of an oasis in a polar desert habitat. It has about 115 species of vascular plants, an unusually rich flora for this latitude. The flora is localised in relatively mild fjords and valleys. Wader studies here in 1966 showed densities of 1.09 pairs km$^{-2}$ for the Knot and 3.04 pairs km$^{-2}$ for the Turnstone (Nettleship 1973 and 1974). Comparing these figures with Table 9.8 shows that these densities are higher for both species than is the case in north-east Greenland with the exception of 1975. It may be noted that 1975 was a good year for breeding birds in the High Arctic generally.

Two Arctic-breeding waders for which very few population data are available are the Rufous-necked Sandpiper *Calidris ruficollis* and the Rock Sandpiper *C. ptilocnemis*. Near Uelen, on the Chukotka Peninsula in the Soviet Union, Rufous-necked Sandpiper densities in favourable habitats usually range from 4 to 6 pairs km$^{-2}$ but can rise locally to 28 pairs km$^{-2}$. Up to 12 pairs km$^{-2}$ have been recorded for the Rock Sandpiper in the same area (Myers *et al* 1982).

The breeding density of a species may vary considerably at a given locality from year to year. For example, at Sarcpa Lake on the Melville Peninsula, the density of Lesser Golden Plovers varied from 65 pairs km$^{-2}$ in 1981 to 35 pairs km$^{-2}$ in 1982, a decrease of 45 per cent. The decrease was attributed to the late spring melt-off in 1982 which apparently prevented many pairs from breeding that year (Montgomerie *et al* 1983).

Data on bird of prey densities in the Arctic includes that by Hansen (1979) on the White-tailed Eagle *Haliaeetus albicilla* in south-west Greenland from 1972 to 1974. The maximum density of breeding birds was 0.58 pairs 100 km$^{-2}$, and in two other areas densities of 0.35 and 0.30 pairs 100 km$^{-2}$ were recorded. The overall breeding density was 0.37 breeding pairs 100 km$^{-2}$. In the case of the Peregrine in west Greenland, an area of 1813 km² was studied in 1972 and 2330 km² in 1973 (Burnham *et al* 1974): in 1972 eight pairs were located giving a density of one eyrie 227 km$^{-2}$, while in 1973 ten eyries were located giving a density of one eyrie 233 km$^{-2}$. About 388 km² of unsuitable Peregrine habitat were included in the 1973 survey area, and excluding this from the calculations gives a density of one eyrie 194 km$^{-2}$. In 1970, a year of peak lemming population on Southampton Island, eleven nests of Snowy Owl were found in an area of approximately 250 km², giving a density of one nest 22 km$^{-2}$; the following year no Snowy Owls were present at all (Parker 1974).

A certain amount of data on the breeding densities of the most characteristic Arctic passerines are available, and some are summarised in Table 9.9. The Lapland

Bunting reaches the highest densities of any Arctic passerine. At Barrow, Alaska, densities reached 250–400 territories km$^{-2}$ (Pitelka 1971), but in subsequent years declined to the 12–15 km$^{-2}$ shown in Table 9.9. Densities on a 16-ha plot of beach ridge habitat averaged 75 pairs km$^{-2}$ (range 50–95 pairs) over the period 1951–1969. Population fluctuations in this species are widespread, as evidenced by the 80 per cent decline in numbers between 1967 and 1968 on the Truelove Lowland (Hussell and Holroyd 1974). The mean density of 46 pairs km$^{-2}$ for Eqabingmiut Nunat, west Greenland, given in Table 9.9 masks pockets of much higher densities in areas of particularly favourable habitat – 64 pairs km$^{-2}$ on north-facing heath/herb slopes, and 128 pairs km$^{-2}$ in dense scrub on south-facing slopes.

Snow Bunting densities apparently never reach those achieved by the Lapland Bunting, and are sometimes very low indeed – for example, 1.1 pairs km$^{-2}$ at Lake Hazen (Savile and Oliver 1964), 1.2 pairs km$^{-2}$ on Ellef Ringnes Island (Savile 1961), and 1.5 pairs km$^{-2}$ on the Foxe Peninsula (Macpherson and McLaren 1959). The highest densities recorded for this species anywhere in the Arctic are 11–13 pairs km$^{-2}$ in north-west Greenland and 11 pairs km$^{-2}$ on the Truelove Lowland (Table 9.9). The breeding density of the Snow Bunting would appear to be largely controlled by the availability of suitable nest cavities.

There have been a number of studies on total population densities of Arctic breeding birds in tundra habitats. There is a certain degree of correlation between the total density of breeding species and latitude,

*Plate 9.23 A White-tailed Eagle photographed near its eyrie in Greenland*

in that density in general decreases the further north one goes. There are, however, as we have already seen, some exceptions to this rule due to the localised occurrence of sites of high primary production and diversity amidst large regions of unproductive polar desert or semi-desert habitats. Data on total breeding bird densities from 25 Arctic localities are presented in Table 9.10, which also shows the number of different breeding species on each study area.

## Marine Birds – A General Discussion

While in the higher latitudes the land provides relatively little in the way of food, the seas can support dense concentrations of animal plankton in the summer when the small planktonic plants on which they feed multiply. There is a clear relationship between the water regime and its productivity, and the distribution of breeding colonies of those marine bird species that live on benthos. A good example of this concerns the Common Eider in the Soviet Arctic where the largest colonies are concentrated on the western coast of the southern island of Novaya Zemlya, the coastal waters of which have the highest index of the biomass of benthos.

The inhabitants of the Arctic marine zone depend upon the marine resources, but because of the rigorous environment the diversity of marine bird species is low. However, because of the scarcity of suitable nesting sites associated with an abundance of nearby food, these few species together comprise enormous populations and may form huge colonies. In large parts of the Arctic, about 95 per cent of the breeding birds consists of only four species – Northern Fulmar *Fulmarus*

*Plate 9.24 On the Chukotka Peninsula the Rock Sandpiper breeds on mesic tundra, usually within 13 km of the coast*

*Plate 9.25 In Siberia the Rufous-necked Sandpiper breeds on high ground on the Chukotka Peninsula*

**Table 9.9:** Breeding Densities of Four Passerine Species at Selected Arctic Localities Expressed as Pairs km$^{-2}$

| Locality | Year | Study Area (ha) | Lapland Bunting *Calcarius lapponicus* | Snow Bunting *Plectrophenax nivalis* | Wheatear *Oenanthe oenanthe* | Horned Lark *Eremophila alpestris* |
|---|---|---|---|---|---|---|
| Sarqaqdalen, NW Greenland | 1965 | 152 | 29.6–36.8 | 11.2–13.2 | 7.2–7.9 | — |
| Eqalungmiut Nunat, west Greenland | 1979 | 57 | 45.6 | — | — | — |
| Truelove Lowland, Devon Island | 1972 | 3,300 | 4.7 | 10.6 | — | — |
| Sarcpa Lake, Melville Peninsula | 1981 | 1,300 | 10.0 | 7.7 | — | 4.6 |
|  | 1982 |  | 15.4 | 7.7 | — | 4.6 |
| Penny Highland, Cumberland Peninsula, Baffin Island | 1953 | 260 | 38.1 | 14.6 | — | 1.1 |
| Barrow, Alaska | 1968 | 17 | 88.2 | — | — | — |
|  | 1972 |  | 11.8 | — | — | — |
|  | 1972 | 25 | 24.0 | — | — | — |
|  | 1973 |  | 32.0 | — | — | — |

Sources: Custer and Pitelka (1977), Fowles *et al* (1981), Joensen and Preuss (1972), Montgomerie *et al* (1983), Pattie (1977) and Watson (1963).

*Plate 9.26 A Knot on its nest on Ellesmere Island in the Canadian High Arctic*

*Plate 9.27 This picture of a Knot incubating in the snow illustrates the harsh conditions that can be experienced by Arctic-breeding waders*

*glacialis*, Kittiwake, Brünnich's Guillemot and Little Auk *Alle alle*. Among Arctic seabirds it is probably the Alcidae (auks) that are ecologically the best adapted. Their arrival on the breeding grounds, for example, is well synchronised with the break-up of winter ice, snow-melt on the breeding sites and a rapid increase in biological production in the sea, due to improved light conditions. When the young are hatched in July, the coastal waters are full of zooplankton and small fishes, the basic food of all auks.

Obviously, those species nesting in large concentrated colonies are the more dependent on the hydrological regime and the biological productivity of the waters. In the case of the Little Auk, the colonies are situated close to the summer rim of the pack-ice, that is to say in the region of massive growth of the mesoplankton (e.g. Copepoda, Amphipoda, Schizopoda and other species) required by the birds. It has been estimated that a colony of 100,000 pairs of Little Auks transports about 71 tonnes of zooplankton to the colony during four weeks of summer (Norderhaug 1980).

In the Arctic seas are currents differing greatly in temperature and salinity and, as discussed in Chapter 4, the areas of turbulence and upwelling where these meet are always suitable feeding areas for large numbers of seabirds. Zones of high productivity occur at the face of glaciers. Here, fresh water produced by the ice, or the streams which flow from it during the summer, meet the warmer saline seawater, thus creating ideal conditions for high planktonic productivity. More than 2,000 Kittiwakes (as well as other species) have been recorded near the snout of a glacier in west Svalbard, feeding mainly on the crustacean *Thysanoessa inermis* which is abundant in these waters. In the Siberian seas,

**Table 9.10:** Total Breeding Bird Densities on Arctic Tundra Habitats Listed in Order of Increasing Latitude

| Locality | Latitude | Year | Census Area (ha) | Habitat | Density (pairs km⁻²) | Total No. of breeding species |
|---|---|---|---|---|---|---|
| Chesterfield Inlet, Northwest Territories | 63 | 1950 | 1,025 | Rock, sedge, lichen, heath | 60 | 39 |
| Frobisher Bay, Northwest Territories | 63 | 1965 | 72 | Heath, sedge, meadow | 20 | ? |
| Foxe Peninsula, Baffin Island | 64 | 1955 | 5,180 | Coastal, little vegetation | 10 | 14 |
| Bowman Bay, Baffin Island (a) | 65 | 1929 | 256 | Grass, with rocks | 55 | ? |
| (b) | | 1929 | 320 | Grass, with rocks, near river | 165 | ? |
| (c) | | 1929 | 256 | Grass, with rocks, near river | 77 | ? |
| Cumberland Peninsula, Baffin Island | 67 | 1953 | 260 | Damp grassy plain, dry heath and rocks | 62 | 27 |
| Sarcpa Lake, Melville Peninsula | 68 | 1981–82 | 1,300 | Fell-field, marsh, vegetated meadows | 35 | 22 |
| Mackenzie delta (a) | 69 | 1973 | 25 | Hilly upland with alder and cottongrass | 168 ⎫ | |
| (b) | | 1973 | 25 | River escarpment with floodplain and upland | 207 ⎬ | 87[a] |
| (c) | | 1973 | 25 | River floodplain with sedge and low willow | 119 ⎭ | |
| Babbage River, Yukon Territory (a) | 69 | 1973 | 40 | Dry sedge, herbs on ridges | 198 | 17 |

$km^{-2}$

| Locality | Latitude | Year | Census Area (ha) | Habitat | Density (pairs km⁻²) | Total No. of breeding species |
|---|---|---|---|---|---|---|
| Babbage River, Yukon Territory (b) | | 1972 | 32 | Sedge, grass meadows | 155 | 14 |
| Prudhoe Bay, Alaska | 69 | 1979 | 100 | Inland coastal tundra | 72 | 18 |
| Firth River, Yukon Territory | 70 | 1972 | 32 | Sedge meadow near coast | 127 | 14 |
| Sarqaqdalen, NW Greenland | 70 | 1965 | 152 | Sedge-marsh and dry upland tundra | 64 | 8 |
| Deadhorse, Alaska | 71 | 1979 | 100 | Wet coastal plain tundra | 126 | 13 |
| Barrow, Alaska | 71 | 1979 | 35 | Wet coastal plain tundra | 52 | 17 |
| Bylot Island, Northwest Territories | 73 | 1954 | 256 | Mosses, sedge, heath | 33 | 52 |
| Truelove Lowland, Devon Island | 74 | 1970–73 | 4,300 | High Arctic lowland oasis | 10.3 | 22 |
| Polar Bear Pass, Bathurst Island | 75 | 1970–73 | 100 | Lowland sedge-moss meadow | 11.75 | >8 |
| | 75 | 1970–73 | 100 | Dry upland saxifrage semi-desert | 4.25 | >7 |
| Isachsen, Ellef Ringnes Island | 79 | 1960 | 3,800 | Largely unvegetated | 2 | ? |
| Alexandra Fjord, Ellesmere Island | 79 | 1980 | 1,200 | High Arctic lowland oasis | 13.3 | 10 |
| Lake Hazen, Ellesmere Island | 82 | 1962 | 2,227 | Largely unvegetated | 4.9 | 17 |

Note: a. Total number of breeding species for the Mackenzie delta as a whole.
Sources: Freedman and Svoboda (1982), Joensen and Preuss (1972), Mayfield (1983), Montgomerie *et al* (1983) and Velzen (1980).

*Plate 9.28 A male Lapland Bunting at the nest*

relatively small colonies of seabirds are unevenly distributed and confined mostly to estuarine areas.

### The Importance of Pack-ice

The sea-ice of the Arctic clearly has a variety of effects on seabirds, particularly in lowering biological productivity and densities of birds in the areas it covers. Prey abundance in inshore areas is reduced as a result of ice-scour. The great extent of the pack-ice, even in summer, reduces the surface area of open water available for feeding and roosting. One important benefit that the sea-ice does provide to seabirds is the in-ice plankton bloom and its associated under-ice fauna, although our understanding of the full significance of this is incomplete. It is probably most important in those areas, such as the Beaufort Sea, where productivity in the water column is low.

Whilst considerable numbers of seabirds are regularly to be found in the summer pack-ice feeding on Arctic Cod *Boreogadus saida* and zooplankton associated with the ice, only the Ross's Gull, Ivory Gull and Black Guillemot *Cepphus grylle* have specific adaptations to the ice environment and depend on the ice-associated fauna for much of their food.

There are other aspects of the important role of the sea-ice. For example, for the young of species such as Brünnich's Guillemot which abandon the nesting ledges while still unable to fly, the ice zone around the coasts represents an essentially unsurmountable barrier. This helps to explain why the breeding colonies of such species (even though the adults can feed in open leads in the ice) are located to the south of the summer rim not only of the pack-ice, but also more often of floating ice. Other colonial seabirds, such as the Her-

*Plate 9.29 A Black Guillemot in breeding plumage*

*Plate 9.30 Little Auks at a breeding site in Svalbard*

ring Gull, Kittiwake and Little Auk, are able to breed under much heavier ice conditions since their young leave the colonies fully developed and capable of flying over extensive areas of coastal ice.

The location of winter concentrations of seabirds is also primarily determined by the ice regime since this controls the presence of open water. For this reason, as well as the high biological productivity of the water, an important area for wintering seabirds is situated by the ice-edge in the Barents Sea and just to the south of it. Here may be seen enormous numbers of Herring and Glaucous Gulls, Brünnich's Guillemots and Little Auks, while Northern Fulmars and Kittiwakes also occur in significant numbers. In the shallower waters Common Eiders, King Eiders and Long-tailed Ducks spend the winter.

### The Importance of Polynas

Polynas were discussed briefly in Chapter 4, and it may safely be assumed that the network of Arctic polynas is important for the wintering of birds in high latitudes. It is probable that the vast majority of Ross's Gulls winter in their vicinity, as for example at the Velikaya Sibirskaya polyna in the Soviet Arctic. Regular winter concentrations of birds occur in polynas north of the pack-ice rim. The vicinity of the northern extremity of Novaya Zemlya, for example, supports wintering populations of Brünnich's Guillemots, Little Auks and Long-tailed Ducks.

Polynas in the Canadian Arctic, including the huge North Water polyna, are discussed in detail by Stirling and Cleator (1981). With the exception of the recurring lead systems in Hudson Bay and Hudson Strait, polynas are not used extensively by over-wintering seaducks in the Canadian Arctic since most winter south of the ice-covered waters. Three species of sea-duck predominate in the Canadian Arctic – Common Eider, King Eider and Long-tailed Duck. Although there are more Common Eider in the area during winter than the other two species combined, most recurring polynas, with the exception of the North Water, are too small to support significant numbers. Some polynas, however, especially those in the western and central Arctic, are important as staging areas prior

to the breeding season. The Cape Bathurst polyna and associated leads are a particularly critical staging area for birds moving east into the central Arctic and south-east into Queen Maud Gulf. The open water of Cape Bathurst polyna and shoreleads occurs over depths shallow enough to permit feeding until nesting areas further north and east are free of snow and ice. Flocks exceeding 50,000 birds have been recorded in the polyna in May (Searing *et al* 1975, Barry 1976).

Polynas are also found off the coasts of Greenland and the most important of these is the West Greenland polyna. It is extremely important in the migratory movements of various populations of Brünnich's Guillemot. This species also winters in the polyna as does the Guillemot *Uria aalge* and it is also an important wintering area for Little Auks from Svalbard, and for the west Greenland populations of Great Cormorants *Phalacrocorax carbo*, Iceland *Larus glaucoides*, Glaucous and Great Black-backed Gulls *L. marinus*.

There is a good correlation between the siting of Arctic seabird colonies and the presence of polynas. The Nørdosvandet polyna within the East Greenland Current stretches south along the east coast from Nordosrundingen, the north-easternmost point of Greenland. This polyna was found to be an isolated northern breeding enclave for the Northern Fulmar by the Danmark Expedition 1906–8, which also noted pre-breeding congregations of King Eider (Hjort *et al* 1983). All the colonies of Northern Fulmar and Brünnich's Guillemot in Arctic Canada and west Greenland are on coasts adjacent to polynas, or to waters covered with unconsolidated pack-ice during the winter. The breeding range of the Little Auk also illustrates the importance of polynas to a High Arctic seabird, in that throughout the entire Arctic all major colonies are beside waters that either never freeze over completely (Thule District in Greenland, west Svalbard, Jan Mayen and Bear Island), or that are more or less ice-free by the time the young hatch in July (Scoresby Sound, northern Novaya Zemlya, Franz Josef Land and Severnaya Zemlya).

### Resource Partitioning

Generally speaking, Arctic seabirds obtain all their

*Plate 9.31 The Turnstone breeds as far north in the Arctic as land extends*

food from the sea but a few, such as the Glaucous Gull and some less polar gulls, make up their diets with a substantial proportion obtained on land. The principal prey items of Arctic seabirds are fish, molluscs and crustaceans. Fish are taken by most species, but principally by guillemots and the Razorbill *Alca torda* which feed on them almost exclusively (up to 95 per cent in the case of Brünnich's Guillemot), and also by most large gulls, the Kittiwake and Arctic Tern.

Molluscs are preyed on by the Black Guillemot (up to about 20 per cent of the diet), Glaucous Gull and Arctic Tern. The Northern Fulmar takes a high proportion of pelagic species, while littoral species are the staple diet of the Common Eider. Pelagic crustaceans are the principal prey of the Little Auk and also form a not unimportant proportion of the diets of Northern Fulmar, Black Guillemot (up to some 20 per cent), and Arctic Tern. Littoral zone species are taken by Common Eider and Glaucous Gulls (up to about 30 per cent of the diet).

While each species tends to specialise in a well-defined sector, these seabird species between them exploit the whole expanse of the Arctic seas. Northern Fulmars and Little Auks feed in the open seas, even during the breeding season, while other species such as the Kittiwake, become pelagic in habit only during the winter. Other species feed in the littoral and inshore zones at distances from the coast which vary according to species and season, but disperse further afield for the winter.

Having discussed the use of marine food resources by Arctic seabirds in general terms it is instructive to take a more detailed look at one particular area. Lan-

caster Sound is critical to the reproduction and survival of a large proportion of the total seabird community in the Canadian High Arctic. Several million seabirds reproduce and spend the summer in this area, and are dependent upon its productivity to meet their energy requirements for growth, reproduction and maintenance. The Northern Fulmar, Glaucous Gull, Kittiwake, Brünnich's Guillemot and Black Guillemot are the principal species. These, together with much lesser numbers of Thayer's *Larus thayeri* and Ivory Gulls, and Arctic Tern, have an estimated total breeding population in Lancaster Sound of 806,650 pairs (Gaston and Nettleship 1981).

As well as the small number of seabird species in Lancaster Sound, there are also relatively few species of fish (only about 30 have been recorded), of which the Arctic Cod is the most important both in numbers and biomass. It is the main food of three of the eight seabird species, and only a little less important in the diet of the Black Guillemot. Arctic Cod *Boreogadus saida* apparently feed on phytoplankton that live on the undersurface of sea-ice, and in Lancaster Sound they hold a dominant position at the intermediate trophic level (Figure 9.2). In practice this means that the greater part of biological production in Lancaster Sound that reaches the top of the food pyramid is channelled through this one species, giving it a pivotal role in the entire marine ecosystem. Since Lancaster Sound is exceptional for its low diversity of species, the situation there cannot be extrapolated to elsewhere in the Arctic, but it is an interesting example of a simple food web in a High Arctic location.

*Plate 9.32 Brünnich's Guillemot—one of the most numerous auks in the Arctic*

*Plate 9.33 Cliffs at Ørsted Dal, Greenland, a breeding site of the Barnacle Goose*

### Connections Across the Land-Marine Boundary

The transfer of nutrients between land and sea generally proceeds in only one direction, with the products of organic processes on land finding their way into rivers which carry them eventually to the sea. Movement in the reverse direction is less common, but seabirds transporting organic material from sea to land are a vital link between the two ecosystems, and waste from seabird colonies is an important source of nutrients to Arctic terrestrial ecosystems, as demonstrated by the rich vegetation beneath the colonies. In turn this vegetation forms the basis for other terrestrial organisms like insects, land birds and various mammals

Seabirds introduce organic nutrients into terrestrial

*Plate 9.34 A Barnacle Goose at its cliff-nesting site in Greenland*

ecosystems in several ways:–

1. Seabird excreta is deposited on their breeding ledges; after drying out, it is transported inland by strong winds, hence fertilising the vegetation.
2. Eggs, chicks, and adults eaten or cached by terrestrial predators such as foxes, falcons, and Ravens, become incorporated into the terrestrial food web.
3. Food obtained from the sea and brought to the colony, either to feed nestlings, in courtship, or for adult consumption, may be discarded, again being incorporated into the food web of the land.

This subject was studied in the course of research on Brünnich's Guillemot in the Digges Sound area of Hudson Strait (Gaston *et al* 1985) and provides a useful illustration. Six trophic levels were identified in the marine food chain which can be summarised as:–

1. Primary producers: the phytoplankton and large benthic algae →
2. Herbivorous zooplankton: e.g. Copepods, *Limacina*
3. Carnivorous zooplankton: e.g. *Parathemis-libellula*, *Sigitta* →
4. Small fish feeding on the larger zooplankton →
5. Fish-eating seabirds and marine mammals →
6. Top carnivores: e.g. Polar Bear, Gyrfalcon, Glaucous Gull, Red Fox.

The terrestrial food chain on East Digges Island consists of only three levels:–

1. Primary producers: green plants
2. Herbivores: e.g. lemmings, geese, ptarmigan
3. Carnivores: foxes, Ravens, and falcons.

This food web, centred on the Brünnich's Guillemot colony at Digges Sound, is illustrated in Figure 9.3 which shows the connections across the marine-terrestrial boundary. The difference in the length of the marine and terrestrial food chains is related to the size of the primary producers.

## Selected Species Accounts

The discussion here follows the sequence of orders as listed in Appendix 1 and the treatment of species is, of necessity, highly selective and concentrates mainly on distribution, population levels and certain aspects of the ecology of the species concerned.

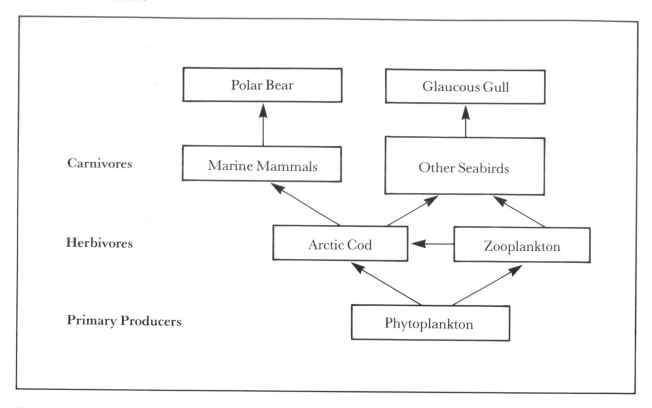

*Figure 9.2: The Position of Arctic Cod* Boreogadus saida *in the Lancaster Sound Ecosystem*
*Source: Gaston and Nettleship (1981).*

### Gaviiformes

The most essentially Arctic of the four breeding species is the White-billed Diver *Gavia adamsii*. In the breeding season it is found along the littoral of the Arctic Ocean within the tundra zone and nests almost exclusively north of the treeline. Even at the present time its detailed distribution is unclear and there is little data on population levels. The only two areas where it may be said to be fairly common are north-east Siberia and Arctic Canada. There is still a paucity of information on habitat requirements, although it has been reasonably well studied in Arctic Alaska (Sage 1971), where it has been found nesting close to the coast (in the Colville delta) and at least 174 km inland up to an altitude of 425 m. Two breeding lakes studied by Sage were about 18 ha and 43 ha in extent, both with a maximum depth of 3 m. In their studies on the Arctic Coastal Plain, Derksen *et al* (1981) found it the least abundant of the three breeding species of diver, and several nests found in the Colville delta in 1976 were all on deep, open lakes with abrupt shores.

### Procellariiformes

The only representative of this order breeding in the Arctic is the Northern Fulmar. Its total population is considerable and it is an important component of the marine ecosystem, breeding as far north as there is open water (north of 80° N in north-east Greenland). In the Barents Sea region it is most abundant in Sval-

*Plate 9.35 Within its Arctic breeding range the White-billed Diver is nowhere numerous*

bard, although numbers there appear to have decreased since the cessation of whaling. It breeds as far east as Franz Josef Land and the northern island of Novaya Zemlya, and also in the Canadian Arctic, western Greenland and on Jan Mayen. Despite the considerable amount of census work on seabirds that has been carried out in the Arctic it is still not possible to give an accurate figure for the breeding population of the area as a whole, although fairly good data are available for some sectors. According to Evans (1984a) the total for Greenland is probably about 200,000–400,000 pairs. The population in Baffin Bay is

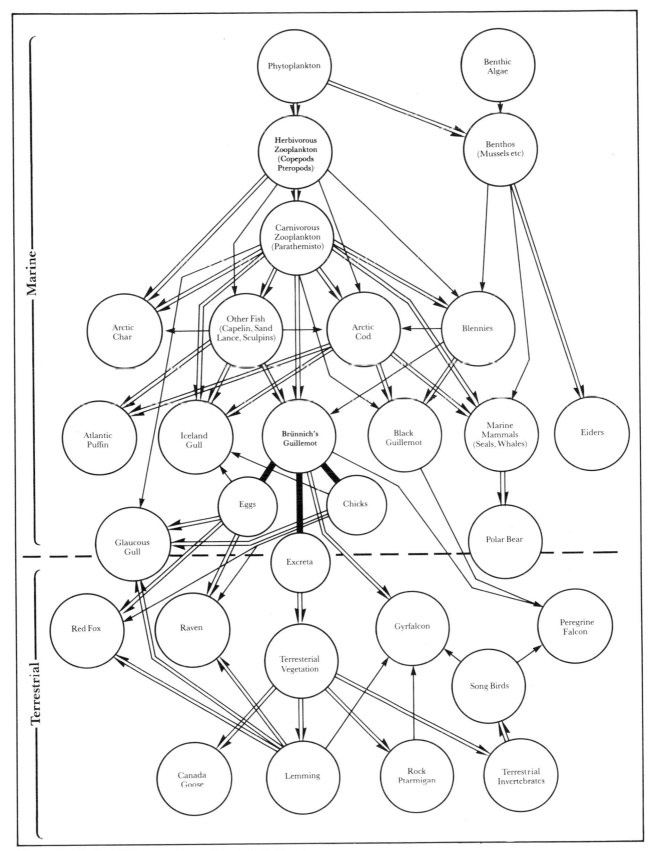

*Figure 9.3: The Food Web Centred on the Brünnich's Guillemot
Colony at Digges Sound, Showing Connections Across the
Marine-Terrestrial Boundary*

*Sources: Gaston, Cairns, Elliott and Noble (1985).*

*Plate 9.36 A Red-breasted Goose at its nest on the Taimyr Peninsula*

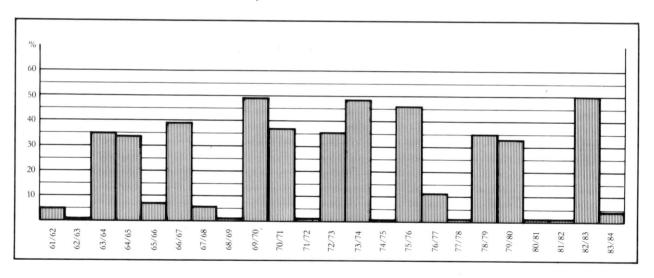

*Figure 9.4: The Percentage of Young Birds in Winter Flocks of Dark-bellied Brent Geese 1961–1962 to 1983–1984*
*Source: Perrins and Birkhead (1983) and the Wildfowl Trust.*

estimated at 250,000 pairs, and in the Davis Strait at 110,000 pairs (Brown and Nettleship 1984). Three colonies on Devon Island probably total up to 200,000+ pairs (Nettleship 1974b) and about 62,000 pairs breed on Prince Leopold Island in Lancaster Sound (Gaston and Nettleship 1981).

### Anseriformes

Among the advantages the Arctic has to offer breeding waterfowl are the excellent wetland habitats with a good food supply and little in the way of competition, and the continuous daylight which enables them to feed for up to 20 hours per day. The most significant disadvantages are the notoriously variable climate and the shortness of the nesting season. It is the climatic factor which periodically results in years of partial or total loss of production.

As an example of the effects of climatic oscillations on breeding success we can take the case of the Dark-bellied Brent Goose *Branta b. bernicla* which is restricted to the Palearctic where it breeds on the Arctic coasts of Siberia eastwards from Kolguev Island to the eastern Taimyr Peninsula and the islands of Severnaya Zemlya. Figure 9.4 shows the percentage of young birds in

*Plate 9.37 The Black Brant* Branta bernicla nigricans *has an extensive breeding range in the North American and Soviet Arctic*

*Plate 9.38 The Emperor Goose nests on the Chukotka Peninsula and thus just qualifies as an Arctic-breeding species*

flocks in Britain and Europe over 23 winters from 1961–1962 to 1983–1984, and the summers when breeding conditions were poor in Siberia stand out quite clearly.

Considerable research has been carried out on Arctic-nesting geese, both on the nesting grounds and in their winter quarters, and some recent population estimates are shown in Table 9.11. These data are not strictly comparable since some counts were done on the breeding grounds and others in winter, but they do give some indication of relative abundance. Most populations of geese breeding in the Arctic increased during the period 1950–1980, but there was considerable variation and some have since declined due to a succession of poor breeding seasons. Detailed population data are

given by Owen (1980). The breeding population of Lesser Snow Geese on Wrangel Island at one time numbered 400,000 (Uspenski 1965), but had declined by 1977 to 50,000 (Table 9.11). In contrast, the McConnell River colony on the west side of Hudson Bay increased from 35,000 birds in 1961 to an estimated 326,000 in 1973 (Kerbes 1975).

The population dynamics of the Wrangel Island Lesser Snow Geese have been reviewed by Bousfield and Syroechkovskiy (1985). Weather conditions influence all aspects of the nesting season, and a late spring results in high nest density in the few snow-free areas available. In 1973 when snow cover lasted well into the spring, 87,000 adult geese were estimated to have arrived on the island, but only 6,000 nests were estimated to be present. In that year (as in most years when there is a shortage of nesting space), intraspecific nest parasitism was widespread and 81.90 per cent of all nests were calculated to contain at least one such egg, and many others were found scattered over the tundra.

Some species of goose breed over many degrees of latitude, whilst others are much more restricted in their range. The essentially Arctic forms include the Greater Snow Goose breeding from 73° N on Bylot Island to 82° N on Ellesmere Island and north-west Greenland; the Greenland White-fronted Goose *Anser albifrons flavirostris* which breeds only in western Greenland; the Barnacle Goose ranging from 70°–80° N with distinct populations in the Siberian Arctic, Svalbard and east Greenland; the Dark-bellied Brent Goose from 71°–81° N; and the Red-breasted Goose *Branta ruficollis* from 68°–76° N with a restricted range on the Yamal,

*Plate 9.39 Ross's Geese on the breeding grounds at Karrak Lake, northern Canada*

Gydan and Taimyr Peninsulas. Another Arctic species of interest is Ross's Goose which is a North American endemic nesting at 68° N, mostly in colonies on islands south of the Queen Maud Gulf, although some probably now breed in all Snow Goose colonies in the Hudson Bay drainage (Frederick and Johnson 1983).

The Red-breasted Goose is endemic to the Soviet Union. They nest on the ground on low hummocks or the tops of riverbank cliffs, virtually always in small colonies close to the eyrie of a Peregrine or other bird of prey. It has in fact been suggested that this goose delays arrival and laying to coincide with the nesting of the birds of prey. The population has probably declined by some 50 per cent in the last 20 years (Ogilvie 1978).

Among the various species of duck that breed in the Arctic, the most northerly ranging are the King Eider and the Long-tailed Duck; even their winter distributions are concentrated in fairly high latitudes. Whilst the Common Eider is essentially colonial in the Arctic, the King Eider is usually a scattered and solitary nester. There may be some vegetation at the nest site, but many are on vast expanses of polar desert consisting of gravel, loose sand and rock. It is probably most abundant in Canada where an estimated 800,000 nest on Victoria Island alone (Barry 1968).

*Plate 9.40 Many Spectacled Eiders nest close to gulls or terns*

*Plate 9.41 Young Peregrines in an eyrie on river bluffs in northern Alaska*

**Table 9.11:** Recent Population Estimates for Some Arctic-Nesting Geese

| Species | Total Numbers | Year | Remarks |
|---|---|---|---|
| Pink-footed Goose<br>*Anser brachyrhynchus* | 12,000–20,000<br>69,000 | 1950s–1960s<br>1977 | Svalbard population<br>Iceland/Greenland population |
| Greenland White-fronted Goose<br>*Anser albifrons flavirostris* | 7,200–7,300 | 1982–1983 | Based on counts on the British<br>wintering grounds |
| Greater Snow Goose<br>*Anser caerulescens atlanticus* | 180,000 | 1980 | Census of the spring population |
| Lesser Snow Goose<br>*Anser c. caerulescens* | 165,000[a]<br>56,400[a]<br>1,069,000[a]<br>50,000 | June 1976<br>June 1976<br>June 1979<br>1977 | W. Canadian Arctic population<br>Central Canadian Arctic population<br>E. Canadian Arctic population[b]<br>Wrangel Island nesting total |
| Ross's Goose<br>*Anser rossii* | 77,300[a] | June 1976 | Central Canadian Arctic endemic |
| Emperor Goose<br>*Anser canagicus* | 12,000–15,000 | 1974 | Chukotka Peninsula population |
| Barnacle Goose<br>*Branta leucopsis* | 80,000–90,000 | Winter 1980–81 | World population – Greenland,<br>Svalbard and Barents Sea |
| Dark-bellied Brent Goose<br>*Branta b. bernicla* | 180,000 | Winter 1979–80 | Siberian Arctic breeding population |
| Light-bellied Brent Goose<br>*Branta bernicla hrota* | 2,200 | Winter 1977–78 | Svalbard population |
| Red-breasted Goose<br>*Branta ruficollis* | 22,000–27,000 | 1978 and 1979 | Post-breeding population of adults<br>and young |

Notes: a. Totals do not include non-breeding birds. b. Includes some colonies outside the boundaries of the Arctic as defined for the purposes of this book.
Sources: Boyd *et al* (1982), Ebbinge (1982), Gauthier *et al* (1984), Kerbes (1983), Kerbes *et al* (1983), Owen (1980), Stroud (1984) and Vinokurov (1982).

*Plate 9.42 White-fronted Geese and other waterfowl may have to begin nesting before the snow has melted*

One other species of eider deserves mention. The Spectacled Eider *Polysticta fischeri* breeds in north-east Siberia and northern Alaska. It requires large areas of coastal shallows (mostly temporarily flooded moss-sedge bog) 0–10 cm deep for summer living. In this habitat its diet consists of hydrophilous larvae of crane flies *Prionocera* spp. and those of various caddis flies (Kistchinski and Flint 1974). There is evidence that this duck often deliberately chooses to nest in colonies of gulls and terns, and that it is only those who do so who successfully incubate their clutches. The outer maritime section of the Indigirka River 40–50 km from the sea has the highest known nesting density, estimated at 17,000–18,000 pairs in 1971. The remainder of the Siberian population being provisionally estimated at 30,000–40,000 pairs.

### Accipitriformes

The most interesting species in this group is the White-tailed Eagle which, in our area, breeds in Greenland and the Soviet Arctic. Its distribution in Greenland is confined to the Low Arctic regions in the west where it nests as far north as about 67° N. The total population in Greenland in 1974 was estimated at

*Plate 9.43 A male Willow Ptarmigan in summer plumage*

*Plate 9.44 A Pacific Golden Plover in the Karyak Highlands, Soviet Union*

85–101 pairs, suggesting that the population had been reduced to a level of only about 25–50 per cent of the original population (Hansen 1979). Six eyries in the sheep-farming areas of southern Greenland were studied from 1976–1980. Fish made up 90 per cent of the diet and various bird species and Arctic Fox 10 per cent. The total intake of an eaglet amounted to 50 kg from hatching to fledging, with a daily requirement of some 800 g of fish (Wille and Kampp 1983).

### Falconiformes

The true Arctic species is the Gyrfalcon with a circumpolar nesting distribution. In Greenland it breeds from 82° N south to 60° N, and in North America from 79° N on Ellesmere Island south to 60° N across Canada, although local populations are found a few degrees further south in Quebec and Alaska. The breeding cycle of this falcon begins earlier than that of any other northern raptor, at a time when winter still prevails. For example, studies in the western Canadian Arctic north of 68° N showed that pairs were present in the nesting area in February about 60 days before egg-laying (Platt 1976).

Throughout most of its range it is almost completely dependent for some seven months of the year on one prey – the ptarmigan – whose populations are cyclic. However, although ptarmigan may be the most important prey (about 88 per cent of the diet on the Arctic Slope of Alaska and 96 per cent in Greenland), most of the available birds and mammals are taken as prey including Snow Bunting (especially when in autumn flocks); in coastal areas, seabirds (gulls, terns, auks);

*Plate 9.45 A female Willow Ptarmigan on its nest blends into its surroundings*

Arctic Lemming *Dicrostonyx groenlandicus* and Arctic Hare (Summers and Green 1974). Studies in western Ellesmere Island showed that Gyrfalcons were able to maintain primary dependence on Arctic Hares throughout the breeding season, although significant numbers of Knot and Turnstone were also taken (Muir and Bird 1984).

Although also circumpolar in distribution, the Peregrine does not in general nest quite so far north as the preceding species. In Alaska and northern Canada both species have long been known occasionally to nest on the same cliff, and in 1984 proof of this was also found in Greenland for the first time. A Peregrine survey in Greenland in 1984 located a total of 70 young at 22 cliffs.

*Plate 9.46 A Peregrine at its eyrie on the Taimyr Peninsula*

*Plate 9.47 A Semipalmated Plover at its nest on the Canadian tundra*

*Plate 9.48 The Western Sandpiper has a restricted breeding range in the Arctic*

In 1976 and 1977 the Wager Bay area in north-east Keewatin and the south-western part of the Melville Peninsula, Canada, were found to be the most productive nesting areas known for this falcon, and more sites producing young were located at Wager Bay than are known to exist in any other area of the North American Arctic. At this locality in 1976, 85 per cent of the sites visited produced young, and the number of young per successful nest averaged 2.45. The comparable figures for 1977 were 84 per cent and 2.95. At least 10 out of 15 occupied eyries on the Melville Peninsula in 1977 produced young and the average number per successful nest was 2.6 (Calef and Heard 1979).

## Galliformes

While the Rock Ptarmigan is completely circumpolar in its distribution, the Willow Ptarmigan is absent from Greenland and Svalbard. Numerous flocks of Willow Ptarmigan are characteristic of the continental tundras of North America and Eurasia. In Arctic Alaska they breed commonly from the Brooks Range to the coast with concentrations in the willow bars and alder scrub along river valleys. Throughout most of their range both species must rely almost entirely on buds, twigs and catkins of deciduous shrubs during the five to seven months when snow covers non-woody plants. The Willow Ptarmigan probably has a more specialised and uniform diet than any other northern animal since during the winter months (in Alaska) up to 94 per cent of its diet consists of buds and twigs of willow, 80 per cent of which may be of a single species – Alaska Willow (West and Meng 1966). In other regions of the circumpolar tundra the food preference may shift according to availability; birch may dominate the diet.

*Plate 9.49 A Long-tailed Skua at its nest among Mountain Avens*

*Plate 9.50 The Pomarine Skua is a major predator of lemmings*

*Plate 9.51 A dark-phase Arctic Skua on the Canadian tundra*

*Plate 9.52 A female Snowy Owl on its nest*

*Plate 9.53 Young Snowy Owls in the nest at Barrow, Alaska, with the bodies of Brown Lemmings on the rim*

### Charadriiformes

Various aspects of the ecology of the 50 species of Arctic-nesting wader have already been discussed, but a few other points of interest may be mentioned here.

The breeding ranges of several wader species reach the highest latitudes. Baird's Sandpiper, for example, breeds from Greenland (to about 80° N) across the high North American Arctic from Ellesmere Island, extending westwards to the Chukotka Peninsula. This distribution places it among the most northerly of the *Calidris* species. The Knot is a highly disjunctive circumpolar species whose distribution is in the High Arctic, in general north of the 4° C July isotherm, extending to the extreme limits of land in Greenland and on Ellesmere Island. A similar disjunctive high latitude distribution is shown by the Sanderling, and by the Purple Sandpiper which is absent from Alaska. The Turnstone on the other hand has a completely circumpolar high-latitude range.

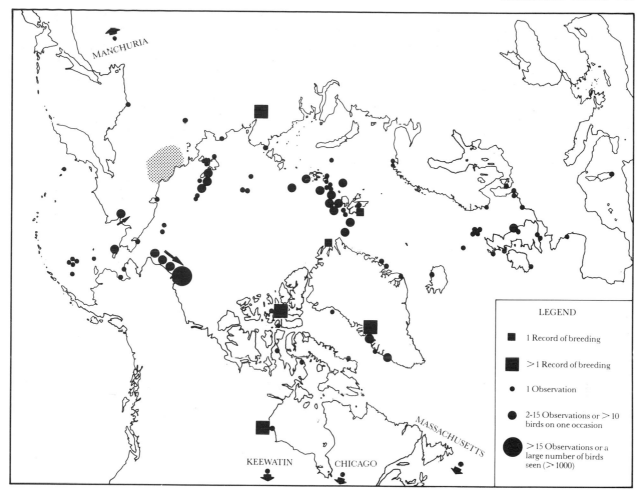

*Figure 9.5: Ross's Gull in the Arctic. Breeding areas (dotted shading). Observed migration movements are marked with arrows*
*Source: Blomqvist and Elander (1981).*

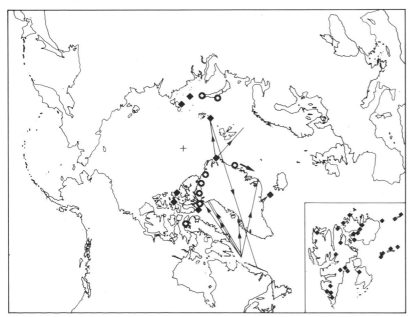

*Figure 9.6: Distribution of the Ivory Gull in the Arctic. The thick arrow represents one observed concentrated migration movement. Ringing places and recovery places are connected by thin arrows. (Note: black diamond=known breeding places; white diamond on black=probable breeding places.)*
*Source: Blomqvist and Elander (1981).*

The closely related Ringed *Charadrius hiaticula* and Semipalmated Plovers *C. semipalmatus* form an interesting species pair. The range of the former extends from extreme north-eastern Canada and Greenland, across northern Eurasia to the Chukotka Peninsula. It is absent from Alaska where it is replaced by the Semipalmated Plover which is also widespread in the remainder of the Canadian Arctic.

Waders with much more restricted distributions include the Western Sandpiper *Calidris mauri* which (in the Arctic), has a small breeding range in north-west Alaska and the north-eastern Chukotka Peninsula; the Rufous-necked Sandpiper which breeds primarily on the Chukotka Peninsula and near the Lena delta, and occasionally at Barrow, Alaska; the Sharp-tailed Sandpiper *C. acuminata* which nests on the Arctic coastal plain of eastern Siberia; the Curlew Sandpiper *C. ferruginea* which breeds only in northern Siberia from the Taimyr Peninsula east to the Kolyma delta, and occasionally in the vicinity of Barrow; and the Rock Sandpiper which is confined to the Chukotka Peninsula.

While there are few data concerning the population size of individual wader species within the Arctic, it is worth noting that Manning *et al* (1956) estimated that in 1952 an adult population of 70,000 Semipalmated Sandpipers, 65,000 Sanderling, 25,000 Baird's Sandpipers, 25,000 White-rumped Sandpipers *C. fuscicollis*, 14,000 Pectoral Sandpipers, and 2,000 Buff-breasted Sandpipers *Tryngites subruficollis* summered on Banks Island (60,100 km²).

Of the four species of skua nesting in the Arctic, the Great Skua is confined to Svalbard and will not be discussed further. There is an extensive literature on the other three species and important papers include those of Korte (1977 and 1984) and Maher (1970a, 1970b and 1974). Although the Pomarine, Arctic and Long-tailed Skuas are all circumpolar in their distribution, the Pomarine is absent from Greenland and Svalbard. While the Arctic Skua is primarily a small-bird predator and utilises this prey predominantly in all situations, the Pomarine and Long-tailed Skuas are both strongly adapted for their role as predators on microtine rodents in Arctic ecosystems, and are geographically and/or ecologically separated on their breeding grounds, although some competition may occur. The Pomarine Skua is an obligate lemming or microtine rodent predator and relies on these for 90–100 per cent of its food, even when not breeding (in years of low rodent populations), and is unable to exploit avian prey effectively. The Long-tailed Skua is also a microtine rodent predator but, unlike the Pomarine Skua, is also able to take avian prey effectively. All these skuas defend large, mutually exclusive, all-purpose territories, which vary in size with different nesting densities.

Ross's Gull is a particularly interesting species whose most important known breeding area is in the Subarctic and boreal parts of north-eastern Siberia. However, within the Arctic it breeds on the Taimyr Peninsula, in a few localities in western and northern

*Plate 9.54 In the Arctic the Bar-tailed Godwit nests mainly on low-lying coastal tundras*

*Plate 9.55 The Hudsonian Godwit* Limosa haemastica *has a very restricted breeding range in the North American Arctic*

Greenland, at Penny Strait near Devon Island and at Churchill on Hudson Bay (Blomqvist and Elander 1981); see Figure 9.5. A few nests have also been found on lakeside tundra in southern Borkha Bay by the Laptev Sea, in northern Yakutsk, where the adults feed on glacier lakes.

The two truly Arctic species are Sabine's Gull *Larus sabini* and the Ivory Gull, the latter being essentially High Arctic with its distribution almost exclusively north of 70° N. Whilst the breeding range of Sabine's Gull is more extensive than that of the Ivory Gull, the breeding area is not completely circumpolar; it nests on level terrain in grass-covered moist tundra or on islets.

The Ivory Gull has on average, the most northerly breeding grounds of all birds (see Figure 9.6). The main populations are on Svalbard (estimated total population 344 pairs), Franz Josef Land (a colony of several thousand has been reported from Cape Mary Harmsworth on flat ground), North Island (Severnaya Zemlya) and apparently the north island of Novaya Zemlya. It breeds also in a few localities in north and east Greenland, usually on nunataks (rocks or mountains projecting out of inland ice) up to 1,900 m a.s.l. and 60 km inland. In Canada it breeds near Bathurst Island, northern Baffin Island, on nunataks in the upland icefields of south-eastern Ellesmere Island (up

*Plate 9.56 A White-rumped Sandpiper at its nest on Jenny Lind Island, Canada*

*Plate 9.57 Sabine's Gull has an extensive breeding range in the Arctic*

to 750 m a.s.l.), and on nunataks in eastern Devon Island (Birkenmajer 1969, Blomqvist and Elander

1981, Frisch 1983, Norderhaug *et al* 1977).

The seasonal occurrence and distribution of Ivory Gulls in Davis Strait and the Labrador Sea may be explained by food concentrations along the pack-ice edge and by reduced light levels and biological production to the north. The species is absent only during the short ice-free period from late June to late October. From February through June, and probably longer, the gulls concentrate near the ice edge, where they feed on lanternfishes (Myctophidae) during April and May in Davis Strait. About 35,000 Ivory Gulls may be present in Davis Strait during March. Hooded Seal *Crystaphora cristata* remains may be seasonally important. The largest gull concentration during March 1978 was at the ice edge near the Hooded Seal whelping patch. Numbers were estimated at 23,800±12,100 near the seal herd (Orr and Parsons 1982).

Turning now to the Alcidae, comment will be confined to two species. Brünnich's Guillemot is a highly specialised seabird and one of the most numerous seabird species in the northern hemisphere, breeding in a relatively small number of very large colonies. An outstanding study of this species in the Canadian Arctic is that by Gaston and Nettleship (1981). Some idea of the sheer abundance of this species can be gained from the fact that the west Greenland population alone was formerly estimated to number $2-3 \times 10^6$ pairs (Evans and Waterston 1978). It was recently estimated (Gaston 1980) that some $3.8 \times 10^6$ of these birds from west Greenland and the Canadian Arctic winter off Newfoundland. Unfortunately, substantial decreases (20–40 per cent) appear to have taken place over much of the species' range in recent years. Recent population estimates are given in Table 9.12, from which it can be seen that the highest numbers are now in Svalbard and west Novaya Zemlya.

**Table 9.12:** Some Recent Population Estimates for Brünnich's Guillemot *Uria lomvia* and the Little Auk *Alle alle* (Figures in Pairs Rounded to the Nearest 1,000)

| Area | Brünnich's Guillemot | Little Auk |
|---|---|---|
| Greenland | 470,000> | 7,506,000–15,506,000 |
| Canada—Baffin Bay | 406,000 | |
|     Davis Strait | 250,000 | |
|     Hudson Strait | 785,000 | |
| Soviet Union—Murman coast of Barents Sea | 19,000 | |
|     West Novaya Zemlya | 1,000,000 | 10,000–50,000 |
|     Franz Josef Land | 100,000 | 250,000 |
|     Kara Sea (E. Novaya Zemlya) | 25,000 | |
|     Laptev Sea | ? | 75,000 |
|     East Siberian Sea | 45,000 | |
|     Chukchi Sea | 19,000 | |
| Svalbard | 1,000,000 | 400,000–1,600,000 |
| Bear Island | 750,000 | 10,000 |
| Jan Mayen Island | 75,000 | 50,000 |
| Totals | 4,909,000> | 8,301,000–17,541,000 |

Sources: Brown and Nettleship (1984), Evans (1984a and 1984b), Golovkin (1984) and Nettleship and Birkhead (1985).

Large though the total population of Brünnich's Guillemot may be, it is exceeded by that of the Little Auk which is the most abundant seabird in the North Atlantic. Its breeding range is Holarctic and it is the most pronouncedly High Arctic of the auks. It breeds in screes, talus slopes and eroded and fissured cliffs from sea level to about 450–500 m, well above the snow line. Given the nature of the breeding habitat and its enormous numbers, obtaining population estimates is difficult. However, recent estimates are given in Table 9.12, and this shows that the present centres of abundance are Greenland and Svalbard.

Studies carried out at 73° N in west Greenland (Evans 1981) showed that Little Auks fed exclusively on copepods and amphipods (94 per cent *Calanus finmarchicus*). This copepod is available in Arctic waters for only a short period of the year and its peak density coincides with the breeding season of the Little Auk. The combined incubation and fledging period of 52 days is the shortest of all the Atlantic Alcidae, consistent with the short time that food is available in abundance. Most food was taken within 2.5 km of the colony, but elsewhere they have been recorded feeding up to 100 km west of colonies in Svalbard and the same distance north-east of colonies on Jan Mayen (Brown 1976).

### Strigiformes

The Snowy Owl is a truly circumpolar species which, when food is available, can live further north in winter than either ptarmigan or the Raven; it has been seen as far north as 82° N on Ellesmere Island. This owl can survive at ambient temperatures below −62.5° C which is about the lowest recorded in the northern hemisphere (Gessaman 1972). The Snowy Owl exhibits marked fluctuations in numbers in relation to availability of prey, and nesting is often sporadic. It breeds beyond the treeline at the highest latitudes, mainly on open tundra and ranging from sea level to upland habitats. On Axel Heiberg and Ellesmere Islands in 1971, three nests were each at a different Snow Goose colony, and on Wrangel Island the tendency of Snow Geese colonies to form around the nests of Snowy Owls has been noted.

On its Arctic nesting grounds the diet is almost entirely lemmings, and Watson (1957) suggested that the mean daily food intake of an adult in the wild was between 150 and 350 g (55–130 kg yr$^{-1}$) or the equivalent of 600–1,600 full grown lemmings per year. In 1971 an early decline of the Brown Lemming population in the Barrow area caused Snowy Owls to turn to young Lapland Buntings as substitute prey (Custer 1973).

### Passeriformes

As stated earlier, many of the 47 breeding passerines of the Arctic are in fact of limited distribution there, and only reach the southern part of the tundra zone. Species that are widespread, however, include the Horned Lark *Eremophila alpestris* and Water Pipit *Anthus spinoletta* (both mostly on alpine tundra), Wheatear, Raven, the redpolls, Lapland and Snow Buntings.

Obtaining food is probably the most crucial problem facing Ravens during the Arctic winter, and most of their time must be spent foraging during the brief daylight hours. Studies at Umiat (69° N) on Alaska's Arctic Slope in the winters of 1966 and 1967 indicated that Ravens obtained half of their energy requirement through predation and half through scavenging. Microtine rodents provided the bulk of the predatory part of the diet, while carcasses of Caribou *Rangifer tarandus* and ptarmigan were the items most often scavenged (Temple 1974).

The taxonomy of the redpolls is somewhat confusing, but the two species recognised here – the Common Redpoll and the Arctic Redpoll – are both circumpolar in distribution although both are absent from Svalbard. They consume primarily birch seeds in winter, and although many migrate south in winter to forested areas, others are present in shrub-tundra habitats throughout the winter where birch is available. The Common Redpoll was formerly a breeding species of only the Low Arctic part of Greenland, but subsequently extended its range to the north as a result of climatic amelioration while the Arctic Redpoll correspondingly withdrew northwards. The Common Redpoll was first recorded as breeding in northern Greenland in 1963, and in 1968 both species were breeding at Scoresby Sound (Waterston and Waterston 1970).

The Lapland Bunting is a characteristic species of the circumpolar tundra biome and in some localities represents a major avian consumer. At Barrow, Alaska, it is an important carnivore in the detritus-based food chain, and the only major passerine in a terrestrial insectivorous guild which otherwise consists mainly of waders. Breeding activities begin there early in June and are highly synchronous, thus allowing the young to reach independence during the peak of insect emergence (Tryon and MacLean 1980). Crane flies are

Plate 9.58 A male Rock Ptarmigan on the Taimyr Peninsula

*Plate 9.59 The Savannah Sparrow penetrates the tundra zone along river valleys*

*Plate 9.61 Within the Arctic the Horned Lark is absent as a breeding species from Greenland and Svalbard*

*Plate 9.60 The Snow Bunting is particularly well adapted to Arctic conditions*

by far the most important component of the nestling diet, and in 1975 over 60 per cent by weight of food given to nestlings at Barrow consisted of the crane fly *Tipula carinifrons* (Seastedt and MacLean 1979). Seeds become progressively more important in the diet later in the summer during the period of moult and pre-migratory drift. The males establish breeding territories while the ground is almost completely covered with snow, and polygamy may occur when the species is nesting at high densities. In contrast to the Lapland Bunting, Smith's Longspur *Calcarius pictus*, has a much more restricted distribution and is a montane species confined to the North American Arctic. In Alaska it occurs in the Brooks Range where it nests in valley bottoms with level areas of sedge-grass marsh with scattered cottongrass tussocks (Sage 1974).

The Snow Bunting is one of those species whose feeding strategies permit them some use of tundra resources before snow-melt, and the males in particular exercise the option of early territory establishment and spend as much as five months annually in High Arctic localities (Pattie 1972), but must do so at the expense of having to compensate metabolically for added heat loss because of wind and low temperatures. Studies over four summers on the Truelove Lowland, Devon Island, showed that Snow Buntings required 53.1 kcal bird$^{-1}$ day$^{-1}$ and derived 6 per cent of their food from spiders, 28 per cent from insects, and 66 per cent from seeds (Pattie 1977).

# 10
# TERRESTRIAL MAMMALS

## Introduction

The total number of species of land mammals occurring in the Arctic is 48 (Appendix 2 shows their distribution in the Soviet Union, North America and Greenland). The nomenclature used here follows Corbet (1978) for the Soviet Union (with minor changes as indicated) and Chapman and Feldhamer (1982) for North America and Greenland. The number of species occurring in each country is Canada 31, Alaska 29, Soviet Union 33 and Greenland 9. It can be seen that out of a world total of about 4,000 species, the variety of terrestrial mammals in the Arctic is low and consists of slightly modified shrews, hares, rodents, wolves, foxes, bears and deer.

The species listed in Appendix 2 include a number whose occurrence in the Arctic as defined here is marginal. These include the Northern Pika *Ochotona hyperborea*, European Water Vole *Arvicola terrestris* and European Mink *Mustela lutreola* in Siberia, and the Porcupine *Erethizon dorsatum*, American Mink *M. vison*, River Otter *Lutra canadensis* and Lynx *Lynx canadensis* in North America. These are primarily species of the taiga and forest-tundra zones who occasionally venture locally onto the true tundra. In the same category is the Snowshoe Hare *Lepus americanus* which only occurs on the tundra when populations are high. In Table 10.1, those small mammals (Insectivora, Lagomorpha and Rodentia) which occur regularly on Arctic tundra are listed by groups according to their primary habitat affinities.

### Some Aspects of Distribution

There are three species present in the Canadian Arctic that are not found in Arctic Alaska: the Arctic Hare, Hudson Bay Lemming *Dicrostonyx hudsonius*, and Muskrat *Ondatra zibethicus*. On the other hand Alaska has the Alaskan (Tundra) Hare *Lepus othus* which does not occur in Canada. There are only eleven species in Canada whose ranges extend beyond the mainland to the islands of the Canadian Arctic Archipelago: Arctic Hare, Arctic (Collared) Lemming, Brown Lemming *Lemmus sibiricus*, Gray Wolf *Canis lupus*, Red Fox *Vulpes vulpes* (only on Baffin Island), Arctic Fox, Polar Bear, Ermine, Wolverine *Gulo gulo*, Caribou and Muskox *Ovibos moschatus*.

The land mammal fauna of Greenland (like that of the Canadian Arctic Islands) is very restricted, comprising only nine species – Arctic Hare, Arctic Lemming, Gray Wolf, Arctic Fox, Polar Bear, Ermine,

Wolverine (only of local occurrence), Caribou and Muskox. The status of Caribou in Greenland has been the subject of recent reports in the literature. For example, Gunn *et al* (1980–1) state that 'Recent work in Greenland suggests that it no longer exists there.' This remark applies to the subspecies *R. t. pearyi* (Peary Caribou) which is said to have formerly occurred in north-west Greenland. According to Stroud (1981), animals of the subspecies *R. t. groenlandicus* are currently found in central-west Greenland where they inhabit an area of about 60,000 km², and in March 1980 were estimated to number about 7,000–9,000.

The species that are Holarctic, and in some cases completely circumpolar, in distribution are listed in Table 10.2. Many probably occupied the Beringian region during the late Pleistocene. Some Beringian forms, however, have remained specifically distinct, for example the Alaska Marmot and the Black-capped Marmot *M. camtschatica*; the Insular (Singing) Vole *Microtus abreviatus* and the Narrow-skulled Vole *M. gregalis*; the Alaskan Hare and the Varying Hare *Lepus timidus* (assuming that these *are* specifically distinct); and the Dall Sheep *Ovis dalli* and Snow Sheep *O. nivicola*. A more detailed discussion of this subject is given by Hoffman *et al* (1979). According to Guthrie

*Plate 10.1 The range of the Arctic Lemming extends north to Greenland*

(1968), the number of small mammal species present in the tundra seems to have increased considerably since the glaciations of the late Pleistocene, primarily by immigration from more southern locations, while the number of large mammals has declined.

It can be seen from Table 10.1 that four groups of small mammals (shrews, hares, sciurid rodents and microtine rodents) occur regularly in Arctic tundra, although their distribution does not always correspond entirely to the distribution of that habitat. Some of the species are tundra-specific and, according to Hoffman

*Plate 10.2 The Brown Lemming exhibits marked population fluctuations*

**Table 10.1:** Some Small Mammals Occurring Regularly in Arctic Tundra, Grouped According to Their Primary Habitat Affinities[a]

|  | Soviet Union | North America |
|---|:---:|:---:|
| **I. Arctic and Arctic-alpine Tundra** | | |
| Lagomorpha | | |
|   Arctic Hare *Lepus arcticus* | | × |
| Rodentia | | |
|   Insular (Singing) Vole *Microtus abreviatus* | | × |
|   Middendorff's Vole[b] *Microtus middendorffi* | × | |
|   Arctic Lemming[b] *Dicrostonyx groenlandicus* | × | × |
|   Hudson Bay Lemming *Dicrostonyx hudsonius* | | × |
|   Brown Lemming[b] *Lemmus sibiricus* | × | × |
| **II. Boreal Forest** | | |
| Insectivora | | |
|   Masked Shrew[b] *Sorex cinereus* | × | × |
|   Large-toothed Shrew *Sorex daphaenodon* | × | |
|   Dusky Shrew *Sorex obscurus* | | × |
| Lagomorpha | | |
|   Alaskan (Tundra) Hare *Lepus othus* | | × |
|   Varying Hare[b] *Lepus timidus* | × | |
| Rodentia | | |
|   Grey Red-backed Vole[b] *Clethrionomys rufocanus* | × | |
|   Northern Red-backed Vole[b] *Clethrionomys rutilus* | × | × |
| **III. Alpine Tundra Habitat** | | |
| Rodentia | | |
|   Alaska Marmot *Marmota broweri* | | × |
|   Black-capped Marmot *Marmota camtschatica* | × | |

| | Soviet Union | North America |
|---|:---:|:---:|
| **IV. Cosmopolitan – Temperate to Arctic Habitats** | | |
| Insectivora | | |
| Arctic Shrew[b] *Sorex arcticus* | × | × |
| Common Shrew[b] *Sorex araneus* | × | |
| Pygmy Shrew *Sorex minutus* | × | |
| Lagomorpha | | |
| Snowshoe Hare *Lepus americanus* | | × |
| Rodentia | | |
| Arctic Ground Squirrel[b] *Spermophilus undulatus* | × | × |
| Narrow-skulled Vole[b] *Microtus gregalis* | × | |
| Tundra (Root) Vole[b] *Microtus oeconomus* | × | × |

Notes: a. See Appendix 2 for taxonomic comments.
b. Relatively widespread in Arctic tundra.
Source: Adapted from Batzli (1981).

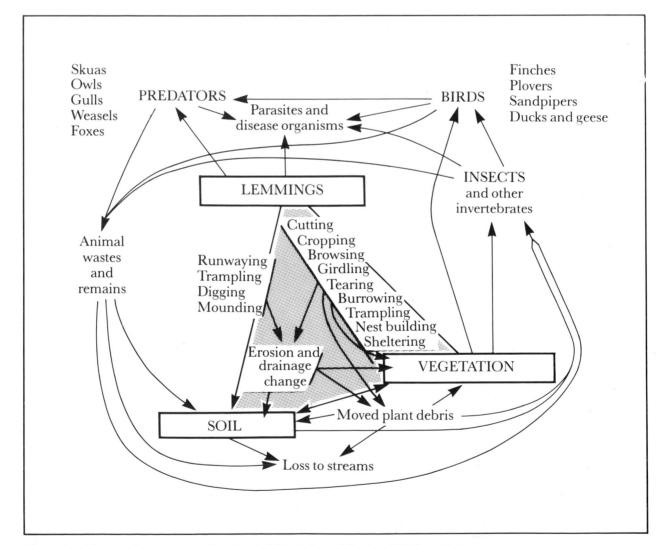

*Figure 10.1: Diagram of Food Web and Lemming Activities in Coastal Tundra of Northern Alaska*
*Source: Pitelka (1957a).*

*Plate 10.3 Lemming runs on the tundra revealed by snowmelt*

**Table 10.2:** Terrestrial Mammals with a Holarctic Distribution

| | |
|---|---|
| Insectivora | Carnivora |
|   Arctic Shrew *Sorex arcticus*[a] |   Gray Wolf *Canis lupus* |
|   Masked Shrew *Sorex cinereus*[a] |   Red Fox *Vulpes vulpes*[a] |
| |   Arctic Fox *Alopex lagopus* |
| Rodentia |   Grizzly Bear *Ursus arctos*[a] |
|   Arctic Ground Squirrel *Spermophilus undulatus*[a] |   Polar Bear *Ursus maritimus* |
|   Tundra Vole *Microtus oeconomus*[a] |   Ermine *Mustela erminea* |
|   Arctic Lemming *Dicrostonyx groenlandicus* |   Least Weasel *Mustela nivalis* |
|   Brown Lemming *Lemmus sibiricus*[a] |   Wolverine *Gulo gulo* |
|   Northern Red-backed Vole *Clethrionomys rutilus*[a] | |
| | Artiodactyla |
| |   Moose *Alces alces*[a] |
| |   Caribou (Reindeer) *Rangifer tarandus* |
| |   Muskox *Ovibos moschatus* |

Note: a. Absent from Greenland.

and Taber (1968), evolved in central Eurasia during the early Pleistocene and migrated to North America. For example, before the last glaciation, the Arctic Ground Squirrel and the Brown Lemming were tundra-specific but confined to Eurasia and the far western parts of North America. Currently both occur in Arctic and alpine tundra on the mainland west of Hudson Bay, and the Brown Lemming has colonised the more southerly islands of the Canadian Arctic Archipelago eastwards to Baffin Island. In his studies of Canadian Arctic mammals, Macpherson (1965) came to the conclusion that the only small mammals which were tundra-specific and widespread before the last glaciation were the Arctic Hare, Arctic Lemming and Hudson Bay Lemming. These three species are still primarily confined to the Arctic tundra in North America, as is the Arctic Lemming also in Eurasia. There can be little doubt that the Arctic Lemming shows the greatest degree of adaptation to the Arctic

winter climate of all the small mammals and its current range extends further north in the High Arctic than that of any other small mammal. Morphological adaptations include shortened tail and, in winter, enlarged claws and white pelage. It also has a highly developed resistance to hypothermic collapse (Ferguson and Folk 1970).

### Population Cycles

Long-term mammalian population cycles have been proposed for several parts of the world, but in the Arctic and Subarctic two cycles stand out particularly clearly: the Snowshoe Hare and the Lynx cycle with a periodicity of about ten years in the boreal forest of the New World, and 4-year cycles for several species of voles and lemmings in the tundra zone around the world (and in some grasslands in lower latitudes). The best known 3–4 year cycle is that of the Brown Lemming, and this is discussed later. Detailed discussion of population cycles will be found in Batzli *et al* (1980), Finerty (1980), Remmert (1980), Southern (1979) and Stoddart (1979). It should be noted that the interval between successive peaks may vary within small limits, and that the regularity of the cycles refers only to the intervals between peaks. The individual peaks may not, of course, necessarily be of the same amplitude. The cycles are typically assymetrical, with populations declining at a greater rate than they increase. As stated by Crawley (1983), there is strong evidence that herbivore population cycles are caused by plant-herbivore interactions (rather than by predator-prey, disease-host, or plant-environment interactions).

### Effects of Grazing by Small Mammals

Analysis of the Arctic land mammal fauna (excluding the eight marginal species mentioned above) according to feeding habits reveals a predominance of herbivores (Table 10.3), and there can be no doubt that small mammals, particularly microtine rodents, play a pivotal role in tundra ecosystems and form a link between many primary producers and secondary consumers. Various workers have diagrammed tundra food webs, and all of them show small mammals in the centre of the web (Figure 10.1). All studies on the feeding habits of Arctic rodents agree that they are herbivorous (Batzli 1975).

In temperate grassland habitats, microtines may only consume 1–35 per cent of available food during any one season (Golley 1960, Batzli and Pitelka 1970), while lemmings may consume nearly all of their accessible winter forage. Anyone who has witnessed a strong fluctuation in a lemming population, such as those which occur periodically at Barrow, Alaska, cannot fail to notice the effects of the massive grazing on the grass-sedge tundra of the coastal plain. These effects clearly indicate a significant impact on the productive potential of the vegetation, and therefore on nutrient cycling and decomposition processes. The immediate effect of small mammal grazing (i.e. reduction of the standing crop) is clear enough, but the long-term effects are much less clear, and may depend on various factors such as the species involved and their density. Many aspects of herbivory on the tundra are discussed in detail by Batzli *et al* (1981) and Crawley (1983).

In the summer following a lemming peak, the monocot standing crop may be depressed by around 50 per cent (Batzli 1975). Where soil has been overturned to gain access to rhizomes production may be reduced by as much as 90 per cent (Pitelka and Schultz 1964). Mosses also can similarly be devastated (Peiper 1963), although both Arctic and Brown Lemmings depend

less on mosses and more on the green stem bases of monocots in the winter. During a winter of high lemming populations, virtually all of the monocot stems are clipped (Pitelka 1957a, Tikhomirov 1959). The effects of microtines on vegetation are not confined to temporary reductions of the standing crop. Tikhomirov (1959) reported that lemming grazing suppresses flowering in cottongrass and Tundra Grass. Controlled experiments with Middendorff's Vole *Microtus middendorffi* and the Tundra Vole *M. oeconomus* (on forest-tundra) indicated that moderate grazing increased production of *Eriophorum* and *Carex* by stimulating new shoot growth (Smirnov and Tokmakova 1971, 1972). However, it was estimated that above an optimal density of 30–50 voles ha$^{-1}$ productivity would be decreased.

Small mammal foraging may also substantially alter the species composition of tundra plant communities. For example, both Tikhomirov (1959) and Pjastalova (1972) suggest that microtine activity enhances the dominance of monocots over mosses in the tundra. The end result of this, they suggest, is the creation of sedge-grass meadows. Other than the microtines, the only other small Arctic mammal that has significant effects on the vegetation is the Arctic Ground Squirrel. Their usual habitat is dominated by *Dryas* and shrubs, but under the influence of feeding and digging, herbs invade and grasses such as *Calamagrostis* and *Poa* become particularly common (Tikhomirov 1959, Carl 1971).

## Insectivora

Shrews are mainly carnivorous and are active throughout the year, hunting in burrows under the snow. Most of the literature on Arctic shrews is concerned with taxonomy and distribution, and nearly all refers to studies in more southerly habitats such as the boreal forest, or even further south. The only detailed paper on the biology of the Arctic Shrew *Sorex arcticus*, for example, is that of Clough (1963) in Wisconsin.

During the period 1959–61, ecological studies were carried out in the vicinity of Cape Thompson, western Alaska. Although not included in the definition used in this book, the area covered by these studies (between 65° and 69° N) is essentially Arctic in character. The terrestrial mammals, reported on by Pruitt (1966), included two species of shrew – Arctic Shrew and Masked Shrew *Sorex cinereus*. In 1959 the vegetation communities used by the shrews were characterised by moist, stable conditions without an excess of water. In 1960 (when population levels were higher), they also

**Table 10.3:** Arctic Land Mammals Classified According to Feeding Habits

|   | Herbivores | Carnivores | Insectivores | Omnivores | Total |
|---|---|---|---|---|---|
|   | 23 | 8 | 8 | 1[a] | 40 |
| % | 57.5 | 20.0 | 20.0 | 2.5 | 100 |

Note: a. The Grizzly Bear is, for present purposes, regarded as an omnivore.

*Plate 10.4 An Arctic Hare photographed in Greenland*

used habitats that were considerably drier, or wetter, or less stable. The Masked Shrew, for example, was found in the *Eriophorum* tussock, *Eriophorum-Carex* wet-meadow (low centre polygons), and *Carex bigelowii* high-centre polygon habitats. These data agree with the hypothesis that at times of low populations, the species are restricted to habitats offering optimal environmental conditions, but during periods of high population levels the species spill over into more marginal or even sub-marginal habitats.

Earlier information on habitat selection in the shrews occurring on the Arctic Slope of Alaska is given by Bee and Hall (1956). Of the three species that occur there, the Masked Shrew is the most tolerant of wet conditions and is commonly found in the low-centre polygon wet meadows, but is also found in almost all plant communities in which microtine rodents are found, and is closely associated with the Brown Lemming on the northern part of the Arctic Slope. The Arctic Shrew is common on hillsides, and when present in valleys with flat floors is associated with ridges and other relief features. The plant communities used are drier than those supporting the Masked Shrew, and lack the high overhead cover usually required by the Dusky Shrew *Sorex obscurus*. On the southern part of the Arctic Slope this shrew is associated principally with the Northern Red-backed Vole *Clethrionomys rutilus*, and to a lesser extent with the Insular Vole *Microtus abreviatus*. Further north, on the coastal plain, it is more often associated with the Arctic than with the Brown

Lemming. The Dusky Shrew is found throughout the Brooks Range and northern foothills, but may only be present on the flat coastal plain where adequate overhead cover is available. It is usually dependent on running water, and its typical habitat is the stream-edge of the floodplain above stream level where willow *Salix* and alder *Alnus* scrub is present.

## Lagomorpha

Two of the five species that occur in the Arctic can be dealt with quickly. The Northern Pika is a species occurring in the Arctic-alpine tundra of north-east Siberia. It is known that the male and female hold a definite territory throughout the year, and each resident reacts to intruders of the same sex, but while females usually remain in their own territories males often range into adjacent territories. The hay piles stored in each territory are consumed by the pair during the winter period. The Snowshoe Hare only appears on the tundra when populations are high and, while occupying a variety of habitats, prefers dense second-growth type forests. The approximately 10-year cycle of this species has been well documented, and one of the striking features is the rapidity with which the populations climb to and decline from the peak, compared with the extended period of low numbers before the rapid rise to the next peak. However, there are areas on the edge of the range where population levels are not cyclic at all (Keith 1963). No other hare in North America exhibits such regular cycles.

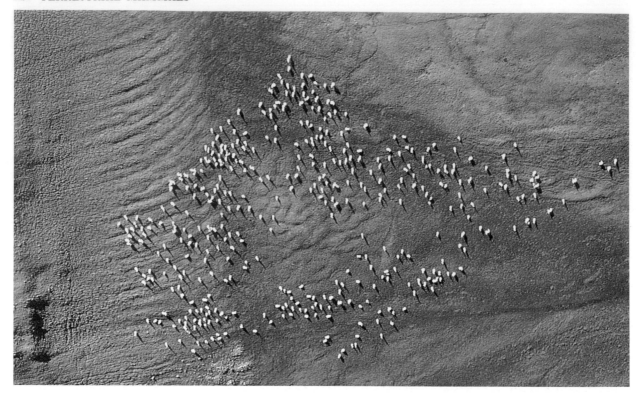

*Plate 10.5 A herd of Arctic Hares on Axel Heiberg in the Canadian Arctic*

### Alaskan Hare

This is one of North America's least known lagomorphs because of its remote and restricted range. It is not common on the Arctic Slope of Alaska, but occurs in the western section and on the north-western slopes of the Brooks Range. One litter is produced annually at about the time of snow-melt. Litter size is 3–8 with a mean of 6.4, and the young are born with open eyes and a full coat. This species has the fastest growth rate of any of the four large lagomorphs found in the Arctic, and this is believed to be an adaptation to the short Arctic growing season (Anderson and Lent 1977). The middle toes have well developed claws enabling the hare to dig through the snow for food, and the most favourable feeding habitat in winter is wind-blown slopes where snow cover is shallow. It is a close relative of the Varying Hare of Eurasia (and may be the same species) for which large gatherings of 100–500 have occasionally been reported (Tikhomirov 1959).

### Arctic Hare

The Arctic Hare probably has the most northerly distribution of any lagomorph in the world, and is widely distributed in the tundra regions of Labrador, northern Canada (including all the islands of the Queen Elizabeth group with the exception of Prince Patrick Island) and coastal Greenland. Its western range terminates near the mouth of the Mackenzie River, and it is replaced by the Alaskan Hare in northern Alaska. Throughout its range it spends the summer north of the treeline, but in winter in the southern part of its range it penetrates 160 km or more into the northern edge of the forest. It is undoubtedly highly adapted to its cold and mostly barren habitat (Wang *et al* 1973).

The habitat of those hares living on the islands of the Canadian Arctic Archipelago is characterised by vast areas of polar desert and semi-desert, and a very small extent (about 3 per cent) of more productive sedge-meadows in the most favourable sites. Hares reach their greatest abundance in the polar semi-desert areas, which are characterised by a scanty plant cover of 10–25 per cent dominated by three species of vascular plants – Purple Saxifrage, Arctic Willow and the sedge *Carex nardina*. The hares probably eat only the Arctic Willow, and if this is the case then they are existing on a very narrow energy base (Wang *et al* 1973). In winter they retreat to windswept and sparsely vegetated slopes where they are able to feed on exposed vegetation. In their extreme High Arctic habitat they are faced with mean monthly ambient temperatures ranging from −38° C for the coldest month, to 6° C for the warmest month, and a wind-packed snow cover that may bury their food supply for 280 days of the year.

The Arctic Hare begins to breed in the High Arctic with the return of long daylight hours in early May. A litter of 5–6 young is born in the latter half of June in a shallow depression scraped out in the gravel and sand, and often behind a rock for protection (Parker 1982).

Although generally common the Arctic Hare is normally solitary, often remaining undetected in the rock-strewn landscape. However, particularly in autumn and winter, they often form large herds. This habit appears to be unique to those populations

*Plate 10.6 The Arctic Ground Squirrel hibernates during the winter months*

inhabiting the High Arctic, and in particular Axel Heiberg and Ellesmere Islands where herds of hundreds of individuals have been reported, and in Greenland. The reason for the formation of these large herds is not clear, but may well be a means of protection against predators. The fact that when danger approaches the whole herd flees (hopping in an upright posture) suggests some sort of social structure, but further research is required. With no vegetation in which to hide, the hares head rapidly towards slopes and hills where they can find concealment in crevices and among boulders.

## Rodentia

Three species – European Water Vole, Muskrat, and Porcupine – will not be discussed here since they are of relatively little importance in the tundra habitat. Neither can anything be said about the vole *Eothenomys lemminus*, about which nothing seems to be known.

### Alaska Marmot

This marmot is found in the Brooks Range of Alaska and possibly occurs also in the Richardson Mountains west of the Mackenzie River in Canada, but the eastern limits of its range do not seem to be known with certainty. Marmots are true hibernators that do not store food for the winter but subsist entirely on fat reserves. In the Alaska Marmot all individuals in a colony hibernate together in a single winter den, and this behaviour also seems to be characteristic of most, if not

all, Eurasian marmots. The use of the plant growing season is maximised by birth of the young before the adults leave the den after hibernation. Even so, young weaned late or during years with a shortened growing season often fail to gain enough weight to survive hibernation (Hoffman *et al* 1979).

### Arctic Ground Squirrel

The Arctic Ground Squirrel population at Point Barrow, Alaska (71° N), represents the most northerly extension of the genus on the North American mainland. In the Brooks Range of Arctic Alaska this squirrel is common to about 1,070 m altitude. Because they require elaborate burrow systems and maintenance of visual contact, permanent colonies are restricted to well-drained sites with low vegetation, as found for example on glacial moraines, along stream banks and old beach ridges on the tundra, and on pingos. On the flat coastal tundra in the Point Barrow area, a relatively low permafrost table exists in certain areas correlated with good drainage, and within these restricted regions the ground squirrels find suitable habitat. On this flat coastal tundra burrows are sited in raised areas with a sandy substrate. Since these sites are of limited extent and rather widely distributed, the coastal plain with its otherwise flat, wet soils, must be regarded as a somewhat marginal habitat (Mayer 1953).

Ground squirrels respond strictly to the progression of the seasons and maintain a cycle of activity that is repeated annually. This is composed of successive periods of fattening, hibernation, and reproduction. In the Brooks Range hibernation usually begins in late September or early October, with emergence in the spring between mid-March and mid-April, but with activity intermittent until late April.

Despite constant daylight, ground squirrels in the Arctic behave as if in response to a regular diurnal light rhythm. The absence of nocturnal activity may result from increased costs of thermoregulation at night, which sharply reduces foraging efficiency. Studies carried out in August on the north slope of the Brooks Range 300–400 m above sea level (Chappell 1981), showed that the squirrels were active from about 06.00 to 20.00 hours. In another study (Vos and Ray 1959) it was found that in June most activity was in the early morning hours, very little in the afternoon, and the animals were inactive from 18.25 to 04.00 hours. On most days, rest periods lasting from 30 minutes to five hours in duration were taken. The rest periods, and each night, were spent in the main den.

The summer activity patterns of the Arctic Ground Squirrel are of particular interest because the species experiences long day lengths within a very short annual activity period. Despite high and stable body temperatures and cool ambient conditions, these squirrels have very low thermoregulatory costs during their summer activity periods. This metabolic efficiency results from moderate body size, low thermal conductance, selective utilisation of sunlit parts of the habitat, cessation of activity during the coldest part of the day, and the use of well-insulated nests. By making maximum use of microclimatic opportunities, enough energy may be saved to increase the rate of accumulation of winter fat by 15–20 per cent, an important advantage for an animal which can forage for only 3–4 months of the year. An adult squirrel stores about 350 g of fat over 60–70 days in preparation for hibernation (Chappell 1981).

**Population Ecology** Unlike most tundra rodents, the ground squirrel maintains a relatively constant population level. According to Carl (1971), they exist in two types of groupings: (a) breeding colonies, which cannot expand because their members are territorial, and (b) refugee populations which do not breed and, being in habitats only periodically suitable for them, are killed off twice each year. In another study, Batzli and Sobaski (1980) working on populations near Atkasook (71° N) on the Arctic Slope of Alaska, a favourable sand dune habitat, concluded that density was regulated at a relatively constant level by aggressive behaviour and dispersal of excess young. Adult females breed every year and July densities reached about 1.5 ha$^{-1}$ after the young emerged. Young animals, particularly males, dispersed in late August, and less than half the female young and one-tenth of the male young survived to the following spring.

**Territories and Burrow Systems** The research carried out by Carl (1971) on the north-west coast of Alaska showed that the breeding populations have two distinct types of territories: (a) breeding territories from May to August, and (b) pre-hibernation territories from August to November. During each phase, surplus animals are driven from the colonies and enter the refugee populations, where they are subjected to

heavy predation by Red Foxes and Grizzly Bears. The relationship between spring territory size (the area actually defended by the territorial male) and home range size (the mean of the area covered for any purpose by each resident of that territory) is shown in Table 10.4. On the 30 ha study area there were 66 single burrow systems, and each had between 20 and 50 surface openings. There were also 23 double burrow systems (the only ones used for breeding). A typical resident burrow system is shown in Figure 10.2

**Feeding Habits** Most foraging occurred within 30 m of burrows but not in the immediate vicinity of burrow entrances. Analysis of stomach contents at Atkasook indicated that ground squirrels ate mostly dicotyledons, including a wide variety of herbs (over 40 species) and shrubs; lichens and evergreen shrubs were generally ignored. Mosses, shoots of monocotyledons, deciduous shrub leaves, dicotyledon roots and animal matter constituted about half the diet in early summer, while herb shoots, seeds and horsetails *Equisetum* made up over 80 per cent of the diet in mid and late summer.

### Voles and Lemmings

Whilst there is an extensive literature on lemmings, studies in the Arctic on the other species are very few. As a general rule it can be said that when *Clethrionomys*

**Table 10.4:** Relationship Between Spring Territory Size and Home Range Size in the Arctic Ground Squirrel *Spermophilus undulatus*. (The home ranges are the average of all the squirrels operating on each territory)

| Territory number | Territory Size (m²) | Mean Home Range (m²) |
|---|---|---|
| 1 | 1,400 | 3,100 |
| 2 | 3,800 | 11,400 |
| 3 | 9,500 | 20,800 |
| 4 | 8,800 | 18,300 |
| 5 | 14,400 | 14,600[a] |
| 6 | 21,700 | 35,500 |
| 7 | 13,600 | 25,200 |
| 8 | 15,900 | 16,100[a] |
| 9 | 21,800 | 20,200[a] |

Note: a. These territories were very near the boundary of the study area and the squirrels on them fed extensively in areas off the study area, hence the home ranges shown are not complete.
Source: Carl (1971).

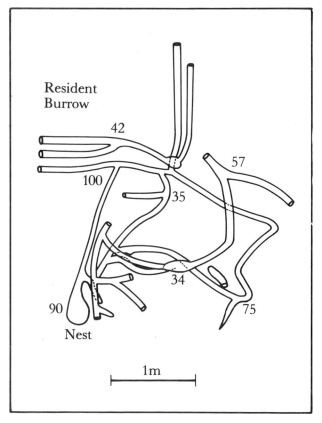

*Figure 10.2: Plan of a Typical Resident Burrow Excavated by Ground Squirrels*
*Source: Batzli and Sobaski (1980).*

**Table 10.5:** Distribution by Habitat of Voles on the Yamal Peninsula, Soviet Union

| Habitat Type | Lichen tundra | Moss-lichen tundra | Moss tundra | Peat-mound tundra | Low marshes | Watershed marshes | Floodplains Meadows of tundra rivers | Meadows on steep tundra slopes | Tundra shrubs |
|---|---|---|---|---|---|---|---|---|---|
| **Species** | | | | | | | | | |
| Narrow-skulled Vole *Microtus gregalis* | | | | | | | ×× | × | |
| Middendorff's Vole *Microtus middendorffi* | | | ×× | × | ×× | ×× | | | |
| Arctic Lemming *Dicrostonyx groenlandicus* | × | × | ×× | ×× | × | ×× | | | × |
| Brown Lemming *Lemmus sibiricus* | | | ×× | ×× | ×× | × | | | ×× |
| Northern Red-backed Vole *Clethrionomys rutilus* | | | | | | | × | | × |

Note: ××=primary habitat. ×=occasional habitat.
Source: Dunaeva (1948).

spp. and *Microtus* spp. do occur in tundra habitats, it is usually at more inland or southern localities, and their distributions overlap those of lemmings. In northern Alaska the species diversity of rodent communities declines from south to north on the Arctic Slope. Near the Brooks Range, five species of microtine and two of sciurid rodents form the community of herbivorous small mammals, but in the extreme northern parts of the coastal plain only two species of microtine and one sciurid remain. In North America *Clethrionomys*, like the Arctic Lemming, is most abundant in well-drained habitats, particularly those where shrubs are present. The Tundra Vole prefers low, wet areas dominated by grasses and sedges, perhaps even more so than the Brown Lemming. The Insular Vole seems to require dry soil adjacent to water and is commonly found on stream banks and lake shores, particularly where willows are spaced so that an understorey is present.

A valuable study relating primarily to the Yamal Peninsula in the Soviet Union is that by Dunaeva (1948). It is shown that the Narrow-skulled Vole occupies sharply limited sections of the tundra and is virtually confined to river valleys, where the preferred habitats are the river banks, riparian willows, steep slopes and pingos. It is the most exacting of the tundra voles in its burrowing requirements, since it is only possible to build wide underground burrows with the deep storerooms characteristic of this rodent where the active layer is deep enough. These conditions, and the preferred food plants, are found along river banks. Middendorff's Vole has a definite preference for moist areas such as marshy moss-dwarf birch-sphagnum moss areas of level tundra, low-lying sedge marshes, and peaty cottongrass tundra on high watersheds. Its characteristic shallow burrows run through the interface of the moss cover and the underlying peat. The nests for nursing the young are located in moss cushions or outside the burrow on the soil surface, under the cover of cottongrass and sedge tussocks.

The local distribution by habitat of voles on the Yamal Peninsula is summarised in Table 10.5.

Studies have been made (Batzli and Jung 1980) of the three species of microtine rodents (Tundra Vole, Arctic and Brown Lemmings) that occur together near Atkasook (71° N) on the Arctic Slope of Alaska. Population densities do not fluctuate as widely as do those of the Brown Lemming near Barrow, where densities may reach >200 ha$^{-1}$. Total microtine densities at Atkasook seldom reach more than 10 ha$^{-1}$, except in the most favourable habitats. Arctic Lemmings, unlike those at Barrow, occur in a wide variety of habitats (as they do in parts of the Soviet Union) and are almost as numerous as Brown Lemmings. Tundra Voles are restricted to habitats where lemmings are uncommon – on stream banks, floodplains, and near human disturbance. The results of studies at Prudhoe Bay (320 km east-south-east of Barrow) suggest that, in contrast to Barrow, the Arctic Lemming may be more abundant than the Brown Lemming, and that the lemming populations at Prudhoe Bay may never reach the magnitude recorded at Barrow (Feist 1975). At Atkasook, mean density of lemming burrows in different habitats varied from 2 to 112 100 m$^{-2}$, with concentrations along the rims of low-centre polygons, in the centres of high polygons and in moist regions of tussock tundra.

**Lemming Population Densities** In a three-year study on the Truelove Lowland, Devon Island (Fuller *et al* 1975, 1977), it was found that the greatest density of Arctic Lemming burrows (533.3 ha$^{-1}$) occurred in peat ice-wedge polygons which occupied well under one per cent of the lowland. Raised beaches had a burrow density of 115.4 ha$^{-1}$ largely associated with frost cracks. Mesic meadows were much less densely settled (26.7 burrows ha$^{-1}$); see Table 10.6.

**Table 10.6:** Proportion of Arctic Lemming *Dicrostonyx groenlandicus* Burrows Located in Different Microhabitats on the Truelove Lowland, Devon Island, Canada, in 1971

| | | | Under Rocks % | Not Under Rocks % | In Ice Wedges % |
|---|---|---|---|---|---|
| Raised Beaches | Crests | | 18 | 29 | 54 |
| | Foreslope | | 56 | 44 | |
| | Backslope | | 96 | 4 | |
| Ice-wedge Polygons | Exposure | North | 14 | | |
| | | South | 36 | | |
| | | East | 12 | | |
| | | West | 13 | | |
| | | Top | 25 | | |
| Hummocky Sedge-moss | Under Rocks | | 67 | | |
| Mesic Meadows | Not Under Rocks | | 33 | | |

Source: Fuller *et al* (1975 and 1977).

At Cape Chelyuskin in the polar desert zone of the Taimyr Peninsula, both Arctic and Brown Lemmings are present and their density is relatively high in spite of the fact that plant cover is sparse and exhibits low productivity. In summer they are confined to rock scatterings, while in winter they are evidently distributed more uniformly, since they utilise the pads of lichens *Cetraria delisei* and *C. ericetorum* for their nests, gnawing them and turning them into debris (Matveyeva and Chernov 1977).

The population densities of both Arctic and Brown Lemmings may show considerable variation between seasons, between different habitats and from one year to the next, and may differ markedly in different areas at the same time of year. At Barrow, Alaska, Brown Lemming densities usually reach their maximum just before snow-melt, after which populations decline. In Table 10.7 sample maximum densities of Arctic and Brown Lemmings are shown for several different Arctic localities. In the case of the Arctic Lemming at Barrow, densities may be as low as 0.1 ha$^{-1}$, and were in fact below 1 ha$^{-1}$ from 1955 to 1970. The peak density of 250 ha$^{-1}$ reported from the Taimyr Peninsula is far higher than any from North America, but was based on sampling in favourable habitats only.

**Habitat Selection and Movements** Although the southern parts of the ranges of both Arctic and Brown Lemmings extend into alpine tundra, both are primarily inhabitants of Arctic coastal plains where grasses (*Arctophila*, *Dupontia*) and sedges (*Carex*, *Eriophorum*) dominate the wet lowlands and polygonal-patterned ground, and decumbent shrubs and herbs (*Salix*, *Dryas*) are dominant on ridges and hummocks. In general the Brown Lemming occupies the wetter habitats and Arctic Lemming the drier, but local exceptions in both directions may occur (e.g. Dunaeva 1948, Batzli and Jung 1980). The seasonal movement patterns of both species appear to be responses to patterns of

**Table 10.7:** Sample Maximum Densities of Lemmings at Arctic Locations

| | Location | Density (no. ha$^{-1}$) |
|---|---|---|
| Brown Lemming | Barrow, N. Alaska | 90–175 |
| *Lemmus sibiricus* | | 75–175 |
| | | 100–200 |
| | Baker Lake, NWT, N. Canada | 75 |
| | Taimyr Peninsula, Soviet Union | 100–350[a] |
| Arctic Lemming | Northern Alaska | 20–30 |
| *Dicrostonyx* | Barrow, N. Alaska | 1–30 |
| *groenlandicus* | Prudhoe Bay, N. Alaska | 7–10 |
| | Devon Island, N. Canada | 2–3 |
| | Baker Lake, NWT, N. Canada | 25 |
| | Churchill, Hudson Bay | 35–40 |
| | | 25 |
| | Taimyr Peninsula, Soviet Union | 250[a] |

Note: a. Data based on sampling in favourable habitats only.
Sources: Batzli (1975), Brooks (1970), Feist (1975), Krebs (1964), Maher (1970a), Schultz (1969), Shelford (1943), Speller (1972), Thompson (1955) and Vinokurov *et al* (1972).

flooding and snow depth. In winter they congregate in lowlands, particularly polygon troughs and meadows where snow is deeper. At melt-off these areas become flooded and lemmings are more concentrated in uplands. As the tundra dries out relative densities increase in the lowlands.

Although occasional mass emigrations by the Norwegian Lemming *Lemmus lemmus* from alpine habitats into agricultural regions are well known, no long emigrations have been reported for the present two species. However, unusual activity may occur during some peak years (Thompson 1955); Gavin (1974) mentions two 'massive scale' movements (presumably by the Brown Lemming) in Canada – one at the Perry River on Queen Maud Gulf stretching for more than 64 km, and one on Victoria Island extending over some 48 km.

**Activity Patterns** The daily activity patterns of Brown Lemmings were studied (Peterson and Batzli 1975 and 1984, Peterson *et al* 1976) at Barrow, Alaska, in the summer of 1973 using radiotelemetry. It was found that activity patterns appeared to change in response to predators, weather and nutritional requirements. During early summer, when daylight is continuous, lemming activity occurred randomly throughout the day and 'night'. But during late summer, when the sun began to set and avian predator activity declined during the dark, lemmings appeared to shift more of their activity to night.

**Breeding and Nest Structure** It should be pointed out that a major difference between the lemmings and other Arctic microtines is the ability of lemmings to breed in the winter. Apparently only the Narrow-skulled Vole and Middendorff's Vole begin breeding before May (Shvarts *et al* 1969). Both the Arctic and the Brown Lemming appear to have a winter and a summer reproductive season. One study of the latter species (Mullen 1968) in which samples were taken throughout the winter, indicated fairly continuous breeding by about 40 per cent of the females from December to April. All breeding ceases at times of snow-melt (spring) or freeze-up (autumn). Maximum breeding occurs during early or mid-summer when nearly all the mature females are pregnant.

In Brown Lemming studies, the proportion of mature females pregnant in the period December–February was 33 per cent, from March–April 29 per cent and in July 70–80 per cent (Krebs 1964, Mullen 1968). In the case of the Arctic Lemming, July pregnancy rates were 85–90 per cent (Krebs 1964, Speller 1972). In actual fact, owing to under-detection of pregnancies, a value of 75 per cent or above indicates that almost all females are pregnant. Available data suggest that breeding in the Arctic Lemming lasts later into May than is the case with the Brown Lemming (Batzli 1975). In both species the population structure shifts from predominantly adult individuals in the spring to predominantly young in the autumn.

All individuals probably construct some form of winter shelter, but only the breeding females elaborate them into large, well-insulated structures. Winter nests of the Arctic Lemming on the Truelove Lowland were constructed from *Carex* shoots and were built predominantly along slopes of raised beaches, the areas with the deepest and most persistent snow cover. Those lemmings not occupying thick, well-insulated nests are living at very low temperatures and may be operating near their maximum metabolic rate where temperatures slightly lower than normal may be critical, especially in relation to winter reproduction. The relationship of snow depth and air temperature to winter breeding is discussed in some detail by MacLean *et al* (1974).

**Feeding Habits** Arctic Lemmings mostly eat dicotyledon leaves, particularly willow, supplemented by small amounts of monocotyledons. Brown Lemmings eat mostly monocotyledons, particularly sedges, and small amounts of mosses (but more in winter when

**Table 10.8:** Percentage Composition of the Diet of Arctic and Brown Lemmings in Tundra Habitats as Determined by Stomach Analyses

| Species | Food type | | | | |
| --- | --- | --- | --- | --- | --- |
| | **Mosses** | **Sedges** | **Grasses** | **Dicots** | **Miscellaneous** |
| Arctic Lemming *Dicrostonyx groenlandicus* | (*Polytrichum, Dicranum*) | (*Carex, Eriophorum*) | (*Dupontia*) | (*Salix, Potentilla, Dryas*) | (lichens) |
| Upland tundra (June) | 4 | 4 | 8 | 83 | 1 |
| Raised beach ridge (September) | | | | (*Dryas, Saxifraga, Salix*) 92 | (unspecified) 8 |
| Brown Lemming *Lemmus sibiricus* | (*Polytrichum, Dicranum, Calliergon*) | (*Carex, Eriophorum*) | (*Dupontia, Poa*) | (*Saxifraga, Stellaria, Draba*) | (liverworts, lichens) |
| Upland tundra (June) | 24 | 30 | 38 | 6 | 2 |
| Marshy tundra (June) | 14 | 20 | 56 | 7 | 3 |
| Low polygons (July) | 24 | 26 | 35 | 13 | 2 |
| Low polygons (January) | 38 | 37 | 18 | 5 | 2 |

Sources: Batzli (1973 and 1975) and Fuller *et al* (1977).

monocots are less available). As pointed out by Batzli (1975), diet does not simply mimic vegetational composition, and where both Arctic and Brown Lemmings occur side by side in upland tundra, their food may be very different. Further light is shed on this subject as a result of feeding trails reported by Batzli and Jung (1980). These indicated that a common sedge *Carex aquatilis* contains a compound(s) deleterious to Arctic Lemmings, and that a common deciduous shrub *Salix pulchra* contains a compound(s) deleterious to Brown Lemmings. Another shrub, the aromatic Labrador Tea contains a compound(s) deleterious to both species of lemming. Apparently each lemming species specialises on particular foods and cannot tolerate the secondary compounds in the other's major food items. Table 10.8 shows the percentage composition (as determined by stomach content analysis) for both species of lemming in various tundra habitats.

The summer nutrition of the Brown Lemming is markedly different from that in winter, the quality and quantity of food changing abruptly with spring growth at melt-off. The importance of Tundra Grass (the most important single species), and the sedges *Eriophorum angustifolium* and *Carex aquatilis* is evident from the data in Table 10.8. The composition of the winter diet is not well known, but data in Batzli (1973) shows the presence of *D. fischeri*, *E. angustifolium* and *C. aquatilis*, with mosses contributing nearly 40 per cent of the diet at that time. Food selection by the Arctic Lemming on Devon Island in September 1971 showed that the animals dug feeding craters to reach favoured food plants. Of 701 craters examined, 95.8 per cent terminated at one of only four species of dicotyledonous plants – Arctic Avens (42.9 per cent), Purple Saxifrage (36.9 per cent), Arctic Willow (12.3 per cent), and *Pedicularis* sp. (3.7 per cent) – all species with high calorific values.

**Lemming Population Cycles** The periodic fluctuations or 'cycles' in lemming numbers are one of the most widely known and best documented of Arctic phenomena. In fact almost all small rodents of the northern hemisphere exhibit marked population changes on a four-year cycle. A recurrent feature of these phenomena is that a species may exhibit very pronounced and regular cycles in population density in one part of its area of distribution, but be relatively

*Figure 10.3: Estimated Brown Lemming Densities Averaged for All Habitats in the Coastal Tundra at Barrow, Alaska, for the Period 1955–1974*

*Source: Based on Batzli, White, MacLean, Pitelka and Collier (1980).*

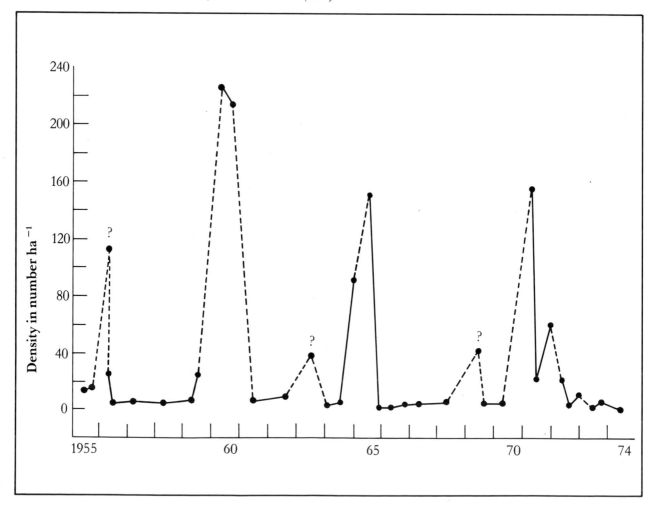

stable in another. Examples are the well known lemming cycles at Barrow, Alaska, which apparently do not occur at Prudhoe Bay only 320 km away or at Atkasook 100 km away (Feist 1975, Batzli and Jung 1980). Another aspect of these population changes is that even during 'low' years, there may be local 'pockets' supporting a denser population. The most pronounced population changes take place with the Brown Lemming. Arctic Lemming populations fluctu-

ate on a much smaller scale, and apparently at much longer intervals. For example, it was suggested by Pitelka (1973) that the higher densities of this species may be reached only occasionally (perhaps every 20 years) at some locations. At Barrow in a 20-year period, 1955–1974, Arctic Lemming numbers were below one ha$^{-1}$, but attained 27 ha$^{-1}$ in 1971.

Figure 10.3 shows the estimated mean densities of the Brown Lemming at Barrow over a period of 20

*Figure 10.4: Diagram of Relationships Among Factors Influencing Lemming Density*
*Source: Based on Batzli, White, MacLean, Pitelka and Collier (1980).*

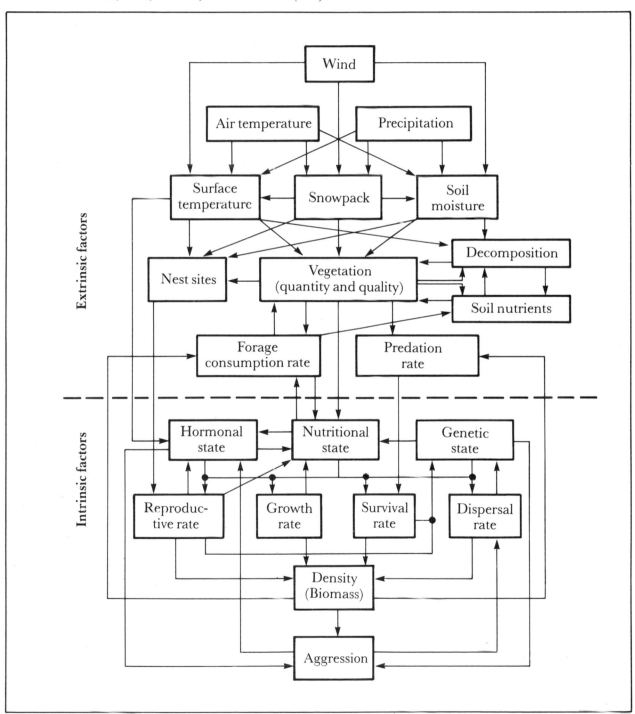

summers. Local densities may depart markedly from overall densities, but the general year to year trends were similar in all habitats. While each cycle has peculiarities of its own, a general sequence of events can be outlined. What may be termed a standard cycle begins with the development of a high population in the winter preceding a population peak late in the following spring. Breeding ceases at the time of the spring snow-melt, although juveniles continue to enter the trappable population until early June. After snow-melt the lemmings are subjected to heavy predation, particularly by Pomarine Skuas, Snowy Owls and Least Weasels. During the summer the population crashes to a low level, where it remains for one to three years. Neither the amplitude or the wavelength of the cycles is always the same. It is possible to recognise four stages in the sequence of events: (a) high, (b) very low, (c) low and (d) medium densities.

Lemming population peaks occurred at Barrow in 1946, 1949, 1953, 1956, 1960, 1965 and 1971, so the period between the peaks varied from three to six years, with an average of 4.2 years. In the summer of 1971 there was a dramatic increase in the population over that of the previous summer. Although the population declined by 80 per cent between mid-June and mid-July as a result of predation, it rose by mid-August to about 60 per cent of the mid-June level. This was a level which, on past experience, was high enough to foretell a peak the next year. Expectations were that the summer of 1972 would see, for the first time in seven years,

a true cyclic high, but it never materialised although lemmings were present in moderate numbers (Figure 10.3). The population did not reach its usual low density of 0.5 ha$^{-1}$ until 1974. The features of each cycle are discussed in detail by Pitelka (1973) and Batzli *et al* (1980).

The role of both extrinsic and intrinsic factors (e.g. behaviour, physiology, genetics) in these remarkable lemming cycles remains the subject of debate and the situation has been summarised by Batzli *et al* (1980) and is set out in Figure 10.4. Whatever the role of intrinsic factors in the population cycle might be, there is no doubt that extrinsic factors exert a powerful and overriding influence. In order for lemming populations to reproduce and grow during winter, good quality forage must be available, the snowpack must be suitable and mammalian predators must be scarce. Only when all three of these conditions prevail can a high population be attained. A high population may begin to decline because of inadequate forage, but only high mortality, resulting from predation or some other factor, and reduced recruitment can make the decline continue through the summer. Therefore, it does not seem that any single extrinsic or intrinsic factor can explain the population dynamics of lemmings. Rather, lemming populations respond to a number of factors that act and interact concurrently to determine the timing and amplitude of fluctuations. Dramatic fluctuations in the lemming population occur because the high reproductive output during a single favourable winter allows them to increase their density by 100-fold or more, and these high levels cannot be sustained.

*Plate 10.7 A Gray Wolf resting*

## Carnivora

### *Gray Wolf*

With the exception of man, the Gray Wolf probably has the greatest natural range of any living mammal. At the maximum extent of the Pleistocene glaciations isolated populations may have survived in various refugia, including western Alaska, eastern Siberia (Beringia) and Greenland. Following the retreat of the glaciers at the end of the Pleistocene, animals from the Greenland refugium probably spread into the northern islands of the Canadian Arctic, and from Beringia eastwards into western and central Canada.

The wolf is a meat-eating animal whose entire digestive system is adapted to a carnivorous diet. The large size of the wolf itself, combined with its habit of travelling in packs, makes it perfectly adapted to feed on larger species of prey. Although capable of eating enormous amounts of food in very short periods, and at frequent intervals, it is also adapted to go for long periods (up to several days) without food. When wolves and ungulates inhabit the same range, ungulates are usually the main prey. Predation by wolves is generally selective, resulting in the removal of very young, very old, sick, wounded or crippled individuals.

The wolf has suffered periodic persecution over most of its range, including the Arctic, for a very long time, and its numbers have fluctuated accordingly. The total wolf population for the whole of Siberia was estimated

to be about 3,000 in 1973. In the tundra and forest-tundra populations, density did not exceed one wolf 1,000 km$^{-2}$ (D. I. Bibokov in Harrington and Paquet 1982). Although wolf densities in Canada's Northwest Territories have been reduced in some areas through man's influence on the ecosystem, they still occupy all of their traditional range (Carbyn 1981). In general, the lowest wolf densities are found on Victoria Island and the Queen Elizabeth Islands, and the highest are found in association with wintering concentrations of Barren-ground Caribou. On southern Ellesmere Island, Riewe (1975) estimated that in the area of maximum wolf concentration, density was only one wolf 900 km$^{-2}$. Kelsall (1968) estimated that there may be 8,000 wolves on all Barren-ground Caribou ranges in Canada combined (one wolf 160 km$^{-2}$), while Parker (1972) estimated wolf density on the Kaminuriak herd's range at about one wolf 500 km$^{-2}$. However, Parker (1973) found one wolf 20 km$^{-2}$ in February 1968 on the winter range of this herd. In April 1979, L. N. Carbyn estimated at least 250 wolves associated with a large segment of the Bathurst Island caribou herd in an area of 1,600 km$^2$ (one wolf 6.4 km$^{-2}$).

**Feeding Habits** The overwhelming dependency of Arctic wolf populations on one or more ungulate species in winter, and continued high dependency in summer, is well known. According to Carbyn (1981), an analysis of population data indicates that rates of increase are primarily determined by the per-capita biomass of their ungulate food supply, and that wolf

*Plate 10.8 The Red Fox usually avoids the exposed tundra and polar desert habitats favoured by the Arctic Fox*

*Plate 10.9 An Arctic Fox in immature coat*

densities in stationary populations are thereby adjusted to total ungulate biomass.

The mortality of newborn Barren-ground Caribou was studied in June and July 1970 on the calving ground of the Kaminuriak caribou herd in Keewatin, northern Canada. Fifty-seven calf carcasses were found of which 31.6 per cent had been killed by wolves (Carbyn 1981). A study of wolf feeding behaviour in the Thelon Game Sanctuary in the Northwest Territories was carried out from 1960 to 1968 (Kuyt 1972). Examination of 595 spring and summer wolf droppings showed that of 1,039 prey items, 38 per cent were remains of adult caribou, and 9 per cent were remains of calves. Clearly, caribou constituted the main prey species of these tundra wolves in spring and summer. In areas temporarily devoid of caribou, a greater average number of different prey items per dropping (2.16 compared to 1.47 for areas north of the Clarke River) is indicative of the resident breeding wolves' greater dependence on prey species other than caribou.

**Movements and Home Range** Numerous studies of North American wolves have shown that in most areas a wolf pack tends to remain in a home range that, although large, remains relatively stable throughout the year. This coincides with the fairly constant availability of prey species which, although often undertaking seasonal movements, do so over relatively short distances. Wolves that depend primarily upon caribou, however, are frequently faced with drastic seasonal fluctuations in prey availability. In the Northwest Territories, Kuyt (1972) found that ear-tagged wolves

moved as much as 360 km during the winter in response to the southward migration of caribou to their winter range – findings that were substantiated by Parker (1973). These and other authors showed that extremely high densities of wolves may occur during the maximum compression of wintering caribou populations.

A study carried out in the western Brooks Range of Alaska (R. Stephenson and D. James in Harrington and Paquet 1982) is of much interest in relation to wolf movements. Aerial surveys in April 1977 indicated that wolf numbers were low, with density along the northern foothills being about one wolf $390\ km^{-2}$. In the northern and western portions of the Arctic Slope, density was about one wolf $520\ km^{-2}$. In the summer of 1977 a pair of wolves were located in the upper Kokalik River area and were radio-collared. They successfuy reared seven pups and remained in an area of about $1,000\ km^2$ throughout the summer and early autumn, relying primarily on caribou for prey. By early December the entire pack was relocated some 80 km south of the 1977 den site.

Another pack ranged over an area of about $2,600\ km^2$ during the summers of 1977 and 1978, although an area of about $1,300\ km^2$ was used more intensively than the remainder. All pack members remained in association with the 1977 den site until late summer when two of the yearling males disappeared. In late November one was located 220 km east of the den site, and the other was trapped 170 km to the east early in December. Thus both packs studied consistently occupied the same summer areas, and both travelled as fairly cohesive units during the winter, but without establishing any apparent territories. There

*Plate 10.10 An Arctic Fox in summer coat in the Canadian High Arctic*

were, however, a number of instances in which individual pack members left the usual pack ranges and dispersed for varying lengths of time.

### Red Fox

The Red Fox occurs in the Arctic in both North America and the Soviet Union, and although perhaps enjoying a more general distribution than the Arctic Fox, it is rarely as abundant locally. There is also a habitat difference in that the Red Fox usually avoids the exposed tundra and polar desert areas frequented by the Arctic Fox, and prefers mountain foothills, valley sides, and canyons. However, in Arctic Canada it competes with the Arctic Fox on at least the tundra of the Ungava Peninsula. It is also present on Baffin Island and Southampton Island, and has occasionally reached Ellesmere and Cornwallis Islands. On the Arctic Slope of Alaska it is generally uncommon on the flat tundra of the coastal plain, but in 1969 when lemmings were common a number of individuals were seen within a few kilometres of the Beaufort Sea and must have been in competition with the Arctic Fox and other predators on lemmings.

### Arctic Fox

The Arctic Fox (like the Arctic Lemming, Arctic Hare, Polar Bear and Musk-ox) is virtually restricted to the Arctic biome, although its range does extend beyond the boundaries of the Arctic as defined for the purposes of this book. Although found throughout the Arctic Slope of Alaska it is most numerous on the coastal plain, as is the case also in the Soviet Union. In Canada

also it is commonest in coastal regions, and its range extends throughout the High Arctic islands to the coastal regions of Greenland. During winter Arctic Foxes disperse widely with many moving far out on the pack-ice; they have been reported within 140 km of the true North Pole, and within 80 km of the northern pole of inaccessibility (the point in the Arctic pack-ice furthest from land).

The Arctic Fox is dimorphic in its winter coat, some individuals being white while others are dark bluish-grey. These genetically distinct phases freely interbreed, and their relative ratios show much variation over the Arctic. In Canada there are less than 1 per cent blue phase animals, and in Siberia 3 to 4 per cent. At the other extreme, on Jan Mayen Island and in parts of Greenland, up to 90 per cent of the population may be of the blue phase (Larson 1960, Finerty 1980).

**Population Density** Considerable data are now available on den density. Macpherson (1969) calculated the mean density of dens for three areas of Canada as one den 36 km$^{-2}$. Boitzov (1937) estimated the density of dens within the tundra zone of the Soviet Union as one den 32 km$^{-2}$, but much higher densities have been reported from individual areas in that country (e.g. one den 1.6 km$^{-2}$ and one den 2.1 km$^{-2}$, but the basis of these calculations is not known). A study in the Colville delta area of northern Alaska (Garrott 1980) revealed at least 40 dens within 1,700 km$^2$ (one den 12.5 km$^{-2}$).

**Denning Habits** The average number of burrow entrances for the dens in the Colville delta area was 33 and ranged from 1 to 85. The surface area of the dens varied from 1 to 625 m², with an average den size of 256 m². These data differ considerably from those of Chesemore (1969) for the Teshekpuk Lake area in northern Alaska where the dens were small with simple burrow systems (mean den size 63 m², average number of entrances twelve). At Prudhoe Bay the mean den size was 150 m² with an average of 26 entrances (Eberhardt 1977).

Prerequisites for a den site are a stable surface deposit and soil structure capable of supporting burrows, and an active layer deep enough to burrow into. In northern Alaska the gently sloping banks of creeks and lakes, banks of terraces, pingos, low mounds and stabilised dune ridges are characteristic sites.

**Behaviour at the Den** The studies by Garrott (1980) in the Colville delta showed that, during the denning season, reproducing Arctic Foxes formed groups consisting of an adult male and female and their progeny. Both adults returned to the den periodically throughout the day with prey for the cubs, but little time was spent there. Social behaviour within the group was most frequently observed between cubs and usually involved some form of play. The most prevalent types of behaviour observed in cubs, however, were nonsocial, such as feeding, resting and solitary play. So although Arctic Foxes form temporary family groups during the spring and summer, interactions between members of the family are limited. The relatively low level of sociality presumably reflects the solitary nature of the species which preys on small birds and mammals that are most easily captured by a single fox.

**Breeding Biology** The Arctic Fox normally gives birth underground in a breeding den which may be used for many years. The cubs are born in the late spring after a gestation period of 51–57 days, and are weaned in mid-summer. In any one year only about one-third of the 1–2 year old vixens breed, whereas about five-sixths of the 3-year and over group breed. A mean litter size of 10.6 was given by Macpherson (1969). Evidence from the Canadian studies suggests that lemming abundance in the breeding season governs the survival of fox cubs.

**Feeding Habits** There is general agreement on the importance of lemmings and other small mammals to Arctic Foxes in inland habitats, but foxes living on islands or in coastal areas may rely to a considerable extent on fish, sea-mammals, seabirds and even marine invertebrates. The propensity of these foxes to eat the remains of seals left on the sea-ice by Polar Bears is well known. The reliance of this fox on lemmings in many areas means that they are profoundly affected by the population cycles of these rodents, and at times of lows in the lemming populations it is those foxes living in coastal regions that are able to compensate most easily by turning to alternative sources of prey. As a predator on birds, the Arctic Fox takes predominantly eggs and young.

In a detailed study of Arctic Fox populations in northern Canada, Macpherson (1969) found that lemmings were by far the largest component in the diet of breeding foxes, averaging up to 90 per cent and never below 50 per cent of total food remains in droppings. Other foods eaten were birds and their eggs, caribou (as carrion), fish, insects and berries. Lemmings were also important in winter, as shown by analysis of digestive tracts. In the Prudhoe Bay region, Underwood (1975) found remains of Brown and Arctic Lemmings in 86 per cent of 50 fresh droppings in an inland area, and in 75 per cent of 24 droppings in a coastal area despite generally low densities of microtines. Bird remains were found in 50 per cent of the droppings from inland and in 63 per cent of the droppings from the coast. Adult foxes appeared to spend large periods of time away from the den sites, and it was assumed that the breeding foxes were occupying large, overlapping feeding ranges.

Research carried out in Jameson Land, east Greenland, in 1984 (Cabot *et al* 1984) indicated the importance of this fox as a predator of young Barnacle Geese. In the case of foxes inhabiting dens near the breeding colonies of these geese, it was found that the latter formed a large proportion of the prey during the period when the goslings left the nest. The foxes are attracted to the colonies by the loud calling which the adult geese make before and during the jump from the nest ledges. Their normal hunting technique is to snatch the goslings among the boulders of the scree where the adult geese are helpless to defend them. Among the prey brought to a den with eight cubs were Barnacle Goose goslings, lemmings, and parts of a nearby Muskox carcase. At another den with five cubs the observed prey included lemmings, chicks of Long-tailed Skua and adult Barnacle Geese taken whilst flightless during the moult.

A good example of the possible scale of predation by this fox on birds concerns Common Eiders nesting on barrier islands at Icy Cape on the Chukchi Sea in north-west Alaska (Quinlan and Lehnhausen 1982). A single fox which crossed mudflats at low tide to one island, then swam the short distance to the eider nesting island where it destroyed the colony, cached an estimated 500 eggs, and killed at least one female eider.

The Arctic Fox is well known in the role of a scavenger of marine mammal remains left by Polar Bears. It is also now known to be an important predator of the pups of the Ringed Seal (Smith 1976). Studies in Prince Albert Sound and the eastern Amundsen Gulf in the Canadian Arctic showed that foxes enter and kill seal pups in their subnivean birth lairs. While predation varied over the three years of study, an average pup predation level of 26.1 per cent in nearshore sea-ice was estimated.

### Grizzly Bear

Throughout the Soviet Arctic the grizzly is a scarce animal on the tundra, probably being most numerous on the Chukotka Peninsula. In northern Alaska it occurs throughout the Brooks Range and the Arctic Slope. It extends across the border into Canada where

*Plate 10.11 The Grizzly Bear ranges widely over tundra habitats*

it does not quite reach as far east as Hudson Bay, and is absent from all of the Canadian Arctic Islands. The northern tundra regions constitute the northern limit of the range of the grizzly.

**Winter Denning** The grizzly requires approximately two weeks to enter the deep 'winter sleep' and, unless disturbed, does not normally waken until spring. During dormancy the drop in body temperature is quite small (only about 5° C on average), and the animal does not feed, urinate or defecate, but utilises the fat reserves laid down before entering the den. Dates of entry into and emergence from the winter den vary in response to weather (especially autumn snowstorms). In the Brooks Range grizzlies usually enter the den sometime during October.

Studies by Reynolds *et al* (1976) in the eastern Brooks Range resulted in the location of 29 active dens (23 excavated and six in caves) for which the winter of use was known, and 23 inactive dens (16 excavated and seven in caves). Of the total of 52 dens, 90 per cent were on southerly slopes, 8 per cent on northerly slopes, and 2 per cent on an easterly slope; most were on slopes of 20–35 degrees. Excluding three dens on the coastal plain, the den sites had a mean elevation of 1,040 m above sea level and 180 m above the valley floor. The preference for southerly-orientated den sites is probably related to soil characteristics: because of permafrost, soils on north-facing slopes may thaw only to depths of 30–60 cm, while on southerly slopes the depth of thaw may reach 2 m.

**Breeding Biology** Detailed research in the Brooks Range by Reynolds (1976, 1978, 1980, 1981, 1982) has thrown considerable light on the breeding biology of the grizzly in that area. First breeding and production of young is probably more related to the nutritional status and weight of a female than to age. Subsequent litters and survival of cubs is also likely linked to nutrition. The age of females at sexual maturity in the eastern Brooks Range has varied from 6.5 to 12.5 years, and in the western Brooks Range the average age at first production of young was 8.1 years. In the northern Yukon Territory of Canada, age at first conception was 7.5 years.

Litter sizes in the Brooks Range ranged from one to three. The mean size of 49 litters over a 5-year period was 2.0. Mortality rates for young were high – cub mortality 46 per cent, yearling mortality 11 per cent and 2-year mortality 16 per cent. Most observed mortality among cubs of the year occurred one to four weeks after emergence from maternal dens. Population structure in the Brooks Range seems to be weighted towards older age classes (Table 10.9).

**Table 10.9:** Age Structure of Brooks Range Grizzly Bear *Ursus arctos* Populations

| | No. of years' data | % cubs | % yearlings | % 2-year olds | % 3–4 year olds | % 5-years+ olds |
|---|---|---|---|---|---|---|
| E. Brooks Range | 3 | 7.9 | 10.9 | 10.9 | 5.0 | 65.3 |
| W. Brooks Range | 2 | 10.8 | 9.5 | 10.8 | 9.5 | 50.0 |

Sources: Reynolds (1976 and 1978).

**Feeding Habits** Grizzlies require large expanses of wilderness with considerable diversity, preferably isolated from human activities. They are omnivorous animals and spend their lives mainly in an intensive search for the most nutritious foods. The diet includes a wide range of animals and plants and varies according to area and season. Animal food includes rodents (particularly ground squirrels), carrion, fish and the occasional Moose or Caribou when these can be caught. Studies in the eastern Brooks Range (Reynolds 1976) showed that from May to early June, carrion, roots (mostly *Hedysarum*) and grasses were the primary food sources; in June and July, grasses and horsetails provided the bulk of the diet; from August to mid-September, Soapberry *Shepherdia canadensis* or Bearberry were the major food items, although hibernating ground squirrels were also dug out. Bears seen after mid-October were utilising carrion.

**Home Range** Evidence from the Brooks Range studies indicated that in that area most grizzlies use a single, well-defined area throughout the year. The home ranges of five breeding males had a mean size of 702 km², while three breeding females had a mean home range size of 382 km², and five females accompanied by cubs had a mean home range size of 280 km². Working with a population of marked animals in the Brooks Range, Reynolds (1978) estimated 121 individuals for a 5,180 km² area, a density of one bear 42.8 km⁻².

### Polar Bear

Polar Bears are widely distributed at low densities over the circumpolar Arctic pack-ice. They are most abundant around the perimeter of the Polar Basin for 200–300 km offshore from the land masses, and have been recorded as far north as 88° N. Their distribution is by no means uniform and much of the pack-ice is a poverty zone so far as the bears are concerned. Research has shown that Polar Bear distribution is related to specific types of ice, presumably because these in turn are related to the abundance and availability of seals. For example, studies by Stirling *et al* (1975) in the area of Victoria and Banks Islands west to the Alaska/Canada border showed that 87 per cent of bear sightings were made in two similar types of habitat which occurred in a relatively narrow band parallel to the mainland coast to Cape Parry, and off the west coast of Banks Island:–

1. 47 per cent of sightings: the active ice habitat – areas of 9/10 or 10/10 ice cover but in 'active zones',

such as around Baillie Island, where wind and sea currents cause much movement of ice, followed by refreezing, creating intermittent lanes or patches of refrozen young ice, bare or only slightly drifted.

2. 40 per cent of sightings: the floe edge habitat – where leads are wide (>1 km), usually with small or refrozen leads parallel to the floe edge or emanating from it; some pressure ridges, occasionally fresh but usually not heavily drifted.

A further 11 per cent of sightings were on flat, landfast ice with stable pressure ridges, drifted with snow and suitable for seal lairs. Polynas (see Chapter 4), such as the Cape Bathurst and North Water polynas of northern Canada, are important feeding areas for bears. Through winter and spring some 1,500–1,800 bears from the western Canadian Arctic population feed at the former, and approximately 1,700 frequent the Canadian side of the huge North Water polyna (Davids 1982).

**Population Data** At one time it was considered that the world population of Polar Bears was a single unit, with individuals living a nomadic existence wandering throughout the circumpolar ice. Subsequent research, however, suggested that most populations are fairly local. Worldwide there may be a dozen or more discrete populations within which are smaller sub-populations. Canada, for instance, may have as many as 15 relatively discrete sub-populations. In Alaska there appears to be two main populations, one on the west coast between Cape Lisburne and Wainwright (ranging westwards to Wrangel Island in the Soviet Arctic), and a north coast population extending eastwards to north-west Canada. In Greenland also there are two populations, one on the west and another on the east coast (wandering eastwards to Svalbard), while another population is found on Svalbard and is augmented by bears roaming westwards from Russia's Franz Josef Land. According to Larsen (1984), Canada's current population is about 15,000 and Alaska's 3,000–4,500. To these must be added the populations of Greenland, Svalbard and the northern Soviet Union, resulting in a world population of about 25,000. Svalbard normally supports about 3,000 bears, but this is estimated to reach 4,000–5,000 when other animals move in from Greenland and Franz Josef Land.

**Breeding Biology** Polar Bears have delayed implantation. That is to say, the fertilised egg does not begin to develop immediately but remains in the uterus in a dormant state. Thus, although mating takes place in May, the fertilised egg does not implant and begin to grow until about September. The species has a slow reproductive rate. In the eastern High Arctic of Canada females first breed at four years of age and give birth about every three years (but sooner if cubs die). In the western Canadian Arctic and in Alaska, most females do not breed until five years old. In contrast, females in the southern part of Hudson Bay have cubs in alternate years, and about 80 per cent of yearling cubs are already weaned, a situation unknown further north.

**Denning Habits** Some time in October pregnant females seek denning areas, and it is usually only these individuals that go into winter dens for extended periods. The cubs are generally born in December and remain in the den with the female until March or early April. Important denning areas at the present time include north-west and north-east Greenland, eastern Svalbard, Franz Josef Land, Wrangel Island, southern Banks Island, the Simpson Peninsula (north-east Keewatin District), eastern Southampton Island, and eastern Baffin Island (Figure 10.5). Other somewhat less important denning areas include the south end of Baffin Island, southern Ellesmere Island, southern Devon Island, and Victoria Island, all in Canada. Dens in Alaska are widely dispersed.

Dens are usually excavated in the dense snowbanks that develop on leeward slopes of coastal hills and valley sides (Harington 1968). Some females give birth out on the pack-ice with little or no protection from the environment. Dens on drifting ice have been recorded only rarely (e.g. Lentfer 1975). Of 113 dens in the Canadian Arctic, about 61 per cent were within eight kilometres of the coast and 81 per cent lay within 16 km of it. The locations ranged from the level of sea-ice to 548 m above sea level. In the Hudson Bay area, two major denning areas are located 20 and 70 km inland. On Russia's Wrangel Island the general number of maternity dens was determined to be 150–200 in 1960, 180–200 in 1970, and about 250 in 1973. The area with the greatest concentration of dens is the small Drem-Khed mountain massif in the north-west of the island. In this area of about 20 km² some 25–50 dens are located annually. The density of dens sometimes reaches one den 50 m⁻².

**Feeding Habits** For the first few days after breaking out of the den, most females seem to dig out and eat ground vegetation. Once back on the sea-ice, however, the diet consists mainly of Ringed Seals and Bearded Seals *Erignathus barbatus*. In the High Arctic of central and eastern Canada, and along south-west Baffin Island, Smith (1980) found that Polar Bear predation of the subnivean lairs of Ringed Seals was common. Although the landfast ice is the most important feeding habitat for these seals, most successful predation by the bears occurs in areas of active or moving pack-ice, and along the edge of the fast-ice or floe edge. The majority of Ringed Seals taken by bears in these ice types are less

*Plate 10.12 A female Polar Bear with cubs of the year*

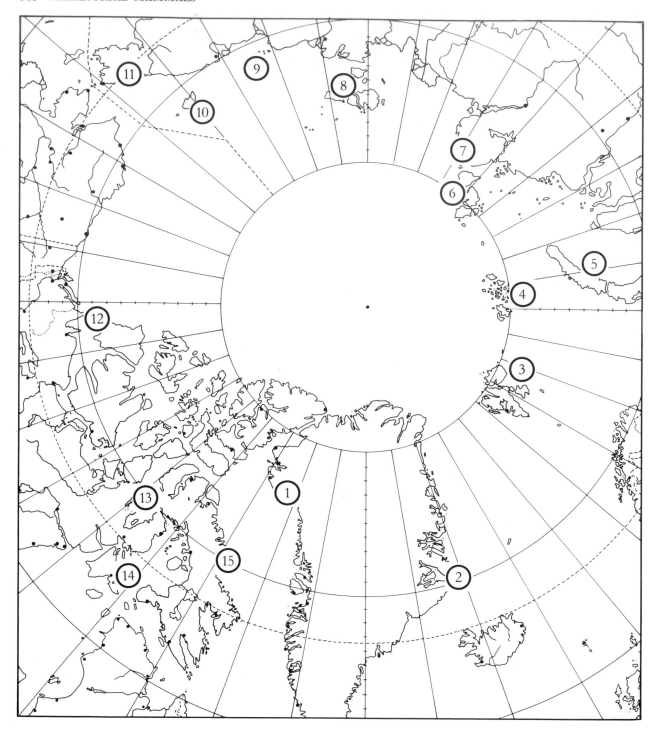

*Figure 10.5: Distribution of Important Polar Bear Denning Areas. (Notes: 1. North-west Greenland; 2. North-east Greenland; 3. East Svalbard; 4. Franz Josef Land; 5. Novaya Zemlya; 6. Severnaya Zemlya; 7. Taimyr Peninsula; 8. New Siberian Islands; 9. Bear Islands; 10. Wrangel Island; 11. Chukotka Peninsula; 12. South Banks Island; 13. Simpson Peninsula; 14. East Southampton Island; 15. East Baffin Island. Sites 5, 6, 7, 8 and 9 are of secondary importance.)*

than two years old. Bearded Seal predation apparently occurs most often in the pack-ice when they are hauled up and lying on ice pans. Bears in the High Arctic tend to hunt more along such features as pressure ridges and edges of rough areas, rather than in the hummock ice habitat exploited by the bears of south-eastern Baffin

Island. The Bearded Seal was found by Stirling and Archibald (1977) to be a more important prey species in the western Arctic than in the High Arctic – clearly a reflection of the greater amount of active ice and floe-edge habitat, which is the preferred winter habitat of the Bearded Seal, present in the Beaufort Sea. Bears

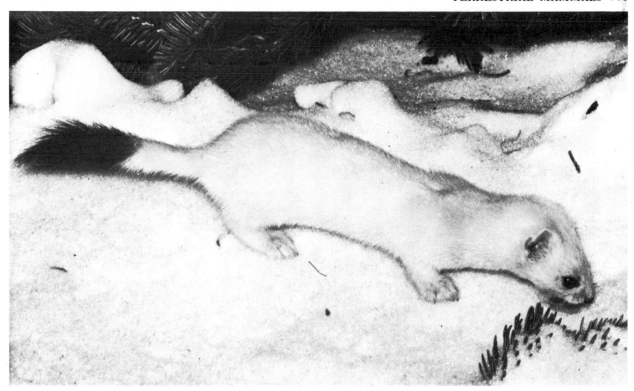

*Plate 10.13 An Ermine in winter coat in Alaska*

that are efficient enough as hunters to afford the luxury of preference, feed primarily on seal blubber and leave the meat.

There are records of Polar Bears catching seabirds by diving and coming up beneath them, and of diving for and eating kelp. They also occasionally kill Musk-oxen or Caribou and it is known that they will take Beluga stranded among icebergs and unable to return to the ocean (see Freeman 1973 for example).

**Movement Patterns** Although Polar Bears are generally faithful to particular areas (Stirling *et al* 1980), considerable movements do occur, particularly in relation to drifting pack-ice. Movement patterns of bears tracked by satellite-monitored radio collars and aerial surveys have revealed travel between Svalbard and Greenland, and between Svalbard and the Soviet Arctic. Among bears tagged off north-east Greenland was a sow with two cubs which, within a month, had travelled 965 km eastwards to Franz Josef Land. Between the Soviet Union and Alaska the movement appears to take place on drifting pack-ice. From Wrangel Island the direction of drift is south-east to western Alaska, north up the coast, and then back again to Wrangel Island. Radio tracking has shown that Polar Bears can walk about 40 km per day for a number of days, and in Alaska up to 80 km in 24 hours has been recorded. The majority of bears tagged off the north coast of Alaska stayed in the area, even though to achieve this meant they had to keep moving against the westward direction of the prevailing ice drift. Radio-collared bears have never been re-located over 161 km from the Alas-

kan coast, and during winter instrumented individuals have seldom been re-located more than 113 km to the north of land (Amstrup 1984).

### *Ermine and Least Weasel*

The Ermine is a circumpolar animal having the most widespread distribution of any species in the family Mustelidae. The primary habitat of this species appears to be boreal coniferous or mixed forests, but within the Arctic it is widespread on the tundra and occurs also in alpine tundra habitats to quite considerable elevations. The Least Weasel also has a circumpolar distribution, but is absent from Greenland and the High Arctic islands.

These are the two smallest species of weasel. The Ermine's total length is 225–340 mm in males and 190–290 mm in females, and the Least Weasel has a total length of less than 259 mm in males and 225 mm in females. They are active on the tundra throughout the year and do not hibernate. In the Arctic both species moult from a brown pelage in summer to a white pelage in winter. However, unlike most Arctic mammals, whose pelage in winter is considerably longer than in the summer, these weasels have relatively short fur in both seasons. Experiments at Point Barrow (Casey and Casey 1979) showed that mean body temperatures at ambient air temperatures ranging from −10° C to −30° C were about 40° C and independent of ambient air temperature.

**Feeding Habits** The main food of these weasels is small mammals, although other prey taken includes birds, young hares and fish. During the winter both species prey heavily on lemmings and are able to pur-

**Table 10.10:** Lemming Winter Nest Density and Intensity of Predation by Least Weasels[a] at Barrow, Alaska

|  | 1968–69 | 1969–70 | 1970–71 | 1971–72 | 1972–73 |
|---|---|---|---|---|---|
| Total number of nests examined | 770 | 0 | 423 | 459 | 209 |
| Number of nests occupied by weasels | 267 | 0 | 25 | 5 | 15 |
| Percentage of nests occupied by weasels | 34.7 |  | 5.6 | 1.1 | 7.2 |
| Number of lemmings eaten at each occupied nest | 1.42 |  | 1.48 | 1.80 | 1.13 |
| Number of study plots searched | 0 | 0 | 12 | 36 | 24 |
| Number of nests/ha | High | 0 | 41.7 | 27.5 | 14.4 |
| Number of lemmings eaten/ha | High | 0 | 3.46 | 0.70 | 1.17 |

Note: a. Ermine are never common near Barrow but are more regular and abundant further inland where more species of small mammals are present.
Source: MacLean *et al* (1974).

sue these into their underground passages, and even live in their nests. Table 10.10 details the predation by Least Weasels on Brown and Arctic Lemmings in their nests at Barrow. Unlike birds, weasels cannot migrate from the tundra when declining lemming numbers and falling snow signal the onset of winter, so the predation on lemmings continues throughout the winter. The weasel population also reaches a high with the lemmings, but then follows the decline of the lemming population to low numbers, usually by the next growing season.

### Wolverine

Although originally an inhabitant of the boreal forests, the Wolverine now ranges widely throughout the circumpolar tundra habitat, including the islands of the Canadian Arctic Archipelago and into northern Greenland, though it cannot be considered abundant anywhere.

Breeding takes place any time between April and late August, but delayed implantation gives rise to births between late January and early April. Litters contain 1–4 young (with an average of 2.5). The den is usually excavated in a deep snow drift and the young are blind at birth.

Adult females are thought to maintain home ranges of 50–350 km², while male territories are much larger (up to 600–1,000 km²) and usually overlap the home ranges of several females, as well as the territories of other males.

**Feeding Habits** Research has shown that the Wolverine is not an efficient hunter, lacking both stealth and speed in pursuit. It is a heavily-built animal (up to 25 kg in weight) with short legs. However, it has an advantage in that its feet are large giving it a low weight load of 27–35 g cm$^{-2}$, with the result that although a Caribou or Moose could elude a Wolverine on tundra or firm snow, deep soft snow gives the Wolverine the advantage. Studies have shown it to be an omnivore in summer, feeding on a large variety of food including carrion, small mammals, eggs and berries, and a meat-eater in winter. Large herbivores are the most important food in winter, but it is probable that the

greater proportion are eaten as carrion. The Wolverine should probably be regarded as a seasonal scavenger on the fringe of the main links of the Arctic food web (Jong 1975). Carcasses of larger prey are not always immediately consumed, but may be dismembered and hidden in widely dispersed caches for use at a later date.

## Artiodactyla

### Moose

This, the largest member of the deer family, is Holarctic in its distribution, having emigrated from Siberia across the Bering land bridge to unglaciated refugia in Alaska during the early Illinoian glaciation of the Pleistocene. In Eurasia it is primarily a coniferous forest species of limited occurrence on the Arctic tundra. In Alaska and Canada, however, it ranges widely over the tundra and reaches the shores of the Arctic Ocean in mid-summer when flies are troublesome further inland. It is absent from the islands of the Canadian Arctic Archipelago. Quite marked changes in distribution have taken place in Alaska and Canada during the present century, with the breeding range extending towards coastal areas, particularly in north-west Canada.

*Plate 10.14 A bull Moose on the tundra in northern Alaska*

*Plate 10.15 Caribou on tundra in northern Alaska*

The history of the Moose in northern Alaska was discussed by Coady (1980). Although having occurred in northern Alaska since the late 1800s, prior to the 1920s most were probably immigrants from south of the Brooks Range. Breeding populations apparently became established in the eastern portion of the Arctic Slope during the 1920s, and in the western portion in the late 1950s and 1960s. The most important factors promoting dispersal to, and an increase in numbers in northern Alaska were probably the temporary cessation of hunting in the north and population increases to the south of the Brooks Range by 1920.

On the Arctic Slope of Alaska at the present time the main habitat is along the river bottoms and valleys near the northern foothills of the Brooks Range, where there are areas of heavy willow growth, especially Alaska Willow which is the preferred browse. Although moderating temperatures in northern Alaska may have resulted in some expansion of growth and distribution of these important alluvial shrub communities, suitable habitat has probably existed throughout the century. While most of the streams and valleys from the Colville River east to the Canning River support Moose populations in winter, their numbers depend to a large extent on snow conditions. Observations by Coady (1980) indicate that snow in winter Moose habitat in northern Alaska is usually 45–60 cm deep and not hard-packed. East of the Canning River (about 146° W longitude), willow stands

tall enough to protrude through the snow cover are of limited occurrence.

Generally speaking, movements of Moose consist of local travel within seasonal ranges, migrations between seasonal ranges, and dispersal to new ranges (as for example movement from south to north through the Brooks Range). They move from willow source to willow source during the winter months and may travel considerable distances as groups. With the commencement of the rut (the peak of which occurs in late September and early October) Moose begin to aggregate. The calves are born between mid-May and early June after a gestation period of 240–250 days, are weaned in the autumn, and remain with the cows through the winter.

### Caribou

The Caribou (Reindeer in Eurasia) is a primitive member of the deer family with a circumpolar distribution. Wild Caribou occurred at the beginning of the Quaternary period in the forests of North America where they were widely distributed. They are believed to have entered Eurasia via the Bering land bridge. For present purposes discussion is confined to wild populations within their natural range, and domesticated herds are excluded. Almost everywhere on the Eurasian tundra wild Reindeer populations have been supplanted by domesticated herds, and in parts of Arctic Alaska domesticated herds occur within the general range of wild Caribou. Reindeer have also been introduced into southern Greenland (primarily in the south-west) where there are now both domesticated and feral populations. There exists a vast literature on this species and the current state of knowledge was largely summarised during the fourth Reindeer/Caribou Symposium held in Canada, in 1985 the proceedings of which were not available at the time of writing.

Within the Arctic the species occurs in six subspecies. In North America these are the Alaskan Barren-ground (or Grant's) Caribou *R. t. granti* found in the Alaskan Arctic and in Canada west of the Mackenzie River; the Barren-ground Caribou *R. t. groenlandicus* ranging from the Mackenzie River eastwards to the west side of Hudson Bay, on Baffin Island and Southampton Island (introduced), and in south-west Greenland from about 62° N to 69° N between Frederikohof and Disko Bay; and the Peary Caribou *R. t. pearyi* inhabiting the islands of the Canadian Arctic Archipelago. The distribution of the various herds within the vast North American area, and the location of the calving grounds, is shown in Figure 10.6. Intergradation occurs between the various subspecies in North America where their ranges overlap. For exam-

ple, intergrades between *R. t. groenlandicus* and *R. t. pearyi* have been found on Banks Island and Victoria Island. Also, since movement across the Mackenzie delta is known to take place, many of the animals in the Porcupine Herd may be *granti–groenlandicus* intergrades.

In Greenland the herds now occupy about 60,000 km² in the central west coastal areas. The Svalbard Reindeer *R. t. platyrhynchus* occurs in four areas as shown in Figure 10.7. The origin of these populations is unknown, but they undoubtedly existed before the first discovery of the islands in 1194. One widely accepted opinion is that they had an eastern origin and migrated to Svalbard from Novaya Zemlya via Franz Josef Land. In the Soviet Arctic the largest remaining population of wild Reindeer *R. t. tarandus* inhabits the western Taimyr Peninsula, while small populations of the subspecies *R. t. pearsoni* survive on Novaya Zemlya and the Novosibirsk Islands.

**Population Statistics** Surveys of Caribou numbers, particularly in North America, have been carried out periodically over many years. Recent population estimates for the Arctic are given in Table 10.11. Caribou herds are currently considered to be groups of animals

*Figure 10.6: Ranges of Caribou Herds in the North American Arctic. (Numbers refer to herds listed in Table 10.11 and the dotted line delimits the range of Peary Caribou.)*
*Source: adapted from Calef (1980).*

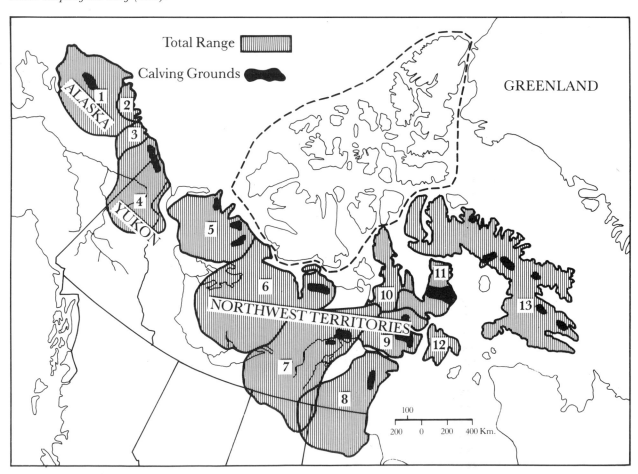

**Table 10.11:** Some Population Estimates for Free-ranging Arctic Caribou and Reindeer *Rangifer tarandus*

|  | **Population Estimate** | **Year** | **Probable Trend** |
|---|---|---|---|
| **Alaska** | | | |
| 1. Western Arctic | 200,000 | 1984 | Increasing |
| 2. Teshekpuk | 10,800 | 1984 | ? |
| 3. Central Arctic[a] | 12,500 | 1983 | Increasing |
| **Alaska/Canada** | | | |
| 4. Porcupine | 150,000 | 1983 | Increasing |
| **Canada** | | | |
| 5. Bluenose | 50,000–80,000 | 1983 | Stable |
| 6. Bathurst | 320,000–450,000 | 1984 | Increasing |
| 7. Beverly | 250,000–420,000 | 1984 | Increasing |
| 8. Kaminuriak | 180,000–280,000 | 1983 | Increasing |
| 9. Wager Bay | | | |
| 10. Lorillard | 110,000–130,000 | 1983 | Stable |
| 11. Melville Peninsula | | | |
| 12. Southampton Island | 1,000 | 1980 | Increasing |
| 13. Baffin Island (north, north-east and south) | 100,000 | 1984 | ? |
| **Peary Caribou *R. t. pearyi*** | | | |
| Banks Island | 5,000 | 1980 | Stable |
| Prince of Wales and Somerset Islands | 4,000–5,000 | 1983 | ? |
| Victoria Island | 7,000–8,000 | 1980 | ? |
| Queen Elizabeth Islands | | | |
| East | 1,500 | 1963 | ? |
| West | 2,700 | 1974 | ? |
| **Greenland** | 7,000–9,000 | 1980 | Decreasing |
| **Svalbard[b]** | | | |
| 1. Nordenskjøldland | 4,500 | 1985 | Stable |
| 2. Reinsdyrsflya | 1,000 | 1985 | ? |
| 3. Nordaustlandet | 500 | 1985 | Stable ? |
| 4. Edgeøya-Barentsøya | 2,500 | 1985 | Stable |
| **USSR** | | | |
| Taimyr Peninsula | 530,000 | 1984 | Increasing |
| Novaya Zemlya | 6,000–7,000 | 1981 | Increasing |
| Novosibirsk Islands | 7,500–16,300 | 1980 | Increasing |
| Chukotka Tundra | 5,000–6,000 | 1981 | Stable |

Notes: The numbers in the left-hand column refer to the herds shown in Figure 10.6.
a. This herd was identified as a distinct subpopulation in 1975.
b. The numbers in the left-hand column refer to the areas shown in Figure 10.7.
Sources: Data taken from 'World Status of Wild Rangifer Populations' by T. M. Williams and D. C. Heard, to be published in the proceedings of the Fourth International Reindeer/Caribou Symposium in 1986, by kind permission of Dr. D. C. Heard, Department of Renewable Resources, Government of the Northwest Territories, Canada. The Greenland figures are from Thing (1984).

which consistently calve in a specific traditional location distinct from calving grounds used by other herds. However, there is evidence to indicate that some herds may have several calving grounds (Calef 1979). Most of the population estimates given here are considered to be acccurate to within 20 per cent.

The fact that Caribou populations fluctuate is well known and has been extensively documented. Among factors which may be responsible for population changes are predation (particularly by wolves), human exploitation, natural mortality, climate, range condition and immigration-emigration. Caribou in west

Greenland undergo periodic population fluctuations with intervals of 58–60 years between the peaks (Vibe 1967). Caribou have recently experienced a rapid decline throughout most of their range in Greenland. The last population maximum occurred at the end of the 1960s and it is estimated to have reached 100,000. Aerial population censuses in March–April of 1977, 1978 and 1980 showed a total population size of 25–30,000, 18–20,000 and 7–9,000 respectively (Thing 1984). The population which formerly inhabited the Thule District, about 79° N in north-west Greenland, is now virtually extinct (Roby *et al* 1984). During the

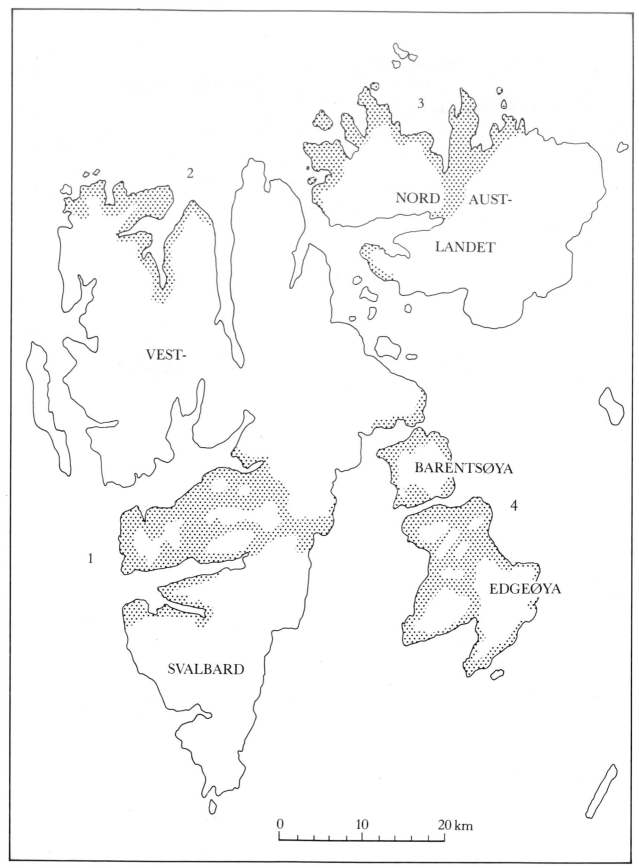

*Figure 10.7: Distribution of Wild Reindeer Populations in Svalbard. (Numbers refer to herds listed in Table 10.11.)*
*Source: Reimers, Villmo, Gaare, Holthe and Skogland (1980).*

*Plate 10.16 Caribou on tundra south of Barter Island in northern Alaska; part of a herd estimated at 80,000–100,000 animals (July 1968)*

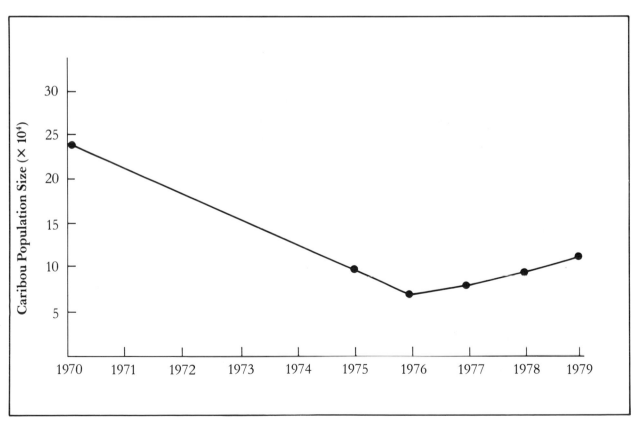

*Figure 10.8: Population Trend in the Western Arctic Caribou Herd of Alaska 1970–1979*
*Source: Based on Davis, Valkenburg and Reynolds (1980)*

winter of 1975–6 on Edgeøya, Svalbard, an estimated 23 per cent of the population starved to death. The surviving animals seemed to recover rapidly which indicates that there was no food shortage, but that adverse snow and ice conditions made it inaccessible (Reimers 1982).

One of the most interesting and best-documented population changes is that of Alaska's Western Arctic Herd which, at one stage, was the largest in North America. The population dynamics of this herd are discussed in detail by Davis *et al* (1980), and Figure 10.8 shows the status of this herd from 1970 to 1979. The population was thought to number 175,000–200,000 in 1961 and reached a high of about 242,000 in 1970. Excessive hunting and substantial predation by wolves were the primary causes of the post-1970 decline. A reduction in hunting pressure and wolf predation, and a probable increase in yearling recruitment allowed the herd to increase in size by 1979 (Davis *et al* 1980), since when the upward trend has continued (Table 10.11). There is little doubt that in the past there were vastly more Caribou in the Arctic than is now the case. According to Kelsall (1968), the prehistoric Caribou of the great barren-lands westwards from Hudson Bay to the Mackenzie River may have numbered 3,000,000.

**Calving Grounds** It seems likely (Calef and Heard 1980) that calving grounds are selected for attributes which optimise neo-natal survival, while summer range with high quality forage is selected to optimise survival. The calving grounds mentioned later in this chapter all have certain features in common (e.g. high, rocky and relatively barren), are avoided by bulls and non-productive animals, and probably have a relatively low level of predation. The calving grounds of the Western Arctic Herd in Alaska lie in an area of cottongrass *Eriophorum vaginatum* tussock tundra, and were studied by Kuropat and Bryant (1980) and Lent (1980). The area was found to be characterised by relatively shallow snow-cover and early snow melt-off, as were the calving grounds of the Porcupine Herd south of Herschel Island. The tussock growth form of the cottongrass creates an environment which allows rapid nutrient absorption and rapid growth at the time of snow ablation, thus providing an abundant food resource immediately following snow-melt; the floral heads are rich in nitrogen and phosphorus which are important nutrients for lactating cows.

Many Caribou herds, particularly but not exclusively those which perform migratory journeys between winter and summer ranges, exhibit post-calving aggregations. On the other hand, there are also herds (for example, the Lorillard, Wager Bay and Melville Peninsula Herds in Canada) that do not behave in this way. Harassment by mosquitos is currently the best hypothesis to explain post-calving aggregation.

**Breeding Biology** In general, Caribou first come into oestrus at about 29 months of age, and under good nutritional conditions some animals can conceive at 17 months. The female has a gestation period of about seven months, the calves are usually born in late May or early June, and there then follows three months' lactation. Studies by Bergerud (1980) of eight herds (including five in the Arctic) representing over 70 per cent of the Caribou in North America, showed that the average pregnancy rate for animals of 2.5 years of age and older was 82 per cent. The average percentage of parous females in seven herds was 86 per cent. In general the reproductive rate showed little variation between years or herds. In contrast to a consistent birth rate the mortality rate of Caribou calves in many herds in North America was variable and exceeded 50 per cent, and was frequently as high as 80–90 per cent. Most of the mortality occurred in the first few months of life and the greatest mortality factor was predation. The annual adult mortality is estimated to be 7–13 per cent (mean 10 per cent) if predators are common, and 5–6 per cent if predators are rare. Predation is considered the chief limiting factor to population growth and sets the level of stocking commonly at 0.4 to 0.8 Caribou $km^{-2}$ or less. Limits imposed by dispersion or food supplies occur at much higher densities.

**Movements** In the Arctic, several individual herds of Caribou carry out distinct annual migrations that appear to have as their focal point restricted calving areas. In the Soviet Arctic the calving grounds of the Taimyr Peninsula herd are on the tundra in the north of the peninsula and the wintering grounds lie astride the Arctic Circle in the boreal forest to the south (see Figure 10.9), thus requiring a twice-yearly movement of some 965 km. Barren-ground Caribou typically make long migrations twice a year between their winter ranges in the boreal forest zone and their calving grounds and summer ranges on the northern tundra. In Alaska, the Western Arctic Herd has its calving grounds on the Arctic Slope west of the Colville River, in the upper reaches of the Mead and Utokuk Rivers. This area has been used for calving for at least 100 years, and possibly for as long as 10 millennia (Humphrey 1970). The wintering grounds of this herd lie in the boreal forest south of the Brooks Range, and the summer range extends north to the Beaufort Sea coast.

The Porcupine Herd is of particular interest since its total range (extending over 250,000 km²) includes part of north-east Alaska, and in Canada the northern Yukon and parts of the Northwest Territories. The calving grounds lie on the coastal tundra and mountain foothills up to 1,100 m above sea level astride the Alaska-Canada border (see Figure 10.10). The winter ranges of this herd are enormous, encompassing over 110,000 km². The main area, some 80,000 km² in extent, includes the headwaters of the Porcupine River and part of the Richardson Mountains. The secondary wintering area is 25,000 km² of the Chandalar-Sheenjek region in Alaska, but major use of this area occurs only sporadically. Spring migration begins with the northward movement of small parties in mid-March, but it is late March or early April before herds of thousands are on the move, and two main routes are

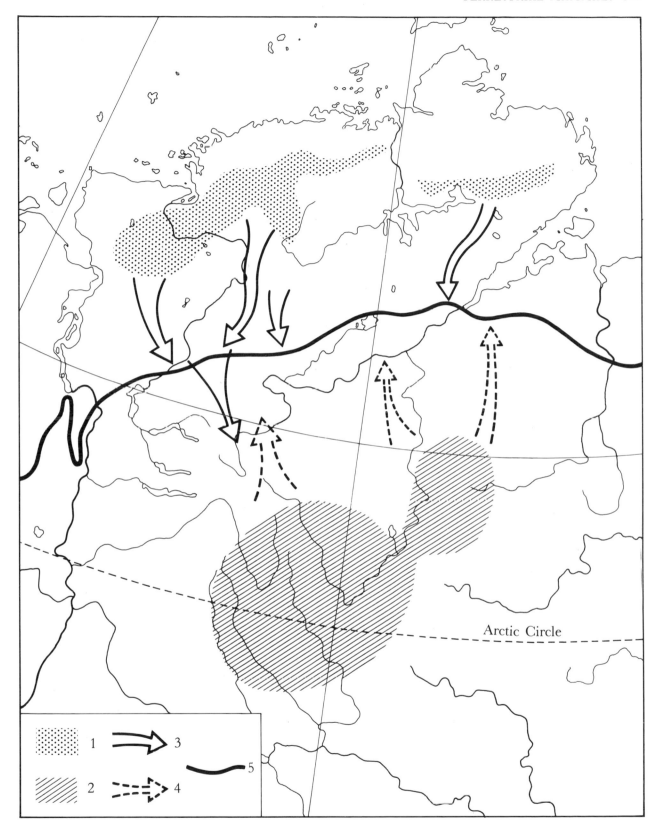

*Figure 10.9: The Annual Life Cycle of the Taimyr Peninsula Wild Reindeer Herd. (1. Calving grounds and concentgration during summer. 2. Basic wintering area. 3. Autumn migration route southwards. 4. Departure from wintering grounds. 5. Limit of the tundra.)*
*Source: Chernov (1985).*

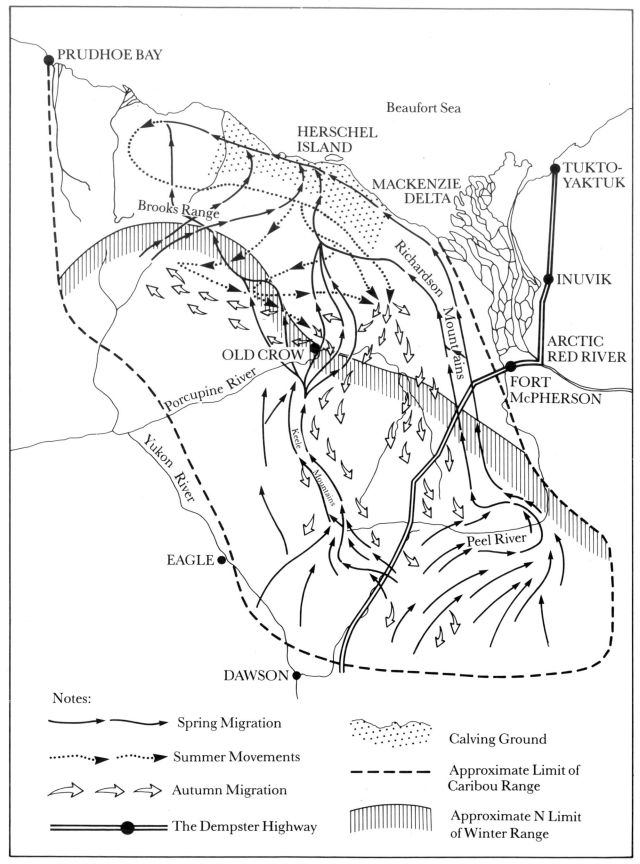

PRUDHOE BAY

Beaufort Sea

HERSCHEL
ISLAND

MACKENZIE
DELTA

TUKTO-
YAKTUK

Brooks Range

Richardson Mountains

INUVIK

ARCTIC
RED RIVER

OLD CROW

Porcupine River

FORT
McPHERSON

Yukon River

Keele

Mountains

Peel River

EAGLE

DAWSON

Notes:

→ Spring Migration

·····▶ Summer Movements

⇨ ⇨ ⇨ Autumn Migration

═══●═══ The Dempster Highway

Calving Ground

Approximate Limit of
Caribou Range

Approximate N Limit
of Winter Range

*Figure 10.10: Range of the Porcupine Caribou Herd Showing Migration Routes Between Wintering Areas and the Calving Grounds*
*Source: LeBlond and Rees (1980).*

used as shown in Figure 10.10. Soon after calving, the cows and calves join the other members of the herd in loose aggregations of 25,000–50,000 animals. By early July most have moved into the mountain foothills to escape the mosquitos, and rapid westerly dispersal takes place early in August. Autumn migration commences early in September but is soon accelerated by the first snowfalls.

**Feeding Habits** The seasonal movements of Caribou and wild Reindeer are partially controlled by the availability and quality of their food resources. Throughout winter and early spring, when forage is often in short supply, Caribou feed extensively on lichens. Studies in the Brooks Range in mid-March (Holleman *et al* 1980) showed that lichen dry-matter intake was 3.0–7.0 kg day$^{-1}$ for an 80 kg Caribou. The mean lichen intake rate was 4.9±0.8 kg day$^{-1}$ which corresponded to a metabolisable energy intake of approximately 38 MJ day$^{-1}$. Caribou have the highest metabolic demands in spring and early summer, when plant growth is most rapid and the nutritive quality of the forage is highest. Peak forage nitrogen and phosphorus concentrations in Arctic tundra forage species are high compared to most temperate and tropical forages. Caribou have the opportunity to maximise forage nutrient quality during spring and summer by migrating north as phenology progresses, and also by selecting among plant species and among local feeding sites.

The mobility of Caribou allows them to make use of many plant species and communities during the summer. At Prudhoe Bay (as on the calving grounds of the Western Arctic Herd) the dominant plant community utilised is the *Eriophorum angustifolium* polygon marsh type. The wet meadows of Tundra Grass are also grazed, and immediately after snow-melt they selectively graze the Arctic Avens dry heath community. It was shown by Skogland (1980) that Caribou at Prudhoe Bay clearly followed a gradient of receding water table during the summer, foraging along a gradient of plant emergence on the plains in response to water level recession.

The food habits of Caribou in west Greenland have been studied by Holt (1980) and Thing (1984). Where food species in early growth stages are available, Caribou tend to concentrate their feeding on them, a form of behaviour most pronounced during spring migration and pre-calving, when intensive foraging takes place on dry slopes which support an early-emerging vegetation. The species particularly involved are Glaucous Spear-grass *Poa glauca* and Alpine Fescue *Festuca brachyphylla*. In the calving season, parturient and nursing cows concentrate on the flat wet sedge meadows which have an abundant supply of emerging *Eriophorum* at this time. They also graze on the gently sloping dwarf shrub heaths when the main attraction are the young leaves of *Poa*. In the short season of post-calving and also during the main summer period, meadows of Common Meadow Grass *Poa pratensis* are the most important feeding habitat, though in the

Søndre Strømfjord area such meadows constitute only 5 per cent of the summer range. In late summer and early September Caribou still utilise *P. pratensis* meadows and wet sedge meadows, but also consume mushrooms which become available at that period. The most important food species in winter were Crowberry, Long-stalked Stitchwort *Stellaria longipes* and various graminoids. In spring and early summer on Svalbard the animals showed high preference for Polar Willow and Alpine Bistort, particularly on *Dryas* and moss tundra. During summer, preference shifted to monocotyledons and Common Horsetail *Equisetum arvense*. In the Arctic bogs, Tundra Grass and *Eriophorum scheuchzeri* dominated, while Alpine Foxtail, Snowgrass *Phippsia algida* and *Poa* spp. were selected on better-drained terrain (Punsvik *et al* 1980).

### Peary Caribou

The Peary Caribou is a subspecies which evolved under harsh climatic conditions and is confined almost entirely to the Canadian Arctic Archipelago. Climatic extremes, especially of snow and ice, cause periodic oscillations in their numbers, and the population dynamics of Peary Caribou are unique among North American ungulates because weather, especially winter weather, dominates not only the reproductive rate but also recruitment and adult survival. The subspecies is thinly scattered over a vast area (see Figure 10.6) and its overall distribution has changed little during historic times. Inter-island movements, special spring-time foraging behaviour, late calving, and probably small group size, are some of the adaptive strategies that Peary Caribou have evolved in response to restricted forage availability (Miller *et al* 1982).

**Population Statistics** The current estimated population of this subspecies is shown in Table 10.11. Populations of Peary Caribou have occupied the larger islands for several years then disappeared from those islands, only to return again some years later. During the period 1960–80, Arctic weather became progressively more severe, and a series of severe winters had a profound effect on Peary Caribou numbers. In the western Queen Elizabeth Islands (including Bathurst, Melville and Prince Patrick Islands) numbers declined from about 24,000 in 1961 to about 2,700 in 1974. Unfavourable winters since then have hindered recovery of the population. However, the estimated size of the inter-island herd on Prince of Wales, Somerset and their satellite islands in July 1980 was 5,022 animals at least one year old, suggesting a relatively stable population (Gunn and Miller 1983). Production of calves or their survival to 1–2 months of age on those islands was zero or low from 1972 to 1976, and recruitment was almost zero (Thomas 1982). The most severe winter was that of 1973–4 when 62 and 68 per cent of the Caribou were lost from Bathurst and Melville Islands respectively.

Many of the Banks Island population died during the winter of 1977–8 after an ice storm in the autumn. At the end of winter, Peary Caribou are in their worst physical condition, and ice conditions during melt and run-off can render much forage unavailable. Ground-fast ice forms under all but the shallowest snow cover and prevents access to most plants. In 1979, ground-fast ice persisted from at least mid-June into the first week of July.

**Breeding Biology** The timing and location of calving may be influenced by the severity and duration of the preceding winter. In 1977, most Caribou appeared to calve in the third week of June on the west coastal area of Somerset Island, but in 1978, after an exceptionally long and severe winter, calving was delayed until the fourth week of June after the cows travelled from Somerset Island to Prince of Wales Island (Miller and Gunn 1979). Cows between 2 years and about 10–13 years of age can potentially produce a single calf each year, but probably rarely do so because of failure to build up adequate fat reserves every year. Pregnancy rates can be highly variable. On the western Queen Elizabeth Islands, for example, pregnancy incidences were 6–7 per cent from 1974 to 1976 (following the particularly severe winter of 1973–4), but recovered to 88 per cent in 1977. The survival of calves during their first winter is usually poor, and the proportion of yearlings recorded has been as low as 3.5 per cent. In the western Queen Elizabeth Islands few, if any calves born in the summer of 1973 survived the following winter.

**Movements** There are extensive intra- and inter-island movements. Peary Caribou in the Parry population migrate in the spring from Prince Patrick and Eglinton Islands to Melville Island, and presumably they return in the early winter. Animals in the Peel population migrate from the Boothnia Peninsula and Somerset Island to Prince of Wales Island in the spring. The movements are seemingly to more favourable feeding areas at both seasons. Other winter movements may be caused by adverse weather rather than being traditional. For example, in the severe winter of 1973–4 some of the Caribou that normally winter on southern Bathurst Island were forced to move east to Cornwallis Island and south to islands in the Barrow Strait in March and April.

**Feeding Habits** Peary Caribou share much of their geographical range in the Canadian High Arctic with Muskoxen, but research has shown that the critical spring feeding ranges are more or less mutually exclusive. Fieldwork on Axel Heiberg and Melville Islands (Parker and Ross 1976) found the most striking contrast in summer habitat use by the Caribou and Muskoxen was the preference of the latter for the sedge-producing hydric meadow type, and the virtual avoidance of that type by Caribou. When feeding, Caribou displayed a greater variety in choice of plant species than Muskoxen, favouring Arctic Willow, grasses, herbs, and the flowers of vascular plants (for example, Purple Saxifrage, *Pedicularis* and Arctic Poppy). On Banks Island they were found to be broad-spectrum grazers specialising on upland monocots, to ingest few lichens, and to exhibit significant seasonal and/or regional differences in diet (Shank *et al* 1977).

A study of diet and habitat selection on eight islands in the Canadian Arctic Archipelago from 1974 to 1977 is reported on by Thomas and Edmonds (1983). Floral composition of the samples was highly variable among sites on some of the islands and among some of the regions. Only a few species dominated the samples from all regions but the apparent winter diets were more diverse and there was more variability among sites on Somerset and Prince of Wales Islands than on the more northerly islands. Monocotyledons (predominantly *Luzula*) and mosses together comprised 33–97 per cent of the rumen contents in the five regions. They and lichens (2–15 per cent) were the only plant groups common to the samples from all regions. High proportions of mosses (34–58 per cent) characterised the rumen samples from Bathurst, Melville and Eglinton/Prince Patrick Islands. Mosses comprised 50 per cent of the rumen contents on Bathurst and Melville Islands in March 1974 when foraging was extremely difficult and malnutrition widespread. In winter the majority of feeding sites were on the tops and sides of ridges and hills with little or relatively soft snow cover, and this is where feeding craters were located.

### Muskox

This is one of the most highly specialised of the Arctic mammals, and the one which has adapted most successfully to the severe environmental conditions of both the tundra and the polar desert, and is the only ruminant whose natural distribution is limited to those regions. Muskoxen were more widely distributed in the past than is the case at present. They thrived in the Siberian Arctic 10,000–12,000 years ago, but climatic changes and the activities of Neolithic hunters extirpated them in this habitat (Trofimenko 1984). Probably never very numerous, they were hunted to extinction on the Arctic Slope of Alaska by 1850–60. The Canadian populations also declined as a result of overhunting.

The present distribution includes the Arctic tundra of mainland Canada and most of the Canadian Arctic islands (but it is absent from Baffin Island). On the mainland, Muskox occur largely in areas with mean annual maximum snow depths of 50 cm or less. They are the only large terrestrial herbivores in north and east Greenland, being present throughout most of the eastern coastal zone from Peary Land (83°N) in the north to Scoresby Sund (70°N) in the south. The species has also been introduced into west Greenland.

Muskoxen from Greenland were introduced to Nunivak Island in the Bering Sea in 1935 where they thrived. In March 1969, 51 animals from Nunivak Island were released on Barter Island in north-east Alaska, and in 1970 13 more were released near the Kavik River. The released animals scattered, some moving east into Canada and others southwards on the Arctic Slope. As a result of these releases herds cur-

*Plate 10.17 A herd of Muskoxen (adults and calves)*

rently exist on the Sadlerochit River, and in the Canning-Tamayariak and Jago-Okerohovik drainages north of the Brooks Range.

The Muskoxen on Svalbard formerly had their main centre of distribution on Nordenskiøld Land, the peninsula between Isfjorden and Van Mijenfjorden. They were the descendants of 17 animals (11 calves and 6 yearlings) introduced from east Greenland to Moskusushavn, Adventfjorden, in 1929 (Alendal 1976). The population numbered about 50 in 1959 but had decreased to one by 1982 due to competition from the native Reindeer (Klein and Staaland, 1984). In the mid-1970s a project began to release animals from Nunivak Island to the Taimyr Peninsula and Wrangel Island in the Soviet Union. Up to 1984 a total of 18 calves had been born to this Soviet stock (Trofimenko 1984). The results of some recent population surveys are summarised in Table 10.12.

**Feeding Habits** In summer Muskoxen appear to select vegetation types on the basis of abundance and phenological stage of preferred forage species. In winter, snow characteristics strongly influence habitat selection. The restricted movements and conservative activity budgets permit minimisation of energy expenditure and forage requirements, thus allowing for a year-long existence in areas of low primary productivity. A daily rhythm of alternately resting and feeding during the summer period is probably consistent for all parts of the species' range. Research in 1973 showed a

**Table 10.12:** Recent Muskox *Ovibos moschatus* Population Data for Parts of the Arctic

| Location | Population Estimate | Date of Survey |
|---|---|---|
| Alaska (NE Arctic Slope) | 235 | 1983 |
| Canada | | |
|   Western Queen | | |
|     Elizabeth Islands[a] | 2,700 | 1974 |
|   Banks Island | 15,000–18,000 | 1980 |
|   Prince of Wales Island | 1,300 | 1980 |
|   Somerset Island | 30 | 1980 |
|   Victoria Island | 12,000 | 1980 |
|   North of Great Bear | | |
|     Lake | 2,000 | 1975 |
|   Thelon Game Sanctuary | 600+500 outside | 1978 |
|   Queen Maud Gulf area | 8,494 (±2,673) | 1982 |
| Greenland | | |
|   North-east | 20,000 | 1983 |
|   West (Søndre Strømfjord) | 700 | 1983 |
| Svalbard | 1 | 1982 |
| Soviet Union | | |
|   Eastern Taimyr Peninsula | 83 | 1983 |
|   Wrangel Island | 21 | 1982 |

Note: a. SW Melville Island is the main centre of distribution.

Sources: Alendal (1976), Chapman and Feldhamer (1982), Gunn *et al* (1984), Klein and Staaland (1984), Reynolds and Ross (1984), Thing *et al* (1984) and Uspenski (1984).

resting:feeding ratio of 0.76:1 on Melville Island and 0.67:1 on Axel Heiberg Island. On Melville Island resting and feeding times averaged 75 and 98 minutes respectively, on Axel Heiberg 91 and 136 minutes, on Bathurst Island approximately 150 minutes each, and on Banks Island 102 and 86 minutes (Parker and Ross 1976).

On the islands of the Canadian High Arctic, the sedge-producing hydric-meadow vegetation type is a highly significant habitat for Muskoxen in summer. In studies on Axel Heiberg and Melville Islands sedges were the most common summer forage, followed closely by willow. On Axel Heiberg the most frequently consumed sedge was *Carex stans*, and on Melville Island *Eriophorum triste*. The willow species concerned in both instances was *Salix arctica*. On Bathurst Island willow was a much smaller component of the diet and, conversely, grasses were far more common. Studies of winter diet on Devon Island and Ellesmere Island in the winters of 1970–1 and 1971–2 showed that sedges were the single most important class of plants consumed in both winters.

### Dall Sheep and Snow Sheep

Both the Dall Sheep in North America and the Snow Sheep in Eurasia, are inhabitants of alpine tundra areas whose range extends southwards beyond the Arctic. In the North American Arctic they are found in the Brooks Range in Alaska, and in the mountains of the Yukon Territory and the Northwest Territories in Canada. In the Soviet Union the Snow Sheep reaches its western limit of distribution in the Lake Ayan region of the Putorana Mountains east of Norilsk, and in the western part of the Taimyr Peninsula. In the Lake Ayan region the sheep are found only on the highest slopes above treeline and around snowbeds, talus, and rock outcrops (Webber and Klein 1977).

**Population Statistics** There is little data on population size for either species. The Snow Sheep population in the Putorana Mountains has been estimated at about 300, mainly in scattered small groups. The Brooks Range is the least known of the Dall Sheep's habitats within Alaska. However, some data are available from studies in the eastern section of these mountains (Roseneau and Stern 1974) which suggests that the drainages of the Canning, Hulahula and Kongakut Rivers support higher populations than elsewhere in the eastern Brooks Range. In 1972 it was conservatively estimated that the Canning River drainage supported 500+, the Hulahula River drainage probably about 650–700, and that of the Kongakut River 200+.

**Breeding Biology** The lambing season for the Dall Sheep in the North American Arctic is usually from about the third week of May into early June. Some ewes mature sexually at 1.5 years, but most mature at 2–2.5 years old and breed annually thereafter. As a

*Plate 10.18 A Dall Sheep ram in its mountain habitat*

result of their harsh environment, lambs have a low survival rate.

**Feeding Habits** On their preferred rough terrain they have little competition for food from other ungulates. The staple foods include grasses *Festuca*, Broad-leaved Willowherb, sedges *Carex*, Richardson's Saxifrage *Boykinia richardsonii*, avens *Dryas* and willow *Salix* (particularly during autumn and winter). Adverse snow and ice conditions may periodically make food inaccessible.

**Movements** The distribution of Dall Sheep (and presumably also Snow Sheep) within a general area is undoubtedly linked to the presence of mineral licks, which are usually the subject of intense activity throughout at least the summer period. The annual movement patterns of these sheep are not fully known. They do not migrate in the usual sense of the word, but in some locations they do move considerable distances between winter and summer ranges. Some areas, however, like parts of the Canning River drainage, appear to support sheep year-round since they contain winter range, summer range, mineral licks and lambing areas. In general, they move to higher elevations during the mid to late summer months. Rams in particular often seek higher and more rugged terrain as summer progresses, partly in response to increased insect harassment.

# 11 MARINE MAMMALS

Dr T.G. Smith

## Introduction

The Arctic, with its vast areas of ice-covered oceans and uninhabited coastlines, is the home of a large number and variety of marine mammals. Seals, Walruses and whales are a conspicuous feature of the Arctic marine habitat. In some situations they are locally very abundant. At certain times of the year Walruses will haul out by the hundreds on small islands and huddle together in great masses during their annual moult. Dense aggregations of Belugas or White Whales, sometimes numbering 3,000–4,000 individuals, congregate in the river channels of certain estuaries during the summer season. A completely different impression of marine mammal abundance is gained in other areas. Hardly a sign can be seen of the abundant but extremely cautious and solitary Ringed Seals. Only a brief glimpse can be caught of their small heads emerging from the water as they take a quick breath.

Two subspecies of Walruses, six species of seals and three whale species are true inhabitants of Arctic waters. In addition, the Harp Seal *Phoca groenlandica*, which migrates to the temperate pack-ice-covered areas of the North Atlantic to whelp, spends most of the year in Arctic areas along ice edges and among the floating ice pans.

The single factor with the most influence on the distribution and abundance of seals, Walruses and whales, is sea-ice (see Chapter 4). Only one species of Arctic marine mammal, the Ringed Seal, is completely adapted to life in areas covered by land-fast sea-ice. Bearded Seals are able to overwinter in such areas by maintaining breathing holes in the same way as the Ringed Seal, but are more typically found in the pack-ice. All other species of seals and Walruses are inhabitants of the pack-ice.

The three Arctic whale species must inhabit the more southerly latitudes of the Arctic during the winter months. In areas of light pack-ice, ocean currents maintain sufficient expanses of open water for them to survive the coldest period of the year. During the summer they move north as the fast-ice melts.

## The Seals: Pinnipedia

The seals are divided into the Otaridae, containing the sea lions and fur seals; the Odobenidae, the walruses; and the Phocidae, the hair seals.

The Otarids have external ears, or pinnae, and are thus termed eared seals as opposed to the Phocids, which have no external appendage at the ear. Fur seals possess a thick layer of under-fur with proper guard hairs. Otarids are able to move easily out of the water and they return to traditional sites on the land to breed. There are no truly Arctic species.

Phocid seals differ in being more specialised as aquatic inhabitants. Their bodies are more streamlined, they have shorter appendages and are much less mobile on land. While some do breed on terrestrial sites, many of the Phocids are also adapted to breeding on sea-ice. Phocids are often called hair seals since they lack true fur and depend entirely on their thick blubber as insulation.

Walruses are a single-species group. They are much larger and heavier than seals. Their prominent tusks and specialised mouth allow them to feed on prey living on the ocean bottom.

### Walrus

The Walrus, sole member of the family Odobenidae, exist as two subspecies: *O. r. rosmarus* in the North Atlantic and *O. r. divergens* in the North Pacific.

Walruses are inhabitants of the pack-ice and ice edges. The southern limit to their distribution in the North Pacific during the warm months appears to coincide with latitudes where air temperatures are less than 20° C (Fay and Ray 1968). In the North Atlantic, Walruses were formerly known to occupy areas as far south as the Magdalen Islands (47° N) in the Gulf of the St Lawrence River. These stocks were completely hunted out by the early nineteenth century (Mansfield 1966). In the north, the number of Atlantic Walruses was severely reduced both in the eastern Canadian Arctic and Greenland during the late 1700s by Bowhead Whale *Balaena mysticetus* hunters, who had turned to them as a further source of oil after depleting the whale population.

Four stocks of Walruses are recognised; the largest, in excess of 200,000, is found in the Bering and Chukchi Sea. Accurate counts have not been possible since this stock is widely dispersed in a vast area. Nevertheless, all indications are that the population has increased significantly in size during the last 20 years (Fay 1982). The Laptev Sea group has been little studied, but is thought to number some 3,000 to 4,000. The stock inhabiting the east Greenland coasts, Svalbard, Franz Josef Land, the Barents, and White Sea is widely dispersed and its numbers are not known. They were apparently once abundant, but now are much reduced because of over-hunting. Though now protected they probably number in the low hundreds (Reeves 1978).

The North Atlantic stock is found primarily in Canada's northern Hudson Bay and Fox Basin, extending north up the east coast of Baffin Island. Mansfield (1966) estimated the stock might number some 25,000 individuals, but this was not based on actual counts. Many of the areas where Walruses were once numerous on the east Baffin coast are no longer occupied. It is unclear whether pressure from the Bowhead Whale hunters in the mid-1800s or over-exploitation by natives has led to their disappearance. Walruses are extremely vulnerable to over-harvesting and are presently protected by management regulations in Canada. Inuit hunters are restricted to four animals per year and uncarved ivory cannot be exported from the Canadian north.

Walruses are the largest of the Arctic pinnipeds, adult males weighing up to 1,600 kg in the Pacific subspecies and 1,200 kg in the Atlantic. The head of the Walrus appears small relative to the rest of the body. Males and females bear tusks, which continue to grow through life and which are modified canine teeth of the upper jaw. The nasal bones are greatly enlarged to support the large tusks which can reach 1 m in length in adult male Pacific Walrus. Atlantic Walruses have much shorter tusks rarely exceeding 35 cm long in adult males. Very noticeable features of the Walrus head are the powerful lips and mystacial pads covered with short stiff vibrissae. These are used to feel out benthic food species along the ocean floor. The hind flippers are used for propulsion while swimming and are rotated forward when the Walrus hauls out on land or ice. The fore flippers, which bear weakly developed claws, are used to aid in support and locomotion out of the water and for steering while swimming.

Little is known of the mating behaviour of the Walrus, which takes place in mid-winter around the floating ice pans and involves underwater vocal displays which have just recently been documented (Ray and Watkins 1975; Stirling *et al* 1983). The actual social system has not yet been described. Adult males appear to be in reproductive condition from as early as November to as late as July. Females ovulate from February until late March. Implantation of the fertilised ovum is delayed for as much as four months followed by the active growth of the foetus over the next eleven months. The single calf is born 15 months after mating during the period mid-April to early June. Calves remain with their dams for up to two years. The actual lactation period probably lasts for 18 months, with the calf learning to feed on benthic organisms during this protracted period of parental care.

The food consists primarily of bottom-living organisms, mainly bivalve molluscs such as *Mya truncata*, a widely distributed Arctic clam. Walruses feed in coastal shelf areas of up to 80 m in depth, usually by making dives two to eight minutes long (Fay 1982). They move along the murky bottom dragging their tusks and locate their food items with the use of their vibrissae. There is little evidence that the tusks are actually used for digging. Most probably the subsurface food items are rooted out with the snout and sucked into the mouth. No hard parts are ingested by the Walruses. They are able to separate off the shells by suction. The heavy lips and tongue along with the small oral aperture form a powerful 'suction pump' which appears to be the principal force used in feeding. Walruses are also occasionally found to have fed on seals, though Mansfield (1958) and Fay (1982) were of the opinion that this was either carrion feeding or only

of sporadic occurrence. More evidence has been accumulated recently, however, which indicates that predation on seals is perhaps more common than was once imagined (Lowry and Fay 1984).

The single largest source of mortality is hunting. In Soviet and Alaskan waters, 3,000–7,000 Walruses are killed annually. The extent of the Canadian harvest on the Atlantic subspecies is not presently known, but might be in the order of 1,000 annually, down from the 3,000 quoted by Mansfield (1966). The decreased harvest has resulted from the reduction in need for dog food, caused by the virtual disappearance of the dog teams as a means of transportation in the Canadian Arctic.

### Common Seals

Five subspecies of Common, or Harbour, Seal are known. Of these only the western Atlantic subspecies *Phoca vitulina concolor*, and the Northern Pacific, *Phoca largha* actually penetrate into Arctic regions. The latter, now considered a separate species and referred to as the Spotted Seal, breeds on the pack-ice and gives birth to a white-coat pup (Shaughnessey and Fay 1977).

The Western Atlantic Harbour Seal *P. v. concolor* is found mainly along the coast of New Brunswick and Nova Scotia in eastern Canada. It penetrates north into Arctic waters along the east and west Greenland coasts, north along the east Baffin coastline and west as far as the west coast of Hudson Bay.

In the Arctic, Harbour Seals, or *Kasigiak*, as they are known by the Inuit, are found in river estuaries. They also often ascend rivers into large lakes. Some groups of Harbour Seals apparently maintain themselves throughout the year in these lakes and have been thought to be isolated populations (Doutt 1942). Reports indicate that Harbour Seals occupy many of the river systems along the coasts of Ungava Bay and Hudson Bay (Mansfield 1967).

The Arctic population of Harbour Seals is apparently very small and almost entirely concentrated in areas of freshwater inflow. The majority of pups shed their white coat in the womb, although about 25 per cent do so shortly after birth. The average length and weight of both sexes as adults is approximately 1.5 m and 95 kg. The pelage pattern is quite varied in its markings, usually with the darkest areas on the back and lighter shades on the sides and belly. Occasionally small rings will be seen which can lead to confusion of identification with the Ringed Seal, which has similar markings. In these cases positive identification must be made from cranial measurements.

Arctic Harbour Seals appear to be mainly fish eaters. Those inhabiting the inland lakes are well able to feed on the northern lake trout *Salvelinus naymacush* (Beck *et al* 1970; Power and Gregoire 1978). In the estuaries of Arctic rivers, they apparently feed on a variety of fish including Arctic Cod, White Fish *Coreogonus clupeaformis* and salmonids.

Pupping occurs in late June or early July in the Arctic, approximately one month later than in the southern part of their range. Female Harbour Seals attain sexual maturity at 4–5 years old and produce a single pup annually, after having attained 7 years of age.

The pelt of the Harbour Seal is sought by the Inuit mainly because it is somewhat different from the more common Ringed Seal. Hunting of this species is sporadic, and because the seals are widespread it will not likely endanger the populations.

### Spotted Seal

Of the Common Seal group, *Phoca largha*, considered by some to be a separate species, is the most adapted to life in ice-filled Arctic waters. It is closely associated with the 'front' zone of the seasonal pack-ice extending along the eastern Siberian coast to Kamchatka. It is also found in the Okhotsk and Po Hai Seas. In Alaska, it extends eastward along the coast, with some specimens being taken as far as Herschel Island in the Canadian Beaufort Sea.

Populations of Spotted Seals are not well known, because of the difficulty in counting widely dispersed animals in the offshore pack-ice zone. Estimates of approximately 200,000 for each of the Bering and Okhotsk Seas have been given (Bonner 1979).

The newborn pup has a long coat of white fur, which is retained for two to four weeks unlike the other Common Seals, which shed it in the uterus. The adult pelage is lighter than the other North Pacific Common Seal species. It is typically silvery with the darker area along the mid-dorsal region. The actual markings give an overall impression of spots, which not uncommonly resemble the rings seen in Ringed Seals. Confusion with the latter species is likely, because they occupy the same areas.

Adult Spotted Seals average 2.1 m in length and 97 kg in weight for both sexes. They attain their full size at approximately 10 years of age. Females give birth to a single pup for the first time when they are approximately 4 years of age. Pups are born in late March to early April on the floating pack-ice. Weaning occurs at 4–6 weeks, at which point the pup must fend entirely for itself.

Spotted Seals feed mainly on pollock *Theragra chalcogramma* when in the pack-ice areas. During the summer, when they leave the pack to occupy nearshore areas, they feed on a variety of fish and shrimps (Lowry *et al* 1979).

Virtually nothing quantitative is known of the natural causes of mortality of Spotted Seals. Killer Whales *Orcinus orca*, Greenland Sharks *Somniosus microcephalus* and Steller's Sea Lions are all documented predators. Present harvests in the Soviet Union and Alaska are between 6,000 and 15,000 animals (Bonner 1979).

### Ribbon Seal

Perhaps the least known species of pinniped in the Arctic, *Phoca fasciata*, occupies the pack-ice of the Okhotsk, Bering and Chukchi Seas. During the winter and spring Ribbon Seals remain with the pack-ice in areas also occupied by Spotted Seals. After the ice has melted, Ribbon Seals apparently remain at sea, since few are ever seen along the coastal regions. Stocks in the Okhotsk and Bering Sea are estimated to be around 240,000 individuals.

Ribbon Seals give birth in the floating pack-ice during April. The white-coated pup, weighing 10 kg at birth, moults its natal coat at three to four weeks of age, which also coincides with the period of weaning. Adults have a distinctive pelage consisting of four pale bands on a dark background. These encircle the neck and posterior trunk and one on each side broadly encircles the fore flippers. Adults average 1.5 m in length and weigh 80 kg.

Like most northern phocids, mating occurs shortly after the pup is weaned. Female Ribbon Seals attain sexual maturity at 3–4 years of age; the males at 4–5 years.

Ribbon Seals feed at sea in Alaskan waters, largely on Pollock and Pandalid Shrimp (Lowry *et al* 1978). Pollock also appears to be the major food item in the Okhotsk Sea.

The Ribbon Seal possesses an air sac, which is connected to the trachea. This overlies the ribs on the right side of the body and is believed to provide additional buoyancy (Burns and Fay 1970). This would seem to be an adaptation to life in the open water, perhaps better enabling the animal to rest in areas where there are no opportunities to haul out.

Nothing is known of the source of natural mortality for this species. Present harvest levels in the Soviet Union are 3,000 annually, reduced from 13,000 in the early 1960s. Less than 100 are taken each year in Alaska.

### Harp Seal

This species forms the largest breeding aggregation of any northern phocid seal. Three breeding stocks are known: one which occupies the Gulf of St Lawrence and the east coast of Newfoundland in Canadian waters, the White Sea, and those of the Greenland Sea north of Jan Mayen. All three stocks migrate south to their breeding areas from their summer feeding areas which are much further north.

Because of the large commercial harvests, this species has been the subject of much population research as well as the target of anti-hunting protests and debate. Estimates of the world population range from 1.3 to 2.5 million animals. The Jan Mayen and White Sea stocks, both of which were severely overharvested, are now under strict management and believed to be increasing. The north-western Atlantic stock, which is now harvested at less than the sustained yield level, is most likely increasing at a rapid rate.

Adult Harp Seals average 1.9 m in length and weigh 125 kg. The dark saddle mark on their back is characteristic of the adult pelage. The pup is born with a white natal lanugo, which it sheds at 2–4 weeks of age. Adolescents have a spotted pelage which changes to the dark harp or saddle mark in the fourth year of life. Adult males have a darker face than do the females.

In the late autumn and early winter, as ice forms in the higher Arctic latitudes, Harp Seals begin to travel south toward the areas which will become their breeding grounds in March and April. There they haul out onto the floating pack-ice and give birth. Female Harp Seals attain sexual maturity at 4–5 years of age; males at 6–7 years. Mating occurs shortly after the pups are weaned at about three weeks of age. There is the usual delay in implantation of the fertilised egg, which remains free floating in the uterus for approximately eleven weeks.

Harp Seals feed on a variety of small fish and crustaceans. In a large part of their range Capelin *Mallotus villosus* is their preferred food item. In the higher latitudes, Arctic Cod and pelagic crustaceans predominate in their diet. Feeding studies of captive Harp Seals indicate that they can maintain themselves on 1.5–5 per cent of their body weight in food consumption per day.

Exploitation of the three stocks of Harp Seals has been severely reduced in recent years due to the ban imposed by the European Economic Community on the importation of white-coat pup pelts. Canadian catches have been reduced by this lowered demand from 167,000 pelts in 1982 to less than 58,000 in 1983. The White Sea quota of 27,000 and Jan Mayen harvest of 15,000 do not appear to be a threat to the present stocks.

### Hooded Seal

The Hooded Seal (or Crested Seal) is an occupant of the north-western Atlantic. Whelping patches are known in the southern Davis Strait, off the north of Jan Mayen in Denmark Strait and off the north-east coast of Newfoundland. It is believed that there is an exchange between the Davis Strait and Newfoundland stock, while the Jan Mayen population remains isolated. Estimates of the Davis Strait stock range from 42,000 to 50,000. The total Jan Mayen stock has not been surveyed, but one moulting patch was estimated to number about 230,000 seals. The total size of Hooded Seal stocks has been estimated to be 300,000 to 505,000 individuals (Scheffer 1958, Oritsland 1960).

Adult male Hooded Seals average 2.5 m in length and weigh 400 kg. Females are somewhat smaller measuring 2.2 m and weighing 350 kg. Pups shed their lanugal hair in the womb and are born with a short-haired coat which is bluish grey in colour and highly prized. The adult pelage is marked over the whole body with dark patches on a silver-grey background.

The name 'Hooded Seal' is derived from the hood which is formed of the enlarged proboscis of the male. This is an enlargement of the nasal cavity which can be inflated to form a crest on the top of the nose. The adult male will usually inflate this when he is making threats towards intruders. Also, a red balloon-like structure can be inflated. This usually projects out of the left nostril and is actually a part of the nasal septum.

Female Hooded Seals, which are sexually mature at 3–4 years old, give birth to their pups on the floating pack-ice. The pup is weaned very quickly in about ten

*Plate 11.1 Walruses hauled out near Uelen, Chukotka Peninsula*

days and mating soon follows. Dominant adult males stay near females with pups waiting for the female to come into oestrus. The term 'family groups' has been applied to such aggregations, but is somewhat misleading. Hooded Seals are either monogamous, or possibly exhibit a limited form of polygyny.

Hooded Seals remain in the offshore areas for most of the year. Their food include fish such as Greenland Halibut *Reinhardtius hippoglossoides*, Redfish *Sebastes marinus*, Capelin and Arctic Cod, as well as some Squid *Gonatus fabricii*.

Polar Bears and possibly Killer Whales are the two main causes of natural mortality. Polar Bears, especially on the northern whelping areas, could cause considerable mortality to newborn pups. Recent exploitation levels were 10,000 to 14,000 for the Newfoundland stock with 90 per cent of the catch made up of newborn pups. The recently severely depressed market for seal pelts reduced the Canadian catch in 1983 to only 128 individuals. The quota for the Jan Mayen stock is presently 30,000 animals. In Greenland up to 2,000 seals are killed annually by Inuit hunters during the summer and autumn months.

### Bearded Seal

The Bearded Seal is distributed throughout the Arctic.

*Plate 11.2 Bearded Seal hauled ashore*

It is widely sought after by the Inuit for its hide, which is used in the fabrication of lines, boot soles and as a covering for skin boats. Two subspecies have been recognized: *E. b. barbatus* found in the Canadian Arctic and Laptev Sea and *E. b. nauticus* found in the Alaska areas as far east as the Beaufort Sea. The exact limits of their distribution is not known and recent work indicates that a single widespread species exists (Smith 1981). Estimates of abundance for this species are difficult to obtain because of its wide distribution in the pack-ice areas. Worldwide estimates range from 500,000 to 700,000 animals, but these figures cannot be considered reliable.

Bearded Seals are distributed along the continental shelf in areas where there is high benthic productivity. In Alaskan waters the wide continental shelf and high production of bottom organisms supports a large number of Bearded Seals. In the Canadian Arctic the major concentrations of Bearded Seals are found in Hudson Bay and Hudson Straits, where there is a wide coastal shelf and benthic production is high. In other Arctic areas small semi-isolated populations of Bearded Seals are found wherever there is a concentration of benthic food.

Bearded Seals are usually found in areas of broken floating pack-ice, but can also maintain themselves in land-fast ice. They are able to keep breathing holes open with the strong claws on their fore flippers, in the same manner as do Ringed Seals. In these situations there are usually areas of high benthic productivity, which provides the food to sustain a year-round resident population of Bearded Seals.

The Bearded Seal is named after its dense mystacial vibrissae, which are used as tactile organs enabling it to find its food on the ocean floor. Bearded Seals are large, adults measuring 2.3–2.4 m and weighing up to 430 kg. There is some indication that adult females are slightly larger than males. The coat of the adults is a fairly uniform grey. Bearded Seals differ from all other northern phocids in having four teats instead of two. They are also distinguishable in having a very heavy fore flipper from which they derive the name 'square flipper'.

Pups are born in early May on the ice. They possess a dark coat showing lighter patches on the neck and back region. This lanugal pelage is shed at the end of lactation, which lasts two to three weeks. Females are sexually mature at 6 years of age and males at 6–7 years. Mating occurs shortly after weaning of the pup, with a delay in implantation of three months and active gestation of nine months (Smith 1981). Once mature, Bearded Seals appear to reproduce annually.

Feeding is primarily on bottom organisms. In the Bering Sea, crabs and crangonid shrimps are the principal food items (Lowry *et al* 1979). There is some indication that at certain times of the year Bearded Seals will feed to a considerable extent on fish such as Saffron Cod *Eleginus gracilis* and Arctic Cod (Johnson *et al* 1966; Smith 1981).

The Inuit of Canada and Alaska hunt Bearded Seals mainly for food and leather. The total Canadian take is unknown, but is probably less than 3,000 annually and is likely decreasing as southern products replace the need for native leather. In Alaska the annual domestic harvest has been as high as 4,700 (Burns 1981). The Soviet commercial catch from pelagic vessels has been up to 7,000 animals, but now is much reduced.

### Ringed Seals

Of all the Arctic pinnipeds, the Ringed Seal is best adapted to life in the land-fast sea-ice. The Inuit along the Arctic coast have lived in intimate contact with this species, which has always been their major resource.

The most widely distributed of the six subspecies currently recognised, *P. h. hispida*, is found throughout the Arctic Ocean and northern Eurasia and all along the coast of Arctic Canada and Greenland. *P. h. kras-chininikovi* occurs in the northern parts of the Bering Sea. Unlike the other Ringed Seals it does not use subnivean lairs, but gives birth on the surface of the pack-ice. *P. h. ochtensis* is found in the Okhotsk Sea south to the Kuril Islands and Sakhalin. *P. h. botnica* is confined to the Baltic Sea, the Gulf of Bothnia and the Gulf of Finland. Two subspecies *P. h. lagodensis* and *P. h. saimensis* occupy the large lakes Lagoda in Russia and Saimaa in Finland. Both these bodies of water are connected to the sea by river systems, but there is no evidence that these seals move up or down these waterways.

The total Arctic population of Ringed Seals has been estimated to be $6–7 \times 10^6$ but this is not considered to be a reliable figure. Only a limited amount of the total range of this species has been surveyed and densities have been shown to vary tremendously from one area to the next. It has also been shown that large annual variation in Ringed Seal densities can occur from year to year in the same region (Stirling *et al* 1977; Smith and Stirling 1978).

The Ringed Seal is a small animal measuring 1.25 m on average and weighing 65 kg. Adults have a pelage which is often marked by pale rings on a darker background. The back is usually darker than the sides and belly, which are grey or silver in appearance. Pups are born with a white lanugo, which is shed in the birth lair 3–4 weeks after they are born.

The Ringed Seal gives birth to its single pup in a sub-snow lair. This is dug out by the female and connected to the ocean by a breathing hole through the sea-ice which the adults keep open by constant scratching with the claws of their fore flippers. Birth lairs provide thermal shelter and protection from predators such as Arctic Foxes and Polar Bears.

Adult females are sexually mature at 4–7 years and males at 7 years. Recent behavioural studies suggest that Ringed Seals are polygamous, with one male attending two to three females (Smith and Hammill 1981). Ringed Seals usually produce pups each year, but recent work has shown that environmental factors can reduce the reproductive rate drastically in certain years. In areas such as the Gulf of Bothnia, low reproductive rates have recently been linked to high PCB levels from industrial pollution (Helle *et al* 1976).

Ringed Seals feed on a wide variety of organisms, from small planktonic crustaceans to Arctic Cod. In the open water season, pelagic and nearshore crustaceans such as *Themisto libellula* and *Mysis occulata* are an important food, especially for the younger seals. During the winter, Arctic Cod and in some areas Squid *Rossia pacifica* form an important part of the diet. Studies on captive seals suggest that they require the equivalent of 3 per cent of their body weight in food as maintenance energy per day.

Ringed Seal populations are thought to be governed by heavy predation from Polar Bears (Stirling and Archibald 1977) and Arctic Foxes (Smith 1976) in the early years of life and by the availability of suitable ice areas for breeding sites.

Because the species is solitary and widely dispersed, there has never been any large-scale organised commercial hunts for Ringed Seals. The Inuit of Canada and Alaska continue to hunt them for food and pelts. In the 1960s and 1970s, up to 90,000 were taken in the Canadian Arctic. This level of exploitation was not considered excessive and because of the reduced demand for seal pelts the harvest has dropped considerably in recent years. The rapidly increasing Inuit population of the Arctic will, in the future, continue to depend on Ringed Seals as an important source of food.

## The Arctic Whales: Cetacea

The order Cetacea is divided into two sub-orders: the Mysticeti, those with baleen plates or whale bone instead of teeth; and the Odontoceti, or Toothed Whales, which include porpoises and dolphins. Only three species are considered true Arctic whales: the Bowhead, a large baleen whale of the family Balaenidae; and two toothed whales, both of the family Monodontidae, the White Whale and the Narwhal. All three species live throughout the year in ice-filled Arctic waters and share as a common adaptation to this environment the absence of a dorsal fin.

### Bowhead Whale

The Bowhead or Greenland Right Whale was hunted almost to extermination by the beginning of the twentieth century. It was widely sought by the European and American whalers and was known as the 'Right' Whale because it was easy to hunt, floated when it was killed and gave a high yield of oil and baleen. The two principal stocks of Bowhead Whales exist in the eastern Canadian Arctic and the Bering, Chukchi and Beaufort Seas. Two additional stocks are known; one around Svalbard, which is thought to be virtually extinct, and a very small group remaining in the Okhotsk Sea.

Most of the research on this species has involved historical studies of whalers' log books, in an attempt to define the geographical location and abundance of stocks prior to the beginning of intensive exploitation. Bowhead Whale hunting in the Davis Strait and west Greenland areas started as early as 250 years ago by the Dutch, who were followed later by the British. By the late 1800s these stocks, including those in Hudson Bay, had been severely depleted, from estimated levels of some 11,000–13,000 whales in the original unexploited population. Present estimates of these stocks are of up to 600 for Baffin Bay and less than 100 for Hudson Bay.

A much larger population of Bowheads is found in the western Arctic. This stock over-winters in the Bering Sea and migrates northward in the summer into the Chukchi and Beaufort Seas. In recent years it has received much attention and study because of the persisting and increasing hunt by the Alaskan Inuit. Recent estimates suggest that some 3,800 individuals remain in this population, which numbered approximately 14,000 to 20,000 animals in the mid-1800s. Hunting of this stock began in 1848 by American whalers, and by 1907 Bowheads in the western Arctic had already become scarce, so with the falling demand for whale products the hunt was abandoned. Presently, the only Bowhead Whales hunted are those taken by the Alaskan Inuit.

The Bowhead gets its name from the curved arching upper jaw. The large number of baleen plates and thick blubber layer made this whale a very profitable catch. At the peak of whale bone and oil prices near the turn of the century, one Bowhead could bring in $10,000. Baleen, a flexible and springy material, was used in a variety of products from corset stays to fishing rods. The Inuit used the shredded baleen for fishing nets, the intestines for waterproof clothing and windows and meat for human and dog food. The most highly prized portion remains the *muktuk*, the epidermis, considered the ultimate delicacy by the Inuit. This continues to be the prime motivation for the modern hunt. *Muktuk*, apart from being a delicacy to the Inuit palate, contains more Vitamin C than any other native food (Geraci and Smith 1979).

Bowheads are large whales sometimes measuring over 15 m in total length. Individuals over 14 m long weigh approximately 3.3 tonnes per m; those under that length, about 1.7 tonnes per m. The head of the whale comes to a peak where the twin blowhole is situated. This might be an adaptation to enable it to breath in areas where emergence from water is somewhat restricted by ice. Bowheads are also known to be able to break sea ice of up to 60 cm in thickness. Their lack of dorsal fin and thick epidermis are adaptations enabling them to live in ice-filled waters. Bowheads are dark in coloration varying from black to dark grey, with a light to white patch under the chin and lighter shading near the genital area.

The life history of the Bowhead is not well known because of the scarcity of specimens available to scientists. Calves are 3–5 m long at birth, which in all likelihood occurs during April and May. Mating also occurs at this time and gestation appears to be about twelve months. Calves apparently are weaned early, but little information is available on the length of the lactation period. Reproductive rates appear very low, which might contradict this short lactation period. Age of sexual maturity is not known because of a problem in determining ages in this species. Estimates range from 5 to 9 years.

Bowheads are filter feeders using their baleen plates to sieve enormous amounts of water containing their prey species. Pelagic crustaceans such as the euphausiid *Thysanoessa raschii*, copepods *Calanus hyperboreus* and amphipods *Parathemisto libellula* are the most common food items found in stomach contents from the Alaskan killed whales (Lowry *et al* 1978). It is believed that the organisms eaten in the four-month summer period spent by Bowheads in the Beaufort Sea would provide sufficient food reserves to maintain the whales throughout the year. Winter feeding in the Bering Sea is not thought to be a significant part of their annual food intake.

Little is known of the sources of natural mortality. Some deaths may be caused by entrapment in the ice, but this is not believed to be very significant. Killer Whales might also play a small part as the only aquatic predator capable of taking such large prey.

## Beluga

Sometimes called the White Whale, the Beluga, a name derived from the Russian *Belukha*, is the most widely distributed of the Arctic odontocetes. Its range is circumpolar Arctic and Subarctic, with world population estimates of up to 58,000 individuals.

More is known of the Canadian stocks of Belugas than those occupying the Alaskan or Asian Arctic. An estimated 32,000 Beluga in seven geographically separate stocks are found in the Canadian Arctic and Subarctic (Smith *et al* 1985). The most southerly stock in the world is found in Canada and numbers 500–700 individuals. This group is located at the mouth of the Saguenay River (45° N), which empties into the Gulf of St Lawrence downstream from Quebec.

Belugas undertake seasonal movements. In the spring as the ice melts and breaks up, they migrate north to areas where they will spend the summer. Belugas seek out the same river estuaries each year, where they aggregate by the thousand in the shallow and relatively warm fresh water. These areas were once thought to be calving grounds, but recently it was found that they serve an entirely different function. The calves in fact are born in July prior to the complete break up of the ice and well before the whales reach their river habitat. In the estuaries, the Belugas move far up the river channels into extremely shallow water. It is not unusual to see them almost completely out of the water, resting with their bellies on the sand or gravel bottom. They are in fact rubbing and scratching themselves, because they are undergoing a pronounced moult. This apparently is the main reason for their occupation of the estuaries. In most years the estuaries

*Plate 11.3 The Ringed Seal is well adapted to life in the land-fast sea-ice zone*

are occupied from early July until mid or late August. There could well be a continuous exchange of animals which come and go during this period. Indications are that individuals probably spend only a few weeks at most in the estuary. This is not surprising, since they do not appear to be feeding at all while they remain in these areas.

By the end of August Belugas begin to move back towards the areas where they will spend the winter. In Canada, the High Arctic stock moves towards Davis Strait and south-western Greenland. Belugas in the Beaufort Sea begin their westward migration to the Bering Sea and those of Hudson Bay migrate north and west to Hudson Strait. All these areas share the common feature of open water throughout the winter, which Belugas need for their survival.

The Beluga is a small whale, adult males measuring up to 4.6 m and weighing 1,400 to 1,600 kg. Calves are born from June to the end of July and are less than one third of the length of their mothers at birth. They are pale grey in colour, often with a mottled or bruised appearance. Yearlings are very dark and at least half the length of the females. Calves apparently stay with their mothers for two to three years. It is not unusual to see females accompanied by yearlings and older calves. It appears in fact that the extended family unit forms the basis of the herd structure; older calves have been observed caring for neonates while the mothers go off to swim by themselves.

By the age of 6 or 7 years, Belugas have assumed the white adult colour. Females attain sexual maturity at this time and produce a calf about every three years. Gestation lasts 14 months with mating taking place between April and May. Nothing is known of the mating behaviour which takes place at sea in ice-filled water. In the summer estuarine habitats, the large males stay together in groups of 10–15 individuals. They interact with each other, often playing for hours on end. Their interaction at this time does not appear to be aggressive. They do, however, occasionally display aggressive behaviour towards the females and calves, which appear to avoid them as much as possible.

Killer Whales are the main predators of White Whales, several attacks having been observed where

*Plate 11.4 A Beluga exhibiting aerial posture*

many Belugas have been killed. While Polar Bears have been observed to stalk and hunt Belugas in the water, no successful kill has yet been seen (Smith 1985).

Because of their habit of congregating in shallow river estuaries Belugas are extremely vulnerable to hunting, and, as with the Bowhead, the Inuit seek them for their white epidermis, which is highly prized *muk-tuk*.

### Narwhal

In many ways the most striking of all the odontocetes, the Narwhal is the only tusk-bearing whale. The name Narwhal is derived from the Scandinavian *nar* meaning corpse. Presumably the grey mottled appearance put the Norse sailors in mind of a floating corpse. The Narwhal is presently found only in the High Arctic areas of Canada, having apparently been extirpated by hunting in the north-eastern part of its range near Novaya Zemlya and Franz Josef Land. The Canadian population has been estimated at 10,000 to 34,000 individuals and recent comprehensive aerial surveys estimate that 20,000–21,000 summer in Lancaster Sound and adjoining waterways (Smith *et al* 1985). An additional unknown number spend their summer along west Greenland, in Fox Basin and south-east Baffin Island.

Adult males measure up to 4.5 m and weigh up to 1,700 kg. Females are slightly smaller. The young are very dark and uniform but develop a mottled appearance of dark patches interspersed with grey areas as they age. The tusk of the Narwhal, normally borne by males only, is its only visible tooth – the upper left canine. Large males have been found with tusks up to 3.3 m in length. The tusk has a left hand spiral which runs down its entire length. Rarely, individuals with two tusks are seen. A variety of theories have been expounded on their use, including an acoustic jousting device and a means of defence against Polar Bears. Recent observations indicate that males do, in fact, use the tusks in displays to establish dominance (Silverman and Dunbar 1980; Best 1981), but little is known of the behaviour and the few studies which have been done were conducted during the summer, well outside the breeding season.

Narwhals overwinter in southern Davis Strait at the

edge of the pack-ice. As the ice recedes in the spring they migrate north to the deep-water fjords of Eclipse Sound, Navyboard Inlet and Admiralty Inlet, on north-eastern Baffin Island.

Adult females probably attain sexual maturity at 6–8 years, and calves are born prior to the Narwhals entering their summer areas, sometimes in mid-July. Breeding is believed to occur in mid-April, which indicates a gestation period of 14.5 months. The lacatation period is probably as long as in the Beluga, resulting in the Narwhal producing a calf about once every three years.

Narwhals appear to feed heavily at the ice edge and in pack-ice areas, but very little in their summering areas. Arctic Cod and Greenland Halibut *Reinhardtius hippoglossoides*, are their most common prey. Halibut and other species such as Polar Cod *Arctogadus glacialus* indicate that Narwhals are capable of feeding in very deep areas (Finley and Gibb 1982).

Predation by both Killer Whales and Polar Bears undoubtedly accounts for some natural mortality. Entrapment in ice, which is known to occur fairly frequently, probably also has some impact (Porsild 1918; Sergeant and Williams 1983). The Inuit hunt mainly male Narwhals, for their tusks. Ivory presently sells for about $100 per pound bringing a yield of $600 for a long tusk. The *muktuk* is used as a preferred food item and some of the meat is also used for human consumption and dog food.

## Management of Arctic Whale and Seal Populations

Without a doubt the single largest source of mortality for all the Arctic marine mammal populations is either commercial or subsistence hunting by man. Canada, Alaska and the Soviet Union have aboriginal cultures which continue to harvest seals and whales as part of their subsistence economy. In addition, Norway has long been a commercial hunter of marine mammals and continues to harvest seals and whales in its own territories as well as in Canadian waters.

The Bowhead Whale, the largest of the Arctic sea mammals and formerly the most valuable, is considered an endangered species. The eastern Canadian Arctic stock numbering in the low hundreds is not presently hunted and will not, according to present Canadian policy, be hunted again in the foreseeable future. The western stock which overwinters in the Bering Sea is hunted by Alaskan Inuit during its migration to the Beaufort Sea. Although this stock has been estimated to number some 3,800 individuals, the apparently extremely low reproductive rate makes the present annual catch of 27 whales worrisome. The International Whaling Commission has repeatedly recommended that this hunt be completely stopped. The Alaskan Inuit on their side argue that the hunt is an integral part of their culture and is essential to its survival. Vast sums have been spent in recent years to improve population estimates and obtain the basic information on mortality and reproductive rates, but a low-density population, which can travel far offshore in ice-filled waters, makes the attainment of better data a very difficult task. Ironically the low numbers of whales harvested also makes improved estimates of reproductive rates difficult.

In general, the increased effort put into Bowhead research has had a positive effect. The dialogue developed between the Alaskan Inuit and the management authorities has made both parties aware of the need for co-operation in such situations. The Inuit have come to realise that they are subject to scrutiny from outside their own small sphere and are increasingly aware of modern management concerns. Recent northern land claim settlements, the creation of Inuit-controlled game advisory groups and the attainment of some autonomy with regard to management of their own renewable resources have all had a positive effect towards creating the understanding and goodwill needed for effective game management in the Arctic. The Bowhead Whale, which is in fact the only truly endangered Arctic species, and which, it must be remembered, was put in that unfortunate position by southern whalers, has served as an important example.

It has been estimated that the Beluga increases at a rate of about 9 per cent annually and that a safe sustained harvest could remove 5 per cent of the population each year. These estimates are based on specimens taken from a large and apparently healthy population of some 11,000 to 12,000 individuals which occupy the coast of western Hudson Bay in the summer. Recent estimates of production based on aerial counts of newborn calves vary between 9 and 14 per cent, but must be viewed with caution, since they may be biased on the high side because of behavioural segregation.

Total annual catches of Belugas are poorly documented, because it is strictly a subsistence fishery. The actual total kill, because of sinking loss, which can be some 30–50 per cent of the animals struck, is difficult to estimate. At present in Canada, three of seven geographically separate stocks are thought to be threatened with reduction in numbers, or harvested close to the sustained level. In the Davis Strait a group of some 500–800 Belugas, which summer in Cumberland Sound, are managed under a quota, which allows 40 individuals to be taken each year. Because of the wounding and sinking loss this level of exploitation is probably near the sustained yield for this stock. Two stocks, occupying the northern Quebec coasts of eastern Hudson Bay and Ungava Bay, are now at a very low level. These were severely over-exploited because of the demand for skins in the nineteenth century. The Hudson Bay Company organised hunting and netting operations, which removed over 5,000 individuals from these populations in the latter half of the 1800s. By placing whale nets in the rivers, or by organising Inuit using numerous boats, it was possible to kill several thousand Belugas at one hunt in the shallow areas where they congregated in summer. The present catch in northern Quebec during the summer is approximately 40–60. No good estimates exist for the stock size, but if the lower guesses of 400–500 individuals are correct, then these stocks are being exploited very near the sustained level. The Ungava Bay stock especially, seems to be severely depleted and warrants the most concern.

Effective management of Beluga stocks in the future will involve quotas and the protection of certain estuaries during the period when the whales occupy them. This is not an easy management strategy to implement, since it is in the estuaries where the Inuit hunters can most effectively kill and retrieve their prey. Protection of major estuaries is most important in areas where few such places of aggregation exist and where the stocks are severely depleted. More data are needed on the identity and discreteness of stocks in order to effectively manage White Whale populations.

Narwhals, because they are hunted largely for their valuable tusk, are somewhat easier to manage. The present village quota system, which permits a maximum of 542 from 21 villages to be taken annually, is both an effective and acceptable management strategy. The chief problem of the managers has been the obtaining of reliable population estimates and estimating the total catch including sinking and wounding loss. With present realistic estimates of some 20,000–21,000 Narwhals in the Canadian High Arctic, the maximum total annual kill represents approximately 3 per cent of the Canadian population, which would seem to be a very safe level of exploitation.

Harp and Hooded Seals, commercially hunted by Canada, Norway and the Soviet Union, have been the main focus of the anti-sealing controversy. Over-exploitation of both species in the past led to reduction in their populations. In recent years, both the Soviet and Canadian stocks have been much studied and management is aimed at harvesting the populations at sustainable levels. The recent ban on the importation to Europe of Harp Seal pup pelts has effectively reduced the catch of Harp Seals in Canadian waters to approximately 30 per cent of the calculated sustainable yield. Hooded Seal catches are also drastically reduced.

The reduced market for seal pelts has had a strong impact on the economy of Inuit villages, which depended on Ringed Seal hunting as one of their sole sources of revenue. The catch of Ringed Seals in Canada has fallen from 70,000–80,000 annually in the mid-1970s to less than 50,000, even though there was no reason for reducing the harvest. The future of the seal skin industry remains very uncertain. Present anti-hunt sentiments from countries which have long abandoned harvesting wildlife populations have exerted strong pressure on the few remaining parts of the world where this is still a way of life. Aboriginal hunters who are still numerous in Canada and Alaska are faced with diminished revenue from hunting and increased costs of hunting equipment. Hunting remains the all-important means of feeding an increasing human population in the north. To make this viable, subsistence hunting in the modern age must include some form of revenue to at least pay for the cost of the hunt. There are very few other sources of cash income in the Arctic. This is one of the major problems facing the Inuit and managers of wildlife in the Arctic today.

# APPENDIX 1
# BREEDING BIRDS OF THE ARCTIC

| | Alaska | Canada | Greenland | Svalbard | Soviet Union |
|---|---|---|---|---|---|
| **Gaviiformes** | | | | | |
| Red-throated Diver or Loon<br>*Gavia stellata* | ✕ | ✕ | ✕ | ✕ | ✕ |
| Black-throated Diver (Arctic Loon)<br>*Gavia arctica* | ✕ | ✕ | | | ✕ |
| Great Northern Diver (Common Loon)<br>*Gavia immer* | ✕[a] | ✕ | ✕ | | |
| White-billed Diver (Yellow-billed Loon)<br>*Gavia adamsii* | ✕ | ✕ | | | ✕ |
| **Podicipediformes** | | | | | |
| *Red-necked Grebe<br>*Podiceps grisegena* | ✕ | ✕ | | | |
| *Slavonian (Horned) Grebe<br>*Podiceps auritus* | | ✕ | | | |
| **Procellariiformes** | | | | | |
| Northern Fulmar<br>*Fulmarus glacialis* | | ✕ | ✕ | ✕ | ✕ |
| **Pelecaniformes** | | | | | |
| *Great Cormorant<br>*Phalacrocorax carbo* | | | ✕ | | |
| Pelagic Cormorant<br>*Phalacrocorax pelagicus* | ✕ | | | | ✕ |
| **Anseriformes** | | | | | |
| *Whooper Swan<br>*Cygnus cygnus* | | | | | ✕ |
| Bewick's/Whistling Swan (Tundra Swan)<br>*Cygnus columbianus* | ✕ | ✕ | | | ✕ |
| *Trumpeter Swan<br>*Cygnus buccinator* | ✕[b] | | | | |
| Bean Goose<br>*Anser fabalis* | | | | | ✕ |
| Pink-footed Goose<br>*Anser brachyrhynchus* | | | ✕ | ✕ | |
| White-fronted Goose<br>*Anser albifrons* | ✕ | ✕ | ✕ | | ✕ |
| *Lesser White-fronted Goose<br>*Anser erythropus* | | | | | ✕[c] |
| Snow Goose<br>*Anser caerulescens* | ✕ | ✕ | ✕ | | ✕ |
| Ross's Goose<br>*Anser rossii* | | ✕ | | | |
| *Emperor Goose<br>*Anser canagicus* | | | | | ✕ |
| Canada Goose<br>*Branta canadensis* | ✕ | ✕ | ✕ | | |
| Barnacle Goose<br>*Branta leucopsis* | | | ✕ | ✕ | ✕ |

| | Alaska | Canada | Greenland | Svalbard | Soviet Union |
|---|---|---|---|---|---|
| Brent Goose (Black Brant)<br>*Branta bernicla* | × | × | × | × | × |
| Red-breasted Goose<br>*Branta ruficollis* | | | | | × |
| *European Wigeon<br>*Anas penelope* | | | | | ×[c] |
| American Wigeon<br>*Anas americana* | × | × | | | |
| Baikal Teal<br>*Anas formosa* | | | | | × |
| Teal (Green-winged Teal)<br>*Anas crecca* | × | × | | | × |
| Mallard<br>*Anas platyrhynchos* | × | × | × | | |
| Pintail<br>*Anas acuta* | × | × | × | | × |
| Northern Shoveler<br>*Anas clypeata* | × | × | | | |
| *Tufted Duck<br>*Aythya fuligula* | | | | | ×[d] |
| Greater Scaup<br>*Aythya marila* | × | × | | | × |
| Lesser Scaup<br>*Aythya affinis* | × | × | | | |
| Eider<br>*Somateria mollissima* | × | × | × | × | × |
| King Eider<br>*Somateria spectabilis* | × | × | × | × | × |
| Spectacled Eider<br>*Somateria fischeri* | × | | | | × |
| Steller's Eider<br>*Polysticta stelleri* | × | | | | × |
| Harlequin Duck<br>*Histrionicus histrionicus* | × | × | × | | |
| Long-tailed Duck (Oldsquaw)<br>*Clangula hyemalis* | × | × | × | × | × |
| Common (Black) Scoter<br>*Melanitta nigra* | × | × | | | ×[c] |
| Surf Scoter<br>*Melanitta perspicillata* | × | × | | | |
| Velvet (White-winged) Scoter<br>*Melanitta fusca* | × | × | | | ×[c] |
| Barrow's Goldeneye<br>*Bucepahala islandica* | | × | ×[e] | | |
| Red-breasted Merganser<br>*Mergus serrator* | × | × | × | | × |

**Accipitriformes**

| | Alaska | Canada | Greenland | Svalbard | Soviet Union |
|---|---|---|---|---|---|
| White-tailed Eagle<br>*Haliaeetus albicilla* | | | × | | × |
| *Hen (Northern) Harrier<br>*Circus cyaneus* | × | | | | ×[c] |
| Rough-legged Buzzard<br>*Buteo lagopus* | × | × | | | × |
| Golden Eagle<br>*Aquila chrysaetos* | × | × | | | ×[c] |

| | Alaska | Canada | Greenland | Svalbard | Soviet Union |
|---|---|---|---|---|---|
| **Falconiformes** | | | | | |
| Merlin (Pigeon Hawk)<br>*Falco columbarius* | × | × | | | × |
| Gyrfalcon<br>*Falco rusticolus* | × | × | × | | × |
| Peregrine<br>*Falco peregrinus* | × | × | × | | × |
| **Galliformes** | | | | | |
| Willow Ptarmigan<br>*Lagopus lagopus* | × | × | | | × |
| Ptarmigan (Rock Ptarmigan)<br>*Lagopus mutus* | × | × | × | × | × |
| **Gruiformes** | | | | | |
| Sandhill Crane<br>*Grus canadensis* | × | × | | | × |
| Siberian White Crane<br>*Grus leucogeranus* | | | | | × |
| **Charadriiformes** | | | | | |
| Oystercatcher<br>*Haematopus ostralegus* | | | | | × |
| Ringed Plover<br>*Charadrius hiaticula* | | × | × | × | × |
| Semipalmated Plover<br>*Charadrius semipalmatus* | × | × | | | |
| *Lesser Sand Plover<br>*Charadrius mongolus* | | | | | ×[f] |
| Dotterel<br>*Charadrius morinellus* | × | | | | × |
| Pacific Golden Plover<br>*Pluvilis fulva* | × | | | | × |
| Lesser Golden Plover<br>*Pluvialis dominica* | × | × | | | |
| Golden Plover<br>*Pluvialis apricaria* | | | ×[g] | | |
| Grey (Black-bellied) Plover<br>*Pluvialis squatarola* | × | × | | | × |
| *Great Knot<br>*Calidris tenuirostris* | | | | | × |
| Knot<br>*Calidris canutus* | × | × | × | × | × |
| Sanderling<br>*Calidris alba* | × | × | × | × | × |
| Semipalmated Sandpiper<br>*Calidris pusilla* | × | × | | | |
| Western Sandpiper<br>*Calidris mauri* | × | | | | × |
| Rufous-necked Sandpiper (Red-necked Stint)<br>*Calidris ruficollis* | ×[h] | | | | × |
| Little Stint<br>*Calidris minuta* | | | | | × |
| Temminck's Stint<br>*Calidris temminckii* | | | | | × |
| Least Sandpiper<br>*Calidris minutilla* | × | × | | | |
| White-rumped Sandpiper<br>*Calidris fuscicollis* | × | × | | | |

| | Alaska | Canada | Greenland | Svalbard | Soviet Union |
|---|---|---|---|---|---|
| Baird's Sandpiper<br>*Calidris bairdii* | × | × | × | | × |
| Pectoral Sandpiper<br>*Calidris melanotos* | × | × | | | × |
| Sharp-tailed Sandpiper<br>*Calidris acuminata* | | | | | × |
| Curlew Sandpiper<br>*Calidris ferruginea* | × | | | | × |
| Purple Sandpiper<br>*Calidris maritima* | | × | × | × | × |
| *Rock Sandpiper<br>*Calidris ptilocnemis* | | | | | × |
| Dunlin<br>*Calidris alpina* | × | × | × | × | × |
| Spoon-billed Sandpiper<br>*Eurynorhynchus pygmeus* | | | | | × |
| *Broad-billed Sandpiper<br>*Limicola falcinellus* | | | | | × |
| Stilt Sandpiper<br>*Micropalama himantopus* | × | × | | | |
| Buff-breasted Sandpiper<br>*Tryngites subruficollis* | × | × | | | ×[i] |
| *Ruff<br>*Philomachus pugnax* | | | | | × |
| Jack Snipe<br>*Lymnocryptes minimus* | | | | | × |
| Common Snipe<br>*Gallinago gallinago* | × | × | | | × |
| *Great Snipe<br>*Gallinago media* | | | | | × |
| Pintail Snipe<br>*Gallinago stenura* | | | | | × |
| Long-billed Dowitcher<br>*Limnodromus scolopaceus* | × | × | | | × |
| Hudsonian Godwit<br>*Limosa haemastica* | | × | | | |
| Bar-tailed Godwit<br>*Limosa lapponica* | × | | | | × |
| Whimbrel<br>*Numenius phaeopus* | × | × | | | ×[c] |
| Spotted Redshank<br>*Tringa erythropus* | | | | | × |
| Lesser Yellowlegs<br>*Tringa flavipes* | × | × | | | |
| *Solitary Sandpiper<br>*Tringa solitaria* | ×[j] | | | | |
| *Wood Sandpiper<br>*Tringa glareola* | | | | | × |
| *Terek Sandpiper<br>*Xenus cinereus* | | | | | ×[d] |
| Spotted Sandpiper<br>*Actitis macularia* | × | × | | | |
| *Polynesian Tattler<br>*Heteroscelus brevipes* | | | | | ×[f] |
| Wandering Tattler<br>*Heteroscelus incanus* | × | | | | × |
| Turnstone<br>*Arenaria interpres* | × | × | × | × | × |

| | Alaska | Canada | Greenland | Svalbard | Soviet Union |
|---|---|---|---|---|---|
| Red-necked (Northern) Phalarope<br>*Phalaropus lobatus* | × | × | × | | × |
| Grey (Red) Phalarope<br>*Phalaropus fulicarius* | × | × | × | × | × |
| Pomarine Skua or Jaeger<br>*Stercorarius pomarinus* | × | × | | | × |
| Arctic Skua (Parasitic Jaeger)<br>*Stercorarius parasiticus* | × | × | × | × | × |
| Long-tailed Skua or Jaeger<br>*Stercorarius longicaudus* | × | × | × | × | × |
| *Great Skua<br>*Stercorarius skua* | | | | × | |
| Sabine's Gull<br>*Larus sabini* | × | × | × | × | × |
| Black-headed Gull<br>*Larus ridibundus* | | | ×[k] | | |
| Common (Mew) Gull<br>*Larus canus* | × | × | | | ×[m] |
| Herring Gull<br>*Larus argentatus* | × | × | | | × |
| Thayer's Gull<br>*Larus thayeri* | | × | × | | |
| Iceland Gull<br>*Larus glaucoides* | | × | × | | |
| Glaucous Gull<br>*Larus hyperboreus* | × | × | × | × | × |
| Great Black-backed Gull<br>*Larus marinus* | | × | × | × | × |
| Ross's Gull<br>*Rhodostethia rosea* | | × | × | | × |
| Kittiwake (Black-legged Kittiwake)<br>*Rissa tridactyla* | × | × | × | × | × |
| Ivory Gull<br>*Pagophila eburnea* | | × | × | × | × |
| Arctic Tern<br>*Sterna paradisaea* | × | × | × | × | × |
| Guillemot (Common Murre)<br>*Uria aalge* | ×[n] | | × | | × |
| Brünnich's Guillemot (Thick-billed Murre)<br>*Uria lomvia* | ×[n] | × | × | × | × |
| Razorbill<br>*Alca torda* | | × | × | | |
| Black Guillemot<br>*Cepphus grylle* | × | × | × | × | × |
| *Pigeon Guillemot<br>*Cepphus columba* | ×[n] | | | | |
| Kittlitz's Murrelet<br>*Brachyramphus brevirostris* | | | | | × |
| Little Auk<br>*Alle alle* | | ? | × | × | × |
| *Crested Auklet<br>*Aethia cristatella* | | | | | × |
| *Least Auklet<br>*Aethia pusilla* | | | | | × |
| *Parakeet Auklet<br>*Cyclorrhynchus psittacula* | | | | | × |
| Common Puffin<br>*Fratercula arctica* | | | × | × | × |

| | Alaska | Canada | Greenland | Svalbard | Soviet Union |
|---|---|---|---|---|---|
| *Horned Puffin <br> *Fratercula corniculata* | ×[n] | | | | × |
| *Tufted Puffin <br> *Lunda cirrhata* | ×[n] | | | | × |
| **Strigiformes** | | | | | |
| Snowy Owl <br> *Nyctea scandiaca* | × | × | × | × | × |
| Short-eared Owl <br> *Asio flammeus* | × | × | | | × |
| **Passeriformes** | | | | | |
| Say's Phoebe <br> *Sayornis saya* | × | × | | | |
| Shore (Horned) Lark <br> *Eremophila alpestris* | × | × | | | × |
| *Sand Martin <br> *Riparia riparia* | | | | | × |
| Cliff Swallow <br> *Hirundo pyrrhonota* | × | × | | | |
| Pechora Pipit <br> *Anthus gustavi* | | | | | × |
| Meadow Pipit <br> *Anthus pratensis* | | | × | | × |
| Red-throated Pipit <br> *Anthus cervinus* | × | | | | × |
| Water Pipit <br> *Anthus spinoletta* | × | × | × | | × |
| Yellow Wagtail <br> *Motacilla flava* | × | × | | | × |
| Citrine (Yellow-headed) Wagtail <br> *Motacilla citreola* | | | | | × |
| White Wagtail <br> *Motacilla alba* | × | | × | | × |
| North American Dipper <br> *Cinclus mexicanus* | × | | | | |
| *Siberian Accentor <br> *Prunella montanella* | | | | | ×[c] |
| Bluethroat <br> *Luscinia svecica* | × | × | | | × |
| *Stonechat <br> *Saxicola torquata* | | | | | ×[c] |
| Wheatear <br> *Oenanthe oenanthe* | × | × | × | | × |
| Gray-cheeked Thrush <br> *Catharus minimus* | × | × | | | × |
| Naumann's Thrush <br> *Turdus naumanni* | | | | | ×[o] |
| *Fieldfare <br> *Turdus pilaris* | | | ×[p] | | ×[c] |
| *Redwing <br> *Turdus iliacus* | | | | | × |
| American Robin <br> *Turdus migratorius* | × | × | | | |
| *Sedge Warbler <br> *Acrocephalus schoenobaenus* | | | | | ×[c] |
| Arctic Warbler <br> *Phylloscopus borealis* | × | | | | × |

| | Alaska | Canada | Greenland | Svalbard | Soviet Union |
|---|---|---|---|---|---|
| *Chiffchaff<br>*Phylloscopus collybita* | | | | | ×[c] |
| *Willow Warbler<br>*Phylloscopus trochilus* | | | | | ×[c] |
| Great Grey (Northern) Shrike<br>*Lanius excubitor* | × | × | | | ×[d] |
| Gray Jay<br>*Perisoreus canadensis* | × | × | | | |
| Raven<br>*Corvus corax* | × | × | × | | × |
| *Tree Sparrow<br>*Passer montanus* | | | | | ×[q] |
| Common Redpoll<br>*Carduelis flammea* | × | × | × | | × |
| Arctic (Hoary) Redpoll<br>*Carduelis hornemanni* | × | × | × | | × |
| Arctic (Japanese) Rosy Finch<br>*Leucosticte arctoa* | | | | | × |
| Grey-crowned Rosy Finch<br>*Leucosticte tephrocotis* | × | | | | |
| Yellow Warbler<br>*Dendroica petechia* | × | × | | | |
| *Northern Waterthrush<br>*Seiurus noveboracensis* | | × | | | |
| Wilson's Warbler<br>*Wilsonia pusilla* | × | × | | | |
| American Tree Sparrow<br>*Spizella arborea* | × | × | | | |
| Savannah Sparrow<br>*Ammodramus sandwichensis* | × | × | | | |
| Fox Sparrow<br>*Zonotrichia iliaca* | × | × | | | |
| White-crowned Sparrow<br>*Zonotrichia leucophrys* | × | × | | | |
| Lapland Bunting<br>*Calcarius lapponicus* | × | × | × | | × |
| Smith's Longspur<br>*Calcarius pictus* | × | × | | | |
| Snow Bunting<br>*Plectrophenax nivalis* | × | × | × | × | × |
| Little Bunting<br>*Emberiza pusilla* | | | | | × |
| *Reed Bunting<br>*Emberiza schoeniclus* | | | | | ×[r] |
| *Pallas's Reed Bunting<br>*Emberiza pallasi* | | | | | × |
| Rusty Blackbird<br>*Euphagus carolinensis* | × | × | | | |
| **Totals 183** | **113** | **105** | **61** | **31** | **136** |

Notes:
a. Probably only a sporadic breeding species north of the Continental Divide of the Brooks Range.
b. A rare nesting species in north-east Alaska.
c. Breeds in the extreme south of the tundra zone, becoming more abundant in the forest-tundra.
d. Extends into the tundra zone only along wooded valleys.
e. Breeds only in the extreme south-west of Greenland.
f. Breeding only on the southern Chukotka Peninsula.

g. First found breeding at Schuchert, east Greenland, in 1962.

h. A rare breeding species on the Arctic Slope of Alaska.

i. Breeds only on Wrangel Island.

j. Has been recorded nesting on the ground near Chandler Lake (68° 15′ N, 152° 40′ W) in the northern foothills of the Brooks Range.

k. In Greenland, first bred in 1969 in Tasiussaq Bay, Nordre Sermilik, and subsequently at other localities. Successful breeding not recorded in 1983, possibly as a result of recent harsh winters.

m. Breeds sporadically in the extreme southern tundra.

n. Breeding only at Cape Lisburne within the Arctic.

o. The northern form of this thrush is regarded by some authorities as a separate species, the Dusky Thrush *Turdus eunomus*.

p. Found breeding near Narssarssuaq in 1972 but not subsequently, and may now be absent from Greenland as a breeding species.

q. Associated with human settlements.

r. Breeds on the Kanin and Yamal Peninsulas.

* Of only marginal occurrence in the Arctic.

# APPENDIX 2
# TERRESTRIAL MAMMALS
# OF THE ARCTIC

|  | Soviet Union | Alaska | Canada | Greenland |
|---|---|---|---|---|
| **Insectivora** | | | | |
| Common Shrew *Sorex araneus* | × | | | |
| Arctic Shrew *Sorex arcticus*[a] | × | × | × | |
| Laxmann's Shrew *Sorex caecutiens* | × | | | |
| Masked Shrew *Sorex cinereus* | ×[b] | × | × | |
| Large-toothed Shrew *Sorex daphaenodon* | × | | | |
| Pygmy Shrew *Sorex minutus* | × | | | |
| Dusky Shrew *Sorex obscurus* | | × | × | |
| Flat-skulled Shrew *Sorex vir* | × | | | |
| **Lagomorpha** | | | | |
| Snowshoe Hare *Lepus americanus*[c] | | × | × | |
| Arctic Hare *Lepus arcticus*[d] | | | × | × |
| Alaskan (Tundra) Hare *Lepus othus*[d] | | × | | |
| Varying Hare *Lepus timidus*[d] | × | | | |
| Northern Pika *Ochotona hyperborea*[e] | × | | | |
| **Rodentia** | | | | |
| Alaska Marmot *Marmota broweri* | | × | ?[f] | |
| Black-capped Marmot *Marmota camtschatica*[g] | × | | | |
| Arctic Ground Squirrel *Spermophilus undulatus*[h] | × | × | × | |
| Insular (Singing) Vole *Microtus abreviatus*[j] | | × | × | |
| Narrow-skulled Vole *Microtus gregalis* | × | | | |
| Middendorff's Vole *Microtus middendorffi*[k] | × | | | |
| Tundra (Root) Vole *Microtus oeconomus* | × | × | × | |
| Meadow Vole *Microtus pennsylvanicus* | | | × | |
| Arctic (Collared) Lemming *Dicrostonyx groenlandicus*[m] | × | × | × | × |
| Hudson Bay Lemming *Dicrostonyx hudsonius* | | | × | |
| Brown (Siberian) Lemming *Lemmus sibiricus* | × | × | × | |
| Grey Red-backed Vole *Clethrionomys rufocanus* | × | | | |
| Northern Red-backed Vole *Clethrionomys rutilus* | × | × | × | |
| *Eothenomys lemminus*[n] | × | | | |

| | Soviet Union | Alaska | Canada | Greenland |
|---|---|---|---|---|
| European Water Vole *Arvicola terrestris*[o] | × | | | |
| Muskrat *Ondatra zibethicus* | | | × | |
| Porcupine *Erethrizon dorsatum*[p] | | × | × | |
| **Carnivora** | | | | |
| Coyote *Canis latrans* | | × | × | |
| Gray Wolf *Canis lupus* | × | × | × | × |
| Red Fox *Vulpes vulpes* | × | × | × | |
| Arctic Fox *Alopex lagopus* | × | × | × | × |
| Grizzly Bear *Ursus arctos* | ×[o] | × | × | |
| Polar Bear *Ursus maritimus* | × | × | × | × |
| Ermine (Stoat) *Mustela erminea* | × | × | × | × |
| Least Weasel *Mustela nivalis* | × | × | × | |
| European Mink *Mustela lutreola* | ×[o] | | | |
| American Mink *Mustela vison* | | ×[p] | ×[p] | |
| Wolverine *Gulo gulo* | × | × | × | × |
| River Otter *Lutra canadensis* | | ×[p] | ×[q] | |
| Lynx *Lynx canadensis* | | ×[q] | ×[p] | |
| **Artiodactyla** | | | | |
| Moose *Alces alces* | ×[s] | × | × | |
| Caribou (Reindeer) *Rangifer tarandus* | × | × | × | × |
| Muskox *Ovibos moschatus*[t] | × | × | × | × |
| Dall Sheep *Ovis dalli* | | × | × | |
| Snow Sheep *Ovis nivicola*[u] | × | | | |
| **Total species 48** | **33** | **29** | **31** | **9** |

Notes:

a. Includes *Sorex tundrensis* regarded by some authors as a separate species.

b. Of marginal occurrence on the tundra in north-east Siberia.

c. Only occurs on the Arctic tundra when populations are high.

d. Corbet (1978) treats all three as races of one species (*Lepus timidus*), but Chapman and Feldhamer (1982) recognise three species, although commenting that *L. timidus* and *L. othus* may be conspecific.

e. Included by Corbet (1978) under *Ochotona alpina*, but here treated as a separate species.

f. The eastern limit of this species' range is not known with certainty.

g. According to Corbet (1978) this species does not occur on the Chukotka Peninsula, but Ognev (1963) clearly states that it does occur there.

h. Corbet (1978) regards *Spermophilus undulatus* and *S. parryi* as separate species, with the latter being the tundra form of north-east Siberia and the North American Arctic, but Chapman and Feldhamer (1982) refer the North American populations to *S. undulatus* and consider this to be conspecific with *S. parryi*.

j. Includes the Singing Vole *Microtus miurus* regarded by some authorities as a separate species.

k. Includes *Microtus hyperboreus* of the Siberian alpine tundra.

m. This is the same species as *Dicrostonyx torquatus* of some authors.

n. Little seems to be known about this vole. According to Corbet (1978) it occurs in north-east Siberia from the mouth of the Lena River east to the Anadyr region.

o. The range of this species just reaches the southern edge of the tundra.

p. Occasionally seen on the Arctic Slope of Alaska, and on the tundra north of the treeline in Canada.

q. Only of marginal occurrence on the tundra.

r. Only a vagrant north of the Brooks Range in Alaska.

s. Primarily a coniferous forest species in Eurasia.

t. Introduced to Svalbard in 1929, and to the Taimyr Peninsula and Wrangel Island in the mid-1970s.

u. May be conspecific with *Ovis dalli*. Occurs in the mountains of north-east Siberia east of the Lena River, and there is an isolated population in the Putorana Mountains east of the mouth of the Yenesei River.

Sources: Banfield (1974), Bee and Hall (1956), Chapman and Feldhamer (1982) and Corbet (1978).

# REFERENCES

Ahlen, I. & Andersson, A. (1970). Breeding ecology of an Eider population on Spitsbergen. *Ornis Scand.* 1: 83–106

Alaska Geographical Society (1982). Alaska's Glaciers. *Alaska Geographic* 9, No. 1: 1–144

Aleksandrova, V. D. (1980). *The Arctic and Antarctic: their division into geobotanical areas.* Translated from Russian by D. Löve. Cambridge University Press, Cambridge

Alendal, E. (1976). The Muskox population (*Ovibos moschatus*) in Svalbard. *Norsk. Polarinst. Arbok* 1974: 159–74

Amren, H. (1964). Ecological studies of zooplankton populations in some ponds on Spitsbergen. *Zool. Bid. Uppsala, Bd.* 36: 161–91

Amstrup, S. C. (1984). Polar bear research in Alaska 1980–82. *Proceedings of Technical Workshop of the IUCN Polar Bear Specialists Group*, February 1983, pp. 1–17. IUCN, Gland

Anderson, H. L. & Lent, P. C. (1977). Reproduction and growth of the Tundra Hare (*Lepus othus*). *J. Mammal.* 58: 53–7

Arctic Institute of North America (1974). *The Alaskan Arctic Coast: A Background Study of Available knowledge.* Dept. of the Army, Alaska District, Corps of Engineers, Anchorage

Armstrong, T. E., Roberts, B. & Swithinbank, C. (1973). *Illustrated Glossary of Snow and Ice* (2nd edn). Scott Polar Research Institute, Cambridge

Armstrong, T., Rogers, G. & Rowley, G. (1978). *The Circumpolar North.* Methuen, London

Asbirk, S. & Franzmann, N. (1978). Studies of Snow Buntings. In *Joint Biological Expedition to North East Greenland 1974*, eds. G. H. Green & J. J. D. Greenwood, pp. 132–42. University of Dundee

Asbirk, S. & Franzmann, N. (1979). Observations on the diurnal rhythm of Greenland Wheatears Oenanthe oe. leucorrhoa Gm. in continuous daylight. *Dansk Orn. Foren. Tidsskr.* 73: 95–102

Babb, T. A. & Bliss, L. C. (1974). Susceptibility of environmental impact in the Queen Elizabeth Islands. *Arctic* 27: 234–7

Banfield, A. W. F. (1974). *The Mammals of Canada.* University of Toronto Press, Toronto

Barnes, D. F. (1960). *An investigation of a perennially frozen lake.* Airforce Surveys in Geophysics No. 129, ARCRL-TN-60-660

Barry, R. G., Courtin, G. M. & Labine, C. (1981). Tundra climates. In *Tundra Ecosystems: A Comparative Analysis*, eds. L. C. Bliss, O. W. Heal & J. J. Moore. Cambridge University Press, Cambridge

Barry, T. W. (1956). Observations of a nesting colony of American Brant. *Auk* 73: 193–202

Barry, T. W. (1968). Observations on natural mortality and native use of eider ducks along the Beaufort Sea coast. *Can. Fld. Nat.* 82: 140–44

Barry, T. W. (1976). Seabirds of the southeastern Beaufort Sea: summary report. *Beaufort Sea Tech. Rep.* 3a. Environment Canada, Victoria, B.C.

Bartels, R. F. (1973). Bird survey techniques on Alaska's north coast. M.S. Thesis, Iowa State University, Iowa

Batzli, G. O. (1973). Population determination and nutrient flux through lemmings. US IBP Tundra Biome Data Report, pp. 79–9.

Batzli, G. O. (1975). The role of small mammals in arctic ecosystems. In *Small Mammals: Their Productivity and Population Dynamics*, eds. F. B. Golley, K. Petrusewicz & L. Ryszkowski, pp. 243–68. Cambridge University Press, Cambridge

Batzli, G. O. (1981). Population and energetics of small mammals in the tundra ecosystem. In *Tundra Ecosystems: A Comparative Analysis*, eds. L. C. Bliss, O. W. Heal & J. J. Moore, pp. 377–96. Cambridge University Press, Cambridge

Batzli, G. O. & Jung, H. J. G. (1980). Nutritional ecology of microtine rodents: resource utilization near Atkasook. *Arct. Alp. Res.* 12: 483–99

Batzli, G. O. & Pitelka, F. A. (1970). Influence of meadow mouse populations on California grassland. *Ecology* 51: 1027–39

Batzli, G. O. & Sobaski, S. T. (1980). Habitat preference and foraging patterns of ground squirrels near Atkasook, Alaska. *Arct. Alp. Res.* 12: 501–10

Batzli, G. O., White, R. G. & Bunnell, F. L. (1981). Herbivory: a strategy of tundra consumers. In *Tundra Ecosystems: A Comparative Analysis*, eds. L. C. Bliss, O. W. Heal & J. J. Moore, pp. 359–75. Cambridge University Press, Cambridge

Batzli, G. O., White, R. G., MacLean, S. F., Pitelka, F. A. & Collier, B. D. (1980). The herbivore-based trophic system. In *An Arctic Ecosystem: The Coastal Tundra at Barrow, Alaska*, eds. J. Brown, P. C. Miller, L. L. Tieszen & F. L. Bunnell, pp. 335–410. Dowden, Hutchinson & Ross Inc., Stroudsburg, Pennsylvania

Beck, B., Smith, T. G. & Mansfield, A. W. (1970). Occurrence of the Harbour Seal, *Phoca vitulina*, Linnaeus in the Thlewiaza River, N.W.T. *Can. Fld. Nat.* 84: 297–300

Bee, J. W. & Hall, E. R. (1956). *Mammals of Northern Alaska.* Museum of Natural History, University of Kansas, Kansas City

Bergerud, A. T. (1980). A review of the population dynamics of Caribou and wild Reindeer in North America. In *Proceedings of the 2nd International Reindeer/Caribou Symposium*, Røros, Norway 1979, eds. E. Reimers *et al*, pp. 556–581. Direktoratet for vilt og ferskvannsfisk, Trondheim

Beschel, R. E. (1963). Hummocks and their vegetation in the High Arctic. *Proceedings of Permafrost International Conference*, Natl. Acad. Sci., Natl. Research Council Pub. 1287, pp. 13–20. Lafayette, Indiana

Beschel, R. E. (1963). Geobotanical studies in Axel Heiberg Island in 1962. In *Axel Heiberg Island Preliminary Report 1961–1962*, F. Muller *et al*, pp. 199–215. McGill University, Montreal

Best, R. (1981). The tusk of the Narwhal (*Monodon monoceros* L.): interpretation of its function (Mammalia: Cetacea). *Can. J. Zool.* 59: 2386–93

Billings, W. D. & Peterson, K. M. (1980). Vegetational change and ice-wedge polygons through the thaw-lake cycle in Arctic Alaska. *Arct. Alp. Res.* 12: 413–32

Birkenmajer, K. (1969). Observations on Ivory Gull, *Pagophila eburnea* (Phipps), in south Vestspitsbergen. *Acta Orn. Warsz.* 11: 461–76. (In Polish.)

Birkhead, T. R. & Nettleship, D. N. (1982). The adaptive significance of egg size and laying dates in Thick-billed Murres *Uria lomvia. Ecology* 63: 300–6

Bliss, L. C. (1962). Adaptations of arctic and alpine plants to environmental conditions. *Arctic* 15: 117–44

Bliss, L. C. (1975). Tundra grasslands, herblands and shrublands and the role of herbivores. *Geoscience and Man* 10: 51–79

Bliss, L. C., ed. (1977). *Truelove Lowland, Devon Island, Canada: A High Arctic Ecosystem*. University of Alberta Press, Edmonton

Bliss, L. C., Heal, O. W. & Moore, J. J., eds. (1981). *Tundra Ecosystems: A Comparative Analysis*. Cambridge University Press, Cambridge

Blomqvist, S. & Elander, M. (1981). Sabine's Gull (*Xema sabini*), Ross's Gull (*Rhodostethia rosea*) and Ivory Gull (*Pagophila eburnea*). Gulls in the Arctic: a review. *Arctic* 34: 122–32 and errata in *Arctic* 34: 388

Böcher, J. (1972). Feeding Biology of *Nysius groenlandicus* (Zelt.) (Heteroptera: Lygaeidae) in Greenland. *Meddr. Grønland* 191(4)

Böcher, T. W. (1963). Phytogeography of Greenland in the light of recent investigations. In *North Atlantic biota and their history*, eds. A. Löve & D. Löve, pp. 285–95. Macmillan, New York

Boitzov, L. V. (1937). Arctic fox: biology, breeding, feeding. *Trans. Arctic Inst. Leningrad* 65: 1–144

Bonner, N. (1979). Harbour (Common) Seal. In *Mammals in the sea*, II: pp. 58–62. Pinniped species summaries and reports on Sirineans. Annex B, Appendices VI and VII of FAO Advisory Comm. on Marine Resources Research Working Party on Marine Mammals. F.A.O. Rome

Bousefield, M. A. & Syroechkovskiy, Ye. V. (1985). A review of Soviet research on the Lesser Snow Goose on Wrangel Island, U.S.S.R. *Wildfowl* 36: 13–20

Boyd, H., Smith, G. E. J. & Cooch, F. G. (1982). The Lesser Snow Geese of the eastern Canadian Arctic. *Can. Wildl. Ser. Occas. Paper* No. 46

Britton, M. E. (1957). Vegetation of the arctic tundra. In *Arctic Biology*, ed. H. P. Hansen, pp. 26–72. Oregon State University Press, Cornvallis

Brooks, R. J. (1970). Ecology and acoustic behavior of the collared lemming *Dicrostonyx groenlandicus* (Trail). Ph.D. Thesis, University of Illinois, Illinois

Brown, J., Haugen, R. K. & Parrish, S. (1975). Selected climatic and soil thermal characteristics of the Prudhoe Bay region. In *Ecological Investigations of the Tundra Biome in the Prudhoe Bay Region, Alaska*, ed. J. Brown. Biological Papers, Special Report No. 2, pp. 3–11. University of Alaska, Fairbanks

Brown, R. G. B. (1976). The foraging range of breeding Dovekies, *Alle alle. Can. Fld. Nat.* 90: 166–8

Brown, R. G. B. & Nettleship, D. N. (1984). The seabirds of northeastern North America: their present status and conservation requirements. In *Status and Conservation of the World's Seabirds*, eds. J. P. Croxall, P. G. H. Evans & R. W. Schreiber, pp. 85–100. ICBP, Cambridge

Burnham, W. A., Clement, D. M., Harris, J. T., Mattox, W. G. & Ward, F. P. (1974). Falcon research in Greenland, 1873. *Arctic* 27: 71–4

Burns, J. J. (1981). Bearded Seal *Erignathus barbatus* Erxleban 1777. In *Handbook of marine mammals*, eds. Sam. H. Ridgeway & R. J. Harnson, pp. 145–70. Academic Press, New York

Burns, J. J. & Fay, F. H. (1970). Comparative morphology of the skull of the Ribbon Seal, *Histriophoca fasciata*, with remarks on the systematics of Phocidae. *J. Zool.* 161: 363–94

Butler, M. G. (1982). A 7-year life cycle for two *Chironomus* species in Arctic Alaskan tundra ponds (Diptera: Chironomidae). *Can. J. Zool.* 60: 58–70

Cabot, D., Nairn, R., Newton, S. & Viney, M. (1984). *Biological Expedition to Jameson Land, Greenland, 1984*. Barnacle Books, Dublin

Cade, T. J., White, C. M. & Haugh, J. R. (1968). Peregrines and pesticides in Alaska. *Condor* 70: 170–8

Cade, T. J. & Fyfe, R. (1970). The North American Peregrine survey. *Can. Fld. Nat.* 84: 231–45

Calef, G. W. (1979). The population status of Caribou in the Northwest Territories. Progress report. N.W.T. Wildlife Service, Yellowknife

Calef, G. W. (1980). Status of *Rangifer* in Canada. 11. Status of *Rangifer* in the Northwest Territories. In *Proceedings of the 2nd International Reindeer/Caribou Symposium*, Røros, Norway 1979, eds. E. Reimers *et al*, pp. 754–9. Direktoratet for vilt og ferskvannsfisk, Trondheim

Calef, G. W. & Heard, D. C. (1979). Reproductive success of Peregrine Falcons and other raptors at Wager Bay and Melville Peninsula Northwest Territories. *Auk* 96: 662–74

Calef, G. W. & Heard, D. C. (1980). The status of three tundra wintering Caribou herds in northeastern mainland Northwest Territories. In *Proceedings of the 2nd International Reindeer/Caribou Symposium*, Røros, Norway 1979, eds. E. Reimers *et al*, pp. 582–94. Direktoratet for vilt og ferskvannsfisk, Trondheim

Cameron, R. D. (1983). Issue: Caribou and petroleum development in Arctic Alaska. *Arctic* 36: 227–31

Carbyn, L. N. (1981). Wolves in Canada and Alaska. *Can. Wildl. Ser. Report Series* Paper No. 45

Carl, E. A. (1971). Population control in Arctic Ground Squirrels. *Ecology* 52: 395–413

Carruthers, D. R. & Jakimchuk, R. D. (1983). The distribution, numbers and movements of the Bluenose Caribou herd, Northwest Territories, Canada. *Acta Zool. Fennica* 175: 141–3

Casey, T. M. & Casey, K. K. (1979). Thermoregulation of Arctic Weasels. *Physiol. Zool.* 52: 153–64

Chapman, J. A. & Feldhamer, G. A. (1982). *Wild Mammals of North America*. Johns Hopkins University Press, Baltimore and London

Chappell, M. A. (1981). Standard operative temperatures and cost of thermoregulation in the Arctic Ground Squirrel, Spermophilus undulatus. *Oecologia (Berl.)* 49: 397–403

Cheesemore, D. L. (1969). Den ecology of the Arctic Fox in northern Alaska. *Can. J. Zool.* 47: 121–9

Chernov, Y. I. (1978). Adaptive features of the life cycles of tundra zone insects. *Zhurnal Obshchoi Biologia* 39: 394–401. (In Russian)

Chernov, Y. I. (1985). *The Living Tundra*. Translated from Russian by D. Löve. Cambridge University Press, Cambridge

Chernov, Y. I., Striganova, B. R. & Ananjeva, S. I. (1977). Soil fauna of the polar desert at Cape Cheluskin, Taimyr Peninsula, Soviet Union. *Oikos* 29: 175–9

Christensen, N. H. (1967). Moult migration of Pink-footed Geese (*Anser fabalis brachyrhynchus*) from Iceland to Greenland. *Dansk. Orn. Foren. Tiddsskr.* 61: 56–66

Clough, G. C. (1963). Biology of the Arctic Shrew, Sorex arcticus. *Amer. Midland Nat.* 69: 69–81

Coady, J. W. (1980). History of Moose in northern Alaska and adjacent regions. *Can. Fld. Nat.* 94: 61–8

Corbet, G. B. (1978). *The Mammals of the Palaearctic Region: A Taxonomic Review*. British Museum (Natural History), London

Corbet, P. S. (1966). Diel patterns of mosquito activity in a high Arctic locality: Hazen Camp, Ellesmere Island, N.W.T. *Canadian Entomologist* 98: 1238–52

Corbet, P. S. (1967). Further observations on diel

periodicities of weather factors near the ground at Hazen Camp, Ellesmere Island, N.W.T. *Defence Research Board of Canada, Dep. Nat. Def. D. Phys. R (G) Hazen* 31

Corbet, P. S. (1972). The microclimate of Arctic plants and animals, on land and in fresh water. *Acta Arctica* 18: 1–43

Corbet, P. S. & Danks, H. V. (1973). Seasonal emergence and activity of mosquitoes in a high Arctic locality. *Canadian Entomologist* 105: 837–72

Craig, P. C. & McCart, P. J. (1975). Classification of stream types in Beaufort Sea drainages between Prudhoe Bay and the Mackenzie Delta, N.W.T., Canada. *Arct. Alp. Res.* 7: 183–98

Crawley, M. J. (1983). *Herbivory: The Dynamics of Animal-Plant Interactions*. Blackwell Scientific Publications, Oxford

Custer, T. W. (1973). Snowy Owl predation on Lapland Longspur nestlings recorded on film. *Auk* 90: 433–5

Custer, T. W. & Pitelka, F. A. (1977). Demographic features of a Lapland Longspur population near Barrow, Alaska. *Auk* 94: 505–25

Dahl, E. (1955). Biogeographic and geologic indications of unglaciated areas in Scandinavia during the glacial ages. *Bulletin of the Geological Society of America* 66: 1499–520

Danks, H. V. & Oliver, D. R. (1972). Seasonal emergence of some high Arctic Chironomidae (Diptera). *Canadian Entomologist* 104: 661–86

Danks, H. V. (1978). Modes of seasonal adaptation in the insects. I. Winter survival. *Canadian Entomologist* 110: 1167–205

Danks, H. V. (1981). *Arctic Arthropods: a review of systematics and ecology with particular reference to the North American fauna*. Entomological Society of Canada, Ottawa

Dau, C. P. & Kistchinski, S. A. (1977). Seasonal movements and distribution of the Spectacled Eider. *Wildfowl* 28: 65–75

Davids, R. C. (1982). *Lords of the Arctic*. Sidgwick & Jackson, London

Davis, J. L., Valkenburg, P. & Reynolds, H. V. (1980). Population dynamics of Alaska's Western Arctic Caribou herd. In *Proceedings of the 2nd International Reindeer/Caribou Symposium*, Røros, Norway 1979, eds. E. Reimers *et al*, pp. 595–604. Direktoratet for vilt og ferskvannsfisk, Trondheim

Derksen, D. V., Eldridge, W. D. & Weller, M. W. (1982). Habitat ecology of Pacific Black Brant and other geese moulting near Teshekpuk Lake, Alaska. *Wildfowl* 33: 39–57

Derksen, D. V., Rothe, T. C. & Eldridge, W. D. (1981). *Use of wetland habitats by birds in the National Petroleum Reserve–Alaska*. US Dept. of Interior, Fish and Wildlife Service, Resource Publication 141

Derksen, D. V., Weller, M. W. & Eldridge, W. D. (1979). Distributional ecology of geese moulting near Teshekpuk Lake, National Petroleum Reserve, Alaska. In *Management and Biology of Pacific Flyway Geese*, eds. R. L. Jarvis & J. C. Bartonek, pp. 198–207. Oregon State University Press, Cornvallis

Derviz-Sokolova, T. G. (1966). Flora of the extreme east of Chukchi Peninsula (Uelen Town–Cape Dezhnev). In *Vascular plants of the Siberian North and the northern Far East*, ed. A. I. Tolmachev, pp. 106–44. Translated from Russian by L. Philips (1969). Israel Program for Scientific Translations, Jerusalem

Doutt, J. K. (1942). A review of the genus *Phoca*. *Annals of the Carnegie Museum*. 29: 61–125

Downes, J. A. (1965). Adaptations of insects in the Arctic. *Annual Review of Entomology*. 10: 257–74

Downes, J. A. (1970). The feeding and mating behaviour of the specialised Empidinae (Diptera): observations on four species of *Rhamphomyia* in the high Arctic and a general discussion. *Canadian Entomologist* 102: 769–91

Dunaeva, T. N. (1948). *Comparative Survey of the Ecology of the Tundra Voles of the Yamal Peninsula*. Translated from Russian by G. MacDonald. Boreal Institute, University of Alberta, Edmonton

Dunbar, M. J. (1968). *Ecological Development in Polar Regions*. Prentice-Hall, New Jersey

Dunbar, M. J. (1982). Arctic marine ecosystems. In *The Arctic Ocean: The Hydrographic Environment and the Fate of Pollutants*, ed. Louis Rey, pp. 233–50. Macmillan Press, London

Ebbinge, B. (1982). The status of *Branta leucopsis* in 1980–81. *Aquila* 89: 151–61

Eberhardt, W. (1977). The biology of Arctic and Red Foxes along the Arctic Slope portion of the trans-Alaska pipeline corridor. M.Sc Thesis, University of Alaska, Fairbanks

Edlund, S. A. (1983). Bioclimatic zonation in a High Arctic region: Central Queen Elizabeth Islands. In *Current Research*, Part A, paper 83-1A, pp. 381–90. Geological Survey of Canada

Elliott, D. L. (1979). The current regenerative capacity of the northern Canadian trees, Keewatin, N.W.T., Canada: some preliminary observations. *Arct. Alp. Res.* 11: 243–51

Evans, P. G. H. (1981). Ecology and behaviour of the Little Auk *Alle alle* in west Greenland. *Ibis* 123: 1–18

Evans, P. G. H. (1984a). The seabirds of Greenland: their status and conservation. In *Status and Conservation of the World's Seabirds*, eds. J. P. Croxall, P. G. H. Evans & R. W. Schrieber, pp. 49–84. ICBP, Cambridge

Evans, P. G. H. (1984b). Status and conservation of seabirds in northwest Europe (excluding Norway and the Soviet Union). In *Status and Conservation of the World's Seabirds*, eds. J. P. Croxall, P. G. H. Evans & R. W. Schreiber, pp. 293–321. ICBP, Cambridge

Evans, P. G. H. & Waterston, G. (1978). The decline of Brunnich's Guillemot in West Greenland. *Ibis* 120: 131–2

Fay, F. H. (1982). Ecology and biology of the Pacific Walrus, *Odobenus rosmarus divergens* Illiger. In *North American Fauna*, No. 74. US Dept. of Interior, Fish and Wildlife Service

Fay, F. H. & Ray, C. (1968). Influence of climate on the distribution of Walruses *Odobenus rosmarus* (Linnaeus) I. Evidence of thermoregulatory behaviour. *Zoologica* 53: 1–18

Feist, D. D. (1975). Population studies of lemmings in the coastal tundra of Prudhoe Bay, Alaska. In *Ecological Investigations of the Tundra Biome in the Prudhoe Bay Region, Alaska*, ed. J. Brown. Biological Papers, Special Report No. 2, pp. 135–43. University of Alaska, Fairbanks

Ferguson, J. H. & Folk, G. E., Jr. (1970). The critical thermal minimum of small rodents in hypothermia. *Cryobiology* 7: 44–6

Finerty, J. P. (1980). *The Population Ecology of Cycles in Small Mammals*. Yale University Press, New Haven and London

Finley, K. J. & Gibb, E. J. (1982). Summer diet of the Narwhal (*Monodon monoceros*) in Pond Inlet, northern Baffin Island. *Can. J. Zool.* 60: 3353–63.

Fitzgerald, B. M. (1981). Predatory birds and mammals. In *Tundra Ecosystems: A Comparative Analysis*, eds. L. C. Bliss, O. W. Heal and J. J. Moore, pp. 485–508. Cambridge University Press, Cambridge

FitzPatrick, E. A. (1980). *Soils: their formation, classification and distribution*. Longman, London and New York

Flint, V. E., Boehme, R. L., Kostin, Y. V. & Kuznetsov, A. A. (1984). *Birds of the USSR*. Princeton University Press, Princeton and London

Fowles, A. P., Fox, A. D. & Stroud, D. A. (1981). Breeding bird census. In *Report of the 1979 Greenland White-fronted Goose Study Expedition to Equalungmiut Nunat, West Greenland*, eds. A. D. Fox & D. A. Stroud, pp. 192–6. Aberystwyth

Frederick, R. B. & Johnson, R. R. (1983). Ross' Geese increasing in central North America. *Condor* 85: 257–8

Freeman, M. M. R. (1973). Polar Bear predation on Beluga in the Canadian Arctic. *Arctic* 26: 163–4

Freedman, B. & Svoboda, J. (1982). Populations of breeding birds at Alexandra Fjord, Ellesmere Island, Northwest Territories, compared with other Arctic localities. *Can. Fld. Nat.* 96: 56–60

French, H. M. (1976). *The Periglacial Environment*. Longman, London and New York

Freuchen, P. & Salomonsen, F. (1958). *The Arctic Year*. Putnam, New York

Frisch, T. (1983). Ivory Gull colonies on the Devon Island ice cap, Arctic Canada. *Arctic* 36: 370–1

Fuller, W. A., Martell, A. M., Smith, R. F. C. & Speller, S. W. (1975). High Arctic Lemmings (Dicrostonyx groenlandicus) 1. Natural history observations. *Can. Fld. Nat.* 89: 223–33

Fuller, W. A., Martell, A. M., Smith, R. F. C. & Speller, S. W. (1977). Biology and secondary production of Dicrostonyx groenlandicus on Truelove Lowland. In *Truelove Lowland, Devon Island, Canada: A High Arctic Ecosystem*, ed. L. C. Bliss, pp. 437–59. University of Alberta Press, Edmonton

Garrott, R. A. (1980). Den characteristics, productivity, food habits, and behavior of Arctic Foxes in northern Alaska. M.Sc Thesis, The Pennsylvania State University, School of Forest Resources

Gaston, A. J. (1980). Populations, movements and wintering areas of Thick-billed Murres (*Uria lomvia*) in eastern Canada. *Can. Wildl. Ser. Note* 110: 1–10

Gaston, A. J., Cairns, D. K., Elliot, R. D. & Noble, D. G. (1985). A Natural History of Digges Sound. *Can. Wildl. Serv. Rep. Ser. Paper* No. 46

Gaston, A. J. & Nettleship, D. N. (1981). The Thick-billed Murres of Prince Leopold Island. *Can. Wildl. Serv. Monogr.* No. 6

Gauthier, G., Bedard, J., Huot, J. & Bedard, Y. (1984). Spring accumulation of fat by Greater Snow Geese in two staging habitats. *Condor* 86: 192–9

Gavin, A. (1974). *Wildlife of the North Slope: a Five Year Study, 1969–1973*, p. 38. Atlantic Richfield Company, Anchorage

Geraci, J. R. & Smith, T. G. (1979). Vitamin C in the diet of Inuit hunters from Holman, Northwest Territories. *Arctic* 32: 135–9

Gessaman, J. A. (1972). Bioenergetics of the Snowy Owl (*Nyctea scandiaca*). *Arct. Alp. Res.* 4: 223–38

Gessaman, J. A. (1978). Body temperature and heart rate of the Snowy Owl. *Condor* 80: 243–5

Gill, D. (1973). Eutrophic lakes in the Mackenzie Delta: their use by waterfowl. *Proceedings, Symposium on the lakes of Western Canada, 1972*, pp. 196–201. Water Resources Center, University of Alberta, Edmonton

Gjaerevoll, O. (1963). Survival of plants on nunataks in Norway during the Pleistocene Glaciation. In *North Atlantic biota and their history*, eds. A. Löve and D. Löve, pp. 261–83. Macmillan, New York

Golley, F. B. (1960). Energy dynamics of a food chain of an old-field community. *Ecol. Monog.* 30: 187–206

Golovkin, A. N. (1984). Seabirds nesting in the USSR: The status and protection of populations. In *Status and Conservation of the World's Seabirds*, eds. J. P. Croxall, P. G. H. Evans & R. W. Schrieber, pp. 473–86. ICBP, Cambridge

Green, G. H., Greenwood, J. J. D. & Lloyd, C. S. (1977). The influence of snow conditions on the date of breeding of wading birds in north-east Greenland. *J. Zool, Lond.* 183: 311–28

Green, G. H. (1978). The census of waders. In *Joint Biological Expedition to North East Greenland 1974*, eds. G. H. Green & J. J. D. Greenwood, pp. 84–9. University of Dundee

Gunn, A., Decker, R. & Barry, T. W. (1984). Possible causes and consequences of an expanding Muskox population, Queen Maud Gulf area, Northwest Territories. In *Proceedings of the First International Muskox Symposium, Biological Papers of the University of Alaska, Special Report* No. 4, eds. D. R. Klein, R. G. White & S. Keller, pp. 41–6

Gunn, A. & Miller, F. L. (1983). Size and status of an inter-island population of Peary Caribou. *Acta Zoologica Fennica* 175: 153–4

Gunn, A., Miller, F. L. & Thomas, D. C. (1980–1). The current status and future of Peary Caribou Rangifer tarandus pearyi on the Arctic Islands of Canada. *Biol. Conserv.* 19: 283–96

Guthrie, R. D. (1968). Paleoecology of a late Pleistocene small mammal community from interior Alaska. *Arctic* 21: 223–44

Halliday, G., Kliim-Nielsen, L. & Smart, I. H. M. (1974). Studies on the flora of the North Blosseville Kyst and on the hot springs of Greenland. *Meddr. Grønland.* 199(2): 1–49

Hansen, K. (1979). Status over bestanden af Havørn Haliaeetus albicilla groenlandicus Brehm i Grønland i arene 1972–1974. *Dansk Orn. Foren. Tidsskr.* 73: 107–30

Harington, C. R. (1968). Denning habits of the Polar Bear. *Can. Wildl. Serv. Rep. Ser. Paper* No. 5

Harrington, F. H. & Paquetm P. C., eds. (1982). *Wolves of the World: Perspectives of Behaviour, Ecology and Conservation*. Noyes Publications, New Jersey

Hattersley-Smith, G. (1974). Present Arctic ice cover. In *Arctic and Alpine Environments*, ed. J. D. Ives and R. G. Barry, pp. 195–223. Methuen, London

Harris, J. T. & Clement, D. M. (1975). Greenland Peregrines at their eyries. *Meddr. Grønland* 205(3): 1–28

Helle, E., Olsson, M. & Jensen, S. (1976). DDT and PCB levels and reproduction in Ringed Seals from Bothnia Bay. *Ambio* 5: 188–9

Hjort, C., Hakansson, E. & Stemmerik, L. (1983). Bird observations around the Nørdostvandet polyna, Northeast Greenland, 1980. *Dansk Orn. Foren. Tidsskr.* 77: 107–14

Hobbie, J. E. (1973). Arctic limnology: A review. In *Alaskan Arctic Tundra*, ed. M. E. Britten. Arctic Institute of North America Technical Paper No. 25, pp. 127–68

Hobson, W. (1972). The breeding biology of the Knot (*Calidris c. canutus*). *Proceedings of the Western Foundation of Zoology*, 2(1): 1–25. Los Angeles

Hoffmann, R. S., Koeppl, J. W. & Nadler, C. F. (1979). The relationships of the Amphiberingian marmots (Mammalia: Sciuridae). *Occas. Papers Univ. Kansas Mus. Nat. Hist.* No. 83: 1–56. Lawrence

Hoffman, R. S. & Taber, R. D. (1968). Origin and history of Holarctic tundra ecosystems, with special reference to their vertebrate faunas. In *Arctic and Alpine Environments*, eds. H. E. Wright & W. H. Osburn, pp. 143–70. Indiana University Press, Bloomington

Holleman, D. F., White, R. G., Luick, J. R. & Stephenson, R. O. (1980). Energy flow through the lichen–Caribou–Wolf food chain during winter in northern Alaska. In *Proceedings of the 2nd International Reindeer/Caribou Symposium, Røros, Norway 1979*, eds. E. Reimers *et al*, pp. 202–6. Direktoratet for vilt og ferskvannsfisk, Trondheim

Holmes, R. T. (1966). Breeding ecology and annual cycle

adaptations in the Red Backed Sandpiper in northern Alaska. *Condor* 68: 3–46

Holmes, R. T. & Pitelka, F. A. (1968). Food overlap among co-existing sandpipers on northern Alaskan tundra. *Syst. Zool.* 17: 305–18

Holt, S. (1980). Vegetation patterns and effects of grazing on Caribou ranges in the Søndre Strømfjord area, west Greenland. In *Proceedings of the 2nd International Reindeer/Caribou Symposium, Røros, Norway 1979*, eds. E. Reimers *et al*, pp. 57–63. Direktoratet for vilt og ferksvannsfisk, Trondheim

Hopkins, D. M., ed. (1967). *The Bering land bridge*. Stanford University Press, Stanford

Hultén, E. (1958). The amphi-Atlantic plants and their phytogeographic connections. *Kungl. Svenska Vetenskapsakademiens Handlingar*, Series 4, vol. 7, No. 1. Almquist and Wiksell, Stockholm

Hultén, E. (1964). The circumpolar plants. I. Vascular cryptogams, conifers, monocotyledons. *Kungl. Svenska Vetenskapsakademiens Handlingar*, Series 4, vol. 8, No. 5. Almquist and Wiksell, Stockholm

Hultén, E. (1971). The circumpolar plants. II. Dicotyledons. *Kungl. Svenska Vetenskapsakademiens Handlingar*, Series 4, vol. 13, No. 1. Almquist and Wiksell, Stockholm

Humphrey, R. L. (1970). The prehistory of the Arctic Slope of Alaska. Pleistocene cultural relationships between Eurasia and North America. Ph.D. dissertation, University of New Mexico, Albuquerque

Hussell, D. J. T. (1972). Factors affecting clutch size in arctic passerines. *Ecol. Monogr.* 42: 317–64

Hussell, D. J. T. & Holroyd, G. L. (1974). Birds of the Truelove Lowland and adjacent areas of northeast Devon Island, N.W.T. *Can. Fld. Nat.* 88: 197–212

Irving, L., West, G. C., Peyton, L. J. & Paneak, S. (1967). Migration of Willow Ptarmigan in Arctic Alaska. *Arctic* 20: 77–85

Ives, J. D. (1974). Biological refugia and the nunatak hypothesis. In *Arctic and Alpine Environments*, eds. J. D. Ives & R. C. Barry, pp. 605–36. Methuen, London

Ives, J. D. & Barry, R. G., eds. (1974). *Arctic and Alpine Environments*. Methuen, London

Jehl, J. R. (1971). Patterns of hatching success in subarctic birds. *Ecology* 52: 169–73

Jepsen, P. U. (1984). Observations of moulting eider and breeding Common Eider *Somateria mollissima* at Nordaustlandet, Svalbard, in 1979. *Polar Res.* 2: 19–25

Joensen, A. M. & Preuss, N. O. (1972). Report on the ornithological expedition to northwest Greenland 1965. *Meddr. Grønland* 191(5): 1–58

John, B. (1978). *The World of Ice: The Natural History of the Frozen Regions*. Orbis Publishing, London

Johnson, M. L., Fiscus, C. F., Ostenson, B. & Barbour, M. K. (1966). Marine Mammals. In *Environment of the Cape Thompson Region, Alaska*, ed. N. J. Wilimovsky, pp. 877–924. U.S. Atomic Energy Commission, Washington, D.C.

Johnson, S. R. (1979). Avian ecology in Simpson Lagoon, Beaufort Sea, Alaska. In *Beaufort Sea Barrier Island-Lagoon Ecological Process Studies*. NOAA/OCSEAP Annual Rep., Res. Unit 467, pp. 1–111

Johnson, S. R. (1984). Prey selection by Oldsquaws in a Beaufort Sea lagoon, Alaska. In *Marine Birds: their feeding ecology and commercial fisheries relationships*, eds. D. N. Nettleship, G. A. Sanger & P. F. Springer, pp. 12–19. Can. Wildl. Ser.

Johnson, S. R. & Richardson, W. J. (1982). Waterbird migration near the Yukon and Alaskan coast of the Beaufort Sea: II. Moult migration of seaducks in summer. *Arctic* 35: 291–301

Jong, C. G. Van Zyll de (1975). The distribution and abundance of the Wolverine (Gulo gulo) in Canada. *Can. Fld. Nat.* 89: 431–7

Kalff, J. (1970). Arctic lake ecosystems. In *Antarctic Ecology*, vol. 2, ed. M. H. Holdgate, pp. 651–64. Academic Press, London

Karlstrom, T. N. V. & Ball, G. E., eds. (1969). *The Kodiak Island refugium: Its geology, flora, fauna and history*. The Ryerson Press, Toronto

Keith, L. B. (1963). *Wildlife's Ten-Year Cycle*. University of Wisconsin Press, Madison

Kelsall, J. P. (1968). The Migratory Barren-ground Caribou of Canada. *Can. Wildl. Ser. Paper* No. 3

Kerbes, R. H. (1975). Lesser Snow Geese in the eastern Canadian Arctic. *Can. Wildl. Ser. Occas. Paper* No. 35

Kerbes, R. H. (1983). Lesser Snow Goose colonies in the western Canadian Arctic. *J. Wildl. Mgmt.* 47: 523–6

Kerbes, R. H., McLandress, M. R., Smith, G. E. J., Beyersbergen, G. W. & Godwin, B. (1983). Ross' Goose and Lesser Snow Goose colonies in the central Canadian Arctic. *Can. J. Zool.* 61: 168–73

Kevan, P. G. (1970). High Arctic insect-flower relations: The interrelationships of arthropods and flowers at Lake Hazen, Ellesmere Island, Northwest Territories, Canada. Unpublished Ph.D. thesis, University of Alberta, Edmonton

Kevan, P. G. (1972). Insect pollination of high Arctic flowers. *J. Ecol.* 60: 831–47

Kevan, P. G. (1973). Flowers, insects and pollination ecology in the Canadian High Arctic. *Polar Record*. 16: 667–74

Kevan, P. G. (1975). Sun-tracking solar furnaces in high Arctic flowers – significance for pollination and insects. *Science* (Washington) D.C., 189: 723–6

Kevan, P. G., Jensen, T. & Shorthouse, J. D. (1982). Body temperatures and behavioral thermoregulation of high Arctic woolly-bear caterpillars and pupae (*Gynaephora rossii*, Lymantriidae: Lepidoptera) and the importance of sunshine. *Arct. Alp. Res.* 14: 125–36

Kevan, P. G. & Shorthouse, J. D. (1970). Behavioural thermoregulation by High Arctic butterflies. *Arctic*. 23: 268–79

King, J. G. (1970). The swans and geese of Alaska's Arctic Slope. *Wildfowl* 21: 11–17

King, R. (1979). Results of aerial surveys of migratory birds on NPR/A in 1977 and 1978. In *Studies of Selected Wildlife and Fish and Their Use of Habitats on and Adjacent to NPR-A 1977–1978*, ed. P. C. Lent, pp. 187–226. U.S. Dept. of Interior, National Petroleum Reserve in Alaska, Anchorage, Field Study 3, vol. 1

Kistchinski, A. A. & Flint, V. E. (1974). On the biology of the Spectacled Eider. *Wildfowl* 25: 5–15

Klein, D. R. & Staaland, H. (1984). Extinction of Svalbard Muskoxen through competitive exclusion: an hypothesis. In *Proceedings of the First International Muskox Symposium, Biological Papers of the University of Alaska, Special Publication* No. 4, eds. D. R. Klein, R. G. White & S. Keller, pp. 26–31

Komárková, V. & Webber, P. J. (1980). Two Low Arctic vegetation maps near Atkasook, Alaska. *Arct. Alp. Res.* 12: 447–72

Köppen, W. (1900). Versuch einer Klassifikation de Klimate, vorzugsweise nach ihren Beziehung zur Pflanzenwelt. *Geog. Zeitschr.* 1900: 593–611

Korte, J. De (1977). Ecology of the Long-tailed Skua (*Stercorarius longicaudus* Vieillot, 1819) at Scoresby Sund, East Greenland. Report of the Nederlandse Groenland

Expeditie Scoresbysund 1973, 1974 and 1975. Part one: Distribution and density. *Beaufortia* 25: 201–19

Korte, J. De (1984). Ecology of the Long-tailed Skua (*Stercorarius longicaudus* Vieillot, 1819) at Scoresby Sund, East Greenland. Part two: Arrival, site tenacity and departure. *Beaufortia* 34: 1–14.

Krebs, C. J. (1964). The lemming cycle at Baker Lake, Northwest Territories, during 1959–62. Arctic Institute of North America, Technical Paper No. 15

Krüll, F. (1976). Zeitgebers for animals in the continuous daylight of High Arctic summer. *Oecologia (Berlin)* 24: 149–57

Kukal, O. (1984). Life history and adaptations of a high Arctic insect, *Gynaephora groenlandica* (Wocke) (Lepidoptera: Lymantriidae). Unpublished M.Sc. Thesis. University of Guelph, Ontario

Kuropat, P. & Bryant, J. P. (1980). Foraging behaviour of cow Caribou on the Utukok calving grounds in northwestern Alaska. In *Proceedings of the 2nd International Reindeer/Caribou Symposium, Røros, Norway 1979*, eds. E. Reimers *et al*, pp. 64–70. Direktoratet for vilt og ferskvannsfisk, Trondheim

Kuyt, E. (1972). Food habits of wolves on Barren-ground Caribou range. *Can. Wildl. Ser. Paper* No. 21

Lachenbruch, A. H. (1968). Permafrost. In *The Encyclopedia of Geomorphology*, ed. R. W. Fairbridge, New York, Reinhold, pp. 833–9

Lamb, H. H. (1982). *Climate, History and the Modern World.* Methuen, London

Larsen, T. (1984). We've saved the ice bear. *International Wildlife* 14: 4–11

Larson, S. (1960). On the influence of the Arctic Fox Alopex lagopus on the distribution of Arctic birds. *Oikos* 11: 276–305

LeBlond, N. R. & Rees, W. E. (1980). An International conservation challenge: the Porcupine Caribou. In *Threatened and Endangered Species and Habitats in British Columbia and the Yukon*, eds. R. Stace-Smith, L. Johns & P. Joslin, pp. 228–40. British Columbia Ministry of Environment, Victoria, B.C.

Leffingwell, E. de K. (1919). The Canning River region, northern Alaska. *US Geol. Survey Professional Paper,* 109

Lent, P. C. (1980). Synoptic snowmelt patterns in Arctic Alaska in relation to Caribou habitat use. In *Proceedings of the 2nd International Reindeer/Caribou Symposium, Røros, Norway 1979*, eds. E. Rimers *et al*, pp. 71–7. Direktoratet for og vilt ferskvannsfisk, Trondheim

Lentfer, J. W. (1975). Polar Bear denning on drifting sea ice. *J. Mammal.* 56: 716–18

Lentfer, J. W. (1983). Alaskan Polar Bear movements from mark and recovery. *Arctic* 36: 282–8

Lewellen, R. I. (1970). *Permafrost erosion along the Beaufort Sea coast.* University of Denver, Colorado

Lindsey, C. C. (1981). Arctic refugia and the evolution of arctic biota. In *Evolution today, Proceedings of the Second International Congress of Systematic and Evolutionary Biology*, eds. G. G. E. Scudder and J. L. Reveal, pp. 7–10. Hunt Institute for Botanical Documentation, Carnegie-Mellon University, Pittsburgh

Löken, O. H. (1966). Baffin Island refugia older than 54,000 years. *Science* 153: 1378–80

Löve, A. (1959). Origin of the arctic flora. In *Problems of the Pleistocene Epoch and Arctic Area*, ed. G. R. Lowther. Museum Publication No. 1: 82–95. McGill University, Montreal

Löve, A. & Löve, D. eds. (1963). *North Atlantic Biota and their History.* Pergamon Press, Oxford

Löve, A. & Löve, D. (1974). Origin and evolution of the Arctic and alpine floras. In *Arctic and Alpine Environments*, eds. J. D. Ives & R. G. Barry, pp. 571–603. Methuen, London

Löve, D. (1970). Subarctic and subalpine: where and what? *Arct. Alp. Res.* 2: 63–73

Lowry, L. F., Frost, K. J. & Burns, J. J. (1978). Food of Ringed Seals and Bowhead Whales near Point Barrow, Alaska. *Can. Fld. Nat.* 92: 67–70

Lowry, L. F., Frost, K. J. & Burns, J. J. (1979). Potential resource competition in the southeastern Bering Sea: Fisheries and Phocid seals. *Proceedings of the 29th Alaska Science Conference*, pp. 287–96

MacInnes, C. D. & Misra, R. K. (1972). Predation on Canada Goose nests at McConnell River, Northwest Territories. *J. Wildl. Mgmt.* 36: 414–22

MacLean, S. F. (1974). Lemming bones as a source of calcium for Arctic sandpipers (Calidris spp.). *Ibis* 116: 552–7

MacLean, S. F. (1975). Ecological adaptations of tundra invertebrates. In *Ecological Investigations of the Tundra Biome in the Prudhoe Bay Region, Alaska*, ed. J. Brown. Biological Papers, Special Report No. 2, pp. 115–23. University of Alaska, Fairbanks

MacLean, S. F., Fitzgerald, B. M. & Pitelka, F. A. (1974). Population cycles in Arctic lemmings: winter reproduction and predation by weasels. *Arct. Alp. Res.* 6: 1–12

Mackay, J. R. (1973). The growth of pingos, western arctic coast, Canada. *Can. Jour. Earth Sci.* 10: 979–1004

Macpherson, A. H. (1965). The origin of diversity in mammals of the Canadian Arctic tundra. *Systematic Zoology* 14: 153–73

Macpherson, A. H. (1969). The dynamics of Canadian Arctic Fox populations. *Can. Wildl. Ser. Paper* No. 8

Macpherson, A. H. & McLaren, I. A. (1959). Notes on birds of southern Foxe Peninsula, Baffin Island, Northwest Territories. *Can. Fld. Nat.* 73: 68–81

McKay, G. A., Findlay, B. F. & Thompson, H. A. (1970). A climatic perspective of tundra areas. In *Productivity and Conservation in Northern Circumpolar Lands*, eds. W. A. Fuller and P. G. Kevan, pp. 10–33. IUCN Publ. No. 16 (New series), Morges

Maher, W. J. (1960). Nesting attempt by a pair of Barn Swallows in northern Alaska. *Condor* 62: 141–2

Maher, W. J. (1970a). The Pomarine Jaeger as a Brown Lemming predator in northern Alaska. *Wilson Bull.* 82: 130–57

Maher, W. J. (1970b). Ecology of the Long-tailed Jaeger at Lake Hazen, Ellesmere Island. *Arctic* 23: 112–29

Maher, W. J. (1974). *Ecology of Pomarine, Parasitic, and Long-tailed Jaegers in northern Alaska.* Cooper Ornithological Society Pacific Coast Avifauna No. 37

Manning, T. H., Hohn, E. O. & Macpherson, A. H. (1956). The Birds of Banks Island. *Natl. Mus. Canada Bull.* 143: 1–144

Mansfield, A. W. (1958). The biology of the Atlantic Walrus *Odobenus rosmarus rosmarus* (Linnaeus) in the eastern Canadian Arctic. *J. Fish. Res. Board Can. Ms. Rep. Ser.* No. 653

Mansfield, A. W. (1966). The Walrus in Canada's Arctic. *Can. Geog. J.* 72: 88–95

Mansfield, A. W. (1967). Distribution of the Harbour Seal, *Phoca vitulina* Linnaeus, in Canadian Arctic waters: *J. Mammal.* 48: 249–57

Marshall, A. J. (1952). Non-breeding among Arctic birds. *Ibis* 94: 310–33

Matthews, J. V. Jr. (1979a). Tertiary and Quaternary environments: Historical background for an analysis of the

Canadian insect fauna. In *Canada and its insect fauna*, ed. H. V. Danks, pp. 31–86. *Memoir of the Entomological Society of Canada* 108

Matthews, J. V. Jr. (1979b). Beringia during the late Pleistocene: Arctic steppe or discontinuous herb tundra: A review of the paleontological evidence. *Geological Survey of Canada Open-File Report*. No. 649

Matthews, J. V., Jr. (1982). East Beringia during late Wisconsin time: A review of the biotic evidence. In *Paleoecology of Beringia*, eds. D. M. Hopkins, J. V. Matthews Jr., C. E. Schweger & S. B. Young, pp. 127–50. Academic Press, New York

Matveyeva, N. V. & Chernov, Y. I. (1976). Poliarnye pustyni Poluostrova Taimyr. *Botanical Journal (Moscow)* 61: 297–312

Mayer, W. V. (1953). A preliminary study of the Barrow Ground Squirrel, Citellus parryi barrowensis. *J. Mammal.* 34: 334–45

Mayfield, H. F. (1983). Densities of breeding birds at Polar Bear Pass, Bathurst Island, Northwest Territories. *Can. Fld. Nat.* 97: 371–6

Mead, C. (1983). *Bird Migration*. Country Life Books, Feltham

Meltofte, H. (1979). The population of waders Charadriidae at Danmarks Havn, Northeast Greenland, 1975. *Dansk Orn. Foren. Tidsskr.* 73: 63–94

Meltofte, H., Edelstam, C., Granstrom, G., Hammar, J. & Hjort, C. (1981). Ross's Gulls in the Arctic pack-ice. *British Birds* 74: 316–20

Miller, F. L., Edmonds, E. J. & Gunn, A. (1982). Foraging behaviour of Peary Caribou in response to springtime snow and ice conditions. *Can. Wildl. Serv. Occas. Paper* No. 48

Miller, F. L. & Gunn, A. (1979). *Inter-island movements of Peary Caribou south of Viscount Melville Sound and Barrow Strait, Northwest Territories, May–July 1978*. Can. Wildl. Ser. (Unpublished report). Canadian Wildlife Service, Edmonton

Miller, F. L., Russell, R. H. & Gunn, A. (1977). Peary Caribou and Muskoxen on western Queen Elizabeth Islands, N.W.T. 1972–74. *Can. Wildl. Serv. Rep. Ser. Paper* No. 40: 1–55

Money, D. C. (1980). *Polar Ice and Periglacial Lands*. Evans Brothers, London

Montgomerie, R. D., Cartar, R. V., McLaughlin, R. L. & Lyon, B. (1983). Birds of Sarcpa Lake, Melville Peninsula, Northwest Territories: Breeding phenologies, densities and biogeography. *Arctic* 36: 65–75

Muir, D. & Bird, D. M. (1984). Food of Gyrfalcons at a nest on Ellesmere Island. *Wilson Bull.* 96: 464–7

Mullen, D. A. (1968). Reproduction in Brown Lemmings (*Lemmus trimucronatus*) and its relevance to their cycle of abundance. *University of California Publications in Zoology* 85: 1–24

Müller, F. (1963). *Observations on Pingos*. National Research Council of Canada, Technical Translation 1073

Müller, F. (1981). *The Living Arctic*. Methuen, Toronto

Murray, D. F. (1981). The role of Arctic refugia in the evolution of the Arctic vascular flora – a Beringian perspective. In *Evolution Today, Proceedings of the Second International Congress of Systematic and Evolutionary Biology*, eds. G. G. E. Scudder and J. L. Reveal, pp. 11–20. Hunt Institute for Botanical Documentation, Carnegie-Mellon University, Pittsburgh

Myers, J. P., Hilden, O. & Tomkovich, P. (1982). Exotic *Calidris* species of the Siberian tundra. *Ornis Fennica* 59: 175–82

Nettleship, D. N. (1973). Breeding ecology of the Turnstone at Hazen Camp, Ellesmere Island. *Ibis* 115: 202–11

Nettleship, D. N. (1974a). The breeding of the Knot *Calidris canutus* at Hazen Camp, Ellesmere Island, N.W.T. *Polarforschung* 44: 8–26

Nettleship, D. N. (1974b). Seabird colonies and distributions around Devon Island and vicinity. *Arctic* 27: 95–103

Nettleship, D. N. & Birkhead, T. R. eds. (1985). *The Atlantic Alcidae*. Academic Press, London

Nordenskjöld, O. & Meckling, L. (1928) *The geography of the polar regions*. American Geographical Society Special Publication No. 8

Norderhaug, M. (1980). Breeding biology of the Little Auk (Plautus alle) in Svalbard. *Norsk Polarinstitutt Skrifter* No. 173

Norderhaug, M., Brun, E. & Møllen, C. U. (1977). Barentshavets sjøfuglressurser. *Norsk Polarinst. Meddr.* 104: 1–119

Norton, D. W. (1972). Incubation schedules of four species of calidridine sandpipers at Barrow, Alaska. *Condor* 74: 164–76

Norton, D. W. (1973). Ecological energetics of calidridine sandpipers breeding in northern Alaska. Ph.D. dissertation, University of Alaska, Fairbanks

Norton, D. W., Ailes, I. W. & Curatolo, J. A. (1975). Ecological relationships of the inland tundra avifauna near Prudhoe Bay, Alaska. In *Ecological Investigations of the Tundra Biome in the Prudhoe Bay Region, Alaska*, ed. J. Brown. Biological Papers, Special Report No. 2, pp. 125–33. University of Alaska, Fairbanks

Ogilvie, M. A. (1978). *Wild Geese*. T. & A. D. Poyser, Berkhamsted

Ognev, S. I. (1963). *Mammals of the USSR and Adjacent countries*, volume 5. Israel Program of Scientific Translations

Orr, C. D. & Parsons, J. L. (1982). Ivory Gulls, *Pagophila eburnea*, and ice edges in Davis Strait and the Labrador Sea. *Can. Fld. Nat.* 96: 323–8

Owen, M. (1980). *Wild Geese of the World*. Batsford, London

Palmer, R. S. (1977). King Eider studies. *British Birds* 70: 107–13

Parker, G. R. (1972). Biology of the Kaminuriak population of Barren-ground Caribou. Part 1: Total numbers, mortality, recruitment, and seasonal distribution. *Can. Wildl. Serv. Paper* No. 20

Parker, G. R. (1973). Distribution and densities of wolves within Barren-ground Caribou ranges in northern mainland Canada. *J. Mammal.* 57: 341–8

Parker, G. R. (1974). A population peak and crash of lemmings and Snowy Owls on Southampton Island. *Can. Fld. Nat.* 88: 151–6

Parker, G. R. (1982). Hordes of hopping hares. *Canadian Geographic* 102: 30–3

Parker, G. R. & Ross, R. K. (1976). Summer habitat use by Muskoxen (*Ovibos moschatus*) and Peary Caribou (*Rangifer tarandus pearyi*) in the Canadian High Arctic. *Polarforschung* 46: 12–25

Patterson, L. A. (1974). An assessment of the energetic importance of the North Slope to Snow Geese (Chen caerulescens caerulescens) during the staging period in September 1973. *Arctic Gas: Biological Report Series* 27: 1–44

Pattie, D. L. (1972). Preliminary bioenergetic and population level studies in High Arctic birds. In *Devon Island I.B.P. Project, High Arctic Ecosystems*, ed. L. C. Bliss, pp. 281–92. University of Alberta, Edmonton

Pattie, D. L. (1977). Population levels and bioenergetics of Arctic birds on Truelove Lowland. In *Truelove Lowland, Devon Island, Canada: A High Arctic Ecosystem*, ed. L. C. Bliss, pp. 413–33

Paulson, D. R. & Erckmann, W. J. (1985). Buff-breasted Sandpipers nesting in association with Black-bellied Plovers. *Condor* 87: 429–30

Peiper, R. (1963). Production and chemical composition of Arctic tundra vegetation and their relation to the lemming cycle. PhD Thesis. University of California, Berkeley

Perrins, C. M. & Birkhead, T. R. (1983). *Avian Ecology*. Blackie, Glasgow and London

Peterson, R. M. & Batzli, G. O. (1975). Activity patterns in natural populations of the Brown Lemming (*Lemmus trimucronatus*). *J. Mammal.* 56: 718–20

Peterson, R. M. & Batzli, G. O. (1984). Activity periods and energetic reserves of the Brown Lemming in northern Alaska. *Holarctic Ecology* 7: 245–8

Peterson, R. M., Batzli, G. O. & Banks, E. M. (1976). Activity and energetics of the Brown Lemming in its natural habitat. *Arct. Alp. Res.* 8: 131–8

Pienkowski, M. W. & Green, G. H. (1976). Breeding biology of Sanderlings in north-east Greenland. *British Birds* 69: 165–77

Pitelka, F. A. (1957a). Some characteristics of microtine cycles in the Arctic. In *Arctic Biology*, ed. H. P. Hansen, pp. 153–84. Oregon State University Press

Pitelka, F. A. (1957b). Some aspects of population structure in the short-term cycle of the Brown Lemming in Northern Alaska. *Cold Spring Harbor Symposia on Quantitative Biology* 22: 237–51

Pitelka, F. A. (1971). Social organization, habitat, utilization and bioenergetics in the Lapland Longspur near Barrow, Alaska. In *The Structure and Function of the Tundra Ecosystem*, Vol. 1 Progress report and proposed abstracts, pp. 107–10. U.S. Tundra Biome Program of the U.S.I.B.P. and U.S. Arctic Research Program

Pitelka, F. A. (1973). Cycling pattern in lemming populations near Barrow, Alaska. In *Alaska Arctic Tundra*, ed. M. E. Britton. Arctic Institute of North America Technical Paper No. 25 pp. 199–215

Pitelka, F. A. (1974). An avifaunal review for the Barrow Region and North Slope of Arctic Alaska. *Arct. Alp. Res.* 6(2): 161–84

Pitelka, F. A., Holmes, R. T. & MacLean, S. F. (1974). Ecology and evolution of social organization in Arctic sandpipers. *Amer. Zool.* 14: 185–204

Pitelka, F. A. & Schultz, A. M. (1964). The nutrient-recovery hypothesis for Arctic microtine rodents. In *Grazing in Terrestrial and Marine Environments*, ed. D. Crisp, pp. 55–68. Blackwell Scientific Publications, Oxford

Pjastolova, O. A. (1972). The role of rodents in energetics of biogeocoenoses of forest tundra and southern tundra. In *Proceedings of the IV International Meeting on the Biological Productivity of Tundra*, eds. F. W. Wielgolasky & T. Rosswall. Leningrad

Platt, J. B. (1976). Gyrfalcon nest site selection and winter activity in the western Canadian Arctic. *Can. Fld. Nat.* 90: 338–45

Pohl, H. & West, G. C. (1973). Daily and seasonal variation in metabolic response to cold during rest and forced exercise in the Common Redpoll. *Comp. Biochem. Physiol.* 45A: 851–67

Polunin, N. (1948). Botany of the Canadian eastern Arctic, Part III, Vegetation and ecology. Bulletin No. 104, National Museum of Canada, Ottawa

Polunin, N. (1951). The real Arctic: Suggestions for its delimitation, subdivision and characterization. *Journal of Ecology* 39: 308–15

Polunin, N. (1959). *Circumpolar Arctic Flora*. Oxford University Press, Oxford

Porsild, A. E. (1951). Plant life in the Arctic. *Canadian Geographical Journal* 42: 121–45

Porsild, A. E. (1955). The vascular plants of the western Canadian Arctic Archipelago. Bulletin No. 135, National Museum of Canada, Ottawa

Porsild, A. E. (1958). Geographical distribution of some elements in the flora of Canada. *Geographical Bulletin* 11: 57–77

Porsild, M. P. (1918). On 'Savssats': crowding of Arctic animals at holes in the sea ice. *Geog. Rev.* 6: 215–28

Portenko, L. A. (1981). *Birds of the Chukchi Peninsula and Wrangel Island*. Volume 1. Smithsonian Institution and the National Science Foundation, Washington, D.C.

Power, G. & Gregoire, J. (1978). Predation by freshwater seals on the fish community of Lower Seal Lake, Quebec. *J. Fish Res. Board Can.* 35: 844–50

Pruitt, W. O. (1966). Ecology of terrestrial mammals. In *Environment of the Cape Thomson Region, Alaska*, eds. N. J. Wilimovsky & J. N. Wolfe, United States Atomic Energy Commission, pp. 519–64

Punsvik, T., Syvertsen, A. & Staaland, H. (1980). Reindeer grazing in Aventdalen, Svalbard. In *Proceedings of the 2nd International Reindeer/Caribtsymposium, Røros, Norway 1979*, eds. E. Reimers *et al*, pp. 115–23. Direktoratet for vilt og ferskvannsfisk, Trondheim

Quinlan, S. E. & Lehnhausen, W. A. (1982). Arctic Fox, Alopex lagopus, predation on nesting Common Eiders, Somateria mollissima, at Icy Cape, Alaska. *Can. Fld. Nat.* 96: 462–6

Raup, H. M. (1963). Turf hummocks in the Mesters Vig district, northeast Greenland. *Proceedings of Permafrost International Conference*, pp. 43–50. Lafayette, Indiana

Raup, H. M. (1965). The structure and development of turf hummocks in the Mesters Vig district, Northeast Greenland. *Meddr. Grønland* 166(3)

Rawson, D. S. (1953). Limnology in the North American Arctic and Sub-arctic. *Arctic* 6: 198–204

Ray, C. G. & Watkins, W. A. (1975). Social function of underwater sounds in the Walrus *Odobenus rosmarus*. In *Biology of the Seal*, eds. K. Ronald & A. W. Mansfield, pp. 524–6. Charlottenlund Slot, Denmark: Rapports et Proces Verbeaux des Reunions. Cons. Inl. pour l'exploration de la mer. 169

Reeves, R. R. (1978). Atlantic Walrus (*Odobenus rosmarus rosmarus*): a literature survey and status report. US Dept. of Interior, Fish and Wildlife Service Research Rep. No. 10

Reimers, E. (1982). Winter mortality and population trends of Reindeer on Svalbard, Norway. *Arct. Alp. Res.* 14: 295–300

Remmert, H. (1980). *Arctic Animal Ecology*. Springer Verlag, Berlin

Rey, L. ed. (1982). *The Arctic Ocean: The Hydrographic Environment and the Fate of Pollutants*. Macmillan Press, London

Reynolds, H. (1976). *North Slope Grizzly Bear Studies*. Alaska Federal Aid in Wildlife Restoration Project W-17-6 and W-17-7

Reynolds, H. (1978). *Structure, Status, Reproductive Biology, Movement, Distribution and Habitat Utilization of a Grizzly Bear Population in NPR-A*. Final Report NPR-A 105 (c) Studies to USFWS

Reynolds, H. (1980). *North Slope Grizzly Bear Studies*. Alaska Federal Aid in Wildlife Restoration Project W-17-11

Reynolds, H. (1981). *North Slope Grizzly Bear Studies*. Alaska Federal Aid in Wildlife Restoration Project W-21-1

Reynolds, H. (1982). *North Slope Grizzly Bear Studies*. Alaska Federal Aid in Wildlife Restoration Project W-21-2

Reynolds, H., Curatolo, J. A. & Quimby, R. (1976). Denning

ecology of Grizzly Bears in northeastern Alaska. In *Bears: their Ecology and Management*, eds. M. Pelton, J. Lentfer & E. Folk, pp. 403–10. IUCN New Series No. 40. IUCN, Gland

Reynolds, P. E. & Ross, D. E. (1984). Population status of Muskoxen in the Arctic National Wildlife Refuge, Alaska. In *Proceedings of the First International Muskox Symposium, Biological Papers of the University of Alaska, Special Publication No. 4*, eds. D. R. Klein, R. G. White & S. Keller, p. 63

Richards, K. W. (1973). Biology of *Bombus polaris* Curtis and *B. hyperboreus* Schonherr at Lake Hazen, Northwest Territories (Hymenoptera: Bombini). *Quaestiones entomologicae*. 9: 115–57

Ricklefs, R. E. (1980). Geographical variation in clutch size among passerine birds: Ashmole's hypothesis. *Auk* 97: 38–49

Riewe, R. (1975). The High Arctic wolf in the Jones Sound Region. *Arctic* 28: 209–12

Risebrough, R. W. (1976). Shorebird dependence on Arctic littoral habitats. In *Environmental Assessment of the Alaskan Continental Shelf*. Volume 2. Marine Birds, pp. 401–55. US Dept of Interior

Roby, D. D., Thing, H. & Brink, K. L. (1984). History, status, and taxonomic identity of Caribou (*Rangifer tarandus*) in northwest Greenland. *Arctic* 37: 23–30

Roen, U. I. (1962). Studies on freshwater entomostraca in Greenland 11. *Meddr. Grønland* 170: 1–243

Romanova, E. N. (1972). Microclimate of tundras in the vicinity of the Taimyr Field Station. *US IBP International Tundra Biome Translation* No. 7: 1–10

Rönning, O. I. (1963). Phytogeographical problems in Svalbard. In *North Atlantic biota and their history*, eds. A. Löve and D. Löve, pp. 99–107. Macmillan, New York

Roseneau, D. G. & Stern, P. M. (1974). Distribution of Moose, Muskox and sheep in northeastern Alaska, 1972. In *Distribution of Moose, Sheep, Muskox and Furbearing Mammals in Northeastern Alaska*, ed. R. D. Jakimchuk, pp. 1–31. Arctic Gas Biological Report Series Volume 6

Ryan, J. K. (1981). Invertebrate faunas at IBP tundra sites. In *Tundra Ecosystems: A Comparative Analysis*, eds. L. C. Bliss, J. B. Cragg, O. W. Heal & J. J. Moore. International Biological Programme No. 25, pp. 517–39. Cambridge University Press, Cambridge.

Ryan, J. K. & Herbert, C. R. (1977). Energy budget for *Gynaephora groenlandica* (Homeyer) and *G. rossii* (Curtis) (Lepidoptera: Lymantriidae) on Truelove Lowland Island, Canada: A High Arctic Ecosystem, pp. 395–409. University of Alberta Press, Edmonton

Ryder, J. B. (1967). The breeding biology of Ross' Goose in the Perry River region, Northwest Territories. *Can. Wildl. Ser. Paper* No. 3

Sage, B. L. (1971). A study of White-billed Divers in Arctic Alaska. *British Birds* 64: 519–28

Sage, B. L. (1974). Ecological distribution of birds in the Atigun and Sagavanirktok River valleys, Arctic Alaska. *Can. Fld. Nat.* 88: 281–91

Sage, B. L. (1981). Conservation of the tundra. In *Tundra Ecosystems: A Comparative Analysis*, eds. L. C. Bliss, O. W. Heal & J. J. Moore, pp. 731–46. Cambridge University Press, Cambridge

Salomonsen, F. (1972). Zoogeographical and ecological problems in Arctic birds. In *Proceedings of the XVth International Ornithological Congress* pp. 25–77

Salomonsen, F. (1979). Marine birds in the Danish Monarchy and their conservation. In *Conservation of Marine Birds of Northern North America*, eds. J. C. Bartonek & D. H. Nettleship, pp. 267–87. US Dept. of Interior

Sater, J. E. (1969). *The Arctic Basin*. 2nd edition. Arctic Institute of North America

Savile, D. B. O. (1961). Bird and mammal observations on Ellef Ringnes Island in 1960. *Natural History Paper* No. 9, National Museum of Canada, Ottawa

Savile, D. B. O. (1972). Arctic adaptations in plants. Monograph No. 6, Canada Department of Agriculture, Ottawa

Savile, D. B. O. & Oliver, D. R. (1964). Bird and mammal observations at Hazen Camp, northern Ellesmere Island, in 1962. *Can. Fld. Nat.* 78: 1–7

Schamel, D. & Tracy, D. (1977). Polandry, replacement clutches and site tenacity in the Red Phalarope (*Phalaropus fulicarius*) at Barrow, Alaska. *Bird-Banding* 48: 314–24

Scheffer, B. (1958). *Seals, Sea Lions and Walruses. A review of the Pinnipedia*. Stanford University Press, Stanford

Schultz, A. M. (1969). A study of an ecosystem: the Arctic tundra. In *The Ecosystem Concept in Natural Resource Management*, ed. G. Van Dyne, pp. 77–93. Academic Press, New York

Schuster, R. M., Steere, W. C. & Thomson, J. W. (1959). The terrestrial cryptogams of northern Ellesmere Island. *Natl. Mus. Canada Bull.* No. 164

Searing, G. F., Kuyt, E., Richardson, W. J. & Barry, T. W. (1975). Seabirds of the southeastern Beaufort Sea: aircraft and group observations in 1972 and 1974. *Beaufort Sea Tech. Rep.* No. 36. Environment Canada, Victoria, B.C.

Seastedt, T. R. & MacLean, S. F. (1979). Territory size and composition in relation to resource abundance in Lapland Longspurs breeding in Arctic Alaska. *Auk* 96: 131–42

Sergeant, D. E. & Williams, G. A. (1983). Two recent ice entrapments of Narwhals, *Monodon monoceros*, in Arctic Canada. *Can. Fld. Nat.* 97: 459–60

Shank, C. C., Wilkinson, P. F. & Penner, D. F. (1977). Diet of Peary Caribou, Banks Island, N.W.T. *Arctic* 31: 125–32

Shaugnessey, P. D. & Fay, F. H. (1977). A review of the taxonomy and nomenclature of North Pacific Harbour Seals. *J. Zool. Lond.* 182: 385–419

Shelford, V. E. (1943). The abundance of Collared Lemmings (*Dicrostonyx groenlandicus*) in the Churchill area, 1929 to 1940. *Ecology* 24: 472–84

Shvarts, S. S., Bolshakov, V. N., Olenov, V. G. & Pjastolova, O. A. (1969). Population dynamics of rodents from northern and mountainous geographical zones. In *Energy Flow Through Small Mammal Populations*, eds. K. Petrusewicz & L. Ryszkowski, pp. 205–20. Polish Scientific Publishers, Warsaw

Silverman, H. B. & Dunbar, M. J. (1980). Aggressive tusk use by the Narwhal (*Monodon monoceros* L.). *Nature* 284: 57–8

Skogland, T. (1980). Comparative summer feeding strategies of Arctic and alpine *Rangifer*. *J. Anim. Ecol.* 49: 81–98

Slessers, M. (1966). Soviet studies in the northward movement of birds. *Arctic* 21: 201–4

Smirnov, V. S. & Tokmakova, S. G. (1971). Preliminary data in the influence of different numbers of voles upon the forest tundra vegetation. *Annales Zoologici Fennici* 8: 154–6

Smirnov, V. S. & Tokmakova, S. G. (1972). Influence of consumers on natural phytocenoses' production variation. In *Tundra Biome. Proceedings of the IV International Meeting on the Biological Productivity of Tundra*, eds. F. E. Wielgolaski & T. Rosswall, pp. 122–7. Leningrad

Smith, T. G. (1976). Predation of Ringed Seal pups (*Phoca hispida*) by the arctic fox (*Alopex lagopus*). *Can. J. Zool.* 54: 1610–6

Smith, T. G. (1980). Polar bear predation of Ringed and Bearded Seals in the land-fast sea ice habitat. *Can. J. Zool.* 50: 2201–9

Smith, T. G. (1981). Notes on the Bearded Seal, *Erignathus barbatus*, in the Canadian Arctic. *Can. Tech. Rep. Fish. Aquat. Sci.* No. 1042

Smith, T. G. (1985). Polar Bears, *Ursus maritimus*, as predators of Beluga Whales, *Delphinapterus leucas. Can. Fld. Nat.* (In press.)

Smith, T. G. & Hammill, M. O. (1981). Ecology of the Ringed Seal, *Phoca hispida*, in its fast-ice breeding habitat. *Can. J. Zool.* 59: 966–81

Smith, T. G., Hammill, M. O., Burrage, D. J. & Sleno, G. A. (1985). Distribution and abundance of Belugas, *Delphinapterus leucas* and Narwhals, *Monodon monoceros*, in the Canadian High Arctic. *Can. J. Aquat. Sci.* (In press.)

Smith, T. G. & Stirling, I. (1978). Variation in the density of Ringed Seal (*Phoca hispida*) birth lairs in the Amundsen Gulf, Northwest Territories. *Can. J. Zool.* 56: 1066–71

Sørensen, T. (1941). Temperature relations and phenology of the northeast Greenland flowering plants. *Meddr. Grønland* 125: 1–305

Southern, H. N. (1979). The stability and instability of small mammal populations. In *Ecology of Small Mammals*, ed. D. M. Stoddart, pp. 103–34. Chapman & Hall, London

Speller, S. W. (1972). Biology of *Dicrostonyx groenlandicus* on Truelove Lowland, Devon Island, N.W.T. In *Devon Island IBP Project, High Arctic Ecosystem*, ed. L. C. Bliss, pp. 257–71. University of Alberta, Edmonton

Steindórsson, S. (1963). Ice age refugia in Iceland as indicated by the present distribution of plant species. In *North Atlantic biota and their history*, eds. A. Löve & D. Löve, pp. 303–20. Macmillan, New York

Stirling, I., Andriashek, D., Latour, P. & Calvert, W. (1975). *Distribution and Abundance of Polar Bears in the Eastern Beaufort Sea*. Beaufort Sea Project, Department of the Environment, Technical Report No. 2. Victoria, B.C.

Stirling, I. & Archibald, W. R. (1977). Aspects of Polar Bear predation. *J. Fish. Res. Board Can.* 34: 1126–9

Stirling, I., Archibald, W. R. & DeMaster, D. (1977). The distribution and abundance of seals in the eastern Beaufort Sea. *J. Fish. Res. Board Can.* 34: 976–88

Stirling, I., Calvert, W. & Andriashek, D. (1980). Population ecology studies of the Polar Bear in the area of southeastern Baffin Island. *Can. Wildl. Ser. Paper* No. 44

Stirling, I., Calvert, W. & Cleator, H. (1983). Underwater vocalization as a tool for studying the distribution and relative abundance of wintering pinnipeds in the High Arctic. *Arctic* 36: 262–74

Stirling, I. & Cleator, H., eds. (1981). Polynyas in the Canadian Arctic. *Can. Wildl. Ser. Paper* No. 45

Stoddart, D. M., ed. (1979). *Ecology of Small Mammals*. Chapman & Hall, London

Stonehouse, Bernard (1971). *Animals of the Arctic; the ecology of the far north*. Ward Lock, London

Stroud, D. A. (1981). Mammal observations. In *Report of the 1979 Greenland White-fronted Goose Study Expedition to Eqalungmiut Nunat, West Greenland*, eds. A. D. Fox & D. A. Stroud, pp. 197–205

Stroud, D. A. (1984). Status of Greenland White-fronted Geese in Britain, 1982/83. *Bird Study* 31: 111–16

Sugden, D. E. & John, B. S. (1984). *Glaciers and landscape*. Edward Arnold, London

Summers, R. W. & Green, G. H. (1974). Notes on the food of the Gyrfalcon *Falco rusticolus* in north-east Greenland in 1972. *Dansk Orn. Foren. Tidsskr.* 68: 87–90

Svoboda, J. (1977). Ecology and primary production of raised beach communities, Truelove Lowland. In *Truelove Lowland, Canada: a High Arctic Ecosystem*, ed. L. C. Bliss, pp. 185–216. University of Alberta Press, Edmonton

Svoboba, J. (1981). The Canadian high north: resource of renewal. In *Proceedings First International Symposium on Renewable Resources and the Economy of the North*, ed. M. R. Freeman, pp. 183–9. Association of Canadian Universities for Northern Studies

Temple, S. A. (1974). Winter food habits of Ravens on the Arctic Slope of Alaska. *Arctic* 27: 41–6

Thing, H. (1984). Feeding ecology of the West Greenland Caribou (*Rangifer tarandus groenlandicus*) in the Sisimiut-Kangerlussuaq regions. *Danish Review of Game Biology* 12(3): 1–52

Thing, H., Henrichsen, P. & Lassen, P. (1984). Status of the Muskox in Greenland. In *Proceedings of the First International Muskox Symposium, Biological Papers of the University of Alaska, Special Report* No. 4, eds. D. R. Klein, R. G. White & S. Keller, pp. 1–6

Thomas, D. C. (1982). The relationship between fertility and fat reserves of Peary Caribou. *Can. J. Zool.* 60: 597–602

Thomas, D. C. & Edmonds, J. (1983). Rumen contents and habitat selection of Peary Caribou in winter, Canadian Arctic Archipelago. *Arct. Alp. Res.* 15: 97–105

Thompson, D. Q. (1955). The 1953 lemming emigration at Point Barrow, Alaska. *Arctic* 8: 37–45

Tieszen, L. L., ed. (1978). *Vegetation and Production Ecology of an Alaskan Arctic Tundra*. Springer-Verlag, New York and Berlin

Tikhomirov, B. A. (1959). *Relationship of the Animal World and the Plant Cover of the Tundra*. Translated from Russian by E. Issakoff & T. W. Barry, Boreal Institute, University of Alberta, Edmonton

Tolmachev, A. I., ed. (1966). *Vascular Plants of the Siberian North and the Northern Far East*. Translated from Russian by L. Philips (1969). Israel Program for Scientific Translations, Jerusalem

Trofimenko, S. (1984). Musk-oxen stand firm in Siberia. *Ambio* 13: 213

Tryon, P. R. & MacLean, S. F. (1980). Use of space by Lapland Longspurs breeding in Arctic Alaska. *Auk* 97: 509–20

Underwood, L. S. (1975). Notes on the Arctic Fox (*Alopex lagopus*) in the Prudhoe Bay area of Alaska. In *Ecological Investigations of the Tundra Biome in the Prudhoe Bay Region, Alaska*, ed. J. Brown. Biological Papers, Special Report No. 2, pp. 144–9. University of Alaska, Fairbanks

Uspenskii, S. M. (1965). The geese of Wrangel Island. *The Wildfowl Trust Sixteenth Ann. Rep. 1963–4*, pp. 126–9

Uspenskii, S. M. (1984a). *Life in High Latitudes*. Amerind Publishing, New Delhi

Uspenskii, S. M. (1984b). Muskoxen in the USSR: some results of and perspectives on their introduction. In *Proceedings of the First International Muskox Symposium, Biological Papers of the University of Alaska, Special Publication* No. 4, eds. D. R. Klein, R. G. White & S. Keller, pp. 12–14

Uspenskii, S. M. & Belikov, S. E. (1974). Research on the Polar Bear in the USSR. In *Bears: their Biology and Management*, eds. M. R. Pelton, J. W. Lentfer & G. E. Folk, pp. 321–3. IUCN, Morges

Vasil'evskaia, V. D., Ivanov, V. V. & Bogatyrev, L. G. (1973). Natural conditions and soils of 'Agapa' Station (Western Taimyr). *International Tundra Biome Translation* No. 8, pp. 28

Veatch, J. O. & Humphreys, C. R. (1964). *Lake Terminology*. East Lansing, Mich: Michigan State University, Dept. of Resource Development, Agricultural Experiment Station (Water Bulletin No. 14)

Vibe, C. (1967). Arctic animals in relation to climatic fluctuations. *Meddr. Grønland* 170: 1–227

Vincent, J.-S. (1982). The quaternary history of Banks Island, N.W.T., Canada. *Geographie physique et Quaternaire* 36: 209–32

Vinokurov, A. A. (1982). Present status of the *Branta ruficollis* population and measures for its conservation. *Aquila* 89: 115–21

Vinokurov, A. A., Orlov, V. A. & Okhotsky, Y. V. (1972). Population and faunal dynamics of vertebrates in tundra biocenosis (Taimyr). In *Tundra Biome. Proceedings of the IV International Meeting on the Biological Productivity of Tundra*, eds. F. E. Wielgolaski & T. Rosswall, pp. 187–9. Leningrad

Voous, K. H. (1963). The concept of faunal elements or faunal types. *Proceedings of the XIII International Ornithological Congress, Ithaca 1962*, pp. 1104–8

Voous, K. H. (1977). *List of Recent Holarctic Bird Species.* Academic Press, London

Vos, A. D. & Ray, E. M. (1959). Home range and activity pattern of an Arctic Ground Squirrel. *J. Mammal.* 40: 610–11

Walker, H. J. & Harris, M. K. (1976). Perched ponds: an Arctic variety. *Arctic* 29: 223–38

Wang, L. C. H., Jones, D. L., MacArthur, R. A. & Fuller, W. A. (1973). Adaptation to cold: energy metabolism in an atypical lagomorph, the Arctic Hare (Lepus arcticus). *Can. J. Zool.* 51: 841–6

Washburn, A. L. (1979). *Geocryology: A survey of periglacial processes and environments.* Edward Arnold, London

Waterston, G. & Waterston, I. (1970). Greenland Redpoll (*Carduelis flammea rostrata*) breeding in High Arctic region. *Dansk Orn. Foren. Tidsskr.* 64: 93–4

Watson, A. (1957). The behaviour, breeding, and food-ecology of the Snowy Owl *Nyctea scandiaca. Ibis* 99: 419–62

Watson A. (1963). Bird numbers on tundra in Baffin Island. *Arctic* 16: 101–8

Webber, P. J. & Klein, D. R. (1977). Geobotanical and ecological observations at two locations in the west-central Siberian Arctic. *Arct. Alp. Res.* 9: 305–15

West, G. C. (1968). Bioenergetics of captive Willow Ptarmigan under natural conditions. *Ecology* 49: 1035–45

West, G. C. (1972). Seasonal differences in resting metabolic rate of Alaskan ptarmigan. *Comp. Biochem. Physiol.* 42: 867–76

West, G. C. & Meng, M. S. (1966). Nutrition of Willow Ptarmigan in Northern Alaska. *Auk* 83: 603–15

West, G. C. & Norton, D. W. (1975). Metabolic adaptations of tundra birds. In *Physiological Adaptation to the Environment*, ed. F. J. Vernberg, pp. 301–29. Intext Educational Publishers, New York

Wille, F. & Kampp, K. (1983). Food of the White-tailed Eagle *Haliaeetus albicilla* in Greenland. *Holarctic Ecology* 6: 81–8

Woodby, D. A. & Divoky, G. J. (1982). Spring migration of eiders and other waterbirds at Point Barrow, Alaska. *Arctic* 35: 403–10

Young, S. B. (1971). The vascular flora of St. Lawrence Island with special reference to floristic zonation in the Arctic regions. *Contributions from the Gray Herbarium*, No. 201. Harvard University

Yurtsev, B. A. (1972). Phytogeography of northeastern Asia and the problem of transberingian floristic interrelations. In *Floristics and paleofloristics of Asia and eastern North America*, ed. A. Graham, pp. 19–54. *Proceedings of symposia for the systematics section, XI International Botanical Congress (1969), Seattle.* Elsevier Publishing, New York

# INDEX